Scholastic SCIENCE Dictionary

MELVIN BERGER

Illustrated by Hannah Bonner

SCHOLASTIC REFERENCE

The author and publisher would like to thank Gary Brockman for his help
in making the book as accurate as possible and John Bollard for his
contributions to the pronunciations and etymologies.

ISBN 0-590-31321-5

Library of Congress Cataloging-in-Publication Data
Berger, Melvin
Scholastic science dictionary / Melvin Berger
p. cm.
Includes index.
Summary: An illustrated dictionary defining scientific terms from "aa" to "zygote."
1. Science — Dictionaries, Juvenile. [1. Science — Dictionaries.] I. Title.
Q123.B46 2000
503—dc21   99-087883
10 9 8 7 6 5 4 3 2 1   0/0 01 02 03 04

Printed in the U.S.A.
First printing, August 2000

Book design by Nancy Sabato • Composition by Kevin Callahan

Introduction

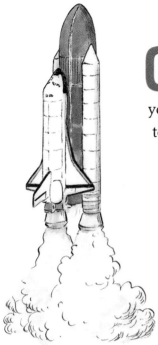

Our twenty-first century is humming with countless new ideas, concepts and technologies. Each day youngsters encounter unfamiliar scientific and technical terms that require explanation and more information.

The purpose of the *Scholastic Science Dictionary* is to give young people a quick and easy way to familiarize themselves with the vocabulary, ideas, objects, and people of science. Since no dictionary can cover *all* the words of science, it was necessary to be highly selective in choosing which words to include. Each entry, therefore, was very carefully drawn from basic elementary school science curricula, from current scientific journals, newspapers, and magazines, and from the author's own experience in writing children's science books for more than 40 years.

The more than 2,400 word entries in the dictionary cover all the major branches of science—astronomy, biology, chemistry, geology, paleontology, and physics. In addition, there are entries for many diseases, drugs, treatments, and specialties in the field of medicine. A distinctive feature of this dictionary is the over 140 biographies of important scientists from diverse backgrounds

The author owes a huge debt of gratitude to the many people who helped create this dictionary, from the scientists who checked the text and illustrations for accuracy, to the editors and book designers who produced the book. A particular word of thanks goes to Hannah Bonner for her exceptionally clear and appealing illustrations, which enrich the meanings and extend the explanations of hundreds of the terms.

While intended for use by elementary school students, the author sincerely hopes readers of all ages will find the *Scholastic Science Dictionary* timely and useful.

Etymologies explain the sources of word entries. They are included only when they are of special interest or helpful in understanding the word.

Word entries are set in bold (**dark**) type and extend into the margin to make them easy to locate. Only proper nouns and acronyms are capitalized.

Pronunciations are given in parentheses following every entry word. The words are broken up into separate syllables. The syllable with the main, heavy accent is printed in bold (**dark**) type. The syllable with a lighter accent is printed in italics (*slanted*) type.

nearsighted (**nir**-*sie*-tid)
Having a defect of **vision** in which nearby objects are seen clearly, but distant objects appear blurred. Nearsightedness can be corrected by **concave lenses** in glasses or contacts. Also called *myopia*.

nebula (**neb**-yuh-luh)
A cloud of gas and dust in space. A nebula may be the place where a new star is forming. From the Latin *nebula*, meaning "mist or cloud."

nebular hypothesis
(**neb**-yuh-luhr hie-**pahth**-uh-sis)
The belief that the **solar system** developed from a huge, hot, spinning **nebula**. It is the most widely accepted idea on the formation of the solar system.

nectar (**nek**-tuhr)
A sugary liquid made by many flowering plants. The nectar of flowers is food for many birds, bats, and insects. Bees make honey from nectar.

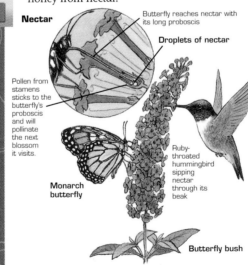

Nectar

Butterfly reaches nectar with its long proboscis

Droplets of nectar

Pollen from stamens sticks to the butterfly's proboscis and will pollinate the next blossom it visits.

Ruby-throated hummingbird sipping nectar through its beak

Monarch butterfly

Butterfly bush

needleleaf tree (**need**-l-*leef tree*)
A tree with needlelike leaves rather than broad leaves. The needleleaf trees include pine, spruce, and fir.

negative (**neg**-uh-tiv)
A number or quantity of less than zero. *Also,* a pole in a battery or electrical device that **electrons** flow away from. *Also,* developed photographic film in which dark and light are reversed. *Also,* the **electrical charge** on a substance that has more **electrons** than normal. From the Latin *negare*, meaning "to say no."

neolithic (*nee*-uh-**lith**-ik)
See **Stone Age**.

neon (**nee**-ahn)
A **chemical element** found in small quantities as a gas in the earth's **atmosphere.** Neon has no **color**, smell, or taste. Passing an **electric current** through a glass tube of neon makes the gas glow with a red-orange light. It is widely used in signs. From the Greek *neon*, meaning "new." (Symbol—Ne)

Neptune (**nep**-toon)
The eighth planet from the sun, except every 248 years when **Pluto** swings in closer and Neptune becomes the ninth planet. The flight of the **spacecraft** *Voyager II* in 1989 showed that winds on Neptune blow up to 1,240 miles (2,000 kilometers) an hour on the surface, and that the planet is surrounded by a number of faint rings and 7 **satellites.**

Average distance from sun—2,796,000,000 miles (4,500,000,000 kilometers)
Length of year—165 Earth years
Length of day—16 hours, 7 minutes
Diameter at equator—30,800 miles (49,500 kilometers)

nerve (**nuhrv**)
One of the cordlike bundles of nerve **cells**, or **neurons**, that connects the brain and **spinal cord** with every part of the body. Nerves carry messages to and from the brain at high speeds.

nerve cell (**nuhrv** *sel*)
See **neuron**.

Cross references tell which word or words defined in the dictionary will give more information on the subject.

Measurements of lengths, area, weight, volume, speed, and temperature are given in both the English, or inch-pound, system used in the United States, and in the metric system, used in many other countries around the world.

This Dictionary

Bold type within a definition shows that that word is defined elsewhere in the dictionary

Guide words tell you the first and last entry words on each page.

nervous system
(**nuhr**-vuhs *sis*-tuhm)
The **network** of **nerves**, brain, and **spinal cord** found in almost all animals. The nervous system reacts to changes in the **environment** and controls the heart, breathing, and digestion. The two parts of the human nervous system are the **central nervous system**, which includes the brain and spinal cord, and the **peripheral nervous system** which runs to the rest of the body.

network (**net**-*wuhrk*)
A **system** that connects two or more **computers**, **telephones**, **radio** or **television** stations, or **electronic** components. *Also,* any connected arrangement of roads, canals, people, **nerves**, and so on.

neuron (**nur**-ahn)
One of the star-shaped **cells** that make up the **nerves** of the **nervous system**. Attached to the cell body is a long tubelike extension called an **axon**. The axon carries messages to other cells. Each cell also has about six shorter branches called *dendrites*. The dendrites receive messages from other cells. Also called *nerve cell*.

neurosis (nu-**roh**-sis)
A mild mental illness. The **symptoms** of neurosis may include anxiety, **depression**, or unreal fears.

neutral (**noo**-truhl)
An **electrical charge** that is neither **positive** nor **negative**. *Also,* a **chemical** that is neither **acid** nor **alkali**.

neutralize (**noo**-truh-*lize*)
The act of adding a **base** (or **alkali**) to an **acid**, or adding an acid to a base, to make the solution **neutral**.

neutrino (noo-**tree**-noh)
A **subatomic particle** with no **electrical charge**. Because it has no electrical charge, a neutrino rarely interacts with

ordinary **atoms** and can pass through planet Earth with little chance of colliding with another particle. In 1998 scientists found that neutrinos have **mass**, which they have not yet been able to measure.

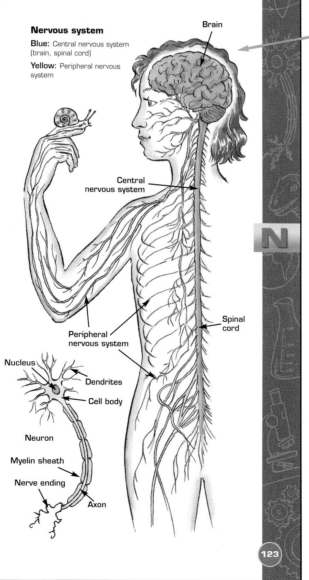

Nervous system
Blue: Central nervous system (brain, spinal cord)
Yellow: Peripheral nervous system

Brain
Central nervous system
Peripheral nervous system
Spinal cord

Nucleus
Dendrites
Cell body
Neuron
Myelin sheath
Nerve ending
Axon

123

Illustrations extend the definitions. Illustration labels that are not entry words are listed in the **Index of Picture Labels** on page 219.

N

Italicized words (*slanted type*) indicate another word for the word being defined or call attention to a word not defined. Italics are also used for foreign words and word parts.

5

aa (**ah**-ah)
A thick bed of **lava** from a **volcano**. Aa becomes rough as it hardens. It is blocky and angular in form.

abdomen (**ab**-duh-muhn)
The part of the human body between the chest and **hips**. *Also,* the abdomen is the third of the three parts of most insect bodies.

abscess (**ab**-ses)
A collection of **pus** in some part of the body caused by an **infection**.

absolute magnitude
(**ab**-suh-*loot* **mag**-nuh-*tood*)
The measure of a star's true brightness. The higher the number the lower the brightness. See also **apparent magnitude.**

absolute zero (**ab**-suh-*loot* **zir**-oh)
The lowest, coldest possible temperature. Absolute zero is -459.67° **Fahrenheit**, -273.15° **Celsius**, or 0° **Kelvin**. Scientists have never been able to cool anything to absolute zero.

absorption (uhb-**sorp**-shuhn)
The process in which one substance or living thing takes in or soaks up another. For example, in plant absorption, the roots take in water. Absorption also refers to substances taking in or holding energy, such as heat, light, or sound.

abyssal (uh-**bis**-uhl)
Describes an area of the **ocean** that is deeper than 2 miles (3.2 kilometers). From the Greek *a,* meaning "without," and *byssos,* meaning "bottom."

AC (**ay**-see)
Short for **alternating current.**

acceleration (ak-*sel*-uh-**ray**-shuhn)
The change in speed or **velocity** of a moving body. Acceleration can mean either slowing down or speeding up.

acid (**as**-id)
A substance that tastes sour and that can burn your skin. Acids turn blue **litmus** paper red and react with **bases** to form **salts**. Lemon juice is a weak acid. **Sulphuric acid** is a strong acid. From the Latin *acidus,* meaning "sour."

acid rain (**as**-id **rayn**)
Rain that is polluted by **acids**. Acid rain forms from gases that come from burning fuels in cars, factories, and power plants. Acid rain harms plants, animals, bodies of water, buildings, and other structures.

acne (**ak**-nee)
A skin condition in which **pimples** appear on a person's body, especially on the face, chest, or back. Acne often occurs when **oil glands** in the skin become blocked.

acoustics (uh-**koo**-stiks)
The science of sound or the quality of sound in a room or concert hall. From the Greek *akouein*, meaning "to hear."

acrylic (uh-**kril**-ik)
A factory-made **plastic** used in the manufacture of **fibers** and paints.

acupuncture (**ak**-yuh-*puhngk*-chuhr)
An ancient Chinese medical system that treats different illnesses by inserting long, thin needles into various parts of the body.

Adam's apple (**ad**-uhmz **ap**-uhl)
See **larynx**.

adaptation (*ad*-ap-**tay**-shuhn)
A change in the body or behavior of a **species** over many **generations**, making it better able to survive in its **environment**. See also **evolution**.

addiction (uh-**dik**-shuhn)
A very strong need to keep using a substance. People with addictions find it very hard to stop taking a drug, even if it causes them harm. From the Latin *addicere*, meaning "to surrender."

addictive (uh-**dik**-tiv)
Causing **addiction**.

adenoids (**ad**-n-*oidz*)
Growths of **tissue** in the top of the throat, just in back of the nose.

adhesion (ad-**hee**-zhuhn)
A **force** that holds two surfaces or different substances together.

adhesive (ad-**hee**-siv, -ziv)
Anything, like paste or glue, that makes things stick together or become sticky.

adobe (uh-**doh**-bee)
A sun-dried brick of clay or mud, or a house made of such bricks. *Also,* the heavy clay soil used to make the bricks.

adolescent (*ad*-l-**es**-uhnt)
A person going through the many physical and emotional changes of growing from childhood to adulthood. The changes usually begin at about age 12 and continue to about age 20.

adrenaline (uh-**dren**-l-in)
A substance released by the adrenal **glands** when you are frightened or

Acid rain
Gases from cars and factories mix with rain to form acid rain, which harms plants and trees.

angry. It is used as a medicine to speed the heart and stop bleeding.

adsorption (ad-**sorp**-shuhn)
The process of one substance collecting on the surface of another substance. In a gas mask, adsorption holds the poison gas on the surface of the **charcoal** pellets in the mask.

aerobic (er-**oh**-bik)
Describes plants and animals that live and grow only where there is **oxygen.** *Also,* describes any exercise that deepens breathing and strengthens the heart.

aerodynamics (*er*-oh-*die*-**nam**-iks)
The branch of **physics** that deals with how objects move through air. Aerodynamics determines the shape of airplanes and automobiles.

aeronautics (*er*-uh-**nawt**-iks)
The science of designing, building, repairing, and flying **aircraft.**

aerosol (**er**-uh-*sawl*)
A mixture of very tiny bits of solids or liquids in gas. Smoke is an aerosol of solid **particles** in air; a cloud is an aerosol of liquid drops in air.

aerospace engineering
(**er**-oh-*spays en*-juh-**nir**-ing)
The branch of **engineering** that designs, builds, and repairs **aircraft** and **spacecraft.**

agar (**ay**-guhr)
A substance similar to **gelatin.** Scientists grow **bacteria** on agar in laboratories.

agriculture (**ag**-ruh-*kuhl*-chuhr)
The raising of crops or livestock.

AI (**ay**-ie)
See **artificial intelligence.**

AIDS (**aydz**)
Short for *Acquired Immune Deficiency Syndrome.* A very serious disease caused by HIV, or *Human Immunodeficiency Virus.* In AIDS the

HIV attacks the body's immune system so that the person cannot fight off other diseases. AIDS is transmitted only through an exchange of bodily **fluids,** such as blood.

air (**er**)
The **mixture** of gases that surrounds the earth. The two main gases in air are **nitrogen** (about 80 percent) and **oxygen** (about 20 percent). Humans and most animals breathe the oxygen in the air. The air also protects us from the sun's harmful **rays** and traps the sun's **heat** to help keep us warm.

air-conditioning
(**er**-kuhn-*dish*-uh-ning)
A way to control the **temperature, humidity,** dust, and movement of air inside buildings, cars, trains, and so on.

aircraft (**er**-kraft)
Any flying machine, such as an **airplane, helicopter, rocket, balloon,** or **dirigible.**

air-cushion vehicle
(**er** *kush*-uhn **vee**-i-kuhl)
See **hovercraft.**

airplane (**er**-playn)
A heavier-than-air machine with a fixed wing. Airplanes carry people or cargo at high speeds through the air. The shape and tilt of the wings and the speed of the airplane cause an upward **air pressure** on the wings that keeps

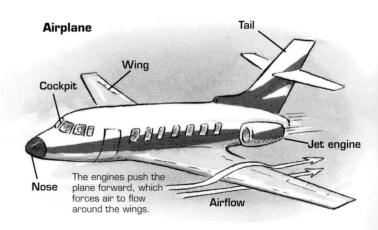

Airplane

Tail

Wing

Cockpit

Jet engine

Nose

The engines push the plane forward, which forces air to flow around the wings.

Airflow

the plane in the air. **Jet engines** or **propellers** move it forward. See also **Bernoulli's principle.**

air pollution (**er** puh-*loo*-shuhn)
See **pollution.**

air pressure (**er** *presh*-uhr)
The weight of air of the **atmosphere** pressing down on Earth. The air pressure at the surface of Earth averages 14.7 pounds (6.6 kilograms) per square inch (6.5 square centimeters).

albumen (al-**byoo**-muhn)
The white of an egg. Albumen protects the developing **embryo** and provides it with food. From the Latin *albus,* meaning "white."

alchemy (**al**-kuh-mee)
A very old form of **chemistry** that tried to change cheap metals into gold and to find ways to cure disease and lengthen life. Alchemy is not considered a true science.

alcohol (**al**-kuh-*hawl*)
A group of **chemicals** that contains **atoms** of **carbon, hydrogen,** and **oxygen.**

algae (**al**-jee)
A group of plantlike **organisms** without true stems, roots, or leaves that grows in water. Algae is the plural of *alga.*

Algorithm

algorithm (al-guh-*riTH*-uhm)
A set of rules used to solve a problem.

alimentary canal
(*al*-uh-**ment**-uh-ree kuh-**nal**)
The long tube in the human body through which food passes and is digested. The alimentary canal in adults is about 30 feet (9 meters) long.

alkali (**al**-kuh-lie) See **base.**

allergy (**al**-uhr-jee)
A bodily reaction to a particular substance that does not cause a reaction in most people. An allergy to dust, certain plant **pollens,** or such foods as chocolate or strawberries, can cause wheezing, sneezing, **hives,** or difficulty in breathing.

alloy (**al**-oi)
A mixture of two or more metals or a metal and a nonmetal. The alloy **brass** is a mixture of **copper** and **zinc; steel** is made from **iron** and **carbon.**

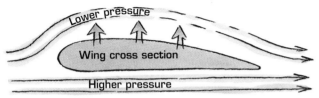

Air flowing over the top of the wing is spread out, which lowers the pressure. Below, higher pressure lifts the plane.

Tilting the wing up and extending the flaps makes the air on top curve more and provide more lift for take off.

In flight the wing is almost flat, with flaps pulled in. There is less lift, but the wing cuts through the air more easily.

alluvial soil (uh-**loo**-vee-uhl **soil**)
Soil deposited by flowing water. Alluvial soil is found in a delta at the mouth of a river and in a **flood plain**. From the Latin *ad,* meaning "up," and *luere,* meaning "wash."

alpha particle (**al**-fuh *pahr*-ti-kuhl)
An **atomic particle** with 2 **protons** and 2 **neutrons** and with a **positive charge.** It is the same as the nucleus of a **helium** atom. Alpha is the first letter of the Greek alphabet.

alternating current
(**awl**-tuhr-*nay*-ting **kuhr**-uhnt)
An **electric current** that reverses its direction of flow many times a second. Alternating current (AC) is produced by **generators** in **power plants.**

alternator (**awl**-tuhr-*nay*-tuhr)
An **electric generator** that produces **alternating current.**

altimeter (al-**tim**-uh-tuhr)
An instrument that measures height above the earth's surface and shows pilots how high they are flying.

altitude (**al**-tuh-*tood*)
The height of an object above the earth's surface, or **sea level.** *Also,* in **astronomy,** altitude is the distance of a **star** or **planet** above the **horizon.**

aluminum (uh-**loo**-muh-nuhm)
A chemical element. Aluminum is a light, silver-colored **metal** that resists **rust,** and is used to make everything from soda cans to airplane bodies. (Symbol—Al)

alveoli (al-**vee**-uh-*lie*)
Tiny air spaces in the lungs. Alveoli is the plural of *alveolus.*

Alzheimer's disease
(**awlts**-*hie*-muhrz di-**zeez**)
A disease of the brain that causes an increasing loss of memory and other mental abilities. First described by the German doctor *Alois Alzheimer* (1864–1915) in 1906.

AM (**ay-em**)
Short for *Amplitude Modulation.* A method of radio broadcasting that uses radio waves of varying height produced in the broadcasting studio. When these waves reach the **receiver,** they reproduce the original sounds. *Also,* morning, or, more exactly, any time from midnight to noon. See also **FM** and **radio.**

amalgam (uh-**mal**-guhm)
A combination of **mercury** with another metal.

amino acids (uh-**mee**-noh **as**-idz)
The **organic acids** that form the **proteins** in living beings. Amino acids contain **carbon, hydrogen, oxygen,** and **nitrogen;** some also contain **sulfur.**

ammeter (**am**-*mee*-tuhr)
An instrument that measures the strength of an **electric current** in units called **amperes.**

ammonia (uh-**mohn**-yuh)
A sharp-smelling, colorless gas consisting of **nitrogen** and **hydrogen.** Ammonia is used to make fertilizers and many other products.

amoeba (uh-**mee**-buh)
A tiny one-celled **protist** that can only be seen through a **microscope.** An amoeba moves by pushing out fingerlike projections. Most amoebas live in water. From the Greek *ameibein,* meaning "to change."

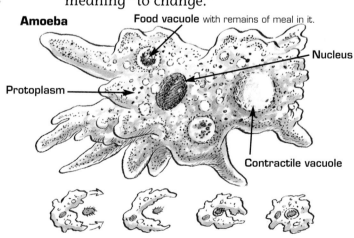

Amoeba — Food vacuole with remains of meal in it. — Nucleus — Protoplasm — Contractile vacuole

An amoeba trapping an even tinier creature.

Ampère (**am**-pir or ahm-**per**), **André** (1775–1836)
A French **physicist** who stated the first theories on **electromagnetism.** Ampère built the first device for measuring **electric current.**

ampere (**am**-pir)
A unit of electric current named after *André Ampère.* Amperes are usually measured with an **ammeter** or a **galvanometer.** Ampere is often shortened to "amp."

amphibian (am-**fib**-ee-uhn)
An animal that lives part of its life on land and part in water, such as a frog, toad, or salamander. Amphibians are **cold-blooded** and hatch from eggs laid in water. From the Greek *amphi,* meaning "on both sides," and *bios,* meaning "life."

amplifier (**am**-pluh-*fie*-uhr)
An **electronic** device that makes weak **electrical signals** stronger. Amplifiers are found in radios, televisions, and **stereo** systems. Some musical instruments, such as electric guitars, use them too.

amplify (**am**-pluh-*fie*)
Increase the strength of a sound or of an electric current by sending it through an **amplifier.**

amplitude (**am**-pluh-*tood*)
The size of something. In science, amplitude usually means the strength, or distance from peak to trough, of a **vibrating wave,** such as a sound wave.

amplitude modulation
(**am**-pluh-*tood* mahj-uh-**lay**-shuhn)
See **AM.**

anaerobic (an-uh-**roh**-bik)
Able to live and grow without **oxygen.**

analgesic (*an*-l-**jee**-zik)
A drug that relieves pain without making a person unconscious.

analog (**an**-l-*awg*)
Using moving parts to show changing information. An analog clock has hands that move as time passes.

analogous structures
(uh-**nal**-uh-guhs **struhk**-chuhrz)
Body parts with different structures but that serve the same purpose. A bird wing and an insect wing are analogous structures.

analysis (uh-**nal**-uh-sis)
The study of a substance or object to learn what it contains.

anatomy (uh-**nat**-uh-mee)
The study of the structure of living things.

android (**an**-droid)
A **robot** that looks and acts like a human being.

anemia (uh-**nee**-mee-uh)
A condition in which blood does not contain enough red blood **cells,** or **hemoglobin.**

anemometer (*an*-uh-**mahm**-uh-tuhr)
An instrument that measures wind speed in **revolutions** per minute. An anemometer usually has 3 or 4 cups at the ends of arms that spin around as the wind blows.

Anemometer

Cups spin in wind.

Spinning is translated into wind speed in miles per hour.

A

aneroid barometer
(**an**-uh-*roid* buh-**rahm**-uh-tuhr)
An instrument that measures **air pressure.**
It is usually a sealed box with a small
amount of air inside and an elastic lid.
High pressure makes the lid push in, low
pressure allows it to push out. The change
moves a pointer over a dial to show the
pressure in bars or millibars.

anesthetic (*an*-uhs-**thet**-ik)
A substance that blocks the feeling of
pain. A general anesthetic puts the
patient to sleep so that he or she feels no
pain. A local anesthetic just causes the
patient to lose feeling in one part of the
body. From the Greek *an,* meaning
"without," and *aisthesis,* meaning
"feeling."

angiosperm (**an**-jee-uh-*spuhrm*)
Any plant whose seeds are protected by
a pod, shell, or fruit. Rosebushes and
apple trees are angiosperms. From the
Greek *angeion,* meaning "vessel," and
sperma, meaning "seed."

angle of incidence
(**ang**-guhl uhv **in**-suh-duhns)
The angle at which a beam of light or
an object meets a surface.

**Angle of
incidence**

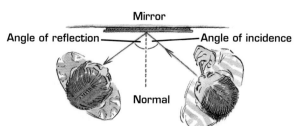
Mirror
Angle of reflection —— Angle of incidence
Normal

animal (**an**-uh-muhl)
Any living thing that moves, eats other
living things, and has thin **membranes**
enclosing its **cells.** From the Latin
anima, meaning "breath" or "soul."

Anning (**an**-ing), **Mary** (1799–1847)
An English **fossil** hunter. Anning started
collecting shells on the beach near her
house. Later she went on to search for
dinosaur bones.

annual (**an**-yoo-uhl)
Coming once a year. An annual plant
is one that lives for only one season.
Tomatoes and peas are annual plants.

anode (**an**-ohd)
A positive **conductor,** or **electrode,** that
passes electricity into or out of electrical or
electronic devices. The anode in a battery
is the little button top. See also **cathode.**

anorexia (*an*-uh-**rek**-see-uh)
A disorder in which a person has no
appetite and becomes dangerously thin.
From the Greek *an,* meaning "without,"
and *orexis,* meaning "appetite."

antenna (an-**ten**-uh)
A device used in television and radio for
sending or receiving **electromagnetic
waves.** *Also,* the long feelers (antennae,
plural of antenna) on the heads of most
insects and many other kinds of
invertebrates, such as crabs and lobsters.

anther (**an**-thuhr)
The part of the **flower** that produces
pollen. The anther is the top part of
the **stamen.**

anthropology (*an*-thruh-**pahl**-uh-jee)
The science that deals with the origin,
development, customs, and beliefs of
groups of people. From the Greek
anthropos, meaning "human being,"
and -*logia,* meaning "science of."

antibiotic (*an*-ti-*bie*-**aht**-ik)
A drug produced by **microorganisms,**
fungi, or manufactured from chemicals.

Antibiotics kill or stop the growth of harmful **bacteria** and other **microbes.** From the Greek *anti,* meaning "against," and *bios,* meaning "life."

antibodies (**an**-ti-*bahd*-eez)
Proteins produced by the body that weaken or destroy invading **bacteria, viruses,** and poisons.

anticyclone (*an*-ti-**sie**-*klohn*)
Winds swirling around a center of high **pressure.** Anticyclones usually bring dry, clear, high-pressure weather and light winds.

antidote (**an**-ti-*doht*)
A substance that prevents a poison from causing harm.

antigen (**an**-ti-juhn)
Any substance that can cause your body to produce **antibodies. Bacteria, viruses,** and poisons are common antigens.

antimatter (**an**-ti-*mat*-uhr)
Subatomic particles that are exactly the same as ordinary **particles**—except that they have opposite **electric** charges. When a particle of antimatter collides with an ordinary particle they destroy each other, producing either **energy** or another particle.

antiseptic (*an*-ti-**sep**-tik)
A substance that kills germs and prevents **infection.** An antiseptic, such as **alcohol** or tincture of **iodine,** is sometimes applied to cuts and scrapes.

anus (**ay**-nuhs)
The lower opening of the digestive tract, through which solid wastes move out of the body.

aorta (ay-**or**-tuh)
The main **artery** in the body. The aorta carries blood from the left side of your heart to all parts of the body, except the lungs.

aphelion (a-**feel**-yuhn)
The point in the **orbit** of a planet or **comet** that is farthest from the sun.

From the Greek *apo,* meaning "away from," and *helios,* meaning "sun."

apogee (**ap**-uh-jee)
The point in the **orbit** of a moon or **satellite** that is farthest from Earth. At apogee, the moon is 252,711 **miles** (406,699 **kilometers**) from Earth. From the Greek *apo,* meaning "away from," and *gaia,* meaning "earth."

apparent magnitude
(uh-**par**-uhnt **mag**-nuh-*tood*)
The brightness of a star as seen in the night sky. See also **absolute magnitude.**

aquarium (uh-**kwer**-ee-uhm)
A glass or plastic tank in which you can keep fish at home. *Also,* a public place where you can see many different kinds of fish and other sea creatures.

aquifer (**ak**-wuh-fuhr)
Water trapped in a layer of **porous** rocks under the ground. You must drill a well down to an aquifer to get water.

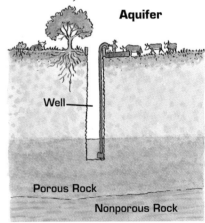

Aquifer

Well

Porous Rock

Nonporous Rock

arachnid (uh-**rak**-nid)
A small animal, such as a spider, tick, or scorpion, similar to an insect, but with some important differences.

ARACHNIDS	INSECTS
8 legs	6 legs
No wings	Most have wings
No antennae	Antennae
2 body parts	3 body parts

archeology (*ahr*-kee-**ahl**-uh-jee)
The study of people, customs, and life of past times. From the Greek *archaios,*

A

meaning "old," and -*logia,* meaning "science of."

Archimedes (*ahr*-kuh-**mee**-deez) (ca. 287–212 B.C.)
A Greek mathematician, scientist, and inventor. Archimedes invented a screwlike device for raising water or grain. He also discovered the principles of **buoyancy** and of the **lever.**

Aristotle (**ar**-uh-*staht*-l) (384–322 B.C.)
A Greek philosopher and scientist who is considered the father of **biology.** Aristotle believed that the best way to understand nature is by observation.

armature (**ahr**-muh-chuhr)
The **coil** suspended in the **magnetic field** of an **electric motor.** When an **electric current flows** through the coil, the coil **rotates.** The spinning coil provides the motor's **mechanical energy** to turn or move something. Also called **rotor.**

artery (**ahr**-tuh-ree)
A blood vessel that carries blood away from the heart to all parts of the body.

artesian well (**ahr**-**tee**-zhuhn wel)
A well that reaches down to water under pressure so that the water flows to the surface without having to be pumped.

arthritis (**ahr**-**thrie**-tis)
A term for over 100 diseases that cause painful swelling of the joints.

arthropod (**ahr**-thruh-*pahd*)
An animal without a backbone that has a **segmented,** or jointed body, and legs. Insects, spiders, shrimp, and lobsters are arthropods. Arthropods are the largest group of animals on Earth.

arthroscopy (ahr-**thrahs**-kuh-pee)
A way of seeing into the body with a long, thin tube that is inserted through

Archeology

a small cut in the skin. Arthroscopy also lets doctors do surgery inside the body through the same cut. From the Greek *arthro,* meaning "joint," and *skopein,* meaning "to look at."

artificial intelligence
(*ahr*-tuh-**fish**-uhl in-**tel**-uh-juhns)
The ability of a computer to perform tasks that usually requires human intelligence. Sometimes shortened to AI.

artificial selection
(*ahr*-tuh-**fish**-uhl suh-**lek**-shuhn)
Breeding plants or animals with certain wanted **traits** so that their offspring will have the same traits.

asbestos (as-**bes**-tuhs or az-**bes**-tuhs)
A grayish **mineral** with **fibers** that can be woven into fabric that does not burn or **conduct** heat. Asbestos is now rarely used, since breathing asbestos fibers can cause lung disease.

aspirin (as-puh-rin, as-prin)
A drug used to relieve pain. The full name of aspirin is *acetylsalicylic acid.* (Formula—$C_9H_8O_4$) See also **analgesic.**

asterism (as-tuh-*riz*-uhm)
A group of stars. The Big Dipper is an asterism within the **constellation** *Ursa Major.*

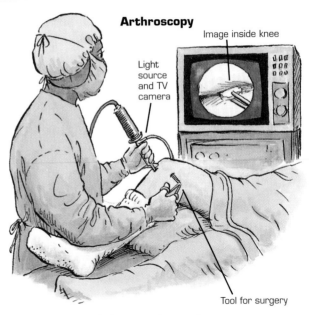

Arthroscopy

Image inside knee

Light source and TV camera

Tool for surgery

asteroid (**as**-tuh-*roid*)
A small rocky object in **orbit** around the sun. Most asteroids are found between the planets **Mars** and **Jupiter.**

asthma (**az**-muh)
A disease of the lungs that causes wheezing and difficulty in breathing. Asthma attacks come when the small air tubes in the lungs are partly blocked by mucus or a tightening of the muscles around the tubes.

astrology (uh-**strahl**-uh-jee)
The nonscientific study of how the stars and planets affect life on Earth.

astronaut (**as**-truh-*nawt*)
A person trained to pilot a **spacecraft** or to conduct medical or scientific experiments in space. From the Greek *astron,* meaning "star," and *nautes,* meaning "sailor."

astronomy (uh-**strahn**-uh-mee)
The scientific study of **galaxies,** stars, planets, and other objects in space. The main tools of the astronomer are **telescopes, spectroscopes,** cameras, **satellites,** and computers.

atmosphere (**at**-muh-*sfir*)
The air that surrounds Earth and other planets. The earth's atmosphere is

Atmosphere
Northern lights (aurora borealis)

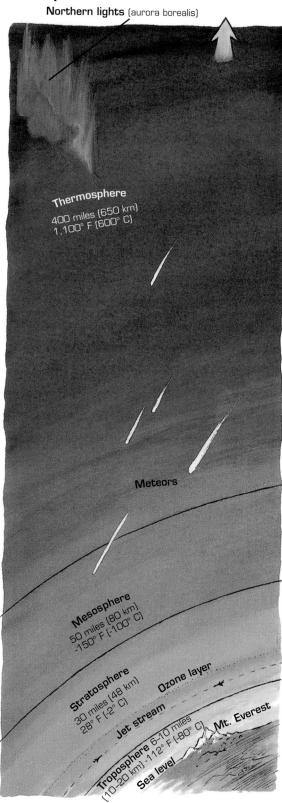

Thermosphere
400 miles (650 km)
1,100° F (600° C)

Meteors

Mesosphere
50 miles (80 km)
-150° F (-100° C)

Stratosphere
30 miles (48 km)
28° F (-2° C)

Ozone layer

Jet stream

Troposphere 6-10 miles
(10-20 km) -112° F (-80° C)

Mt. Everest

Sea level

composed of **nitrogen** (78 percent), **oxygen** (21 percent), other gases (one percent), plus **water vapor** (the amount varies considerably), and tiny **particles** (dust, sand, plant **pollens**, salt from the oceans, and **microbes**). The earth's atmosphere is made up of four layers: The thermosphere gradually gives way to airless outer space.

atoll (**a**-tohl or **a**-tahl)
A ring of **coral** in the sea. Soil often builds up on the atoll and plants start to grow. In time this creates an island.

atom (**at**-uhm)
The smallest part of a **chemical element** that has all the properties of that element. Nevertheless, each atom contains still smaller particles—**protons, neutrons,** and **electrons.** The protons and neutrons are crowded into the **nucleus** at the center of the atom. The electrons whirl around the nucleus.

atomic energy (uh-**tahm**-ik **en**-uhr-jee)
See **nuclear energy.**

atomic number
(uh-**tahm**-ik **nuhm**-buhr)
The number of **protons** in the **nucleus** of an **atom,** which is also equal to the number of **electrons** spinning around

Atoll

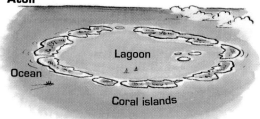

Ocean

Lagoon

Coral islands

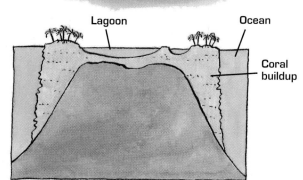

Lagoon

Ocean

Coral buildup

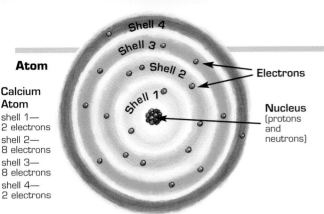

Atom

Calcium
Atom

shell 1—
2 electrons
shell 2—
8 electrons
shell 3—
8 electrons
shell 4—
2 electrons

Shell 4
Shell 3
Shell 2
Shell 1
Electrons
Nucleus
(protons
and
neutrons)

the nucleus. **Hydrogen**, for example, has an atomic number of 1.

atomic weight (uh-**tahm**-ik **wayt**)
The weight or **mass** of an **atom** compared to the weight or mass of a **carbon** atom. **Hydrogen** has an atomic weight of 1.

atom smasher (**at**-uhm *smash*-uhr)
See **particle accelerator**.

attraction (uh-**trak**-shuhn)
The force that pulls two things together. A **magnet** has an attraction for **iron**.

aurora australis
(uh-**ror**-uh aw-**stray**-luhs)
Colorful bands of light appearing in the far southern sky at night. The aurora australis is caused by **electrically charged particles** from the **sun** striking the earth's atmosphere. Also called southern lights. See also **aurora borealis.**

aurora borealis
(uh-**ror**-uh *bor*-ee-**al**-uhs)
Colorful bands of light appearing in the far northern sky at night. The aurora borealis is caused by **electrically charged particles** from the **sun** striking the earth's atmosphere. Also called northern lights. See also **aurora australis.**

automation (*aw*-tuh-**may**-shuhn)
The use of machines such as robots to do work that had been done by humans, for example, assembling cars in automobile factories.

autonomic nervous system
(*aw*-tuh-**nahm**-ik **nuhr**-vuhs *sis*-tuhm)
The part of the **nervous system** that controls such automatic activities as breathing and digestion.

autumn (**aw**-tuhm)
The season between summer and winter. Autumn in the northern hemisphere starts on or about September 22 (**autumnal equinox**) and ends on December 21 (winter **solstice**). In the southern hemisphere, autumn starts on or about March 21 and ends on or about June 21. Since many trees drop their leaves during autumn, the season is also called *fall.*

autumnal equinox
(aw-**tuhm**-nuhl **ee**-kwuh-nahks)
The time at the beginning of **autumn** when day and night are the same length all over Earth. The autumnal equinox is on or around September 22.

avalanche (**av**-uh-*lanch*)
A mass of snow or ice suddenly sliding down the side of a mountain.

Avogadro's law
(*ah*-vuh-**gah**-drohz **law**)
The statement that equal volumes of different gases at the same temperature and pressure have the same number of either **atoms** or **molecules**. The law is named after the Italian physicist *Amedeo Avogadro* (1776–1856).

axis (**ak**-sis)
An imaginary straight line that passes through an object and around which the object spins. The axis of Earth passes between the North and South poles. *Also,* axis is the side or bottom line of a graph.

axle (**ak**-suhl)
A rod or bar around which a wheel turns. An automobile has two axles— one for the front wheels and one for the rear wheels.

axon (**ak**-sahn)
The long, thin part of a **nerve cell** that carries messages from the **cell**.

Babbage (**bab**-ij), **Charles** (1791–1871)
An English mathematician and father of modern computers.

backbone (**bak**-bohn)
See **spine**.

Bacon (**bay**-kuhn), **Roger** (1214–1292)
An English philosopher and scientist who helped lay the foundation for modern science. Bacon believed in doing **experiments**, rather than accepting the word of others.

bacteria (bak-**tir**-ee-uh)
Tiny, one-celled **organisms** that can only be seen through a **microscope**. Certain bacteria cause human diseases, such as **whooping cough** and **tuberculosis**. Others are useful, such as those that change milk into cheese. Bacteria is the plural of *bacterium*.

bacteriology (bak-*tir*-ee-**ahl**-uh-jee)
The scientific study of **bacteria**.

balance (**bal**-uhns)
An instrument for weighing objects. A basic balance has two pans hanging from a horizontal bar. See also **scale**.

Balance

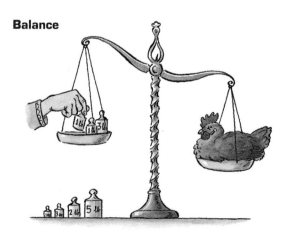

balance of nature (**bal**-uhns uhv **nay**-chuhr)
See **ecosystem**.

baleen (buh-**leen**)
Thin plates that hang from the upper jaws of some whales. These whales use baleen to strain their food from the water. Baleen is often called whalebone.

ball bearing (**bawl ber**-ing)
A small metal ball held in a groove to help parts of machines slide more easily against each other.

ballistics (buh-**lis**-tiks)
The science that deals with bodies moving through the air, such as bullets, bombs, **rockets**, and **missiles**.

bar code (**bahr** *kohd*)
A rectangle of bars of different widths and spacings which contains information that can be read by a computer. The bar code is sometimes called *Universal Product Code* (**UPC**).

barometer (buh-**rahm**-uh-tuhr)
An instrument used for measuring the pressure of the **atmosphere**. Weather forecasters mostly use **mercury** barometers to predict the weather. See also **aneroid barometer**.

basalt (buh-**sawlt** or **bay**-sawlt)
A hard, dark-colored rock formed by **lava** from a **volcano**. Basalt makes up most of Hawaii, and other volcanic islands.

base (**bays**)
A substance that tastes bitter and reacts with an **acid** to form salt and water. A base turns red **litmus** paper blue. Also called *alkali*.

Baleen

The whale takes in a huge mouthful of water and small sea creatures.

The whale squeezes out the water with its tongue; the baleen traps the sea creatures inside.

bathysphere (**bath**-uh-*sfir*)
A watertight chamber with thick walls and glass windows. Scientists in bathyspheres dive deep into ocean waters to study undersea life.

battery (**bat**-uh-ree)
A container filled with metal plates and **chemicals** that react to produce a small **electric current.** The dry cell battery, used in flashlights, wears out in a fairly short time. The storage battery, used in automobiles, can be recharged and lasts far longer.

beaker (**bee**-kuhr)
A glass or plastic container with a spout but no handle. Scientists use beakers to pour liquids.

Beaufort wind scale
(**boh**-fuhrt **wind** *skayl*)
A way of measuring wind speeds by noting the effects of the wind. The scale ranges from zero (smoke goes straight up) to 17 (destruction of buildings). It was devised in 1805 by British Rear Admiral *Sir Francis Beaufort* (1774–1857).

Becquerel (*bek*-uh-**rel** or beh-**krel**), **Antoine-Henri** (1852–1908)
A French **physicist** who discovered natural **radioactivity** in 1896. Becquerel found that **uranium** and other radioactive substances give off invisible **rays.**

bedrock (**bed**-*rahk*)
The solid rock beneath the soil and broken rocks on the surface of Earth.

behavior modification
(bi-**hayv**-yuhr *mahd*-uh-fi-**kay**-shuhn)
Changing the way a person or animal behaves by rewarding wanted behaviors and punishing unwanted behaviors.

Bell (**bel**), **Alexander Graham** (1847–1922)
A Scottish-American inventor who built the first telephone. Bell's interest in teaching speech to deaf children led him, in 1876, to create the telephone.

bell curve (**bel** *kuhrv*)
A curved line, shaped like a bell, that shows the rate at which certain things normally occur. A bell curve showing how tall people are, for example, starts low to show that just a few people are very short. The line then rises to show that more and more people are close to **average** height. And then the line goes down showing fewer and fewer who are very tall.

Bell curve

Number of cows

All black   Half black, half white   All white

Bernoulli's principle
(bur-**noo**-leez **prin**-suh-puhl)
A law named after the Swiss **physicist** *Daniel Bernoulli* (1700–1782). Bernoulli's principle states that as the speed of a liquid or gas increases, the **pressure** at right angles to the movement decreases. It explains how airplane wings keep planes in the air.

beta particle (**bay**-tuh *pahr*-ti-kuhl)
An **electron** or **positron** given off by a **radioactive atom**. A stream of these tiny **particles** is called a *beta ray.* Beta is the second letter of the Greek alphabet.

biennial (bie-**en**-ee-uhl)
Coming every two years. A biennial plant lives for only two growing seasons. Carrots, beets, and turnips are biennial plants.

bifocals (**bie**-*foh*-kuhlz)
Eyeglasses or contact lenses with **lenses** divided into two parts. The upper part is for seeing distant objects; the lower for seeing things that are nearby.

Big Bang (**big bang**)
A **theory** that the **universe** was created billions of years ago in a tremendous explosion. The Big Bang theory is based on the fact that the **galaxies** are moving apart. Today, astronomers believe the galaxies were all together at the time of the Big Bang.

bile (**bile**)
A yellow or green liquid produced by the **liver**. Bile helps the body digest fats. Also called **gall**.

binary star (**bie**-nuh-ree **stahr**)
Two stars that are linked by **gravity** and **revolve** around each other.

binary system
(**bie**-nuh-ree **sis**-tuhm)
A number system, used in computers, with only two digits, 0 and 1, because their **electronic circuits** exist in only two states—on (or 1) and off (or 0). For example, in the binary system the number 5 is written as 101.

binoculars (buh-**nahk**-yuh-luhrz)
Telescopes for both eyes.

binocular vision
(buh-**nahk**-yuh-luhr **vizh**-uhn)
Seeing with two eyes that are slightly apart. Binocular vision helps you to judge depth and distance.

biochemistry (*bie*-oh-**kem**-uh-stree)
The **chemistry** of living things.

biodegradable
(*bie*-oh-di-**gray**-duh-buhl)
Describes anything that can be broken down into simpler elements by living things. Most plant and animal matter is biodegradable.

biodiversity
(*bie*-oh-duh-**vuhr**-suh-tee)
A wide variety of plant and animal species living in one area.

Biome—Desert
Climate—Dry, with hot days and cold nights
Plants—Cactus, sagebrush, and mesquite
Animals—Lizards, rats, snakes, and insects

Biome—Grassland
Climate—Temperate with little rainfall
Plants—Grasses
Animals—Originally antelope and bison; now widely used for grazing cattle and sheep

bioethics (*bie*-oh-**eth**-iks)
The study of whether things done to humans or animals are right or wrong. Bioethics seeks to answer such questions as: Is it right to hurt an animal while testing a drug for a human disease?

biofeedback (*bie*-oh-**feed**-bak)
A way of learning to control your own heartbeat, body **temperature**, blood flow, and brain waves. Biofeedback can sometimes help to lower high blood pressure and relieve headaches.

biogenesis (*bie*-oh-**jen**-uh-sis)
The development of living things from other similar living things.

biological clock
(*bie*-uh-**lahj**-i-kuhl **klahk**)
The internal rhythm of living things that makes you hungry at mealtimes and sleepy at bedtime.

biology (bie-**ahl**-uh-jee)
The science of living things. Biology is divided into special areas: **zoology**, the study of animals; **botany**, the study of plants; and **microbiology**, the study of **microscopic organisms**. From the Greek *bios*, meaning "life," and *-logia,* meaning "science of."

bioluminescence
(*bie*-oh-*loo*-muh-**nes**-uhns)
The ability of certain animals and plants to give off light. Bioluminescence is the result of **chemical reactions** within the **tissue** of fireflies, glowworms, and many other creatures.

biome (**bie**-ohm)
A community of plants and animals that extends over a large area. A biome is largely defined by **climate** and soil type. The living things in each biome are well **adapted** for life in that

Biome—Taiga (boreal forest)
Climate—Cold winter, short summer
Plants—Evergreen (coniferous) trees, such as spruce and fir
Animals—Bear, wolf, and moose

Biome—Tropical rain forest
Climate—Always warm and wet
Plants—Great variety of trees and vines
Animals—Monkeys, sloths, birds, insects, and snakes

Biome—Temperate deciduous forest
Climate—Cool winters, warm summers, moderate rainfall
Plants—Deciduous trees, which shed their leaves every winter, such as elm, maple, and oak
Animals—Deer, fox, squirrel, raccoon

Biome—Tundra
Climate—Cold and dry, with the soil under the surface permanently frozen
Plants—Moss, lichen, and stunted trees
Animals—Caribou, polar bear, Arctic fox, and Arctic hare

community. There are 6 major biomes—desert, grassland, temperate deciduous forest, taiga or boreal forest, tropical rain forest, and tundra.

biosphere (bie-uh-*sfir*)
The parts of the land, sea, and air where life can be found.

biotechnology
(*bie*-oh-tek-**nahl**-uh-jee)
Human interference in the natural functions of plants or animals. Biotechnology uses **genes, bacteria,** and other **microbes** to alter **organisms** or to create new ones. Also called **genetic engineering.**

biped (bie-ped)
An animal with two feet. Humans and birds are bipeds.

bird (buhrd)
An animal that is **warm-blooded,** and has wings, feathers, and two legs. All birds lay eggs, and most can fly.

birth (buhrth)
Being born. Birth in most **mammals** occurs when the offspring emerges from its mother's body.

bit (bit)
The smallest basic unit of information in a computer. The two kinds of bits are 0 for off and 1 for on. Bit is short for *binary* dig*it*. See also **binary system.**

black boxes (blak bahk-siz)
Devices in airliners that record the details of the plane's flight, including instrument readings and talk between the crew and air traffic controllers.

black hole (blak hohl)
A very dense area of **matter** and **energy** found in space. The **gravity** in a black hole is so powerful that nothing, not even light, can escape from it. This makes the black hole invisible. Star-sized black holes are believed to be the last

stages of giant stars that have collapsed into themselves.

blind spot (blinde *spaht*)
A small area of the **retina** of the eye that is not sensitive to light. It is where the **optic nerve** enters the eye.

blood (bluhd)
The red liquid in the **veins** and **arteries** of all animals with backbones. Blood carries **oxygen** and digested food to all parts of the body and takes away waste materials. Blood also fights invading **bacteria,** keeps the body temperature steady, and plugs broken blood vessels to stop bleeding.

Blood

Plasma
(watery liquid—carries nutrients and hormones)

blood clot (bluhd *klaht*)
A mass or lump of dried blood that forms when you cut yourself. **Platelets** in the blood stick together to form a plug that stops the bleeding.

blood pressure (bluhd *presh*-uhr)
The **pressure** of the blood against the walls of the blood vessels. It is caused by the pumping of the heart.

blood vessel (bluhd *ves*-uhl)
A tube in the body through which blood circulates. The main blood vessels are the **arteries, veins,** and **capillaries.**

blubber (bluhb-uhr)
A thick layer of fat under the skin of whales and other sea **mammals.**

Bohr (bor), Niels (1885–1962)
A Danish **physicist** who proposed a model of the **atom** with a **positively charged nucleus** and **negatively** charged **electrons** whirling around the nucleus.

boiling point (**boi**-ling *point*)
The temperature at which a heated **liquid** bubbles and changes into a **gas** or **vapor**. The boiling point of water is 212° **Fahrenheit** (100° **Celsius**).

bone (**bohn**)
The hard material that makes up the **skeleton** of animals with backbones. Bones, with the help of muscles, move the different parts of the body. The ends of some bones are held together with **ligaments** to form **joints**.

botany (**baht**-n-ee)
The study of the structure, growth, and diseases of plants.

Boyle's law (**boilz law**)
The discovery by the Irish scientist *Robert Boyle* (1627–1691) that as a gas is squeezed, its **pressure** increases. You can feel this when you blow up a balloon. It gets harder and harder as you squeeze in more air.

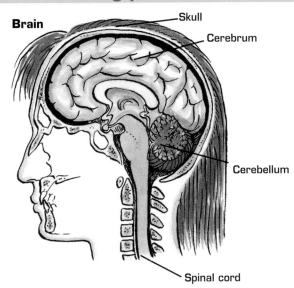

Brain
Skull
Cerebrum
Cerebellum
Spinal cord

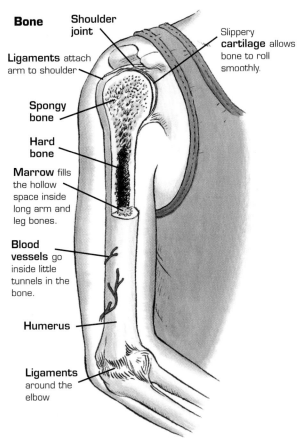

Bone
Shoulder joint
Slippery **cartilage** allows bone to roll smoothly.
Ligaments attach arm to shoulder
Spongy bone
Hard bone
Marrow fills the hollow space inside long arm and leg bones.
Blood vessels go inside little tunnels in the bone.
Humerus
Ligaments around the elbow

Brahe (**brah** or **brah**-hee), Tycho (1546–1601)
A Danish **astronomer** who made precise **observations** of the planets and stars before the invention of the **telescope**.

brain (**brayn**)
The central controlling **organ** of the **nervous system**. The brain is the center for thinking and feeling. It receives and sends messages throughout the body.

brass (**bras**)
A yellow metal that is an **alloy** of **copper** and **zinc**. Brass is harder than copper and is widely used in musical instruments and hardware.

breathing (**bree**-THing)
Taking in **oxygen** and letting out **carbon dioxide**. **Mammals**, birds, **reptiles**, and adult **amphibians** breathe with their lungs; insects breathe through holes in their sides; and fish breathe with their **gills**. See also **respiration**.

breeding (**bree**-ding)
Improving the quality of plants or animals by controlling their mating. Breeding helps farmers get better-tasting fruit and ranchers get faster-growing cattle.

broadleaf (**brawd**-leef)
See **deciduous**.

bronchial tubes
(**brahng**-kee-uhl **toobz**)
Tubes that bring air from the mouth and nose to the lungs. The main bronchial tube is the **trachea**, or windpipe.

bronze (**brahnz**)
A brown metal that is an **alloy** of **copper** and **tin**, sometimes with **zinc** as well. Bronze is often used in statues and bells.

Brownian motion
(**brou**-nee-uhn **moh**-shuhn)
The constant movement of tiny **particles** in a liquid or gas. Brownian motion is named after the Scottish botanist *Robert Brown* (1773–1858).

browser (**brou**-zuhr)
An animal that eats the leaves and bark of trees and shrubs. Deer, giraffes, and cattle are browsers. *Also,* a computer **software program** used to move around the **Internet.**

bubble (**buhb**-uhl)
A thin film of liquid surrounding a quantity of air or other gas.

bud (**buhd**)
A small swelling on a plant that will grow into a flower, leaf, or branch. Many buds appear in the spring.

Bunsen burner   *bec Bunsen*
(**buhn**-suhn *buhr*-nuhr)
A gas burner with a small, hot flame that is often used in **laboratories.** It was developed by the German chemist *Robert Bunsen* (1811–1899).

buoyancy (**boi**-uhn-see)
The upward **force** on an object in a liquid or gas. Buoyancy allows boats to **float** and makes a rock feel lighter in water than in air.

burn (**buhrn**)
To give off heat and light as part of a **chemical reaction.** In order to burn, a substance almost always needs **oxygen.** *Also,* an injury caused by heat, flame, or **acid.**

Burnell (buhr-**nel**), Jocelyn Bell
(born 1943)
A British astronomer who was the first person to detect a **pulsar,** in 1967, while a student at Cambridge University.

byte (**bite**)
A unit of information in a computer that stands for a letter, number, or symbol. A byte usually consists of eight **bits.**

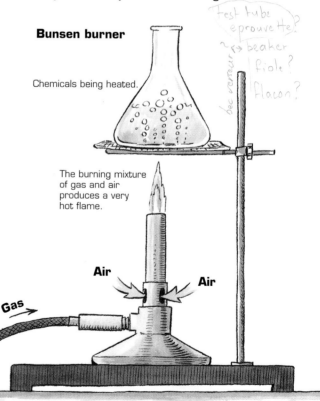

Bunsen burner

Chemicals being heated.

The burning mixture of gas and air produces a very hot flame.

Air

Air

Gas

C (see)
Short for **Celsius scale**.

cable television
(**kay**-buhl **tel**-uh-*vizh*-uhn)
A way of sending television programs from the TV station to home television receivers through wires. Cable television provides good-quality picture and sound.

caffeine (ka-**feen**)
A **chemical** found in coffee, tea, and cola drinks. Caffeine is a **stimulant** that makes the heart beat faster.

calcium (**kal**-see-uhm)
A soft, silver-white metallic **element** found in chalk, **marble**, and **gypsum** and in milk and green vegetables. Calcium is important for building strong bones and teeth. (Symbol—Ca)

calculator (**kal**-kyuh-*lay*-tuhr)
A machine used to add, subtract, multiply, or divide.

calorie (**kal**-uh-ree)
A unit for measuring the amount of **energy** in food. A calorie is the heat necessary to raise the temperature of 1 pound of water 4° Fahrenheit (1 kilogram of water 1° **Celsius**).

cambium (**kam**-bee-uhm)
The layer of **cells** in the roots and stems of certain plants. New cells for the growth of the plant form in the cambium.

Cambrian period
(**kam**-bree-uhn **pir**-ee-uhd)
The period of **geological history** from about 570 to 500 million years ago. During the Cambrian period, life existed only in the sea. **Trilobites** and other shelled animals were common.

camcorder (**kam**-*kor*-duhr)
Short for *camera recorder*. A camcorder is a video camera you use to record motion pictures and sound on a videotape.

camera (**kam**-uh-ruh or **kam**-ruh)
A machine that records a light image onto photographic film. Cameras can be used to make still or motion pictures.

Camouflage

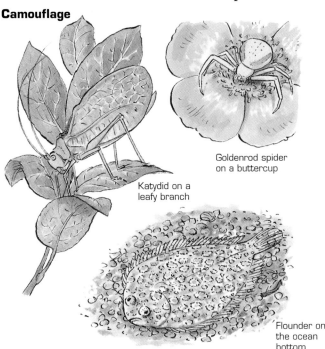

Goldenrod spider on a buttercup

Katydid on a leafy branch

Flounder on the ocean bottom

camouflage (**kam**-uh-*flahzh*)
Coloring and markings on animals or plants that help them blend in with their surroundings and hide from their enemies and victims.

cancer (**kan**-suhr)
A number of serious diseases in which some abnormal body **cells** multiply without stop, damaging healthy **organs** and **tissue**. Cancer is treated in three main ways: surgery—cutting out the cancer cells; **chemotherapy**—using drugs that kill or stop the growth of the cancer; and

radiation—destroying the cancer cells with **X rays** or **radioactive elements**.

canopy (**kan**-uh-pee)
The layer of the rain forest high above the ground. The canopy is made up of the crowns, or tops, of very tall trees.

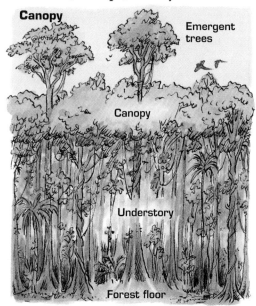

capacitor (kuh-**pas**-uh-tuhr)
A device used to store an **electric charge**. The simplest capacitor consists of two metal plates separated by an **insulator**, such as air. Sometimes called a **condenser**.

capillary (**kap**-uh-*ler*-ee)
A very tiny, narrow blood vessel. Capillaries connect the **arteries** with the **veins**. From the Latin *capillus*, meaning "hair."

capillary action
(**kap**-uh-*ler*-ee **ak**-shuhn)
The rise of a liquid through a tiny opening or tube. Narrow tubes in plants carry water from the roots to the leaves by capillary action.

carbohydrate (*kahr*-boh-**hie**-drayt)
A major **nutrient** of such foods as bread, pasta, corn, rice, and sugar. Carbohydrates are an important source of **energy**. They contain the **elements carbon**, **hydrogen**, and **oxygen**.

carbon (**kahr**-buhn)
A common **chemical element** that occurs in several forms—from superhard diamonds to the soft graphite in pencils. Scientists find carbon in the **tissue** of all animals and plants. (Symbol—C)

carbon dating (**kahr**-buhn **day**-ting)
See **radiocarbon** dating.

carbon dioxide
(**kahr**-buhn die-**ahk**-side)
A colorless, odorless gas that humans and animals produce and release into the **air** when they breathe out. The bubbles in soda are also carbon dioxide. Carbon dioxide has one **atom** of **carbon** joined to two atoms of **oxygen**. (Formula—CO_2)

Carboniferous period
(*kahr*-buh-**nif**-uhr-uhs **pir**-ee-uhd)
The period of **geological history** from about 360 to 290 million years ago. During the Carboniferous period fish and **amphibians** were plentiful and the first **reptiles** appeared. Some of today's coal formed from the remains of plants that became buried under sand during this period. See also **geological history**.

carbon monoxide
(**kahr**-buhn muh-**nahk**-side)
A colorless, odorless gas that is a deadly poison. Carbon monoxide forms when a substance containing **carbon** burns without enough **oxygen**. Automobile exhaust and cigarette smoke contain carbon monoxide. Carbon monoxide has one **atom** of carbon joined to one atom of **oxygen**. (Formula—CO)

cardiology (*kahr*-dee-**ahl**-uh-jee)
The branch of medicine that deals with the diagnosis and treatment of diseases of the heart. From the Greek *cardia*, meaning "heart," and *-logia*, meaning "science of."

caries (**ker**-eez)
Decay of the teeth, bones, or **tissue**. Caries are sometimes called *cavities*.

carnivore (**kahr**-nuh-*vor*)
An animal that eats the flesh of other animals. From the Latin *caro,* meaning "flesh," and *vorare,* meaning "to eat greedily."

carrier wave (**kar**-ee-uhr *wayv*)
A constant **radio wave** from a radio or television **transmitter.** The carrier wave "carries" the waves that represent the sounds or pictures being broadcast from the transmitter.

carrion (**kar**-ee-uhn)
Remains of dead animals. **Scavengers,** such as hyenas, vultures, and jackals, eat carrion.

Carson (**kahr**-suhn), **Rachel** (1907–1964)
An American marine **biologist** who called attention to the dangers of **DDT** and some other **pesticides.** Carson wrote several books, including *Silent Spring* (1962).

cartilage (**kahrt**-l-ij)
Flexible **tissue** that connects bones in humans and animals. Cartilage is the material that supports your ears and nose. A shark's **skeleton** is all cartilage.

Carver (**kahr**-vuhr), **George Washington** (1864–1943)
An American scientist who did important **research** in the field of agriculture. Carver is famous for discovering how to make over 300 products from peanuts. He was born into slavery on a farm in Missouri.

catalyst (**kat**-l-ist)
A substance that starts or speeds up **chemical reactions** without itself being changed. The **enzyme** *ptyalin* in **saliva** is a catalyst that speeds up digestion.

catastrophe (kuh-**tas**-truh-fee)
A major disaster, such as a flood, earthquake, or erupting **volcano.**

cathode (**kath**-ohd)
A **conductor,** or **electrode,** that passes electricity into or out of an **electrical** or **electronic** device. The cathode is the **negative** electrode in batteries. See also **cathode ray.** See also **anode.**

cathode ray (**kath**-ohd *ray*)
A beam of **electrons** coming from a **cathode.**

cathode ray tube (**kath**-ohd *ray toob*)
A **vacuum** tube that is used as a television screen or computer monitor. In a cathode ray tube, the **images** are formed by **electrons** striking the **fluorescent** end of the tube. Often shortened to *CRT.*

CAT scan (**kat** *skan*)
Short for Computerized Axial Tomography. A CAT scan is an **X-ray** picture of a cross

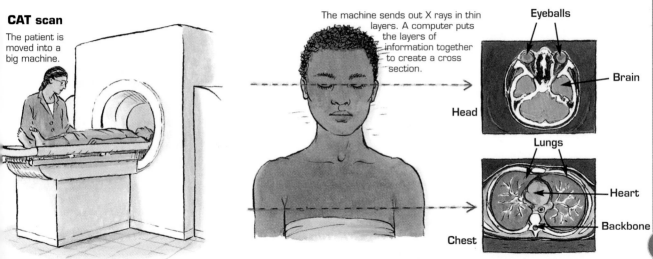

CAT scan

The patient is moved into a big machine.

The machine sends out X rays in thin layers. A computer puts the layers of information together to create a cross section.

Eyeballs

Brain

Head

Lungs

Heart

Backbone

Chest

section of the body. Sometimes simply called *CT* for computerized *t*omography.

Cavendish (**kav**-uhn-dish), **Henry** (1731–1810)
An English **chemist** who discovered **hydrogen.** Cavendish also proved that water is a **compound** containing hydrogen and **oxygen,** not an **element.**

cavity (**kav**-uh-tee)
Common name for **caries.**

CB radio (**see**-*bee* **ray**-dee-*oh*)
Short for Citizens' *B*and radio, a system for short distance communications.

CD (**see dee**)
See **compact disc.**

CD-ROM (**see**-*dee*-**rahm**)
Short for *C*ompact *D*isc *R*ead-*O*nly *M*emory. CD-ROM is a **compact disc** that stores **data** for computers.

cell (**sel**)
The smallest unit of a living thing that can grow, **reproduce,** and die. Some **organisms** have only one cell. But most have huge numbers of cells. Cells are so tiny that they can be seen only under a **microscope.** Inside the cell is the **cytoplasm,** a jellylike substance, surrounded by a thin **membrane.** Within the cytoplasm is the **nucleus,** which contains the **chromosomes** and **genes.** *Also,* a device that produces electricity. *Also,* short for **cellular telephone.** *Also,* an area in which the cellular phone operates.

cellular telephone (**sel**-yuh-luhr **tel**-uh-*fohn*)
A portable telephone that is really a small radio **transmitter** and **receiver.** A cellular telephone picks up and sends radio signals through an **antenna** that serves an area called a **cell.**

cellulose (**sel**-yuh-*lohs*)
The material that makes up the walls of plant **cells.** Cellulose is used in the manufacture of paper and textiles.

Celsius scale (**sel**-see-uhs *skayl*)
A temperature scale developed by the Swedish astronomer *Anders Celsius* (1701–1744). In the Celsius scale, the **freezing point** of water is 0° and the **boiling point** is 100°. Sometimes called the *centigrade scale* and often abbreviated to C. See also **Fahrenheit** and **Kelvin.**

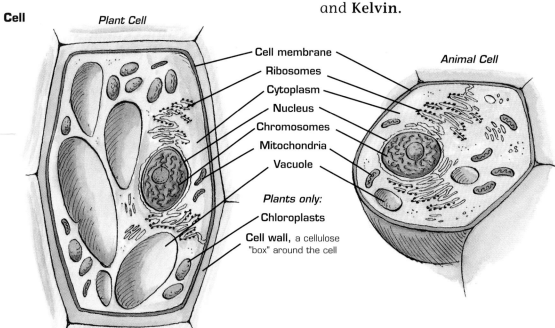

Cell

Plant Cell

Animal Cell

Cell membrane
Ribosomes
Cytoplasm
Nucleus
Chromosomes
Mitochondria
Vacuole

Plants only:

Chloroplasts

Cell wall, a cellulose "box" around the cell

cement (si-**ment**)
A gray powder that is a mixture of crushed **limestone** and clay. Cement is widely used to pave roads. When water and sand are added to cement it forms the *mortar* used to hold bricks together. When water, sand, and gravel are added to cement it forms **concrete**. As cement dries it becomes as hard as rock. *Also*, any substance that joins two things together, such as **rubber cement**.

Cenozoic era (*see*-nuh-**zoh**-ik **ir**-uh)
The most recent **era** of **geological history**, which began about 65 million years ago and is still going on. Dinosaurs disappeared just before the start of the Cenozoic era and **mammals** became much more common. Humans appeared only in the last 2 million years.

center of gravity
(**sen**-tuhr uhv **grav**-uh-tee)
The point in a solid on which the object can be balanced. You must hold a tray of dishes under its center of gravity or the dishes will crash to the floor.

centigrade scale (**sen**-tuh-*grayd skayl*)
See **Celsius scale**.

central nervous system
(**sen**-truhl **nuhr**-vuhs *sis*-tuhm)
The part of the **nervous system** that includes the brain and **spinal cord**. Humans, other **mammals**, birds, fish, **reptiles**, **amphibians**, and some worms and insects have a central nervous system (*CNS*). The CNS controls and directs the entire nervous system.

central processing unit
(**sen**-truhl **prahs**-es-ing *yoo*-nit)
See **CPU**.

centrifugal force
(**sen**-**trif**-uh-guhl **fors**)
The tendency of an object turning around a center to move away from the center. Whirl a rock tied to a string around your head. The centrifugal force sends the rock

away from you and keeps the string straight. It is the opposite of **centripetal force**. From the Latin *centrum*, meaning "center," and *fugere*, meaning "to flee."

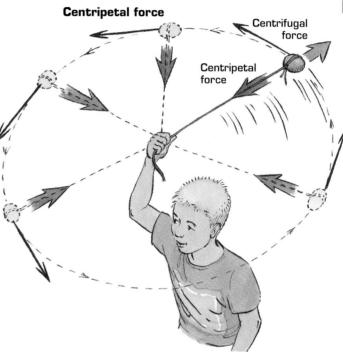

Centripetal force

Centrifugal force

Centripetal force

centripetal force (sen-**trip**-uht-l **fors**)
The force that pulls an object turning in a circle inward toward the center. When you whirl a rock tied to a string around your head, the string is the centripetal force that keeps the rock from flying off into space. Centripetal force is the opposite of **centrifugal force**—and the two always work together. From the Latin *centrum*, meaning "center," and *petere*, meaning "to seek."

ceramic (suh-**ram**-ik)
A hard, strong material usually made from clay. Among the common ceramics are bricks, **cement**, and the *porcelain* used to make dishes and bowls.

cetacean (si-**tay**-shuhn)
A member of a group of **mammals** that includes whales, dolphins, and porpoises. A cetacean has lungs, breathes air, and has flippers for its front limbs.

CFCs (see-*ef*-**seez**)
Short for *ChloroFluoroCarbons*. CFCs are **compounds** that contain **chlorine,** fluorine, and **carbon** and are used in **aerosol** cans and air-conditioning units. CFCs are damaging the **atmosphere** and many countries no longer allow their production.

chain reaction
(**chayn** ree-**ak**-shuhn)
A process, such as **nuclear fission,** in which splitting one **radioactive atom** releases **neutrons,** which split other radioactive atoms, which release more neutrons, and so on. **Nuclear power plants** and **nuclear bombs** produce their energy through chain reactions. *Also,* a **chemical reaction** in which one reaction causes other reactions.

chalk (**chawk**)
A soft white material used for writing on chalkboards and for whitening toothpaste. Chalk is formed from the shells of tiny sea animals that died millions of years ago. (Formula—$CaCO_3$)

chaos (**kay**-ahs)
A new branch of science that studies very complex systems in nature. Scientists use chaos **theory** to try to learn how small events can bring about major changes.

character (**kar**-ik-tuhr)
A single letter, number, or symbol. In computers, a character is the same as a **byte.**

characteristic (*kar*-ik-tuh-**ris**-tik)
A feature or **trait** that is **inherited** by a plant or animal from its parents. Eye color in humans is an example of an inherited characteristic.

charcoal (**chahr**-kohl)
A form of **carbon** made by heating wood in little or no air. Charcoal is used as a **fuel,** in black paints and inks, to make drawing pencils, and to remove smells and flavors from liquids or gases by **adsorption.**

charge (**chahrj**)
The amount of electricity in an object. An object can have a **negative** charge or a **positive** charge.

chemical (**kem**-i-kuhl)
Any substance with a definite composition made up of one or more **elements.**

chemical bond (**kem**-i-kuhl **bahnd**)
The force that joins **atoms** together to form **molecules.** Chemical bonds form solids, liquids, and gases.

chemical engineering
(**kem**-i-kuhl *en*-juh-**nir**-ing)
The branch of **engineering** that deals with changing **chemical** raw materials into useful products.

chemical reaction
(**kem**-i-kuhl ree-**ak**-shuhn)
A process in which one substance changes into another. For example, a chemical reaction combines **sodium** (symbol—Na) with **chlorine** (symbol—Cl) to form **salt** (formula—NaCl).

chemistry (**kem**-uh-stree)
The science that studies the makeup, structure, and properties of matter. Chemistry determines what substances contain, how they behave, and how they change.

chemotherapy
(*kee*-moh-**ther**-uh-pee)
The use of poisonous chemicals to attack harmful **cells** or **microbes** without damaging healthy **tissue.** Today, chemotherapy usually refers to the use of drugs to treat various kinds of **cancer.**

chicken pox (**chik**-uhn *pahks*)
A usually mild, **contagious** disease caused by a **virus.** The first **symptom** is a skin rash of red spots. Those who have had chicken pox generally do not get it again. A **vaccine** also may protect you from the disease.

Chip

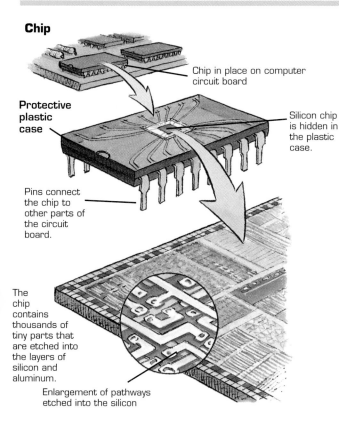

Chip in place on computer circuit board

Protective plastic case

Silicon chip is hidden in the plastic case.

Pins connect the chip to other parts of the circuit board.

The chip contains thousands of tiny parts that are etched into the layers of silicon and aluminum.

Enlargement of pathways etched into the silicon

chip (**chip**)
A complete **electric circuit** on a tiny, flat piece of **silicon** no bigger than your fingernail. A chip stores and processes **data** in a computer. Also called *microchip, silicon chip,* or *integrated circuit.*

chitin (**kie**-tin)
The hard, horny material that forms the shells of **insects**, spiders, and lobsters.

chlorine (**klor**-een)
A green-yellow poisonous gas **element** that irritates the eyes, nose, and throat. Chlorine is added to drinking water to kill germs in the water. (Symbol—Cl)

chlorofluorocarbons
(*klor*-oh-*flur*-oh-**kahr**-buhnz)
See **CFCs.**

chlorophyll (**klor**-uh-*fil*)
The green coloring in many plants, which is produced when the plant is exposed to sunlight. Chlorophyll and the sun's light **energy** help the plant manufacture its food by **photosynthesis.**

cholesterol (kuh-**les**-tuh-*rawl*)
A fatty substance produced by the body that also comes from such foods as meat, egg yolks, and milk products. Cholesterol is necessary for digestion and to make certain **hormones.** Too much cholesterol is believed to be a cause of heart disease.

chromatography
(*kroh*-muh-**tahg**-ruh-fee)
A way to separate the substances in a mixture of liquids or gases. The mixture moves over a surface or through a tube and forms different spots. Each spot contains a substance from the original mixture. From the Greek *chroma,* meaning "color," and *graphein,* meaning "write."

chromium (**kroh**-mee-uhm)
A hard, gray metal **element** that becomes bright and shiny when polished. Chromium is also added to **iron** to make stainless **steel.** (Symbol—Cr)

chromosome (**kroh**-muh-*sohm*)
A tiny threadlike structure found in the **cells** of all living things. Chromosomes consist largely of strands of **DNA.** The DNA contains the necessary information to make new cells. Along the DNA strands are many units called **genes.** They determine the **characteristics** of an offspring. Most humans have the same number of chromosomes—23 pairs.

chronic (**krahn**-ik)
Describes a disease that lasts a long time.

chronometer (kruh-**nahm**-uh-tuhr)
A very accurate clock. A ship uses a chronometer to determine its exact **longitude.**

chrysalis (**kris**-uh-lis)
The third stage, or **pupa**, of a butterfly. Inside the hard outer shell of the chrysalis the pupa changes into an adult butterfly.

C

cilia (**sil**-ee-uh)

Thin, long, hairlike projections that stick out of certain **cells.** Cilia in your nose, ears, and lungs push out any dust or dirt that enters. Many one-celled **organisms** have cilia to help them move.

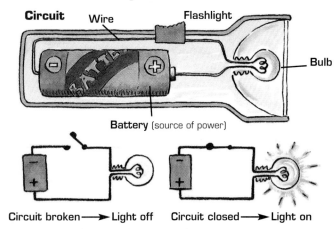

Circuit **Wire** **Flashlight**

Bulb

Battery (source of power)

Circuit broken ➞ Light off   Circuit closed ➞ Light on

circuit (**suhr**-kit)

A path along which electricity flows. A circuit consists of a source of power, such as a **generator** or a battery, wired to a lamp or appliance and wired back to the power source. From the Latin *circuitus,* meaning "going around."

circuit breaker (**suhr**-kit *bray*-kuhr)

A device that automatically breaks, or opens, a **circuit** when too much **current** is flowing. The circuit breaker prevents damage and avoids fires.

circulatory system
(**suhr**-kyuh-luh-*tor*-ee *sis*-tuhm)

The **network** that carries blood throughout the body. The heart pumps the blood out through **arteries** to tiny **capillaries** and to **veins** that carry the blood back to the heart.

cirrus (**sir**-uhs)

A high, wispy cloud made up of small ice **crystals.** From the Latin *cirrus,* meaning "a curl."

civil engineering (**siv**-uhl *en*-juh-**nir**-ing)

The branch of engineering that deals with designing and building roads, bridges, tunnels, dams, and so on.

clairvoyance (kler-**voi**-uhns)

See **extrasensory perception.**

class (**klas**)

A similar group of **organisms** in the **classification** plan.

classification
(*klas*-uh-fi-**kay**-shuhn)

A grouping of living things based on ways in which they are alike. For example, human beings belong to the:

Kingdom — Animalia (all animals)
Phylum — Chordata (backbone)
Class — Mammalia (nurse their young)
Order — Primate (superior brains, hands, and feet)
Family — Hominidae (stand straight and walk on two legs)
Genus — *Homo* (humanlike)
Species — *sapiens* (modern humans)

There are also classification systems for such things as rocks and **chemicals.**

climate (**klie**-mit)

The usual weather in a certain area over many years. Climate is mostly based on temperature, **humidity**, wind, sunshine, and **precipitation** (rain or snow).

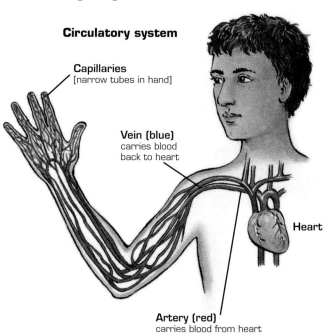

Circulatory system

Capillaries
[narrow tubes in hand]

Vein (blue)
carries blood back to heart

Heart

Artery (red)
carries blood from heart

Cloud

Cirrus

Cumulus

Stratus

Nimbostratus

clinical psychology
(**klin**-i-kuhl sie-**kahl**-uh-jee)
The branch of **psychology** that helps
people deal with their problems and
with the world around them. *Clinical
psychologists* mainly treat patients and
do **research.**

clone (**klohn**)
A plant or animal grown from a **cell**
taken from one parent. In 1997, a sheep
named Dolly was the first animal to be
cloned from a cell taken from an adult.
Also, a copy of a device that works like
the original. A clone of an IBM computer
works exactly like one made by IBM, but
is made by a different company.

clot (**klaht**)
See **blood clot.**

cloud (**kloud**)
Condensed water **vapor** that rises from
bodies of water on Earth. A cloud floats
in the air as tiny drops of water or
crystals of ice. See also the four major
types of clouds: **cirrus, cumulus,
nimbostratus,** and **stratus.**

cloud chamber (**kloud** *chaym*-buhr)
A device for tracing the trail of tiny
water drops left by **subatomic particles**
as they pass through.

clutch (**kluhch**)
The eggs laid at one time by a **female
animal.** *Also,* the part of a car or
machine that connects the **engine**
and **transmission** to make it go.

coagulant (koh-**ag**-yuh-luhnt)
Any substance that causes a liquid to
thicken and harden. Vitamin K is a
coagulant in your blood that stops
bleeding and helps to form a **blood clot.**

coal (**kohl**)
Soft rock that burns easily. Coal began
to form hundreds of millions of years
ago when the earth was covered with
giant plants. As they died, the **pressure**
and heat gradually turned them into
coal. Today, coal is mostly used in
power plants to make steam and
produce electricity.

coaxial cable
(koh-**ak**-see-uhl **kay**-buhl)
An electric wire that consists of a central
wire or **conductor** surrounded by another
conductor, separated by **insulation.**
Coaxial cable is used in television and
other forms of communication.

cocci (**kahk**-sie, **kahk**-see)
Bacteria that are round or spherical in
shape. **Staphylococci** are bacteria that
cause several different kinds of **infections.**

cochlea (**koh**-klee-uh or **kahk**-lee-uh)
A part of the inner ear that has a spiral
shape. The cochlea contains the **organs**
needed for hearing. From the Greek
kochlias, meaning "snail."

cocoon (kuh-**koon**)
The soft, silky protective covering spun by the larvae of certain insects, such as moths. Inside the cocoon, the **larva** turns into a **pupa**. In time the pupa becomes an adult insect. *Also,* the case in which a spider lays its eggs.

cohesion (koh-**hee**-zhuhn)
The force that holds the **molecules** of the same material together. Cohesion is strongest in solids, weaker in liquids, and is weakest in gases.

coil (**koil**)
Anything that is wound around and around in the shape of a circle. A coil of wire is used in **electric motors** and **electric generators.**

cold (**kohld**)
A **virus** infection of the nose and throat. The usual **symptoms** are coughing, a runny **nose**, sore **throat, fever,** and headache. There is no cure; the usual treatment is rest and lots of fluids.

cold-blooded (**kohld bluhd**-uhd)
Describes an animal that cannot control its own body temperature, but is warmed or cooled by the surrounding air or water. All animals are cold-blooded, except **mammals**, birds, and certain fish, which are **warm-blooded.** Also called *ectothermic.*

colloid (**kahl**-oid)
A mixture of tiny **particles** of one substance scattered evenly throughout another substance. A colloid can be either liquid (milk, which is liquid fat in water), gas (smoke, which is ash in air), or solid (stained glass, which is metal in glass).

color (**kuhl**-uhr)
The effect of different **wavelengths** of light on the eye. We see the longest wavelengths as the color red, and the shortest as the color violet. We see an equal mixture of all wavelengths as white.

color-blind (**kuhl**-uhr *blinde*)
Being unable to tell certain colors apart. People who are color-blind find it hardest to see the difference between red and green.

coma (**koh**-muh)
A deep state of unconsciousness. It is very hard, or impossible, to wake someone who is in a coma. *Also,* the gas cloud around the **nucleus** of a **comet.**

combustion (kuhm-**buhs**-chuhn)
Another word for burning. Combustion is a high-speed **chemical reaction** of a fuel, such as wood, with **oxygen.** The reaction gives off heat and light.

Compact disk

Sound waves from singer's mouth

Microphone changes sound waves into electrical pulses.

Pickups in the guitar change the vibrations of the strings into electrical pulses.

Wires carry pulses to a mixing board.

Mixing board combines the pulses. **DAT recorder**

Pulses enter a tape recorder that changes sound into binary code on a digital audio tape (DAT for short).

Tape goes to CD manufacturer. **DAT tape**

Laser etches CD.

The binary code is translated into pits (0) and smooth spaces (1) called lands.

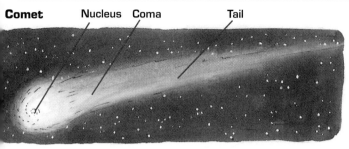

Comet — Nucleus — Coma — Tail

comet (**kahm**-uht)
A small object in **orbit** around the
sun. A comet usually has three parts:
the **nucleus**, a small, solid center of
ice and frozen gases with dust mixed
in; the **coma** or head, a gas cloud
around the nucleus; and the tail, dust
and gas trailing like hair behind
the coma. From the Greek *kome*,
meaning "hair."

commensalism
(kuh-**men**-suh-*liz*-uhm)
Animals or plants living together where
one is helped and the other is neither
helped nor harmed. Commensalism
is found between small fish called

remoras and sharks, for example.
Remoras spend their lives attached to
sharks and eat bits of food too small
for the shark to eat. From the Latin
com, meaning "with," and *mensa,*
meaning "table."

community (kuh-**myoo**-nuh-tee)
All the plants and animals that live in
one area and depend on each other for
survival.

commutator (**kahm**-yuh-*tay*-tuhr)
A device to reverse the direction of the
electric current in an **electric
generator** or motor.

compact disc (**kahm**-pakt **disk**)
A flat, round, plastic disk that is often
called a *CD*. A compact disc records
sounds in a spiral track containing
millions of tiny pits. In a CD player,
a **laser** beam reads the pits on the
rapidly spinning disc, producing
electrical signals, which are then
converted into sound. The **CD-ROM**

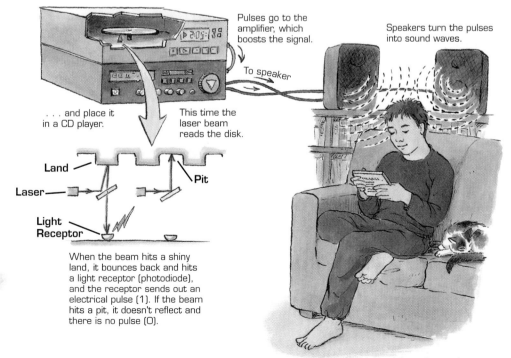

Pulses go to the amplifier, which boosts the signal.

Speakers turn the pulses into sound waves.

To speaker

. . . and place it in a CD player.

This time the laser beam reads the disk.

From the master disk that the laser etched, the manufacturer makes a mold and presses many copies. You buy one . . .

Land — Pit
Laser —
Light Receptor

When the beam hits a shiny land, it bounces back and hits a light receptor (photodiode), and the receptor sends out an electrical pulse (1). If the beam hits a pit, it doesn't reflect and there is no pulse (0).

And you hear the music almost exactly as it was played.

is a similar disk that stores **data** for computers.

compass (**kuhm**-puhs)
A device that points in the north-south direction. Most often it has a **magnetized** needle that is attracted to the earth's north magnetic pole, while the other end points to the south magnetic pole.

compost (**kahm**-pohst)
Rotted plant and food waste. People add compost to soil to make it richer and looser.

compound (**kahm**-pound)
A substance containing **atoms** of two or more **elements.** The compound holds the atoms together in identical units called **molecules.** Water, for example, is a compound in which each molecule contains 2 atoms of **hydrogen** and 1 atom of **oxygen** (formula—H₂O).

compound eye (**kahm**-pound **ie**)
An eye made up of many tiny **lenses.** Compound eyes are common in insects and **crustaceans,** such as crabs and lobsters. Some insects have as many as 20,000 lenses.

compression (kuhm-**presh**-uhn)
Making something smaller or shorter by pressing or squeezing it.

computer (kuhm-**pyoo**-tuhr)
A high-speed machine for calculating and handling information. A computer has two main parts—**hardware** and **software.** The hardware is the machine itself. It includes ways to enter or input information or **data** (keyboard); ways to process the data (**CPU** or *Central Processing Unit*); ways to store the data (**memory chip**); and ways to display the results, or output (**monitor** or **printer**). Other parts are the **mouse,** to operate the computer, and a **modem,** which connects the computer to a telephone line.

The software is the instructions, or **program,** that direct the computer. A computer with several different software programs can get on the **Internet,** send **e-mail,** write stories, get information from an encyclopedia, play games, correct spelling mistakes, and much more.

concave (kahn-**kayv**)
A surface that is bent inward or "caved in" like the inside of a soup bowl. Concave

Computer

Motherboard, with CPU, memory, and other chips attached.
CD-ROM drive
Floppy disk drive
Monitor
CPU chip
Central Processing Unit
Speaker
Video card
Hard drive
Modem
Printer
CD-ROM
Keyboard
Mouse
Mouse pad
Floppy disk

lenses are used to make eyeglasses for **nearsighted** people. From the Latin *concavus,* meaning "hollow."

concentration
(*kahn-suhn-tray-shuhn*)
The amount of one substance **dissolved** in another. One spoonful of salt in a glass of water is a lower concentration than three spoonfuls.

concrete (**kahn**-kreet)
A building material made of **cement,** sand, gravel, and water. When workers combine the ingredients and place the wet mixture into a form, it dries as hard as rock.

condensation
(*kahn-duhn-say-shuhn*)
The change of a gas into a liquid when it is cooled. Clouds are the condensation of water vapor when moist air is cooled in the upper **atmosphere.**

condenser (kuhn-**den**-suhr)
Another name for **capacitor.** *Also,* a device used in **chemistry** to change a gas into a liquid by cooling. *Also,* a system of **lenses** or mirrors that **focuses** light.

conduction (kuhn-**duhk**-shuhn)
The transfer of **energy** through a substance. Conduction sends heat energy through a metal rod when one end is hot. *Also,* the carrying of a signal by a **nerve** or other **tissue.** Conduction sends messages to your brain and muscles.

conductor (kuhn-**duhk**-tuhr)
Any material through which **energy** can flow. A **copper** wire is a good conductor of electricity; glass is not. A metal rod is a good heat conductor; wood is not. Air is a good conductor of sound; a pillow is not. From the Latin *conducere,* meaning "to lead" or "to bring together."

cone (**kohn**)
A **cell** in the back wall, or **retina,** of the eye that can see the colors blue, green, and red. *Also,* the seed-carrying part of a **conifer,** called a *pinecone.*

conifer (**kahn**-uh-fuhr)
A tree or shrub that produces its seeds in cones. Conifers generally stay green throughout the year and have thin, needle-shaped leaves. Pines, firs, cedars, and yews are some common conifers. From the Latin *conus,* meaning "cone," and *ferre,* meaning "to bear."

conservation (*kahn-suhr-vay-shuhn*)
The protection and wise use of natural resources, such as air, water, land, plants, animals, and the **minerals** in the earth.

constellation (*kahn-stuh-lay-shuhn*)
A group of stars seen in one part of the night sky. Ancient **astronomers** saw patterns among the stars and named them after animals (Leo the Lion, Taurus the Bull, and so on) or figures from Greek myth (Orion the Hunter, Gemini the Twins, and so on). Modern astronomers recognize 88 constellations. From the Latin *com,* meaning "together," and *stella,* meaning "star."

Constellation
Orion the Hunter

contagious (kuhn-**tay**-juhs)
Easily spread by contact. For example, a cold is a contagious disease that can quickly pass from person to person.

continent (**kahnt**-n-uhnt)
A landmass that is several million square miles (kilometers) in area. The 7 continents are Africa, Antarctica, Asia, Australia, Europe, North America, and South America.

continental drift (**kahnt**-n-*ent*-l **drift**)
See **plate tectonics.**

continental shelf
(**kahnt**-n-*ent*-l **shelf**)
The underwater land around the edges
of the **continents.** The continental shelf
starts at the shoreline and extends out
about 50 miles (80 kilometers) on
average. Beyond the continental shelf
is the much steeper *continental slope.*

contrail (**kahn**-trayl)
Thin lines of clouds that form behind
airplanes flying at very high **altitudes.**
Contrails contain tiny drops of water or
ice **crystals.** Also called *vapor trail.*

control (kuhn-**trohl**)
Part of an **experiment** that stays the
same while other parts change. For
example, a control group drinks the
same amount of milk every day. Another
group drinks an extra glass of milk every
day. The groups are then compared to
see the effect of the additional glass of
milk on the second group.

Convection

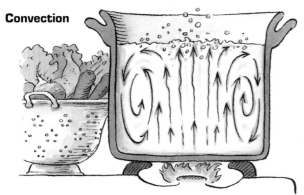

convection (kuhn-**vek**-shuhn)
Rising or falling movement within a liquid
or gas caused by heating or cooling.
Convection occurs when you heat a pot of
water on a hot stove. The hot water at the
bottom moves up to the top. From the
Latin *convectio,* "a bringing together."

convex (kahn-**veks**)
Curved outward like the outside of a
baseball. The **lens** in a magnifying
glass is convex.

copepod (**koh**-puh-*pahd*)
A large group of tiny animals in
oceans or fresh water. Copepods are
an important food for many sea
creatures.

Copernicus (kuh-**puhr**-ni-kuhs),
Nicolaus (1473–1543)
A Polish **astronomer** who believed that
Earth moved in a circle around the sun.
His idea that Earth was a moving planet
was correct. But he was wrong about the
sun being the center of the universe and
Earth's **orbit** being a circle.

copper (**kahp**-uhr)
A soft, reddish-brown metal **element.**
Copper is a good **conductor** of electricity
and is widely used for electrical wire. It is
also mixed with other metals to make
brass and **bronze.** (Symbol—Cu)

coral (**kor**-uhl)
Tiny sea creatures that live in warm ocean
water. The **skeletons** of millions of corals
form underwater **reefs** and islands.

core (**kor**)
The center of planet Earth. The inner
core reaches about 800 miles (1,300
kilometers) from Earth's center. The outer
core reaches about 1,400 miles (2,250
kilometers) beyond that. *Also,* the central
part of a **nuclear reactor** where **fission**
occurs. *Also,* a long, thin sample dug out
of earth, rock, or ice to study the layers
it contains.

cornea (**kor**-nee-uh)
The tough, transparent, outer part of the
eye. The cornea covers the **pupil** and **iris.**

corona (kuh-**roh**-nuh)
The outer atmosphere of the sun or
another star. You can see the sun's
corona only during a **solar eclipse.** From
the Latin *corona,* meaning "crown."

coronary (**kor**-uh-*ner*-ee)
Having to do with the heart. *Also,* a
popular term for heart attack, which is
the blockage of a coronary **artery.**

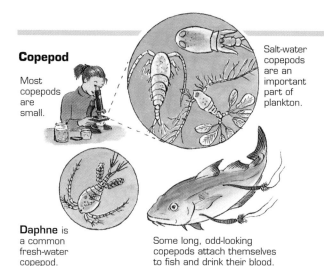

Copepod

Most copepods are small.

Salt-water copepods are an important part of plankton.

Daphne is a common fresh-water copepod.

Some long, odd-looking copepods attach themselves to fish and drink their blood.

corpuscle (**kor**-*puhs*-uhl)
A small rounded body. A blood corpuscle is a **red blood cell** or a white blood cell (**leukocyte**).

corrosion (kuh-**roh**-zhuhn)
The slow eating away of a material by a liquid or gas. You most often see corrosion in metals, such as iron. When water or moist air reacts with iron we get rust. From the Latin *corrodere,* meaning "to gnaw to pieces."

cosmic rays (**kahz**-mik **rayz**)
High-**energy particles** from the sun, stars, and **galaxies**. Cosmic rays travel at nearly the speed of light.

cosmic strings (**kahz**-mik **stringz**)
In **theory**, endless structures that were formed immediately after the **Big Bang.** Some believe that cosmic strings hold the **galaxies** together.

cosmology (kahz-**mahl**-uh-jee)
The study of the **universe**, including how it began, what it contains, and how it is changing. See also **Big Bang.**

cosmonaut (**kahz**-muh-*nawt*)
A Russian astronaut.

cotyledon (*kaht*-l-**eed**-n)
Part of a plant seed. Some plants have one; others have as many as 15. Also called a *seed leaf.*

covalent bond (koh-**vay**-luhnt **bahnd**)
See **ionic bond.**

CPR (see-*pee*-**ahr**)
Short for *CardioPulmonary Resuscitation.* CPR is a way to help someone whose breathing and heartbeat have stopped. It includes breathing into the victim's mouth to get **oxygen** into the lungs and pressing on the victim's chest to force blood through the heart.

CPU (see-*pee*-**yoo**)
Short for *Central Processing Unit.* The heart of a computer. Instructions from the user go to the CPU, which then guides the computer's operations.

crater (**kray**-tuhr)
A bowl-shaped hollow found at the tops of **volcanoes** or where large **meteorites** from space have landed.

Cretaceous period
(kri-**tay**-shuhs **pir**-ee-uhd)
The period in **geological history** from about 138 to 65 million years ago. Flowering plants became common during this period and the dinosaurs died out at the end.

Crick (krik), **Francis H. C.** (born 1916)
An English scientist who discovered the shape of the **DNA molecule** in 1953 with **James D. Watson.**

Cro-Magnon
(kroh-**mag**-nuhn or kroh-**man**-yuhn)
Prehistoric people who lived in Europe and Asia from about 40,000 to 10,000 years ago. Cro-Magnons were an early form of today's human beings. They were named after a cave in France where their remains were found in 1868.

crop (**krahp**)
Plants grown for food. *Also,* a sac in the **esophagus** of some birds, earthworms, and insects, where food is stored.

CRT (see-*ahr*-tee)
Short for **cathode ray tube.**

crust (**kruhst**)
The hard, rocky covering of the earth. The crust is about 5 miles (8 kilometers) thick under the oceans and 25 miles (40 kilometers) thick under the **continents.** See also **Earth.**

crustacean (kruh-**stay**-shuhn)
An animal that has a hard outer shell, no bones inside its body, and legs with many joints. Most crustaceans, including crabs, shrimps, and lobsters, live in the sea. From the Latin *crusta,* meaning "hard shell."

cryogenics (*krie*-uh-**jen**-iks)
The study of very low temperatures, below about -238° **Fahrenheit** (-150° **Celsius**). From the Greek *kryos,* meaning "cold," and *-genes,* meaning "born."

crystal (**kris**-tuhl)
A solid with its **atoms** arranged in a regular shape. A crystal has smooth, flat surfaces that meet at sharp angles. Most minerals are made up of crystals.

CT (**see-tee**)
Short for Computerized Tomography, another name for **CAT scan.**

culture (**kuhl**-chuhr)
The **laboratory** growth of **cells** or **microbes** in a **nutrient.** Scientists use cultures for **research,** to identify different diseases, and to manufacture various drugs.

culture medium
(**kuhl**-chuhr *mee*-dee-uhm)
A substance used in **laboratories** for growing **microorganisms.** Also called *medium.*

cumulus (**kyoo**-myuh-luhs)
A rounded, fluffy, fair-weather cloud. From the Latin *cumulus,* meaning "heap" or "pile."

Curie (**kyur**-ee), **Marie** (1867–1934) and **Pierre** (1859–1906)
Wife and husband team of French scientists who studied **radioactivity** and discovered the **elements radium** and polonium.

current (**kuhr**-uhnt)
The flow of electricity through a wire or other **conductor.** *Also,* a stream of water moving within another body of water. The Japan current flows through the Pacific Ocean. From the Latin *currere,* meaning "to run."

cursor (**kuhr**-suhr)
A symbol that moves on a computer screen to mark a position.

cyberspace (**sie**-buhr-*spays*)
Everything that can be seen or heard through a computer. Cyberspace lets users feel that they are entering a different world. See also **virtual reality.**

cycle (**sie**-kuhl)
Any series of events or actions that happens over and over again. Examples of cycles are day and night, the seasons, and the **water cycle.** From the Greek *kyklos,* meaning "circle."

cyclone (**sie**-klohn)
A **low-pressure area** in the **atmosphere** with winds blowing inward to form a spiral. A small, strong cyclone is a **tornado.** If a cyclone in a tropical area has winds of over 74 miles (119 kilometers) an hour it is called a **hurricane.**

cyclotron (**sie**-kluh-*trahn*)
A **particle accelerator** that shoots particles in a huge circle.

cytology (sie-**tahl**-uh-jee)
The study of **cells.** From the Greek *kytos,* meaning "hollow vessel," and *-logia,* meaning "science of."

cytoplasm (**site**-uh-*plaz*-uhm)
All the material in a **cell,** except what is in the **nucleus.**

D

Dalton (**dawlt**-n), **John** (1766–1844)
An English chemist who helped develop modern **atomic theory**. Dalton found that each **chemical element** has its own kind of **atoms**, all with the same relative **atomic weight**.

dam (**dam**)
A barrier across a stream or river that holds back flowing water. A dam is usually made of earth, rock, or **concrete**. Some animals, such as beavers, also build dams.

dark matter (**dahrk mat**-uhr)
The invisible substance that makes up most of the **mass** of **galaxies**. Dark matter neither gives off nor reflects light. Astronomers believe it makes up over 90 percent of the mass of the **universe**.

Darwin (**dahr**-win), **Charles** (1809–1882)
An English scientist who is famous for his **theory** of **evolution**. Darwin believed that all living things have developed gradually over time by the process of **natural selection**.

DAT (**dat**)
Short for *Digital Audio Tape*. DAT is used to make **digital** cassette recordings of music or speech. The tape itself is a long **magnetic tape**.

data (**day**-tuh or **dat**-uh)
Facts, numbers, or words that provide you with information. Data is the plural of *datum*, a word that is seldom used.

database (**dayt**-uh *bays* or **dat**-uh-*bays*)
Related and organized **data** that is stored in **electronic** form in a computer memory or on a computer **disk**.

Davy (**day**-vee), **Sir Humphry** (1778–1829)
An English chemist who discovered how to split a **compound** into its **elements** by passing electricity through the compound. In this way, he was the first to isolate **sodium, potassium, calcium**, and several other elements. See also **electrolysis**.

day (**day**)
The time it takes a planet to spin completely around its **axis**. A day on Earth lasts about 24 hours. A day on **Jupiter** lasts only about 10 hours.

dB (**dee-bee**)
Short for **decibel**.

DC (**dee-see**)
See **direct current**.

DDT (**dee**-*dee*-tee)
Short for *Dichloro-Diphenyl-Trichloroethane*. DDT is a powerful **insecticide**. When farmers spread it on their crops, it remains in the plants and

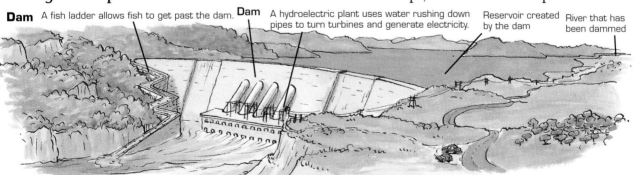

Dam A fish ladder allows fish to get past the dam. **Dam** A hydroelectric plant uses water rushing down pipes to turn turbines and generate electricity. Reservoir created by the dam. River that has been dammed

harms animals that eat the plants and humans who eat the plants or animals. DDT is little used in the United States, but is freely used in many other countries.

debug (dee-**buhg**)
To correct a problem in a computer's **hardware** or **software**. The name arose in the early days of computers when scientists had to remove insects from inside the huge machines.

decay (di-**kay**)
The slow, steady breaking down of dead plants or animals into simpler **compounds**. *Also,* the natural breakdown of **radioactive elements** into other elements of lighter weight.

decibel (**des**-uh-*bel*)
A unit for measuring the **volume**, or loudness, of a sound. The decibel is named after **Alexander Graham Bell**, who did important sound **experiments**. A sound of 10 decibels can barely be heard; 140 decibels hurts your ears. (Symbol—dB)

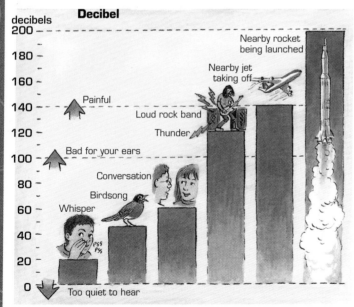

deciduous (di-**sij**-oo-uhs)
Having leaves that fall off each year. Deciduous trees include maples, elms, and most oaks. Their leaves are broad and flat. Their wood is harder than the wood of **needleleaf trees**. Also called

broadleaf trees. *Also,* deciduous teeth is another name for baby teeth.

decomposition (dee-*kahm*-puh-**zish**-uhn)
The **decay** or rotting of dead plants and animals. *Also,* the breaking down of a **chemical compound** into its parts.

deduction (di-**duhk**-shuhn)
Arriving at a conclusion from studying evidence collected in **experiments** or by **observation**. The process of deduction is called *deductive reasoning.* From the Latin *deductio,* meaning "leading away."

deforestation (dee-*for*-uh-**stay**-shuhn)
Cutting down the trees and destroying a forest. In *slash-and-burn* deforestation, workers cut down all the trees that can be used for lumber and burn the rest.

degree (di-**gree**)
A unit of temperature measurement. *Also,* a unit for measuring angles, or arcs, in **astronomy** and **mathematics**. From the Latin *de,* meaning "down," and *gradus,* meaning "step."

dehydration (*dee*-hie-**dray**-shuhn)
The removal of water from a substance. Dehydration preserves foods and makes them lighter and easier to transport. *Also,* extreme loss of water from the body, which can cause a fast heartbeat and low blood pressure, or even death.

delete (di-**leet**)
To remove a character, **data**, or a **file** from a computer's memory or **disk**.

delta (**del**-tuh)
A flat, triangular area of **sediment** left by a river as it enters the sea. *Also,* the triangle-shaped, 4th letter of the Greek alphabet.

Democritus (di-**mahk**-ruh-tuhs) (ca. 460–370 B.C.)
A Greek philosopher who believed that everything is made up of tiny **particles** that he called **atoms**—and that these particles could not be broken down.

Density

Cork: Molecules are farther apart than those of water, so it is less dense and floats.

Water molecules are closer together.

Iron atoms are packed tightly. The iron screw is denser and sinks in water.

density (**den**-suh-tee)
How tightly the matter of an object is packed together. For example, the density of iron is greater than the density of wood.

deoxyribonucleic acid
(dee-**ahk**-see-*rie*-boh-noo-**klay**-ik **as**-id)
See **DNA**.

deposit (di-**pahz**-it)
Soil and rocks dropped by flowing water, moving ice, or blowing wind. From the Latin *de*, meaning "away," and *ponere*, meaning "put."

depressant (di-**pres**-uhnt)
A drug that lessens pain, causes sleep, or reduces anxiety. Depressants can also slow the activity of **organs**, such as the brain.

depression (di-**presh**-uhn)
A region of lower **pressure** in the **atmosphere**. *Also,* a mental state in which a person feels sad and hopeless. *Also,* a low area on the surface of a planet.

dermatology (*duhr*-muh-**tahl**-uh-jee)
The branch of medicine that **diagnoses** and treats diseases of the skin, nails, and hair. From the Greek *derma*, meaning "skin," and *-logia*, meaning "science of."

desert (**dez**-uhrt)
An area that receives less than 10 inches (25.4 centimeters) of rain a year. See also **biome**.

designer genes (di-**zine**-uhr **jeenz**)
Popular name for **genes** that are changed so that they can carry different **traits**. See also **gene splicing** or **genetic engineering**.

Devonian period
(di-**voh**-nee-uhn **pir**-ee-uhd)
The period of **geological history** from about 395 to 360 million years ago. Fish filled the seas and the first forests appeared during the Devonian period.

dew (**doo**)
Small drops of water that collect, or **condense**, on cool surfaces during the night.

dew point (**doo** *point*)
The temperature at which the moisture in the air begins to **condense** into fog, clouds, frost, or dew.

diabetes (*die*-uh-**bee**-tuhs)
A disease in which the body cannot absorb normal amounts of sugar. People with diabetes have too much sugar in their blood, and produce large amounts of **urine**. The full name of the disease is *diabetes mellitus*.

diagnosis (*die*-ig-**noh**-sis)
Deciding a patient's disease by examination and test results. The diagnosis helps the doctor choose the best way to treat the condition. From the Greek *dia*, meaning "through," and *gignoskein*, meaning "to know."

diagnostic (*die*-ig-**nahs**-tik)
A program used to test the different parts of a computer to find whether the various parts are working correctly.

diamond
(**die**-muhnd or **die**-uh-muhnd)
A **crystal** substance formed of pure **carbon**. Diamond is the hardest natural

substance. It is widely used in jewelry and to make very strong, hard, cutting and grinding tools.

diaphragm (**die**-uh-*fram*)
A large, flat muscle that separates the chest from the **abdomen.** *Also,* a device on a camera or **microscope** that controls the amount of light that passes through. *Also,* a thin disk that **vibrates** when receiving or producing sound waves.

diarrhea (*die*-uh-**ree**-uh)
A condition of frequent and watery bowel movements. Diarrhea may come from eating spoiled food.

diatom (**die**-uh-*tahm*)
A tiny, one-celled, hard-shelled **organism.** Diatoms are a kind of **algae.** They are part of the **plankton** found in the ocean.

dicotyledon (*die*-kaht-l-**eed**-n)
Any flowering plant that has two seed leaves, a **network** of **veins** in the leaves, and stems that form rings every year. Dicotyledons include bean plants, lettuce, geraniums, and most **hardwood** trees. The name is often shortened to *dicot.*

diesel engine (**dee**-zuhl **en**-juhn)
A kind of **internal combustion engine.** The diesel engine is mostly used in big trucks, buses, tractors, and locomotives. It was named after its German inventor, *Rudolf Diesel (1858–1913),* in 1892.

diffraction (di-**frak**-shuhn)
The breaking up of light, sound, or water waves as they pass around the edge of an object or through an opening. The diffraction of white light, for example, produces the entire **spectrum** of all colors. From the Latin *dis-,* meaning "apart," and *frangere,* meaning "to break."

diffusion (di-**fyoo**-zhuhn)
The spreading out of the **atoms** or **molecules** of one substance among those of another. Diffusion occurs most often in liquids and gases. *Also,* the scattering of light when passing through **translucent** material or reflected off a rough surface.

digest (die-**jest**)
To change or break food down into a form the body can use. From the Latin *dis,* meaning "apart," and *gerere,* meaning "to carry."

digestion (die-**jes**-chuhn)
The breaking down of food in the body so that its **nutrients** can enter the

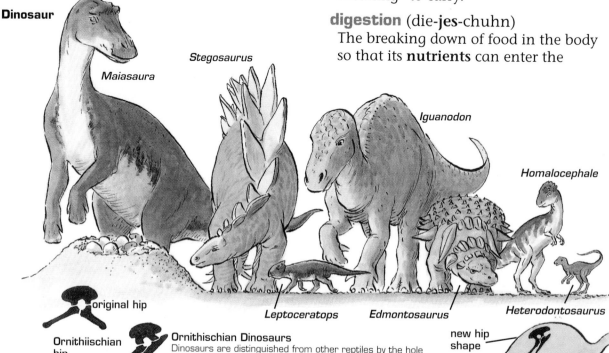

Dinosaur

Maiasaura

Stegosaurus

Iguanodon

Homalocephale

original hip

Ornithiischian hip

Leptoceratops

Edmontosaurus

Heterodontosaurus

new hip shape

Ornithischian Dinosaurs
Dinosaurs are distinguished from other reptiles by the hole in their hip socket. Ornithischians developed a variation on this in which both long bones point back.

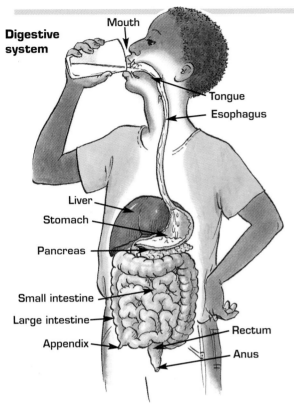

Digestive system

- Mouth
- Tongue
- Esophagus
- Liver
- Stomach
- Pancreas
- Small intestine
- Large intestine
- Appendix
- Rectum
- Anus

bloodstream and be carried throughout the body.

digestive system (die-**jes**-tiv *sis*-tuhm)
The **organs** of digestion. The digestive system in humans includes the mouth, tongue, **esophagus**, stomach, **pancreas**, **gall bladder**, **liver**, **small** and **large** **intestines**, **rectum**, and **anus**.

digital (**dij**-uht-l)
Using numbers to present information or measurements. See also **analog**.

digital versatile disk (**dij**-uht-l **vuhr**-suht-l disk)
See **DVD**.

digital video disk (**dij**-uht-l **vid**-ee-*oh* disk)
See **DVD**.

dinosaurs (**die**-nuh-*sorz*)
A large group of extinct animals that lived from about 220 to 65 million years ago. From the Greek *deinos*, meaning "terrible," and *sauros*, meaning "lizard."

diode (**die**-ohd)
An **electronic** device that allows **electric current** to flow in only one direction. A diode is used to change **alternating current** into **direct current**.

Tyrannosaurus

Diplodocus

Dinosaur

Oviraptor

Plateosaurus

Velociraptor

Sinosauropteryx   *Compsognathus*

Saurischian Dinosaurs
Saurischians kept the original hip shape but developed a fancy new hand shape with fingers of different sizes.

old hip shape

new hand shape

direct current (duh-**rekt kuhr**-uhnt)
An **electric current** that flows in one direction only. Direct current is produced by batteries, **fuel cells**, and **photoelectric cells**. Often shortened to *DC*. See also **alternating current**.

dirigible (duh-**rij**-uh-buhl)
A large balloon airship that is lighter than air and can carry numbers of people. Dirigibles have engines and can be steered.

disc (**disk**)
See **disk**.

disease (di-**zeez**)
Sickness or ill health. Diseases are caused by **bacteria, viruses,** or other **microorganisms,** by exposure to poisons in the **environment;** are inherited; or result from a poor diet, smoking, or a poorly functioning **organ** or **system** of the body.

disinfectant (*dis*-in-**fek**-tuhnt)
Any substance that kills germs on objects. Some common disinfectants are **alcohol,** and **compounds** with **iodine, chlorine,** and **ammonia.** A substance used to kill germs on people is called an **antiseptic.**

disk (**disk**)
A round, flat piece of plastic used for storing information in computers, or for recording and playing back sound and pictures. See also **compact disc, CD-ROM, DVD.**

diskette (dis-**ket**)
A flat, square **magnetic memory** device, 3½ x 3½ inches (8.9 x 8.9 centimeters), that is used to store information that can be read by a computer.

dispersion (dis-**puhr**-zhuhn)
The separation of light or other **electromagnetic waves** into different **wavelengths.** Dispersion occurs when you shine light through a **prism** and make a **spectrum** of many colors. *Also,* the scattering of **particles** of one substance throughout another.

displacement (dis-**plays**-muhnt)
The weight of the fluid that is pushed out of the way by an object in the fluid. The weight of the pushed-out fluid equals the weight of the object.

dissect (di-**sekt**, die-)
To cut an animal or plant into parts in order to see its inside structure. From the Latin *dis,* meaning "apart," and *secare,* meaning "to cut."

dissolve (di-**zahlv**)
To add a solid or gas to a liquid so that the solid or gas disappears. Sugar or salt dissolves in water.

distillation (*dist*-l-**ay**-shuhn)
A way of separating substances from a **solution.** Distillation involves heating a liquid and **condensing** the different gases or **vapors** that form.

DNA (dee-*en*-**ay**)
The material in the **genes** that passes **characteristics** from one generation to

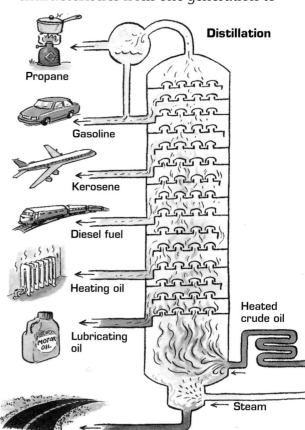

Distillation

Propane

Gasoline

Kerosene

Diesel fuel

Heating oil

Lubricating oil

Heated crude oil

Steam

Tar and asphalt

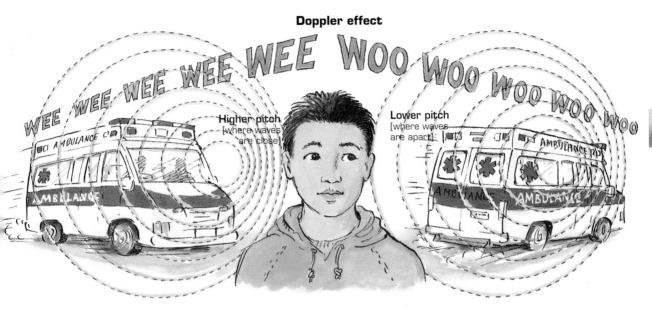

Doppler effect

WEE WEE WEE WEE WEE WOO WOO WOO WOO WOO

Higher pitch
[where waves
are close]

Lower pitch
[where waves
are apart]

the next. The DNA **molecule** is made up of two spiral threads that are connected to each other in a shape called a **double helix**. DNA is short for *DeoxyriboNucleic Acid*.

document (**dahk**-yuh-muhnt)
A **file** of **data** or text that is stored in the computer's memory. *Also,* any piece of paper with important or official information.

dominant (**dahm**-uh-nuhnt)
The one **trait** of a pair of **inherited** traits that appears in an animal or plant. For example, if you inherit a **gene** for blue eyes from one parent and a gene for brown eyes from the other, your eyes will be brown because brown eyes are dominant over blue. *Also,* the animal that is strongest and the leader of a group.

Doppler effect (**dahp**-luhr i-*fekt*)
The change in sound, light, or other waves that occurs when either the wave source or the observer is moving. When an ambulance siren comes toward you, the sound waves shorten and the **pitch** goes up. As it speeds away, the sound waves spread out and the pitch goes down. Named after the Austrian physicist, *Christian Doppler* (1803–1853), who described the effect in 1842.

dorsal (**dor**-suhl)
The back part of something. The dorsal fin of a shark, for example, is on its back.

DOS (**dahs**)
Short for *Disk Operating System*. A **program** that directs a computer.

double helix (**duhb**-uhl **hee**-liks)
The shape of a **molecule** of **DNA**. The double helix is made up of two spiral chains with short links connecting the chains. It looks like a twisted ladder.

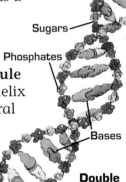

Sugars

Phosphates

Bases

Double Helix

double star (**duhb**-uhl **stahr**)
Two stars that appear to the naked eye as a single point of light.

down (**doun**)
Describes a computer that is not working. *Also,* the soft feathers next to a bird's body. The down is **insulation** for the bird.

download (**doun**-*lohd*)
To move a computer **file** from one computer to another or to a **disk**.

Down syndrome
(**doun** *sin*-drohm)
A form of mental retardation that appears at birth and is caused by a defect in a **chromosome**. The condition is named after *John Down* (1828–1896), who described it in 1866. Also called *Down's syndrome*.

drag (**drag**)
The push that holds an object back as it moves through a gas or liquid. The drag of the wind slows down airplanes.

drought (**drout**)
A lack of rain over a long period of time. Drought causes a shortage of water for use by people, animals, and plants.

drug (**druhg**)
Any substance, other than food, that produces a change when taken into the body. Drugs are usually used to prevent or cure disease. Sometimes, people take illegal drugs to change their moods. Illegal drugs can be very harmful and lead to **addiction.**

dry cell (**drie** *sel*)
A battery that produces **electric current** to operate toys and small **electronic** devices.

dry ice (**drie ise**)
A very cold, white, solid form of the gas **carbon dioxide.** People use dry ice for cooling foods or medicines. It changes from a solid to a **gas** without passing through the liquid state.

ductility (duhk-**til**-uh-tee)
The ability to take on a new shape without breaking. Ductility in metals lets them be drawn out into thin wires or hammered into different shapes.

dump (**duhmp**)
To print material stored in a computer or on a **disk.**

duodenum (*doo*-uh-**dee**-nuhm or du-**ahd**-n-uhm)
The upper end of the **small intestine,** just below the stomach.

DVD (**dee**-*vee*-**dee**)
Originally short for *Digital Video Disk.* A DVD is a large flat **disk** that is "read" by a **laser.** People use DVDs to show movies or television programs on television or computer screens. The DVD takes the place of video cassettes. *Also,* short for *Digital Versatile Disk.* This DVD is for **audio** recordings. It carries more music and produces sound of higher quality than CDs. See also **laser disk.**

dynamite (**die**-nuh-*mite*)
A powerful **explosive** used to blast rock for digging mines and canals, building foundations, and so on. It was invented in 1867 by the *Swedish* chemist **Alfred Nobel.**

dynamo (**die**-nuh-*moh*)
A machine that changes **mechanical energy,** such as water power, into electric energy and **electric current.** A dynamo is sometimes called a **generator.**

dyslexia (dis-**lek**-see-uh)
A reading disability that occurs when the brain confuses signals from the eyes. Dyslexia can cause people to mix up words and letters, so that they read "rat" as "tar," for example.

ear (ir)

The **organ** for hearing. The 3 parts are: outer ear, which is the part you see; middle ear, which **amplifies** the sound; and inner ear, which sends a signal to the brain. The inner ear also helps people keep their balance. *Also,* the seed-containing part of some grain plants, such as an ear of corn.

eardrum (ir-*druhm*)

A thin layer of **tissue** between the outer and middle ear. The eardrum picks up sound **vibrations** in the air and passes them to the tiny bones in the middle ear. An eardrum is also called a *tympanum.*

earphones (ir-*fohnz*)

See **headphones.**

Earth (uhrth)

The third planet from the sun in the **solar system.**

Average distance from sun: 92,960,000 miles (149,600,000 kilometers)
Diameter at equator: 7,926 miles (12,756 kilometers)

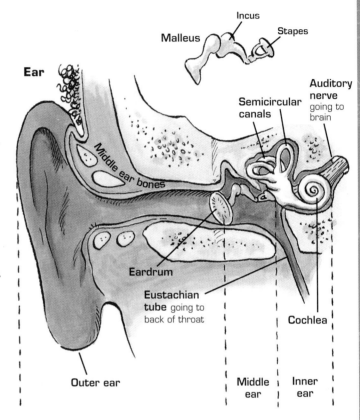

Ear

Incus
Stapes
Malleus
Middle ear bones
Semicircular canals
Auditory nerve going to brain
Eardrum
Eustachian tube going to back of throat
Cochlea
Outer ear
Middle ear
Inner ear

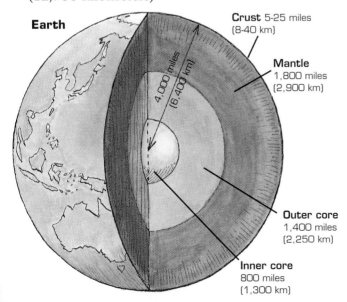

Earth

Crust 5-25 miles (8-40 km)
4,000 miles (6,400 km)
Mantle 1,800 miles (2,900 km)
Outer core 1,400 miles (2,250 km)
Inner core 800 miles (1,300 km)

Length of day: 23 hours, 56 minutes, 4 seconds
Length of year: 365.25 earth days.

The inside of the earth is divided into four layers. The hard, rocky **crust** averages about 5 miles (8 kilometers) thick under oceans and about 25 miles (40 kilometers) thick under **continents.** The **mantle** is a layer of semisolid rock about 1,800 miles (2,900 kilometers) thick.

The **outer core** is 1,400 miles (2,250 kilometers) thick. It is thought to be made of melted iron and nickel.

The **inner core** starts 3,100 miles (5,000 kilometers) down and runs 900 miles (1,440 kilometers) to the center of the earth. The inner core is probably made of solid iron and nickel.

earthquake (**uhrth**-*kwayk*)
A violent shaking of the ground due to sudden shifts in parts of the earth's **crust**. Earthquakes usually occur along a **fault**, which is a break in the crust where the plates that make up the earth's crust rub against each other. See also **plate tectonics.**

ebb tide (**eb** *tide*)
The flow of ocean water away from the coast as low tide approaches. Also called *ebb current.*

echo (**ek**-oh)
A sound that bounces back from a distant object. The echo is heard after the original sound because of the time it takes for sound to travel. An echo is produced by sound waves reflected off a wall or building.

echolocation (*ek*-oh-loh-**kay**-shuhn)
A way to find objects by listening for **echoes**. Echolocation is used by bats, dolphins, and some other animals to avoid danger and find food.

eclipse (i-**klips**)
The temporary blotting out of the light of a heavenly body. A **solar eclipse** is when the moon passes between the earth and sun. A **lunar eclipse** is when the moon passes through the earth's

shadow. From the Greek *ex*, meaning "out," and *leipein*, meaning "to leave."

ecliptic (i-**klip**-tik)
The pathway of the sun over a year as seen against the background of the stars.

ecology (i-**kahl**-uh-jee)
The study of the relationships among plants, animals, and other living things in their **environments**. Ecology is concerned with **populations**—the members of the same **species** living in one area; **communities**—the different plant and animal species in an area; and **ecosystems**—communities and their environments. From the Greek *oik*, meaning "environment," and *-logia*, meaning "science of."

ecosystem (**ek**-oh-*sis*-tuhm)
All the living things in an area. An ecosystem also includes the climate, water supply, **nutrients**, and soil. Every ecosystem can be divided into 5 main parts:

Source of energy—The sun is the major source of **energy.**
Primary producers—Green plants and plantlike **protists** that make their own food by **photosynthesis.**
Primary consumers—Animals, such as

Eclipse

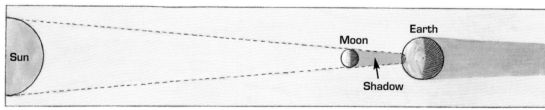

Solar eclipse

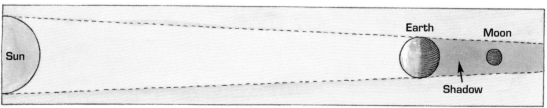

Lunar eclipse

Ecosystem

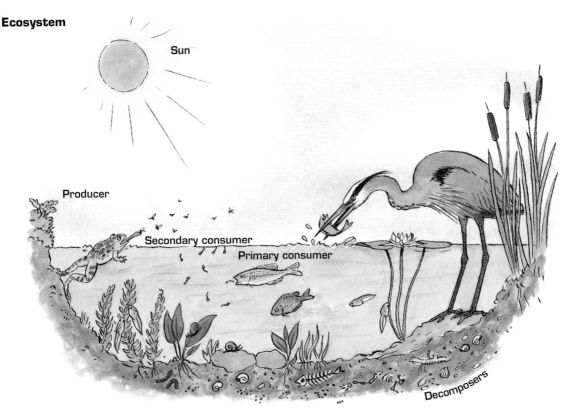

Sun

Producer

Secondary consumer

Primary consumer

Decomposers

rabbits and cows, that eat primary producers.

Secondary consumers—Animals, such as wolves and foxes, that eat other animals, and some birds.

Decomposers—**Bacteria** and other **microbes** that break down dead producers and consumers into simple **nutrients**, which go back into the soil.

ectothermic (*ek*-toh-**thuhr**-mik)
See **cold-blooded.**

eczema (**ek**-suh-muh, ig-**zee**-muh)
A condition in which the skin is dry, rough, itchy, and inflamed. Eczema can be treated with special skin creams. From the Greek *eks,* meaning "out," and *zein,* meaning "to boil."

Eddington (**ed**-ing-tuhn), **Sir Arthur** (1882–1944)
A British astronomer who made important discoveries on the life **cycle** of stars. Eddington's observations helped prove **Einstein's Theory of Relativity.**

Edison (**ed**-uh-suhn), **Thomas Alva** (1847–1931)
An outstanding American inventor. Edison patented the **electric** lightbulb, the phonograph, and more than 1,000 other inventions. He also improved the **telephone**, the typewriter, motion pictures, electric **generators**, and set up the first electric power systems.

efficiency (ee-**fish**-uhn-see)
The work a machine does compared to the **energy** needed to run the machine. The efficiency of most automobile engines, is only about 30 percent. The rest of the energy is lost in heat and **vibrations.**

egg (**eg**)
The **reproductive cell** produced by a female **organism.** When an egg is **fertilized** by a male **sperm** cell, the fertilized egg starts to grow into a new being. Birds, **reptiles**, fish, and **amphibians** lay eggs outside their body. The eggs of most **mammals** develop inside the body of the female.

egg tooth (eg *tooth*)
A small, sharp structure on the upper beak of baby birds and turtles used to help the young animal break out of its egg.

Ehrlich (er-lik), Paul (1854–1915)
A German bacteriologist who found ways to treat various diseases with **chemicals.**

Einstein (ine-stine), Albert (1879–1955)
A German-born American physicist and one of the outstanding scientists of all time. Einstein is best known for stating the two **theories of relativity** and working on a **unified field theory.** His famous equation $E=mc^2$ led to the development of **nuclear energy.**

elasticity (i-*las*-tis-uh-tee)
The ability of a solid to return to its original size and shape after being squeezed, stretched, or bent. Some elasticity is present in all solids. Metal springs and rubber bands are especially elastic.

electrical engineering (i-lek-tri-kuhl *en*-juh-nir-ing)
The branch of **engineering** that deals with developing, making, and testing **electrical** and **electronic** devices.

electric circuit (i-lek-trik suhr-kit)
The path along which an **electric current** flows. An electric circuit consists of a source of electricity (such as a battery or **generator**), devices (such as lamps) that need **electricity, conductors** (such as wires) to carry the electricity, and switches to open or close the circuit.

electric current (i-lek-trik kuhr-uhnt)
The flow of **electric charges** through a **conductor.** The electric current is carried by **electrons** flowing from **atom** to atom through the conductor. Electric current can flow back and forth (**alternating current**) or in one direction (**direct current**).

electric eye (i-lek-trik ie)
A device that produces an **electric current** when light shines on it. The electric eye contains material that gives off **electrons** when struck by light. Electric eyes are used to open doors and turn on street lights. Also called **photoelectric cell** or *photocell.*

electricity (i-*lek*-tris-uh-tee)
A form of **energy** produced by the movement of **electrons.** Electricity comes from such sources as electric **generators** and batteries. The flow of electricity gives us heat and light, creates **electromagnets,** and powers everything from tiny toys to giant machines. From the Greek *elektron,* meaning "amber," since rubbing amber produces **static electricity.** See also **static electricity.**

electric motor (i-lek-trik moh-tuhr)
A machine that uses **electric energy** to make something move. Electric motors turn the blades in electric fans and move the hands in electric clocks, for example.

electrocardiograph (i-*lek*-troh-kahr-dee-uh-*graf*)
An instrument that records the heart's electrical activity. To use the electrocardiograph, the doctor places **electrodes** on the patient's chest, arms, and legs. The electrodes pick up tiny electrical signals from the heart and produce the *electrocardiogram* (called an *ECG,* or *EKG*). The ECG shows the heartbeats, which the doctor studies to see the condition of the patient's heart.

electrode (i-lek-*trohd*)
A conductor, usually metal, that brings **electric current** into or out of an **electric** device. All batteries have two electrodes, labeled (+) and (-).

electrolysis (i-*lek*-trahl-uh-sis)
Passing an **electric current** through a liquid to break it down into its **elements.**

For example, electrolysis separates water into **hydrogen** and **oxygen.** If a liquid has metal in **solution,** electrolysis removes the metal. *Also,* a way to destroy hair roots by **electric current.**

electrolyte (i-lek-truh-*lite*)
A liquid or a paste that **conducts electricity.** You can find electrolytes in most batteries. Electrolytes are also used in **electrolysis** and **electroplating.**

electromagnet (i-*lek*-troh-**mag**-nit)
A temporary magnet created when **electric current** flows through a **conductor.** Most electromagnets consist of a **coil** of wire wound around an iron **core.** When electric current flows through the wire, the iron becomes a **magnet.** When the electric flow stops, the iron loses its magnetism.

electromagnetic induction (i-*lek*-troh-mag-**net**-ik in-**duhk**-shuhn)
Using **magnetism** to produce an **electric current.** Electromagnetic induction occurs in a **coil** of wire when you move a magnet past the coil or move the coil past a magnet. **Generators** use electromagnetic induction to produce electricity.

electromagnetic spectrum (i-*lek*-troh-mag-**net**-ik **spek**-truhm)
Electromagnetic waves of all different lengths. The spectrum ranges from short **gamma waves** to long radio waves.

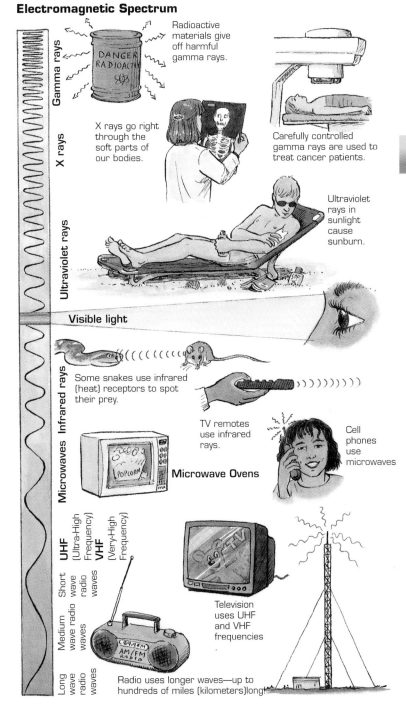

Electromagnetic Spectrum

Gamma rays

Radioactive materials give off harmful gamma rays.

X rays

X rays go right through the soft parts of our bodies.

Carefully controlled gamma rays are used to treat cancer patients.

Ultraviolet rays

Ultraviolet rays in sunlight cause sunburn.

Visible light

Infrared rays

Some snakes use infrared (heat) receptors to spot their prey.

TV remotes use infrared rays.

Cell phones use microwaves

Microwave Ovens

Microwaves

UHF (Ultra-High Frequency)

VHF (Very-High Frequency)

Short wave radio waves

Television uses UHF and VHF frequencies

Medium wave radio waves

Long wave radio waves

Radio uses longer waves—up to hundreds of miles (kilometers) long.

electromagnetic waves (i-*lek*-troh-mag-**net**-ik **wayvz**)
Waves of **electrical** and **magnetic** force created by the **vibration** of **electrons.** Electromagnetic waves travel at the speed of light and can be reflected, bent, and scattered like visible light. See also **electromagnetic spectrum.**

electromotive force
(i-*lek*-troh-**moh**-tiv **fors**)
The force that makes **electrons** move through an **electric circuit**. Electromotive force, or *emf,* comes from a source of **electrical energy,** such as a battery or **generator.** Also called **voltage.**

electron (i-**lek**-trahn)
A tiny **particle** within an **atom** that carries a **negative electric charge.** The electrons travel at great speed in **orbits** around the atom's **nucleus.**

electronics (i-*lek*-**trahn**-iks)
The study of electrical signals in such devices as computers, radios, and televisions. Electronic equipment usually contains **semiconductors** and **transistors.**

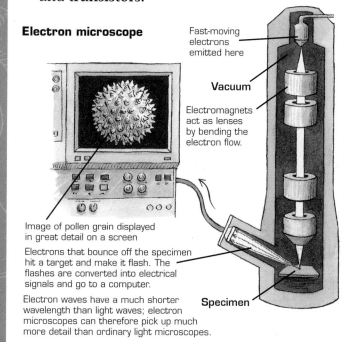

Electron microscope

Fast-moving electrons emitted here

Vacuum

Electromagnets act as lenses by bending the electron flow.

Image of pollen grain displayed in great detail on a screen

Electrons that bounce off the specimen hit a target and make it flash. The flashes are converted into electrical signals and go to a computer.

Electron waves have a much shorter wavelength than light waves; electron microscopes can therefore pick up much more detail than ordinary light microscopes.

Specimen

electron microscope
(i-**lek**-trahn **mie**-kruh-*skohp*)
A very powerful **microscope** that sends a beam of **electrons,** instead of regular light, onto or through an object. An electron microscope can magnify a specimen up to a million times. An ordinary light microscope can only magnify about 1,500 times.

electrophoresis (i-*lek*-troh-fuh-**ree**-sis)
A way of using electricity to separate and break apart large biological **molecules.**

electroplating (i-**lek**-truh-*play*-ting)
Putting a thin layer of metal on an object. Workers place an object in a **solution** of the metal, and pass an **electric current** through the solution. This causes **atoms** of the metal to stick to the object.

electroscope (i-**lek**-truh-*skohp*)
An instrument that detects an **electric charge.**

element (**el**-uh-muhnt)
A **chemical** substance that contains only one kind of **atom** and that cannot be broken down into simpler substances. There are 103 known elements. They are arranged and described in the **periodic table.**

ellipse (i-**lips**)
An oval. The **orbits** of **planets, asteroids,** and **comets** around the **sun** are ellipses.

El Niño (*el* **neen**-yoh)
A **current** of warm water in the Pacific Ocean that runs south along the western coast of South America. El Niño occurs every few years and causes major changes in the world's weather. From the Spanish *el niño,* meaning "the child" or "the Christ Child," since El Niño usually comes around Christmas.

e-mail (**ee**-*mayl*)
Short for *electronic mail,* a message sent from one computer to another.

embryo (**em**-bree-*oh*)
An animal or plant at a very early stage in its development. An animal embryo starts to grow when a male **sperm cell** fertilizes a female **egg** cell. *Also,* the part of a plant seed from which a new plant grows.

E = mc²
A **formula** developed by **Albert Einstein** showing that a great deal of **energy** (E) is

produced if a small amount of **mass** (m) is changed into energy. The c^2 is the **speed of light** squared. See also **relativity**.

emf (ee-*em*-ef)
Short for **electromotive force**.

emission (i-**mish**-uhn)
Any release of **matter** or **energy**, including heat, light, sound, radio waves, or tiny **particles**.

empirical (em-**pir**-i-kuhl)
Something learned from experiment or experience. From the Greek *en*, meaning "in," and *peiran*, meaning "to try."

emulsion (i-**muhl**-shuhn)
A mixture of two liquids that do not **dissolve** in each other. Milk is an emulsion of butterfat in water.

endangered species
(in-**dayn**-juhrd **spee**-sheez or **spee**-seez)
Any **species** of plant or animal that may become **extinct** because there are so few of them living today. Today's endangered species include tigers, blue whales, green pitcher plants, and Santa Cruz cypresses.

endocrine system
(**en**-duh-krin *sis*-tuhm)
A group of **glands** in the bodies of humans and animals. The endocrine glands release **chemicals**, called **hormones**, into the blood and **lymph**. The hormones control various body activities, from growth and development to digestion.

endorphin (en-**dor**-fuhn)
A substance in the **nervous system** of humans and animals. Endorphins help relieve pain and give a feeling of well-being.

endoskeleton (*en*-doh-**skel**-uht-n)
The **skeleton** or bones found inside the bodies of animals with backbones.

energy (**en**-uhr-jee)
The ability to do work, such as moving things or giving heat or light. Energy also is the ability of living things to grow.

Humans get their energy from the food they eat. Earth gets most of its energy from the **sun**. Energy cannot be created or destroyed, but it can be changed from one form to another. From the Greek *en*, meaning "in," and *ergon*, meaning "work."

engine (**en**-juhn)
A device that changes one kind of **energy** into another. For example, an automobile engine changes heat energy from burning gasoline into **mechanical energy** that turns the wheels of the car. See also **motor**. From the Latin *in*, meaning "in," and *gignere*, meaning "to produce."

engineering (*en*-juh-**nir**-ing)
The profession that uses science to design new machines, find better sources of power, build roads and bridges, and discover ways to make our lives easier and safer.

entomology (*ent*-uh-**mahl**-uh-jee)
The study of insects.

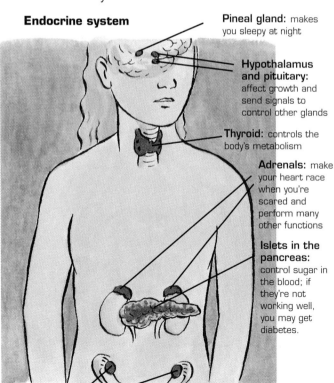

Endocrine system

Pineal gland: makes you sleepy at night

Hypothalamus and pituitary: affect growth and send signals to control other glands

Thyroid: controls the body's metabolism

Adrenals: make your heart race when you're scared and perform many other functions

Islets in the pancreas: control sugar in the blood; if they're not working well, you may get diabetes.

Gonads (ovaries in women, testicles in men): control sexual characteristics, such as breasts in women and beards in men

entropy (**en**-truh-pee)
A measure of the disorder or random nature of a system. Entropy is almost always increasing, going from order to disorder. For example, water **molecules** in ice are locked in a certain order. As the ice melts, the molecules scatter. The entropy increases. When the water **evaporates**, the molecules of water **vapor** in the air show even more entropy.

environment (in-**vie**-ruhn-muhnt)
Everything around a living thing. Your environment includes the climate, soil and water quality, food supply, buildings, plants and animals, **microorganisms**, and people that surround you. From the French *environner,* meaning "to surround."

enzyme (**en**-zime)
A **protein molecule** that starts or speeds up **chemical reactions** within living things without changing itself. Living things depend on enzymes for every part of their life **cycle**. Enzymes are also known as **catalysts**. From the Greek *en,* meaning "in," and *zyme,* meaning "yeast."

Eocene epoch (ee-oh-*seen* **ep**-uhk)
The **period** of **geological history** from 55 to 38 million years ago. The first cats, horses, monkeys, and whales appeared during the Eocene epoch.

epicenter (**ep**-i-*sen*-tuhr)
The point on the surface of the earth directly above the center or focus of an **earthquake**.

epidemic (*ep*-uh-**dem**-ik)
An outbreak of disease that strikes many people in the same area at about the same time. From the Greek *epi,* meaning "on," and *demos,* "people."

epidermis (*ep*-uh-**duhr**-mis)
The outer layer or skin of an animal. The epidermis is also the outer layer of **cells** of a plant.

epilepsy (**ep**-uh-*lep*-see)
A disorder of **nerve cells** in the brain. Epilepsy can cause a person to pass out and sometimes thrash about.

epiphyte (**ep**-uh-*fite*)
A plant that grows on another plant. Epiphytes get the **nutrients** they need from the air and rainwater, not from the plant on which they grow. **Mosses, lichens,** ferns, and orchids can grow as epiphytes. From the Greek *epi,* meaning "on," and *phyton,* "plant."

epoch (**ep**-uhk)
A division of the earth's **geological history** that is shorter than a **period**. The most recent period, the **Quaternary period,** is divided into the **Pleistocene epoch** and the **Holocene epoch**.

epoxy (i-**pahk**-see)
A plastic material used to make very strong glues and **adhesives**.

equation (i-**kway**-zhuhn)
A statement showing two equal amounts. An example of a **chemical** equation is: $2H_2 + O_2 \rightarrow 2H_2O$. It shows that two **molecules** of **hydrogen** ($2H_2$) plus one molecule of **oxygen** (O_2) produces ($\rightarrow$) two molecules of water ($2H_2O$).

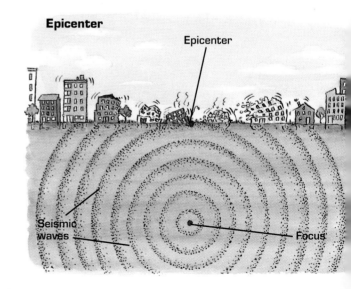
Epicenter
Epicenter
Seismic waves
Focus

equator (i-**kway**-tuhr)
An imaginary line around a **planet** halfway between its north and south poles. The equator divides the planet into a Northern Hemisphere and a Southern Hemisphere.

equilibrium
(*ee*-kwuh-**lib**-ree-uhm)
A state of balance. Equilibrium in **chemistry** means that there will be no further change. In **physics** it means that the forces acting on an object are balanced.

equinox (ee-kwuh-*nahks*)
One of the two times a year when the sun passes over the **equator** and day and night are equally long. The equinoxes in the Northern Hemisphere come around March 21 (start of spring) and September 22 (start of autumn). From the Latin *equus,* meaning "equal," and *nox,* meaning "night."

era (**ir**-uh or **er**-uh)
A large division of time in the earth's **geological history.** The three major eras are **Paleozoic era, Mesozoic era,** and **Cenozoic era.**

erg (**uhrg**)
A very small unit of work or **energy.**

ergonomics (*uhr*-guh-**nahm**-iks)
The study of the relationship between humans and the things around them. **Engineers** use ergonomics to devise safe and comfortable furniture, tools, and work **environments.**

erosion (i-**roh**-zhuhn)
The gradual wearing away of soil and rock from Earth's surface. In erosion, the materials are broken apart and carried away by wind, rain, and flowing water. From the Latin *ex,* meaning "away," and *rodere,* meaning "to gnaw."

erythrocyte (i-**rith**-ruh-*site*)
Another name for a **red blood cell.**

escape velocity
(is-**kayp** vuh-*lahs*-uh-tee)
The speed an object must reach to break free of the **gravitational** pull of a **planet.** The escape velocity for a rocket leaving Earth is about 7 miles (11 kilometers) a second.

esophagus (i-**sahf**-uh-guhs)
The tube that carries food from the mouth to the stomach. Muscles in the wall of the esophagus help to push the food down. Also called *gullet.*

ESP (ee-*es*-**pee**)
See **extrasensory perception.**

estivate (**es**-tuh-*vayt*)
To spend hot, dry periods of the summer in a sleeping state. Several kinds of frogs, snails, insects, and fish estivate. Their breathing and heartbeat slow down a great deal. From the Latin *aestivus,* meaning "relating to summer."

estuary (**es**-choo-*er*-ee)
The wide mouth of a river where it flows into a sea. The water in an estuary is a mix of salt water and freshwater.

Ergonomics
Good computer ergonomics

Monitor directly in front so your head doesn't have to turn

Look slightly down

Good back support

Wrists straight, hands relaxed

Adjustable keyboard tray

Adjustable chair height

Feet firmly on the floor or on a footrest

ethology (ee-**thahl**-uh-jee)
The study of animal behavior and **instincts** in the wild. Ethologists look at how animals communicate, care for their young, defend their territory, mate, and so on. From the Greek *ethos,* meaning "habit," and *-logia,* meaning "science of."

evaporate (i-**vap**-uh-*rayt*)
To change from a liquid to a gas. Liquids evaporate faster when heated. From the Latin *e,* meaning "from," and *vapor,* meaning "steam or vapor."

evening star (**eev**-ning **stahr**)
Either the planet **Venus** or **Mercury** and not a star at all. It shines in the western sky just after sunset.

evergreen (**ev**-uhr-*green*)
A plant that remains green throughout the year. Evergreen trees include pine, fir, and spruce. Ivy is an evergreen vine. Box is an evergreen shrub.

evolution (*ev*-uh-**loo**-shuhn)
The changes in plants and animals over a long period of time. Much of the **theory** of evolution is based on the work of **Charles Darwin.** He realized that individuals within a **species** varied. Those with the most useful **traits** were more likely to survive than the others, and would have more offspring with the useful traits. As a result, over many generations, the species gradually changed, or evolved. See **adaptation, survival of the fittest,** and **natural selection.**

excretion (ik-**skree**-shuhn)
The process of removing waste from cells, or from the body of living organisms. Human excrement includes liquid **urine,** solid **feces,** and **carbon dioxide** gas. From the Latin *excretus,* meaning "separated."

exoskeleton (*ek*-soh-**skel**-uht-n)
The hard, stiff, outside covering of **invertebrate animals,** such as lobsters, crabs, and insects.

exosphere (**ek**-soh-*sfir*)
The top layer of Earth's **atmosphere.** The exosphere starts about 400 miles (650 kilometers) above the surface. The air in the exosphere is so thin that it is impossible to say exactly where the exosphere ends and space begins.

expanding universe (ik-**span**-ding **yoo**-nuh-*vuhrs*)
The accepted belief that the **universe** is growing bigger and the **galaxies** are moving away from one another.

expansion (ik-**span**-chuhn)
The increase in **volume** of a substance or object. Expansion occurs in most solids, liquids, and gases when they are heated.

experiment (ik-**sper**-uh-muhnt)
A controlled scientific test. An experiment usually starts with an idea or **hypothesis.** The scientist then tests the idea, observing and measuring the results. Finally, the scientist decides whether the hypothesis is correct, or whether a new hypothesis is needed. From the Latin *experiri,* meaning "to try."

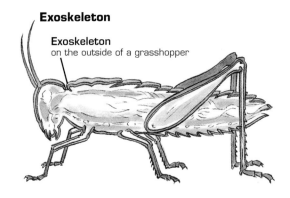

Exoskeleton

Exoskeleton on the outside of a grasshopper

Endoskeleton inside a mouse

expiration (*ek*-spuh-**ray**-shuhn)
Breathing out or exhaling.

explosion (ik-**sploh**-zhuhn)
A sudden blast or release of **energy** that produces a rapidly expanding **volume** of gas. In an explosion, there is often intense heat and shock waves.

explosive
(ik-**sploh**-siv)
Any material that blows up or produces a **volume** of rapidly expanding gas when triggered. Some common explosives are gunpowder, **dynamite**, and **TNT**.

extinction (ik-**stingk**-shuhn)
The dying out or disappearance of a plant or animal **species**. **Fossil** records show that millions of species have suffered extinction on Earth. Dinosaurs went through a mass extinction about 65 million years ago. From the Latin *exstinguere*, meaning "to destroy or kill."

extrasensory perception
(**ek**-struh-**sen**-suh-ree puhr-**sep**-shuhn)
Being aware of something without using any of the known senses. Extrasensory perception includes *telepathy*—knowing what someone is thinking, or mind reading; *clairvoyance*—knowing that something is happening far away; and *precognition*—knowing of a future event. Many scientists doubt that extrasensory perception exists. Extrasensory perception is often shortened to *ESP*. See also **parapsychology**.

extraterrestrial
(**ek**-struh-tuh-**res**-tree-uhl)
Having to do with outer space. *Also,* an object or being not of this world. Sometimes shortened to *ET*.

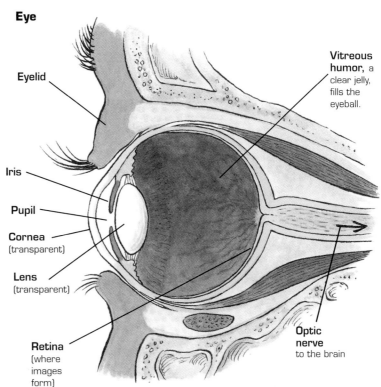

Eye

Eyelid

Iris

Pupil

Cornea
(transparent)

Lens
(transparent)

Retina
(where images form)

Vitreous humor, a clear jelly, fills the eyeball.

Optic nerve
to the brain

E

extrusion (ik-**stroo**-zhuhn)
Forcing something out through a small opening. Extrusion can shape solid metal or plastic into strips, tubes, or threads. *Also,* the way **lava** comes out of some **volcanoes**. From the Latin *ex*, meaning "out," and *trudere*, meaning "to thrust."

eye (**ie**)
The **organ** of sight. The round opening in the **iris**, called the **pupil**, determines how much light enters the eye through the **lens**. The light falls on the **retina**, the lining of the back of the eyeball. The **optic nerve** carries the signals to the brain, which interprets the signals. *Also,* the calm center of a **hurricane** that is usually about 14 miles (22 kilometers) across. See also **hurricane**.

eyepiece (**ie**-*pees*)
The **lens** or lenses of a **microscope** or **telescope** closest to the eye of the user. The eyepiece makes the **image** appear larger. Also called the **ocular**.

facsimile (fak-**sim**-uh-lee)
See **fax**.

Fahrenheit (**far**-uhn-*hite*)
A scale for measuring temperature. In the Fahrenheit, or F scale, 32 degrees is the freezing point of water and 212 degrees is the boiling point. The scale was named for the German physicist *Daniel Gabriel Fahrenheit (1686–1736)*.

fall (**fawl**)
See **autumn**.

falling star (**faw**-ling **stahr**)
Not a star, but a **meteor**. Also called a **shooting star**.

fallout (**fawl**-*out*)
The **radioactive particles** that fall to earth after a **nuclear explosion**.

family (**fam**-uh-lee or **fam**-lee)
In **classification**, a group of related **genera** (plural of genus) of animals or plants. For example, squirrels and chipmunks are two members of the *Sciuridae* family.

Faraday (**far**-uh-*day*), **Michael** (1791–1867)
An English physicist and chemist who discovered **electromagnetic induction**, which is used in **generators** to produce **electricity**.

farsighted (**fahr**-*site*-uhd)
Having a defect of vision in which you are able to see distant things more clearly than near ones. Farsightedness is also called *hyperopia*.

fat (**fat**)
A **compound** that contains **carbon**, **hydrogen**, and **oxygen**. Fat provides **energy** to the body. Liquid fats are called **oils**. See also **fatty acids**.

fatty acids (**fat**-ee **as**-idz)
The substances that make up fats. Certain fatty acids are necessary for growth and development.

fault (**fawlt**)
A break in the earth's **crust** where sections of rock often slide past each other. The best-known fault in North America is the San Andreas fault. From the Latin *fallere*, meaning "to deceive."

fauna (**faw**-nuh)
The animals of a certain region or a certain time. From the Latin *Fauna*, the name of a woodland goddess.

fax (**faks**)
A copy of text or pictures sent from one fax machine to another. The first fax machine changes the dark and light parts on the page into electrical signals. The signals go through telephone lines to the second fax machine, which prints out the original document. Fax is short for *facsimile*.

feather (**fe**TH-uhr)
One of the light, thin structures that cover a bird's skin. Feathers allow a bird to fly and help it keep a steady body temperature. Feathers are made of **keratin**.

feces (**fee**-seez)
The solid waste matter that remains after food is digested. Feces leave the body as **excretion** through the **anus**.

feedback (**feed**-*bak*)
Information from an **organism** or machine that allows it to correct and control itself. *Also,* the loud, whistling noise you hear when someone holds a **microphone** too close to an **amplifier**.

feldspar (**feld**-*spahr*)
A hard **mineral** found in many kinds of rocks. Feldspar is one of the most abundant minerals on the earth's surface.

female (**fee**-mayl)
The sex that produces eggs or bears young.

femur (**fee**-muhr)
The thighbone in humans. The femur is the longest and strongest bone of the human body.

fermentation (*fuhr*-muhn-**tay**-shuhn)
A chemical change in a substance caused by **bacteria, molds,** or **yeast.** Fermentation is important in making bread, cheese, and **alcohol.**

Fermi (**fer**-mee), **Enrico** (1901–1954)
An American physicist, born in Italy. Fermi built the first **nuclear reactor** in 1942 and also helped to develop the atomic bomb.

fern (**fuhrn**)
A plant with roots, stems, and leaves, but no flowers. A fern reproduces by means of **spores** instead of seeds.

fertile (**fuhrt**-l)
Describes an animal or plant able to produce offspring. *Also,* describes soil rich in **nutrients.**

fertilization (*fuhrt*-l-uh-**zay**-shuhn)
The joining of male and female **sex cells** to form a new individual. Fertilization is the first step in **sexual reproduction.**

fertilize (**fuhrt**-l-*ize*)
To join an **egg cell** and a **sperm** cell. *Also,* to improve soil quality by adding **nutrients** to the soil.

fertilizer (**fuhrt**-l-*ize*-uhr)
Material added to soil to produce bigger and better plants.

fetus (**fee**-tuhs)
A **vertebrate** during the later stages of its development before birth.

fever (**fee**-vuhr)
A condition in which the body temperature is higher than normal, which is 98.6° **Fahrenheit** (37° **Celsius**). Fever is a common symptom of disease.

fiber (**fie**-buhr)
Any long, thin, threadlike material. Fiber may be natural, such as cotton, or **synthetic,** such as nylon. *Also,* a **nutrient** found in cereal, fruits, and vegetables. Fiber helps move food through your **intestines.**

fiberglass (**fie**-buhr-*glas*)
Fibers of glass used to make fabrics, auto bodies, and other materials.

fiber optics (**fie**-buhr **ahp**-tiks)
Sending light through very thin **fibers** of glass or plastic. Fiber optic cables carry light signals. See also **optical fiber.**

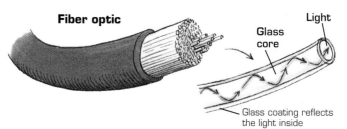

Fiber optic · Light · Glass core · Glass coating reflects the light inside

fibrin (**fie**-brin)
A tough, elastic, yellowish **protein** found in blood **clots.** Fibrin works to stop the bleeding from a cut.

field (**feeld**)
The space in which a force, such as **gravity, magnetism,** or **electricity,** acts. The gravitational field around Earth pulls objects down toward Earth.

filament (**fil**-uh-muhnt)
A very thin wire or thread. The filament in an electric lightbulb glows and gives off light when an **electric current** flows through it. *Also,* the stalk of a **stamen.** *Also,* the threadlike **cells** in **algae.**

file (**file**)
A **document** or complete unit of **data** stored in a computer's memory or on a

diskette. *Also,* a tool with a rough surface used to make things smooth.

filter (**fil**-tuhr)
A device with tiny holes that strains out solids from a liquid or gas. *Also,* a device that removes certain **frequencies** from **electronic circuits.** *Also,* a device that removes particular colors from light rays.

filtration (fil-**tray**-shuhn)
Using a **filter** to remove something unwanted. Air filtration removes dust and dirt from the air.

fire (**fire**)
The flame, heat, and light produced by burning. Fire is a **chemical reaction.** It can only start if **oxygen,** heat, and fuel are present.

fish (**fish**)
An animal with a backbone that lives in freshwater or saltwater. Nearly all fish are **cold-blooded,** mainly breathe through **gills,** and are usually covered with scales. Fish range in size from a goby, less than one half inch (1 centimeter) long, to the whale shark, over 40 feet (12 meters) long.

fission (**fish**-uhn)
Splitting the **nucleus** of an **atom,** which releases a tremendous amount of **energy.**

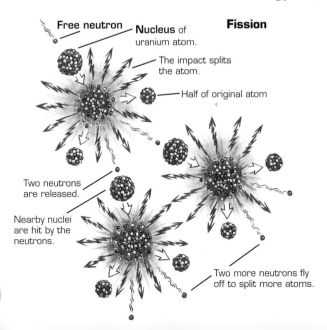

Free neutron — Nucleus of uranium atom.

Fission

The impact splits the atom.

Half of original atom

Two neutrons are released.

Nearby nuclei are hit by the neutrons.

Two more neutrons fly off to split more atoms.

In fission, **neutrons** strike the nuclei (plural of nucleus) of **uranium** or **plutonium** atoms. This splits the nuclei and releases more neutrons, which strike other nuclei and continue the fission in a **chain reaction.** Fission produces the energy in **nuclear reactors.** *Also,* in biology, the splitting of a **cell** into two or more parts. From the Latin *fissus,* meaning "split."

flagellum (fluh-**jel**-uhm)
A long, thin, whiplike part of some **cells** or **microbes.** The flagellum helps the **organism** move about in water. Plural is flagella. From the Latin *flagellum,* meaning "whip."

flammable (**flam**-uh-buhl)
Easily set on fire. Oddly enough, flammable and **inflammable** have the same meaning.

Fleming (**flem**-ing), Sir Alexander (1881–1955)
A British bacteriologist who discovered **penicillin** in 1928. Fleming's discovery gave doctors an important new way to destroy disease-causing **bacteria.**

flint (**flint**)
A hard **mineral** that makes a **spark** when struck sharply against iron or steel. Flint can be used to start fires.

float (**floht**)
To stay on top of a liquid or gas. To float, an object must weigh less than an equal **volume** of the surrounding liquid or gas. For example, a boat floats in water because the air within the boat weighs less than the water that could fit inside.

floe (**floh**)
A slab of ice floating in a cold ocean.

flood (**fluhd**)
A flow of water over normally dry land. A flood can follow a heavy rainfall or melting winter snow that causes rivers or lakes to overflow their banks. **Hurricanes** may also lead to floods.

flood plain (**fluhd** *playn*)
A low, flat area alongside a river that floods when the river overflows its banks.

floppy disk (**flahp**-ee **disk**)
A flat **magnetic disk** that stores information and **programs** for computers. See also **diskette**.

flora (**flor**-uh)
The plants of a certain region or time. From the Latin *Flora*, the name of the ancient Roman goddess of flowers.

flow (**floh**)
To move along smoothly. Fluids, such as water or air, can flow; electricity also flows.

flower (**flou**-uhr)
The part of a plant that produces the seeds and/or fruit necessary for **reproduction**. All flowers have either male (**stamen**) or female (**pistil**) parts—or both.

flu (**floo**)
See **influenza**.

fluid (**floo**-id)
Any liquid or gas that flows easily.

fluorescent (flu-**res**-uhnt)
Describes something that glows or gives off light when exposed to **electric current**, light, **X rays**, or **ultraviolet rays**.

fluoridation (*flur*-uh-**day**-shuhn)
The adding of small amounts of fluoride to drinking water or toothpaste to help teeth resist decay. Fluoride is a **compound** containing fluorine.

flux (**fluhks**)
The lines of magnetic force that run from one pole of a magnet to the other. The flux of the earth's magnetism makes compass needles point north. *Also,* the rate of flow of **matter** or **energy** across a surface. *Also,* a substance that can be added to another substance to make it melt at a lower temperature. *Also,* a substance added to an **ore** before melting to remove impurities.

flywheel (**flie**-weel or **flie**-hweel)
A heavy wheel set in a machine. The flywheel keeps on spinning once it is set in motion. It helps the machine keep running at an even speed.

FM (**ef-em**)
Short for *Frequency Modulation*. FM is a method of radio broadcasting that uses radio waves of varying **frequency**. When these waves reach the **receiver**, they reproduce the sounds sent out from the broadcasting studio. FM broadcasts have less noise than **AM** broadcasts.

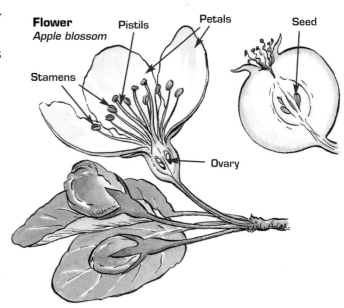

Flower
Apple blossom

Stamens · Pistils · Petals · Seed · Ovary

focus (**foh**-kuhs)
The point where rays of light meet after being bent by a **lens** or curved mirror. Also called *focal point*. From the Latin *focus*, meaning "fireplace or hearth," since the fireplace was the center of home life.

fog (**fawg** or **fahg**)
Fine drops of water that float in the air just above the earth's surface. Fog is really a low-flying cloud. It forms when air containing water **vapor** is cooled so that the water vapor **condenses** into water droplets.

Fold mountain

fold mountain (**fohld** *mount*-n)
A mountain that forms when two sections of the earth's **crust** collide, causing their edges to form long parallel folds.

follicle (**fahl**-i-kuhl)
A small, baglike structure in the body. Hair grows from follicles in the skin. From the Latin *folliculus,* meaning "small bag."

font (**fahnt**)
A complete set of type in a **printer**, printing press, or **word processor**. Each font contains letters, numbers, and symbols of one style.

food additive (**food ad**-uh-tiv)
A substance added to food by the manufacturer or the user to improve quality. Food additives include **vitamins** and **minerals** to make food healthier; spices and flavors to improve taste; colors to make food look better; thickeners to improve texture; and preservatives to make food last longer without spoiling.

food chain (**food** *chayn*)
A grouping of living things in a **community** in which each member feeds on the member below it in the chain. See also **ecosystem**.

food web (**food** *web*)
All the **food chains** in a **community**.

foot (**fut**)
A unit of length equal to 12 inches (30.48 centimeters). Its plural is feet.

foot-pound (**fut**-*pound*)
A unit of **work** or **energy**. A foot-pound of work is done when a force of 1 pound (0.4 kilograms) moves an object 1 foot (30.5 centimeters). A foot-pound of energy is the energy needed to move a 1-pound object 1 foot.

force (**fors**)
Energy that changes the motion or shape of an object. You use force when you hit a baseball or squeeze some clay.

forensic science (fuh-**ren**-sik **sie**-uhns)
The science used to solve crimes. Forensic scientists collect evidence, **analyze** the evidence, and present the evidence.

forest (**for**-uhst)
A thick growth of trees and other plants covering a large area of land.

formula (**for**-myuh-luh)
A short way of showing what is in a **chemical compound** or **molecule**. The formula for water, H_2O, shows that each molecule of water contains 2 **atoms** of **hydrogen** and 1 atom of **oxygen**.

Fossey (**fahs**-ee or **faw**-see), **Dian** (1932–1985)
An American **zoologist** who studied mountain gorillas in Africa. Fossey was the first to observe the day-to-day behavior of gorillas in the wild.

fossil (**fahs**-uhl)
The hardened remains or marks of a living thing that died millions of years ago. From the Latin *fossilis,* meaning "dug up."

fossil fuels (**fahs**-uhl *fyoo*-uhlz)
Coal, oil (**petroleum**), and **natural gas**, which are burned to release **energy**. Fossil fuels formed millions of years ago from the remains of plants (coal) or buried bodies of sea creatures (oil and natural gas).

Foucault pendulum
(foo-**koh pen**-juh-luhm)
A **pendulum** invented by the French scientist *Jean Foucault* (1819–1868) that always swings in the same direction, yet seems to change direction, because of the **rotation** of Earth.

fracture (**frak**-chuhr)
A broken bone. *Also,* a break in a rock or a rock layer.

Franklin (**frangk**-lin), **Benjamin** (1706–1790)
An American statesman, scientist, and inventor whose **experiments** proved that lightning is electricity. His inventions include the lightning rod, **bifocal** eyeglasses, and the Franklin stove.

Franklin (**frangk**-lin), **Rosalind** (1920–1958)
A British biologist whose **X-ray** studies of **DNA** helped reveal the structure of the DNA **molecule.** See also **Francis H. C. Crick** and **James Dewey Watson.**

freeze (**freez**)
To change from a liquid to a solid when cooled. Liquid water freezes to become solid ice.

freezing point (**free**-zing *point*)
The temperature at which a liquid freezes. The freezing point of pure water at sea level is 32° **Fahrenheit** (0° **Celsius**).

frequency (**free**-kwuhn-see)
The number of complete **cycles** per second of sound, radio, or light waves. For example, orchestras tune to the note A, which has a frequency of 440 vibrations per second. From the Latin *frequens,* meaning "crowded."

frequency modulation (**free**-kwuhn-see *mahj*-uh-*lay*-shuhn)
See **FM.**

freshwater (**fresh**-*wawt*-uhr)
Water that is not salty like ocean water. Freshwater is found in lakes, rivers, and streams. Also called *sweet water.*

Freud (**froid**), **Sigmund** (1856–1939)
An Austrian doctor who developed **theories** on the importance of the **unconscious** part of people's minds. Freud devised a treatment, called **psychoanalysis,** to explore the unconscious and treat mental illness.

friction (**frik**-shuhn)
The force that tends to stop objects from sliding. Friction is helpful when sneakers keep you from slipping, and harmful when parts rub against each other in a machine. From the Latin *fricare,* meaning "to rub."

front (**fruhnt**)
In weather, the boundary between two different air masses. In a *warm front,* warm air slides over cold air, bringing warmer weather and light rain. In a *cold front,* cold air moves in under warm air, bringing colder weather and heavy rain. In an *occluded front,* a fast-moving cold front meets a warm front, usually bringing milder weather.

Frequency

Dog bark: 15 hertz

The "A" orchestras tune to: 440 hertz

Bat: 60,000 hertz

Lowest piano key: 27 hertz

Highest piano key: 4,000 hertz

Grasshopper song: 15,000 hertz

frost (frawst)
Ice **crystals** that form on grass, windows, and other surfaces on very cold nights. It comes from water **vapor** in the air that **condenses** on a surface and turns to ice when the temperature is below freezing. *Also,* below-freezing temperatures that are harmful to plants.

frostbite (frawst-*bite*)
An injury to the body caused by intense cold when ice **crystals** form inside body **tissue.**

fruit (froot)
The part of a plant that contains the **seeds**; it is the ripened **ovary** of a flower. Peaches and cherries are fruits with large seeds. Strawberries and tomatoes have small seeds. From the Latin *fructus,* meaning "fruit."

fuel (fyoo-uhl)
Something that stores **energy** and can later supply heat. Fuels that are burned include oil, coal, gas, and wood. Food is fuel for our bodies.

fuel cell (fyoo-uhl *sel*)
A device that uses **chemical reactions** to produce electricity. Fuel cells combine **hydrogen** and **oxygen** to supply electricity for **space shuttles.**

fulcrum (ful-kruhm)
The base or pivot on which a **lever** turns when moving or lifting something. The fulcrum of a seesaw is the bar on which the board rests. From the Latin *fulcire,* meaning "to prop up."

fungus (fuhng-guhs)
Living things that look like plants, but they have no roots, leaves, or **chlorophyll.** Fungi (plural of fungus) **reproduce** with **spores.** Mushrooms, **yeasts,** and **molds** are fungi.

funnel (fuhn-l)
A wide, cone-shaped tube with a narrow spout that is used to pour things into containers with small openings. *Also,* a type of cloud formed by a **tornado.** From the Latin *fundere,* meaning "to pour."

fur (fuhr)
The thick, hairy growth that covers the skin of many kinds of animals.

fuse (fyooz)
A safety device placed in an electric **circuit.** A fuse breaks the circuit if too much **current** is flowing or if the wiring becomes too hot. The fuse is usually a thin wire that melts and breaks before damage can occur. *Also,* a device used to set off an explosive charge.

fusion (fyoo-zhuhn)
Combining the nuclei (plural of **nucleus**) of two or more **atoms** to form another atom. The fusion of two **hydrogen** atoms produces an atom of **helium** and releases tremendous amounts of **energy.** Fusion only occurs at very high **pressures** and temperatures inside the sun and other **stars,** in fusion reactors, and in hydrogen bombs. Also called *thermonuclear reaction. Also,* the joining together of plastics or metals by melting.

Fusion

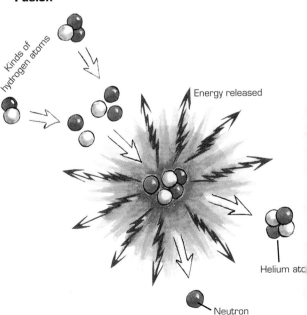

Kinds of hydrogen atoms

Energy released

Helium atom

Neutron

G (jee)

A symbol for the force of **gravity**. One G is the normal force of gravity. A rider in a speeding vehicle, from a car to a spacecraft, may feel two or more Gs. At five Gs, a person may become **unconscious**. *Also*, a unit of **acceleration** equal to 32.16 feet (9.8 meters) per second.

Galápagos Islands
(guh-**lahp**-uh-*gohs* ie-luhndz)

Nineteen tiny islands in the Pacific Ocean, about 600 miles west of Ecuador. Because they are so small and isolated, the Galápagos Islands are the perfect place to study differences within and between **species**. On the Galápagos Islands **Charles Darwin** made **observations** and collected **specimens** that led to his **theory** of **natural selection**.

galaxy (**gal**-uhk-see)

A system of stars, dust, and gas held together by **gravity**. Our galaxy is known as the **Milky Way**. It got this

Galaxy
Our galaxy (Milky Way)   Center   Spiral arms

Our solar system is in this part of the galaxy.

name because the band of stars we can see looks like spilled milk across the sky. Astronomers believe there are more than 50 billion galaxies in space. From the Greek *gala*, meaning "milk."

gale (**gayl**)

A very strong wind with speeds from 25 to 75 miles (40.3 to 120.8 kilometers) an hour.

Galen (**gay**-luhn) (ca. 129–210 A.D.)

A famous doctor of the Roman Empire who was the first to do **experiments** on animals in order to learn more about the human body. Galen's books on **anatomy** and how to treat disease were used for hundreds of years.

Galileo (*gal*-uh-**lay**-oh or *gal*-uh-**lee**-oh) (1564–1642)

An Italian astronomer, physicist, and mathematician. Galileo was the first person to use a **telescope** to observe stars and planets. He discovered craters on the moon, four of the moons around **Jupiter**, **sunspots**, the basic laws of falling bodies and **pendulums**. His full name was Galileo Galilei.

gall (**gawl**)

A substance produced by the **liver** and stored in the **gall bladder** of animals. Gall, also known as **bile**, helps to digest, or break down, **fat**. *Also*, a growth on plants caused by insects or **bacteria**.

gall bladder (**gawl** *blad*-uhr)

A sac attached to the **liver** that stores **gall** until needed.

gallon (**gal**-uhn)

A unit of liquid volume or capacity. One gallon equals 4 quarts (3.785 **liters**) or 231 cubic inches (3,785 cubic centimeters).

Galvani (gahl-**vah**-nee), **Luigi** (1737–1798)
An Italian doctor who found that the legs of a dead frog moved when touched by two different metals, showing that electricity can be produced by a **chemical reaction.**

galvanize (**gal**-vuh-*nize*)
To apply an **electric current** to something. *Also,* to cover iron or **steel** with a thin coating of **zinc** to prevent **rust.** Named after **Luigi Galvani.**

galvanometer (*gal*-vuh-**nahm**-uh-tuhr)
An instrument that detects and measures **electric currents.** Named after **Luigi Galvani.**

gamete (**gam**-eet)
A male or female **sex cell.** One gamete unites with another gamete to form a **fertilized** cell. From the Greek *gametes,* meaning "husband."

gamma rays (**gam**-uh *rayz*)
Electromagnetic radiation given off by **radioactive** substances. Gamma rays are like **X rays,** but have a shorter **wavelength.** Gamma is the third letter of the Greek alphabet.

gas (**gas**)
A substance without a fixed shape or **volume.** A gas can expand to fill any container. *Also,* short for gasoline. *Also,* a fuel that is burned to provide heat. See also **natural gas.**

gasoline (*gas*-uh-**leen**)
A mixture of **hydrocarbons** made from **petroleum** that burns very easily. Gasoline is used as a fuel to power engines. Gasoline is also called gas.

gastric (**gas**-trik)
Having to do with the stomach.

gauge (**gayj**)
An instrument for measuring. A **steam** gauge, for example, measures the **pressure** of steam.

gauss (**gous**)
A measure of the strength of a magnet. The earth's magnetic field is about one half gauss. Gauss is named after the German mathematician, *Carl Friedrich Gauss* (1777–1855).

Gay-Lussac (*gay*-luh-**sak**), **Joseph** (1778–1850)
A French chemist who discovered that gases combine in simple proportions. For example, water is formed of two parts **hydrogen** (H_2) and one part **oxygen** (O).

gear (**gir**)
A wheel with teeth along the edge. The teeth of one gear can fit into the teeth of another gear. If you attach one gear to a source of power, it can turn other gears. If the other gears are bigger, they will turn more slowly. If they are smaller, they will turn faster.

Gear

Slow

Fast

Geiger counter (**gie**-guhr *koun*-tuhr)
A device that detects **radioactivity,** such as **gamma rays** and **alpha** and **beta particles.** The Geiger counter is named after the German **physicist** *Hans Geiger* (1882–1947), who invented it in 1912. Also called the *Geiger-Müller counter.*

gelatin (**jel**-uht-n)
An animal **protein** substance. Gelatin is made from animal skins and bones. It becomes a jelly, like Jell-O, when dissolved in hot water and cooled.

Gell-Mann (gel-**mahn**), **Murray** (born 1929)
An American physicist who suggested that **neutrons** and **protons** were made

up of simpler, smaller **particles.** Gell-Mann called these particles **quarks.**

gem (jem)
A precious stone or pearl that is polished and used in jewelry or for decoration. Some well-known gems are diamonds, rubies, opals, and emeralds. Most gems are minerals, but pearls and amber come from living things. Also called *gemstones.*

gene (jeen)
The part of a **chromosome** that determines one or more **characteristics** or group of characteristics that living things **inherit** from their parents. These characteristics include everything from the shape of a leaf to the height, hair color, and eye color of a child. Genes are made of **DNA.**

gene mapping (jeen *map*-ing)
A way of locating and identifying **genes** on **chromosomes.** In 1990, scientists started the Human **Genome** Project to map and identify the millions of genes in the human body.

generation (*jen*-uh-**ray**-shuhn)
A group of animals or plants born about the same time. Parents belong to one generation; offspring belong to the next. *Also,* the production of electricity.

generator (jen-uh-*ray*-tuhr)
A machine that produces electricity by changing **mechanical energy** into **electrical energy.** In the generator, a **coil** of wire is moved past a magnet or the magnet is moved past the coil to produce an **electric current** in the coil.

gene splicing (jeen *splie*-sing)
Taking a **gene** from one **organism** and joining it with **DNA** from a different organism or from the same organism. See **genetic engineering.**

gene therapy (jeen *ther*-uh-pee)
Replacing a patient's faulty or missing **gene** with a normal gene from another individual. Gene therapy is still a rare, unproven method of treatment. See **gene splicing.**

genetic engineering (juh-**net**-ik *en*-juh-**nir**-ing)
Changing the **genes** in living things to introduce desired **characteristics** in offspring or to get rid of disease. The changed genes are sometimes called *designer genes.* Genetic engineering is used to produce drugs and grow better crops. See also **gene splicing.**

genetics (juh-**net**-iks)
The study of how **characteristics** are passed on from parents to their offspring.

genitals (jen-uht-lz)
The external male and female reproductive **organs.**

genome (jee-nohm)
All the **genes** in an individual. See also **gene mapping.**

genus (jee-nuhs)
The name of a group of closely related animals or plants. The *Canis* genus, for example, includes dogs, wolves, and coyotes. See also **classification.**

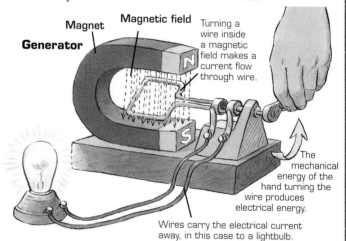
Generator
Magnet
Magnetic field
Turning a wire inside a magnetic field makes a current flow through wire.
The mechanical energy of the hand turning the wire produces electrical energy.
Wires carry the electrical current away, in this case to a lightbulb.

geode (jee-ohd)
A hollow lump of stone, often lined with **crystals.** Geodes are usually found in **limestone** or **shale.**

geography (jee-**ahg**-ruh-fee)
Study of the **continents,** countries, climate, peoples, and products on Earth. From the Greek *ge,* meaning "earth," and *graphein,* meaning "to write."

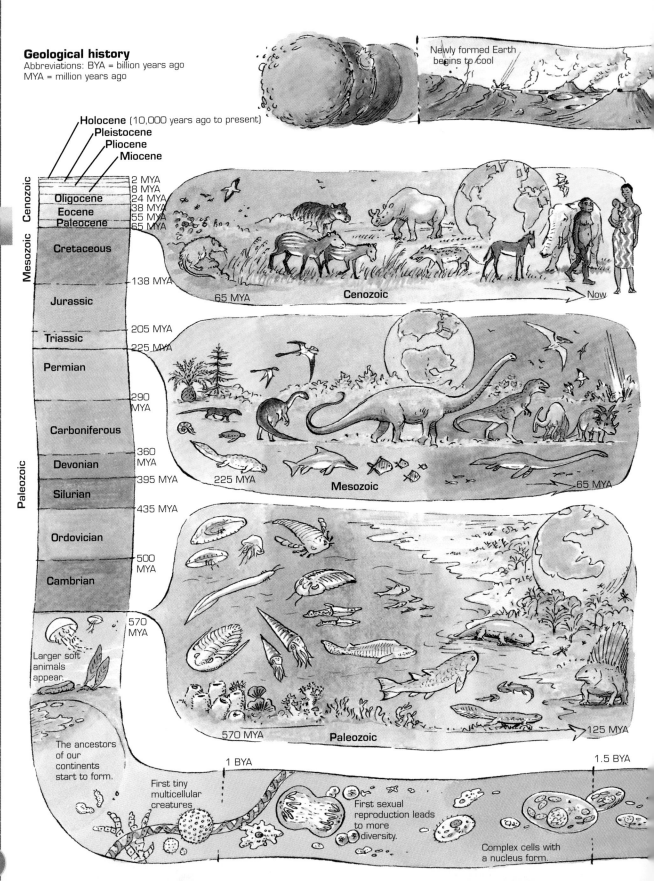

Geological history

Abbreviations: BYA = billion years ago
MYA = million years ago

Newly formed Earth begins to cool

Holocene (10,000 years ago to present)
Pleistocene
Pliocene
Miocene

Cenozoic

Oligocene — 2 MYA
— 8 MYA
— 24 MYA
Eocene — 38 MYA
Paleocene — 55 MYA
— 65 MYA

Mesozoic

Cretaceous

— 138 MYA

Jurassic

— 205 MYA
Triassic
— 225 MYA
Permian

— 290 MYA

Paleozoic

Carboniferous

— 360 MYA
Devonian
— 395 MYA
Silurian
— 435 MYA
Ordovician

— 500 MYA
Cambrian

— 570 MYA

Larger soft animals appear.

The ancestors of our continents start to form.

65 MYA — Cenozoic — Now

225 MYA — Mesozoic — 65 MYA

570 MYA — Paleozoic — 125 MYA

1 BYA

First tiny multicellular creatures

First sexual reproduction leads to more diversity.

1.5 BYA

Complex cells with a nucleus form.

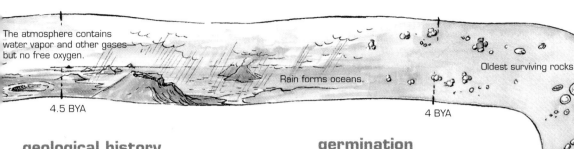

The atmosphere contains water vapor and other gases but no free oxygen.

Rain forms oceans.

Oldest surviving rocks

4.5 BYA

4 BYA

Oceans become a rich mineral soup.

3.5 BYA

First life appears.

Bacteria

Cyanobacteria start producing oxygen.

3 BYA

Cyanobacteria form mats called stromatolites.

2.5 BYA

2 BYA

Oxygen from the oceans escapes into the air.

As oxygen builds up in the oceans, dissolved iron rusts and covers the bottom

The ozone layer forms and protects Earth from too much ultraviolet radiation.

geological history
(*jee*-uh-**lahj**-i-kuhl **his**-tuh-ree)
The story of what has happened on and to Earth over the past 4.6 billion years.

geology (jee-**ahl**-uh-jee)
The science of the earth. Geology studies how it was formed, its history, and the ways in which it changes.

geomagnetism
(*jee*-oh-**mag**-nuh-*tiz*-uhm)
The earth's **magneticism.** Scientists believe that geomagnetism comes from **molten** rock in the earth's outer **core.**

geothermal power
(*jee*-oh-**thuhr**-muhl **pou**-uhr)
Energy that comes from hot rocks below the earth's surface. The rocks make water hot enough to turn into **steam. Power** companies pump the hot water or steam to the surface to run **generators.**

geriatrics (*jer*-ee-**a**-triks)
The study of diseases of the elderly.

germ (**juhrm**)
A tiny, living **organism** that causes disease. **Bacteria, viruses,** fungi (plural of **fungus**), and **protozoa** are different kinds of germs. A germ is also called a **pathogen.**

germ cell (**juhrm** *sel*)
An egg or **sperm cell.** When the two kinds of germ cells come together they can produce a new individual.

germination
(*juhr*-muh-**nay**-shuhn)
The sprouting of a seed or **spore.** Most germination occurs in the spring.

gestation (jes-**tay**-shuhn)
The time during which some female **organisms** carry their unborn young within their body before birth. Human gestation is 9 months. Gestation is also called **pregnancy.** From the Latin *gestare,* meaning "to carry."

geyser (**gie**-zuhr)
A **spring** that sends blasts of hot water and **steam** into the air from time to time. A famous geyser is Old Faithful in Yellowstone National Park.

giga- (**gig**-uh)
A prefix in the **metric system** that means one billion. A computer with a gigabyte of memory can hold a billion **bytes.** From the Greek *gigas,* meaning "giant."

gill (**gil**)
The breathing **organ** of fish and most other animals that live in water. The two gills

remove **oxygen** from the water and release **carbon dioxide** from the body.

gizzard (**giz**-uhrd)
A part of the **digestive system** of birds and some other animals. Tiny stones in the gizzard break up and grind food that is hard to digest.

glacier (**glay**-shuhr)
A large mass of ice that moves slowly down a mountain or along a valley. Some glaciers, called ice caps, cover vast areas of **polar** land. Ice caps flow slowly into the sea.

gland (**gland**)
An **organ** that releases **chemical** substances into the blood or into small ducts, or tubes. Gland chemicals control everything from growth to digestion. The **thyroid, pituitary,** and adrenals are some well-known glands.

glass (**glas**)
A hard, brittle material that often can be seen through. Glass is made by melting sand with **soda ash** and **limestone.**

glider (**glie**-duhr)
An aircraft that looks like an airplane, but has no engine. A glider must be towed into the air, where it is held up by the shape of the wings and rising air currents. Also called *sailplane.*

Global Positioning System (**gloh**-buhl puh-**zish**-uh-ning *sis*-tuhm)
A system based on **satellites** in space that allows people in cars, planes, or ships to determine their exact position on Earth.

global warming (**gloh**-buhl **wor**-ming)
The apparent rise in the earth's temperature. It is caused by an increase in the amount of **carbon dioxide, methane,** and other gases in the air. They trap the sun's heat in the atmosphere. Also called *greenhouse effect.*

globular cluster (**glahb**-yuh-luhr **kluhs**-tuhr)
A ball-shaped group of thousands of stars held together by **gravity.** About 100 globular clusters are found near the center of the **Milky Way galaxy.**

glucose (**gloo**-kohs)
A simple kind of sugar found in fruits and green plants. Glucose is the main source of **energy** for most living **organisms,** including humans. (Formula—$C_6H_{12}O_6$) From the Greek *gleukos,* meaning "sweet wine."

glue (**gloo**)
A sticky substance used to hold objects firmly together.

gluon (**gloo**-ahn)
A type of **subatomic particle.** Gluons carry the force that holds together such particles as **protons** and **neutrons.**

gneiss (**nise**)
A coarse-grained, **metamorphic** rock with dark- and light-colored bands. Gneiss forms when **granite** is subjected to great heat and **pressure.**

Goddard (**gahd**-uhrd), **Robert Hutchings** (1882–1945)
An American pioneer in rocket science. Goddard launched the first liquid-fueled rocket in 1926.

goiter (**goi**-tuhr)
An enlarged **thyroid gland.** The goiter forms a swelling on the front of the neck. From the Latin *guttur,* meaning "throat."

gold (**gohld**)
A bright yellow metal **element** that is used for making coins and jewelry. Gold is a soft metal that can be drawn into wire or hammered into flat sheets and does not rust or tarnish. (Symbol—Au)

Goodall (**gud**-awl), **Jane** (born 1934)
An English zoologist famous for her work with chimpanzees. Goodall discovered that chimpanzees use tools.

Gorgas (**gor**-guhs), **William**
(1854–1920)
An American doctor who found that
mosquitoes carried the germs that
caused **malaria** and **yellow fever.**

gorge (**gorj**)
A deep, narrow valley, usually between
steep mountains.

Gould (**goold**), **Stephen Jay**
(born 1941)
An American paleontologist famous
for his writings on **evolution.** Gould
believes that evolution is not a
gradual process, but occurs in sudden,
irregular spurts.

governor (**guhv**-uhr-nuhr)
An automatic device that keeps a
machine running at the proper speed.
Governors work by controlling the flow
of fuel or **steam** to the machine.

GPS (**gee**-*pee*-**ess**)
Short for Global Positioning System. See
Global Positioning System.

gradient (**gray**-dee-uhnt)
The rate at which temperature or **pressure**
changes. *Also,* the slope of a surface.

grafting (**graf**-ting)
Attaching a cutting from one plant to
another to grow a new plant. *Also,*
moving bone or skin to a different
place in the body or to a different
body so that it can grow there.

grain (**grayn**)
The seeds of wheat, corn, rice, oats,
and similar cereal grasses. *Also,* a very
small unit of weight equal to 0.002
ounces (0.065 **grams**). *Also,* the
arrangement of **fibers** in wood, leather,
or stone. *Also,* the small **crystals** that
make up a metal or rock.

gram (**gram**)
A unit of weight in the **metric system.**
A gram is equal to 0.037 ounces. It is
used to weigh very light substances.

granite (**gran**-it)
A hard, rough-grained, **igneous** rock
that is gray, white, or pink in color.
Workers use granite to construct
buildings and monuments.

graph (**graf**)
A drawing that compares changing
quantities. You could make a graph to
show how many pupils are in school
each day, for example.

Graph

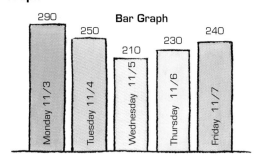

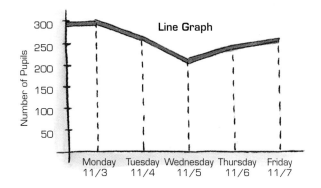

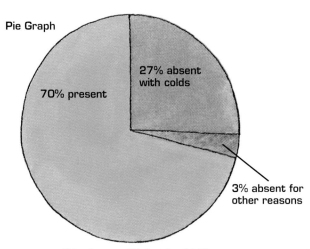

Attendance on Wednesday, 11/5,
when colds were going around the school.

graphics (**graf**-iks)
The creation and use of **images**—
drawings, charts, diagrams, or **graphs**—
in a computer, on television, or on paper.

grassland (**gras**-*land*)
An open, generally flat area covered
with tall or short grasses and few trees
or shrubs. **Prairies** and **steppes** are two
kinds of grasslands. See also **biome.**

gravitation (*grav*-uh-**tay**-shuhn)
The natural force that attracts one object
to another. The pull of gravitation
depends on the **mass** of the objects and
how close they are. The greater and closer
the mass, the stronger the gravitational
attraction. See also **gravity.** From the
Latin *gravitas,* meaning "heavy."

gravity (**grav**-uh-tee)
The force of **gravitation** felt on Earth
and other bodies in **space.** Gravity pulls
objects toward Earth. It also keeps the
planets in **orbit** around the sun.

grazer (**gray**-zuhr)
An animal that mostly eats grass. Deer,
cattle, and sheep are grazers.

greenhouse effect
(**green**-hous i-*fekt*)
See **global warming.**

grippe (**grip**)
See **influenza.**

groundwater (**ground** *wawt*-uhr)
Water trapped in holes and cracks in
rocks beneath the earth's surface. It
can be brought to the surface by wells.
Springs bring groundwater up naturally.

grub (**gruhb**)
The young form, or **larva,** of some insects.
A grub looks like a tiny white worm.

guard cell (**gahrd** *sel*)
One of a pair of **cells** around each
stoma in a plant leaf. The guard cells
control the amount of water that
evaporates through the stoma.

gullet (**guhl**-it)
See **esophagus.**

gully (**guhl**-ee)
A narrow ditch made by running water.

gunpowder (**guhn**-*pou*-duhr)
A powder that explodes with great force
when burned. The burning gunpowder
quickly produces high-pressure gases
that can propel a bullet from a gun
barrel. Gunpowder is also used for
blasting and in fireworks.

gut (**guht**)
The **intestine** of a living creature.

gymnosperm (**jim**-nuh-*spuhrm*)
A kind of plant with seeds that are not in a
pod, flower, or fruit. A gymnosperm such
as the pine tree, for example, has seeds
on cones. From the Greek *gymnos,*
meaning "naked," and *sperma,*
meaning "seed."

gynecology (*gie*-nuh-**kahl**-uh-jee)
A branch of medicine that deals with
the female body and diseases of women.
From the Greek *gyne,* meaning "women,"
and -*logia,* meaning "science of."

gypsum (**jip**-suhm)
A soft white **mineral.** Heating gypsum
produces a fine white powder called
plaster of Paris. When water is added,
it becomes hard as stone and is mostly
used to make small statues and casts
for broken bones.

gyrocompass (**jie**-roh-*kuhm*-puhs)
A device that determines direction more
accurately than a magnetic **compass.** It
points to the geographic North Pole, not
the magnetic North Pole.

gyroscope (**jie**-ruh-*skohp*)
A device that uses a spinning wheel to
hold a steady direction. A gyroscope
keeps ships and airplanes on course.
The name is sometimes shortened
to *gyro.*

H

habitat (**hab**-uh-*tat*)
The place in nature where a plant or animal usually lives. A habitat can vary from the top of a mountain to the bottom of the ocean, from a desert sand dune to a single tree in a rain forest.

hacker (**hak**-uhr)
A slang term for anyone who uses a computer to enter another computer system illegally.

hail (**hayl**)
Frozen drops of rain that fall as lumps of ice called hailstones.

hair (**her**)
Threadlike strands that grow from the skin of humans and other **mammals.** Hair mostly provides animals with warmth and protection.

half-life (**haf**-*life*)
The time it takes a **radioactive element** to lose half its **radioactivity** and become a different element. Half-lives vary from millions of years to a tiny fraction of a second. See also **radiocarbon dating.**

Halley's comet (**hal**-eez **kahm**-it)
A very bright **comet** that can be seen every 75 or 76 years. Halley's comet is named after *Edmond Halley* (1656–1742), who first predicted the return of the comet. It was last seen in 1986.

hallucination (huh-*loo*-suh-**nay**-shuhn)
A mental state in which a person sees, hears, tastes, smells, or feels things that are not really there. From the Latin *allucinari,* meaning "to dream."

hallucinogen (huh-**loo**-suh-nuh-juhn)
A drug that temporarily changes the **chemistry** of the brain. Hallucinogens affect emotions, thoughts, senses, and

bodily control. The drugs may also cause **hallucinations.**

halo (**hay**-loh)
A bright ring or disk of light that appears around an object. You can sometimes see a halo around the moon in cool, moist weather.

halogen (**hal**-uh-juhn)
One of a group of five chemical **elements: chlorine** (Cl), **fluorine** (F), **iodine** (I), **bromine** (Br), and astatine (At). Halogens react with metals to form **salts.** From the Greek *hals,* meaning "salt," and *genes,* meaning "born."

Hamilton (**ham**-uhl-tuhn), **Alice** (1869–1970)
An American doctor who studied the health of factory workers and found

Hail

Each time an updraft blows a speck of ice back up into a cloud, the speck adds a coat of ice until it becomes so heavy that it falls to Earth.

some were being poisoned by dangerous substances in the workplace.

haploid number
(**hap**-loid *nuhm*-buhr)
The number of **chromosomes** in a **sex cell.** The haploid number is half the number found in a body cell. In humans, this number is 23.

hard copy (**hahrd kahp**-ee)
Output from a computer that is printed on paper.

hard disk (**hahrd disk**)
The main memory or storage medium within a computer.

hardness (**hahrd**-nis)
A measure of the **resistance** of a substance to being scratched or dented. The hardness of **minerals** is often measured on the **Mohs' scale.**

hardware (**hahrd**-*wer*)
The mechanical parts of a computer. Hardware includes the **keyboard, electronic circuits, monitor, printer,** and so on. See also **computer.**

hard water
(**hahrd wawt**-uhr)
Water containing **dissolved mineral salts** (usually **calcium**). Hard water stops **soaps** from forming a thick lather.

hardwood (**hahrd**-*wud*)
Wood from trees with broad leaves, such as maple, oak, or cherry.

harmonics (hahr-**mahn**-iks)
Sounds barely heard within a musical tone that are higher in **pitch** than the basic tone. The harmonics of a violin string, for example, are produced because the string vibrates in parts as well as a whole. Also called *overtones.*

harvest moon (**hahr**-vist **moon**)
The full moon that appears on or about September 22 in the Northern Hemisphere. It is so bright that farmers can harvest into the night.

Harvey (**hahr**-vee), **William**
(1578–1657)
An English doctor who discovered that the heart is a pump that moves blood throughout the whole body.

hatch (**hach**)
To break out of an **egg.** *Also,* to warm an egg, by sitting on it or by placing it in warm ground or in the **sun.**

Hawking (**haw**-king), **Stephen**
(born 1942)
A British **physicist** who has done important work with **gravity** and **black holes.** Hawking suffers from a serious **disease** and can barely move or speak.

hay fever (**hay** *fee*-vuhr)
A common autumn **allergy** to the **pollen** of ragweed and other plants. Hay fever **symptoms** include red eyes, a runny nose, and sneezing.

hazardous waste
(**haz**-uhr-duhs **wayst**)
See **toxic waste.**

H-bomb (**aych**-bahm)
See **hydrogen bomb.**

HDTV (**aych**-dee-*tee*-vee)
Short for *High Definition TeleVision.* HDTV uses a **digital signal,** which produces sharper pictures and better quality sound than standard television. The HDTV set is

Harmonics

Whole string vibrates

String vibrates in halves

String vibrates in quarters

shaped more like a movie screen than the older shape. HDTV began to be used in the 1990s.

head (**hed**)
The top or front part of an animal's body. *Also,* the part of computers and **tape recorders** that enters or reads the **signals.** *Also,* the central part (**nucleus** and **coma**) of a **comet.** *Also,* the source or origin of a river or stream. *Also,* a cluster of flowers on a stem.

headphones (**hed**-*fohnz*)
Small **speakers** that fit in or over the ears. Headphones allow people to listen to music without bothering those around them.

heart (**hahrt**)
A hollow, muscular **organ** that pumps blood throughout the body. Your heart is about the size of your fist. See also **circulatory system.**

heart attack (**hahrt** uh-*tak*)
A blockage in an **artery** that supplies blood to the heart. The heart attack may damage the heart muscle and can result in death if untreated.

heartwood (**hahrt**-*wud*)
The dead inner wood found in old trees. It supports the tree, but no longer carries sap. When the tree is cut, the heartwood makes high-quality lumber.

heat (**heet**)
A form of **energy.** Heat on Earth comes from several sources, including the sun, electricity, fire and other **chemical reactions, friction,** and **nuclear energy.**

heat exchanger
(**heet** iks-*chayn*-juhr)
A device that transfers heat from a warmer object to a cooler one. A car radiator is a heat exchanger that picks up heat from the engine and gives it up to the air.

heat pump (**heet** *puhmp*)
A device that transfers heat from a cooler object to a warmer one. A

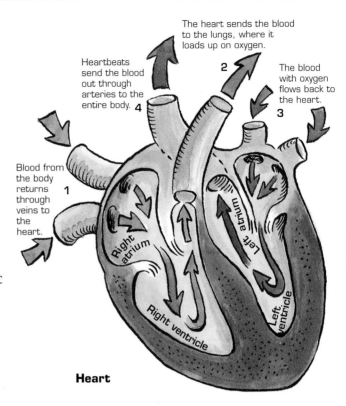

The heart sends the blood to the lungs, where it loads up on oxygen.

Heartbeats send the blood out through arteries to the entire body. **4**

The blood with oxygen flows back to the heart. **3**

Blood from the body returns through veins to the heart. **1**

Right atrium

Left atrium

Right ventricle

Left ventricle

Heart

refrigerator is a heat pump. It absorbs heat from the food on the inside and releases it into the outside air.

heavy water (**hev**-ee **wawt**-uhr)
Water that contains a special form, or **isotope,** of **hydrogen,** called deuterium. Heavy water is used in some **nuclear reactors** to control the **energy** released. (Formula—D_2O or ^2H_2O)

Heisenberg (**hie**-zuhn-*buhrg*), **Werner** (1901–1976)
A German physicist who developed the **uncertainty principle** in 1927.

helicopter (**hel**-uh-*kahp*-tuhr)
An aircraft that is lifted into the **air** by one or two whirling propeller-like **rotors.** A helicopter can take off or land straight up or down and can hover in the air. From the Greek *helix,* meaning "spiral," and *pteron,* meaning "wing."

heliocentric (*hee*-lee-oh-**sen**-trik)
Describes the **solar system,** with the sun at the center. From the Greek *helios,* meaning "sun," and *kentron,* meaning "center."

heliotropism (*hee*-lee-**ah**-truh-*piz*-um)
The turning of plants toward the sun.
From the Greek *helios,* meaning "sun,"
and *tropos,* meaning "turn."

Heliotropism
A growth hormone
called auxin makes
the shady side of
the stem grow
faster than the
sunny side,
bending the plant
toward the light.

helium (**hee**-lee-uhm)
A very light, colorless, odorless gas.
Helium is one of the most common
elements in all the stars in the **universe,**
but is rare on Earth. From the Greek
helios, meaning "sun," since helium was
first found on the sun. (Symbol—He)

helix (**hee**-liks)
A spiral shaped like a coiled **spring**
or the thread of a screw. The **DNA**
molecule is a double helix. From the
Greek *helix,* meaning "spiral."

Helmholtz (**helm**-hohlts), **Hermann
von** (1821–1894)
A German physicist who stated the law
of the **conservation of energy.**

hematite (**hee**-muh-*tite*)
A reddish-brown **mineral** found in the
earth that supplies most of the world's
iron. Hematite is a compound of iron
and **oxygen.** From the Greek *haimatites,*
meaning "bloodlike." (Formula—Fe_2O_3)

hemisphere (**hem**-uh-*sfir*)
One half of planet Earth. *Also,* half of
the brain's **cerebrum.** From the Greek
hemi, meaning "half," and *sphaira,*
meaning "sphere."

hemoglobin (**hee**-muh-*gloh*-buhn)
A substance in **red blood cells.**
Hemoglobin carries **oxygen** throughout
the body and gives blood its red color.

hemophilia (*hee*-muh-**fil**-ee-uh)
An **inherited** disease in which the blood
does not *clot* normally. A person with
hemophilia, called a *hemophiliac,* can
lose lots of blood from a small cut.

hemorrhage (**hem**-uh-rij)
Heavy bleeding from the **skin** or within
the body. A hemorrhage usually comes
from a cut or break in a blood vessel.

Henry (**hen**-ree), **Joseph** (1797-1878)
An American physicist whose **research** led
to the development of **electric motors,** the
telegraph, and other electrical devices.

herb (**uhrb** or **huhrb**)
A plant used to treat or prevent disease,
to flavor foods, or to make perfume. *Also,*
any plant without a "woody" stem that
dies at the end of the growing season.

herbicide (**uhr**-buh-*side* or
huhr-buh-*side*)
A **chemical compound** used to control
or destroy unwanted plants. Also called
a *weed killer.*

herbivore (**uhr**-buh-*vor* or
huhr-buh-*vor*)
An animal that mostly eats plants. Some
herbivores, such as cows and horses, eat
grass. Others, including many birds,
mostly eat seeds.

hereditary (huh-**red**-uh-*ter*-ee)
Describes a **trait** in animals and plants
that is passed on from parents to
offspring. Hereditary traits include size,
body shape, and other characteristics.

heredity (huh-**red**-uh-tee)
The passing of **traits** from parents to
their offspring by means of the **genes**
from the two parents.

hermaphrodite (huhr-**maf**-ruh-*dite*)
A plant or an animal, such as the

earthworm, with both male and female sex **organs**.

hermetic (huhr-**met**-ik)
Closed so tightly that air cannot get in.

Hero of Alexandria
(**hir**-oh) (1st century A.D.)
A Greek inventor and mathematician, famous for inventing the first **steam** engine.

heroin (**her**-oh-in)
A powerful, illegal, habit-forming drug made from the opium poppy plant.

herpes (**huhr**-peez)
A disease of the skin or **mucous membranes** caused by a **virus**. Herpes can produce painful blisters.

herpetology
(*huhr*-puh-**tahl**-uh-jee)
The science that studies **reptiles**, such as snakes, and **amphibians**, such as frogs.

Herschel (**huhr**-shuhl), **Caroline**
(1750–1848)
The first well-known woman astronomer. She discovered several **comets** and also located a number of **nebulae.**

Herschel (**huhr**-shuhl), **William**
(1738–1822)
A noted British astronomer who studied star systems outside the **solar system** and discovered the planet **Uranus.** He worked with his sister, **Caroline Herschel.**

hertz (**huhrts**)
The unit used to measure **frequency** of **electromagnetic waves.** One hertz equals one **cycle** per second. Named for *Heinrich Hertz* (1857–1894). (Symbol—Hz)

Hertzsprung-Russell diagram
(**huhrt**-sprung-**ruhs**-uhl **die**-uh-*gram*)
A chart that relates the brightness of stars to their temperature. It is named after *Ejnar Hertzsprung* (1873–1967) of Denmark and

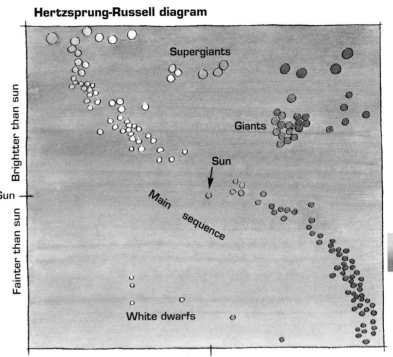

Hertzsprung-Russell diagram

Henry Russell (1877–1957) of the United States, two scientists who worked out the idea independently in the early 1900s.

heuristic (hyu-**ris**-tik)
A way of solving a problem by suggesting an explanation that may be wrong, but that will help to find the right answer. Also called a trial-and-error approach.

hibernate (**hie**-buhr-*nayt*)
To spend the winter asleep or in an inactive state. Among the animals that hibernate are bats, woodchucks, frogs, turtles, and snakes. From the Latin *hibernare,* meaning "to spend the winter."

high blood pressure
(**hie bluhd** *presh*-uhr)
See **hypertension.**

high definition television
(**hie** *def*-uh-**nish**-uhn **tel**-uh-*vizh*-uhn)
See **HDTV.**

high pressure air (**hie presh**-uhr er)
A large mass of air in the **atmosphere** with a high barometric **pressure.** High pressure air usually brings clear weather.

high tide (**hie tide**)
The rise of ocean water higher and farther up on a beach or coastline. High tide is caused by the pull of the moon's gravity. In most places on Earth it usually occurs about twice a day. See also **tide.**

hilum (**hie**-luhm)
The mark or scar on a seed at the point where it is attached to the fruit in which it grew. The eye of a bean is a hilum.

hip (**hip**)
The part of a person's body where the legs join the trunk. You have a right hip and a left hip.

Hipparchus (hi-**pahr**-kuhs) (ca. 180–125 B.C.)
A Greek astronomer who discovered that stars appear to shift to the east.

Hippocrates (hi-**pahk**-ruh-teez) (ca. 460–380 B.C.)
A Greek physician who is often called "the father of medicine." He believed that sickness had natural causes and should be treated by natural means.

histamine (**his**-tuh-*meen*)
A chemical substance released in the blood of someone suffering from an **allergy** or under stress. It may cause **hives,** sneezing, or difficulty in breathing.

histology (hi-**stahl**-uh-jee)
The study of the **tissue** of different living things. *Histologists* usually stain the tissue and examine it under a **microscope.**

HIV (**aych**-*ie*-vee)
Short for *Human Immunodeficiency Virus,* the **virus** that causes **AIDS.** HIV attacks the body's immune system, making patients more likely to get other illnesses.

hive (**hive**)
A natural or manufactured place where bees live.

hives (**hivez**)
A skin rash usually caused by an **allergy** to a food or drug. The medical term for hives is *urticaria.* See also **histamine.**

holistic medicine (hoh-**lis**-tik **med**-uh-sin)
Health care that focuses on treating the whole person, not just the disease. The holistic approach combines medical treatment with help in developing good health habits. From the Greek *holos,* meaning "whole," and the Latin *medicus,* meaning "doctor."

Holocene epoch (**hoh**-luh-*seen* **ep**-uhk)
The most recent **epoch** of **geological history,** from 10,000 years ago to the present. During the Holocene epoch, humans tamed animals, started farming, and began to use metals.

hologram (**hahl**-uh-*gram* or **hoh**-luh-*gram*)
A three-dimensional **image** made by **lasers.** The hologram image seems to float in space. From the Greek *holos,* meaning "whole," and *gramma,* meaning "something written."

homeopathy (*hoh*-mee-**ahp**-uh-thee)
A way of treating disease. The homeopathic doctor gives the patient a very small quantity of a substance that in a larger quantity would cause **symptoms** similar to those of the disease being treated. The amount is so small that it can't harm you.

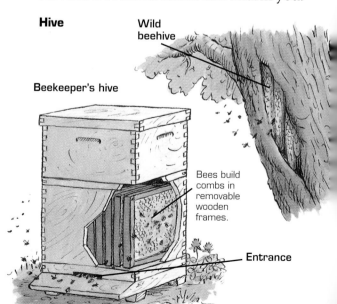

Hive

Wild beehive

Beekeeper's hive

Bees build combs in removable wooden frames.

Entrance

homeostasis (*hoh*-mee-oh-**stay**-sis)
A state of stability within a living **organism** achieved by adjusting to changes in the outside **environment**. See also **biofeedback**. From the Greek *homos,* meaning "same," and *stasis,* meaning "the act of standing."

hominid (**hahm**-uh-nid)
A modern human being or any one of the extinct recent ancestors. ***Homo sapiens*** are the only living hominids. From the Latin *homo,* meaning "human being."

Homo erectus (**hoh**-moh i-**rek**-tuhs)
An **extinct species** of early humans, or **hominids,** that lived from about 1.6 million to 250,000 years ago. From the Latin *homo,* meaning "human being," and *erectus,* meaning "upright."

homogenize (huh-**mahj**-uh-*nize*)
To mix together substances that usually do not mix. Homogenized milk has fat spread throughout the milk instead of floating on top as cream. From the Greek *homos,* meaning "same," and *genos,* meaning "kind."

Homo habilis (**hoh**-moh **hab**-uh-lis)
One of the earliest humans; **fossil** remains date back about 2 million years. From the Latin *homo,* meaning "human being," and *habilis,* meaning "handy."

homologous structures
(hoh-**mahl**-uh-guhs **struhk**-chuhrz)
Body parts in different creatures that are similar in origin and structure; they may be used in the same or different ways. For example, a seal's flippers and a calf's forelegs are homologous structures. See **analogous structures.**

Homo sapiens
(**hoh**-moh **say**-pee-uhnz)
The **species** of human beings after *Homo erectus* that includes all modern humans. *Homo sapiens* first appeared between 400,000 and 300,000 years ago. See also **Neanderthals.** From the Latin *homo,* meaning "human being," and *sapiens,* meaning "wise."

Homo sapiens sapiens (**hoh**-moh **say**-pee-uhnz **say**-pee-uhnz)
Modern humans, a subspecies of *Homo sapiens.* They developed about 100,000 years ago in the Middle East or Africa. Individuals have bigger chins, higher foreheads, less protruding faces, a smaller ridge over the eyes, and more rounded skulls than other *Homo sapiens.*

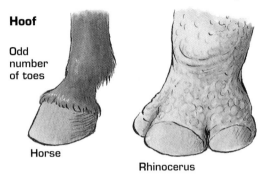

Hoof
Odd number of toes

Horse

Rhinocerus

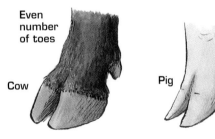

Even number of toes

Cow

Pig

hoof (**huf** or **hoof**)
The hard, horny covering on the feet of horses, cattle, pigs, zebras, etc. A hoofed animal is also called an **ungulate.**

Hooke (**huk**), **Robert** (1635–1703)
An English scientist who first used the word **cell** to describe the microscopic units he saw in plants.

Hooke's law (**huks law**)
A discovery made by **Robert Hooke** that an elastic body bends or stretches in direct proportion to the force acting on it.

Hopper (**hahp**-uhr), **Grace** (1906–1992)
An American computer scientist who developed programming languages that made it easier for people to use computers.

horizon (huh-**rie**-zuhn)
The distant, slightly curved line where the earth and sky seem to meet. If you

are at sea level, the horizon is about 2½ miles (4 kilometers) away. From the Greek *horizon,* meaning "boundary."

hormone (**hor**-mohn)
One of several **chemical** messengers that control the **organs** of the body. Hormones are produced within living things or can also be made in a **laboratory.** From the Greek *horman,* meaning "to stir up."

horn (**horn**)
A hard, pointed growth on the heads of many **mammals,** such as cattle and goats. Horns are usually found in pairs.

horoscope (**hor**-uh-*skohp*)
A chart showing the position of the stars and planets when you were born, which some believe can describe your character. Scientists doubt that the stars and planets influence people's lives.

horsepower (**hors**-*pou*-uhr)
A unit for measuring the power of engines and motors. One horsepower equals 550 foot-pounds per second, or 746 **watts.**

horticulture (**hort**-uh-*kuhl*-chuhr)
The science of growing flowers, fruit, vegetables, and ornamental trees and shrubs. From the Latin *hortus,* meaning "garden," and *cultura,* meaning "the practice of growing crops."

host (hohst)
A plant or animal on which or in which a **parasite** lives and feeds.

hot spring (**hot spring**)
A natural **spring** that sends hot water or **steam** bubbling up out of the ground.

hour (**our**)
A period of time equal to 60 minutes or 3,600 seconds. There are 24 hours in a day on Earth.

hovercraft (**huhv**-uhr-*kraft*)
A vehicle that rides on a cushion of air. Also called *air cushion vehicle.*

hp (*aych*-**pee**)
See **horsepower.**

Hubble (**hub**-uhl), Edwin Powell (1889–1953)
An American astronomer. Hubble found that all the **galaxies** are moving away from Earth, which means that the **universe** is expanding.

human being (**hyoo**-muhn **bee**-ing)
An **organism** that belongs to the subspecies *Homo sapiens sapiens.*

human immunodeficiency virus (**hyoo**-muhn *im*-yuh-*no*-duh-**fish**-uhn-see *vie*-ruhs)
See **HIV.**

humerus (**hyoo**-muh-ruhs)
The long bone in the upper arm of humans. The humerus extends from the shoulder to the elbow. *Also,* the long bone in the front legs of four-legged animals.

humidity (hyoo-**mid**-uh-tee)
The amount of water **vapor** in the air. The humidity is high over oceans and forests, and low over deserts.

humus (**hyoo**-muhs)
The dark brown part of soil that helps plants to grow. Humus forms when decayed leaves and other vegetable matter mix in with the soil.

hurricane (**huhr**-uh-*kayn*)
A powerful, whirling storm. Hurricanes have wind speeds between 74 miles (119 kilometers) and 150 miles (240 kilometers) an hour, and usually very

Hovercraft

Air in

Fan #2 propels it forward, which is easy because there is little friction between the hovercraft and the water.

Rubber skirt

Fan #1 pushes air down under the skirt, compressing it until it lifts the craft up off the water's surface.

Hydrofoil

Low speed

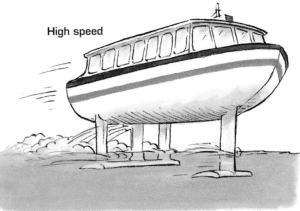

High speed

The foils generate lift the same way an airplane wing does.

heavy rain. A hurricane has at its center a calm, clear zone called the eye.

Huygens (**hie**-guhnz or **hoi**-guhnz), **Christian** (1629–1695)
A Dutch scientist who stated in 1678 that light travels as waves. Huygens improved the **telescope** and used it to identify the rings around **Saturn**.

hybrid (**hie**-brid)
The offspring of a plant or animal whose parents belong to two different **species**. A mule is a hybrid, the offspring of a male donkey and a female horse.

hydraulics (hie-**draw**-liks)
The science dealing with the actions of water and other liquids—from water supply systems to hydraulic brakes. From the Greek *hydor*, meaning "water," and *aulos*, meaning "pipe."

hydrocarbon (*hie*-droh-**kahr**-buhn)
A **chemical compound** that contains only **hydrogen** and **carbon**. Gasoline is a mixture of hydrocarbons.

hydrochloric acid (*hie*-druh-**klor**-ik **as**-id)
A powerful, colorless, strong-smelling **chemical** that is widely used in industry. Hydrochloric acid contains the **elements** **hydrogen** and **chlorine**. (Formula—HCl)

hydroelectric (*hie*-droh-i-**lek**-trik)
Having to do with producing electricity by water power. In a hydroelectric plant, water flowing over a dam or waterfall spins **turbines** in electric **generators**.

hydrofoil (**hie**-druh-*foil*)
A boat that moves above the surface of the water when traveling at high speeds. The hydrofoil has underwater *foils* that look like airplane wings and lift the boat's hull.

hydrogen (**hie**-druh-juhn)
The most common **chemical element** in the **universe**. The hydrogen **atom** is the smallest and lightest of all atoms, with just one **proton** and one **electron**. Hydrogen is usually a gas that combines with other elements to form **compounds**, such as water (H_2O). From the Greek *hydor*, meaning "water," and *genes*, meaning "born." (Symbol—H)

hydrogenation (hie-*drahj*-uh-**nay**-shuhn)
A **chemical** process that adds **hydrogen** to a **compound**, changing liquid oils into solid fats. Margarine is hydrogenated vegetable oil.

hydrogen bomb (**hie**-druh-juhn **bahm**)
A nuclear weapon that explodes as a result of **nuclear fusion**, releasing a tremendous amount of **energy** and causing many deaths and much destruction. Also called *H-bomb* or *thermonuclear bomb*.

H

hydrologic cycle
(*hie*-druh-**lahj**-ik **sie**-kuhl)
See **water cycle.**

hydrolysis (hie-**drahl**-uh-sis)
A **chemical** reaction in which water changes certain substances into other substances. In digestion, hydrolysis breaks complex **sucrose molecules** down into simple **glucose** molecules. From the Greek *hydor,* meaning "water," and *lysis,* meaning "loosening."

hydrometer (hie-**drahm**-uh-tuhr)
An instrument used to measure the **density** of water and other liquids. One kind of hydrometer tests the **acid** level in car batteries.

Hydrometer
Checking a saltwater aquarium with a hydrometer

Hydrometer sinks if water isn't salty enough

Adding salt makes the water denser and the hydrometer floats higher.

Correct salinity level

hydrophone (hie-druh-*fohn*)
A device for picking up sound waves underwater and changing them into patterns of **electric current.** Hydrophones are used in **sonar** and other **research** in the water.

hydroplane (hie-druh-*playn*)
A high-speed motorboat that skims along, or "planes," on the surface of the water. *Also,* one of a pair of fins on the sides of a submarine that help to raise or lower the submarine in the water. See also **hydrofoil.** *Also,* to skim over water. Cars hydroplane when they skid on wet roads.

Hydroponics

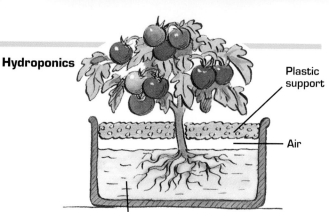

Plastic support

Air

Water with nutrients added

hydroponics (hie-druh-**pahn**-iks)
Growing plants in water, gravel, or other materials. The plants are fed liquid **nutrients.**

hydrosphere (**hie**-druh-*sfir*)
All the water on and above the earth's surface. The hydrosphere includes oceans, rivers, lakes, and other groundwater, the frozen ice caps, water in the soil, and the water **vapor** in the air.

hydrotropism (hie-druh-**troh**-*piz-uhm*)
Moving or leaning toward water. Plant roots often show hydrotropism by growing toward a water source. From the Greek *hydor,* meaning "water," and *tropos,* meaning "turn."

hygiene (**hie**-jeen)
The science of keeping clean in order to stay healthy. Good hygiene includes washing hands before meals.

hygrometer (hie-**grahm**-uh-tuhr)
An instrument used to measure the amount of **humidity,** or water **vapor,** in the air.

Hygrometer
The needle is attached to a coil of two-sided material. One side is absorbent and swells when there is moisture in the air, opening the coil and tilting the needle.

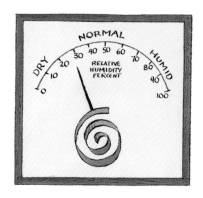

hyperon (**hie**-puh-*rahn*)
A **subatomic particle** that usually has a life of less than one-thousandth of one-billionth of a second.

hyperopia (*hie*-puh-**roh**-pee-uh)
See **farsighted.**

hypertension
(*hie*-puhr-**ten**-chuhn)
The medical term for *high blood pressure.* Hypertension can damage the heart or **kidneys,** as well as the blood vessels themselves.

hypertext (**hie**-puhr-*tekst*)
A computer link between related bits of information. Hypertext makes it possible to jump quickly from one topic to another connected topic.

hyperthermia
(*hie*-puhr-**thuhr**-mee-uh)
Very high body temperature. From the Greek *hyper,* meaning "over," and *therme,* meaning "heat."

hypnosis (hip-**noh**-sis)
A state resembling deep sleep. But in hypnosis a person is able to move about and tends to follow the suggestions of others. From the Greek *Hypnos,* the ancient god of sleep.

hypochondriac
(*hie*-puh-**kahn**-dree-*ak*)
A person who always worries about his or her health. A hypochondriac often suffers from imaginary illnesses.

Hypodermic

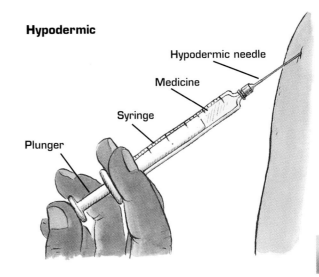

Hypodermic needle
Medicine
Syringe
Plunger

hypodermic (*hie*-puh-**duhr**-mik)
A hollow needle used to inject medicine under the skin. From the Greek *hypo,* meaning "under," and *derma,* meaning "skin."

hypothalamus (*hie*-puh-**thal**-uh-muhs)
A small area at the base of the brain that controls the body's breathing and heartbeat. It also directs body temperature, sleep, hunger, thirst, and emotions.

hypothermia (*hie*-puh-**thuhr**-mee-uh)
Very low body temperature. Your body fights hypothermia by shivering. From the Greek *hypo,* meaning "under," and *therme,* meaning "heat."

hypothesis (hie-**pahth**-uh-sis)
A possible explanation for something observed. To test a hypothesis, scientists do **experiments** or make **observations.**

ibuprofen (*ie*-byoo-**proh**-fuhn)
A drug that relieves pain and reduces **fever** and **inflammation**.

ice (**ise**)
Frozen water. Ice forms when water is cooled below 32° **Fahrenheit** (0° **Celsius**). Snow, sleet, frost, and hail are all forms of ice.

Ice Age (**ise** *ayj*)
A period of the earth's history when **glaciers** covered large areas of land most of the time. The last ice age lasted from about 1.6 million to 10,000 years ago. Also called the **Pleistocene epoch.**

iceberg (**ise**-buhrg)
A huge ice mass that breaks off from a **glacier** and floats in the sea. Only about one-tenth of an iceberg shows on the surface. The rest is hidden under the water.

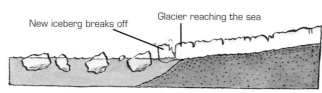

New iceberg breaks off Glacier reaching the sea

Iceberg

ice cap (**ise** *kap*)
A thick layer of **ice** and **snow** covering a land area. Ice caps are found in the **polar** regions and on some mountaintops. The ice cap in Antarctica is over 2 **miles** (3.2 **kilometers**) deep.

ichthyology (*ik*-thee-**ahl**-uh-jee)
The branch of science that deals with fishes. From the Greek *ichthys,* meaning "fish," and *-logia,* meaning "science of."

icicle (**ie**-sik-uhl)
A pointed piece of ice hanging down from a building, tree, or other structure. An icicle is formed when dripping water freezes.

igneous rock (**ig**-nee-uhs **rahk**)
Rock formed of molten **magma** from deep within the earth or from **lava** above the surface. **Granite, basalt,** and **obsidian** are igneous rocks. From the Latin *ignis,* meaning "fire."

ignition (ig-**nish**-uhn)
A system that sets fire to a mixture of fuel and air in an **internal combustion** engine. The ignition system of an automobile uses sparks from spark plugs to set fire to the fuel-air mixture. *Also,* the blasting off of a rocket. See also **internal combustion engine.**

image (**im**-ij)
A picture or **graphic** formed by a computer, camera, **microscope, telescope,** or television screen.

Imhotep (im-**hoh**-tep) (ca. 2950 B.C.)
An Egyptian doctor whom people worshiped as a god. Imhotep is the first doctor whose name is known.

immunity (i-**myoo**-nuh-tee)
The ability of the body to defend itself against germs and other causes of disease.

impedance (im-**peed**-ns)
Resistance to the flow of electricity in an **alternating-current circuit**. Impedance is measured in **ohms.**

impermeable (im-**puhr**-mee-uh-buhl)
Describes a material that does not permit gases or liquids to pass through. For example, rubber is impermeable to water.

implant (im-**plant**)
To insert living or artificial material into the body. Dentists sometimes implant teeth into the jaw, for example. *Also,* the material itself is called an implant (**im**-plant). Thus, the dentist sets an implant into the jaw.

impulse (**im**-puhls)
A message that travels along **nerve** pathways to the brain. The impulse is received by the brain, which decides on the action that should be taken. *Also,* a short burst of electric power or a force that sets an object in motion.

inactive (in-**ak**-tiv)
Not active. An inactive substance in **chemistry** is one that does not easily combine with other **elements** or **compounds.**

inbreeding (**in**-*bree*-ding)
Producing offspring by **breeding** closely related animals or plants. Inbreeding in humans occurs when closely related people mate.

incandescent
(*in*-kan-**des**-uhnt)
Giving off light when heated. When **current** flows through an incandescent bulb, the **filament** glows white hot. From the Latin *in,* meaning "within," and *candere,* meaning "to glow."

inch (**inch**)
A small unit of length. An inch equals 2.54 centimeters or one-twelfth of a foot. From the Latin *uncia,* meaning "one twelfth."

incidence (**in**-suh-duhns)
The rate at which something happens. The incidence of people catching cold is higher in winter than in summer. *Also,* the direction in which a thing or **ray** strikes a surface. Also called the **angle of incidence.**

incinerate (in-**sin**-uh-*rayt*)
To burn something until only ashes remain. From the Latin *in,* meaning "into," and *cinis,* meaning "ashes."

incisor (in-**sie**-zuhr)
One of the front teeth. You have eight incisors for cutting and tearing your food.

inclined plane (in-**klinde playn**)
A sloping plank or ramp that makes it easier to raise heavy loads. For example, pushing a heavy wagon up an inclined plane takes less force than lifting it.

Inclined plane

Incubate

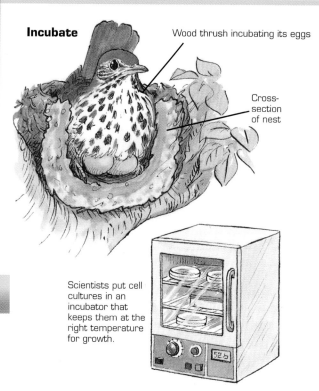

Wood thrush incubating its eggs

Cross-section of nest

Scientists put cell cultures in an incubator that keeps them at the right temperature for growth.

incubate (**ing**-kyuh-*bayt*)
To keep eggs or very young **organisms** warm so that they will hatch or grow. *Also,* to grow **bacteria** or other **microbes** from a **culture**.

incubation period
(*ing*-kyuh-**bay**-shuhn **pir**-ee-uhd)
The time period between when germs enter your body and when the **symptoms** of a disease appear.

indigenous (in-**dij**-uh-nuhs)
Native to the area or country where found. Lions are indigenous to Africa.

induction (in-**duhk**-shuhn)
A process by which an electrically charged object **charges** a nearby object without actually touching it. *Also,* using specific **observations** to arrive at a general rule or principle. See also **electromagnetic induction**.

induction coil (in-**duhk**-shuhn *koil*)
A device that produces high-**voltage current** from lower-voltage current. An induction coil is also used to change **direct current** into **alternating current**.

inert (in-**uhrt**)
Describes a **chemical element** that does not easily combine with other elements. For example, **helium** is an inert gas.

inertia (in-**uhr**-shuh)
The tendency of an object to stay still, or to continue moving in the same direction and at the same speed, unless a force makes it change. Thus, a book on a table stays there unless someone pushes it off. A thrown ball keeps moving until **gravity** and **friction** with the air slow it down and change its direction. The greater the **mass** of an object, the greater its inertia.

inertial guidance
(in-**uhr**-shuhl **gide**-ns)
A way to keep rockets, airplanes, submarines, and other vehicles on course. Inertial guidance uses various instruments to keep checking the position of the vehicle and make necessary adjustments.

infection (in-**fek**-shuhn)
The body's **reaction** to an invasion by **bacteria, viruses**, or other **microorganisms**.

infertile (in-**fuhrt**-l)
Unable to **reproduce**. An infertile male or female cannot produce any offspring.

Induction coil

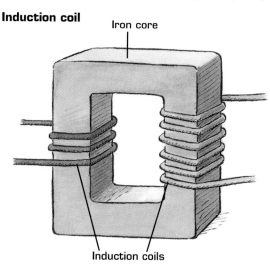

Iron core

Induction coils

A device used in transformers in which low voltage coming in through a coil with few turns around the core—produces higher voltage in a coil with many more turns around the core

infinity (in-**fin**-uh-tee)
A quantity or distance that has no limits, boundaries, or end. From the Latin *in,* meaning "not," and *finitus,* meaning "enclosed."

inflammable (in-**flam**-uh-buhl)
Easily set on fire. For example, paper is inflammable. Inflammable has the same meaning as **flammable.** From the Latin *in,* meaning "in," and *flammare,* meaning "to burn or set on fire."

inflammation (*in*-fluh-**may**-shuhn)
Swelling, redness, pain, and heat in some part of the body. Inflammation can result from an **infection,** injury, poison, or some other cause.

influenza (*in*-floo-**en**-zuh)
A serious disease caused by the influenza **virus.** Influenza has all the **symptoms** of a bad cold, but is much worse and can be very dangerous. Also called *flu* or *grippe.*

information (*in*-fuhr-**may**-shuhn)
In computers, the summary and conclusions reached after collecting **data,** which are raw facts.

information theory
(*in*-fuhr-**may**-shuhn *thee*-uh-ree)
The study of how messages are sent and received **electronically** by computer, radio, telephone, and television. Scientists use information theory to improve the workings of these devices and help people communicate with one another.

infrared rays (*in*-fruh-**red rayz**)
Invisible **electromagnetic rays** that are also called heat **rays.** The sun sends out powerful infrared rays. The remote control for a television sends out weak infrared rays.

ingest (in-**jest**)
Take food into the body. From the Latin *in,* meaning "into," and *gerere,* meaning "to carry."

inhabit (in-**hab**-it)
Live in a place. Penguins inhabit the land around the South Pole. From the Latin *in,* meaning "in," and *habitare,* meaning "to dwell."

inherit (in-**her**-it)
To receive a specific body **trait** from one's parents. The trait is passed from **generation** to generation by **genes.** For example, a child can inherit his or her father's red hair.

inject (in-**jekt**)
To force a liquid into the body, usually with a **hypodermic** needle. Doctors often inject medicine into a patient's arm. From the Latin *in,* meaning "in," and *jacere,* meaning "to throw."

innate (i-**nayt**)
A behavior that is **inherited,** not learned. For example, a bird's song is innate. From the Latin *in,* meaning "in," and *nasci,* meaning "be born."

inner core (**in**-uhr **kor**)
The center region of the inside of Earth. The inner core starts about 3,200 miles (5,150 kilometers) below the surface. It reaches to the center of Earth, 4,000 miles (6,400 kilometers) down. The inner core is probably solid **iron** and **nickel.** The temperature may reach 13,000° **Fahrenheit** (7,000° **Celsius**). See also **Earth.**

inner ear (**in**-uhr **ir**)
Part of the ear within the **skull.** The inner ear sends **nerve impulses** to the hearing center of the brain. It is also responsible for a person's sense of balance. See also **ear.**

inoculation (i-*nahk*-yuh-**lay**-shuhn)
The injecting of dead or weakened germs into the body. The inoculation produces a mild form of the disease so that the person does not later get that disease. Inoculation has rid us of the disease smallpox. *Also,* the placing of **microbes** into a **culture** to grow.

inorganic (*in*-or-**gan**-ik)
Not from an animal or plant. **Minerals** are inorganic. Inorganic chemistry is the study of the **chemical elements** and their **compounds**, except most **carbon** compounds.

input (**in**-put)
Data that are entered into a computer. The input can come from a human operator, another computer or **diskette**, or any device that counts, reads, or measures sources outside the computer. *Also,* the **energy** supplied to a machine or **electronic** device.

insanity (in-**san**-uh-tee)
Mental illness so severe that the individual cannot be held responsible for his or her acts.

insect (**in**-sekt)
A small animal with three pairs of legs, a body divided into three parts, and usually two pairs of wings. Insects make up 80 percent of all animals on Earth.

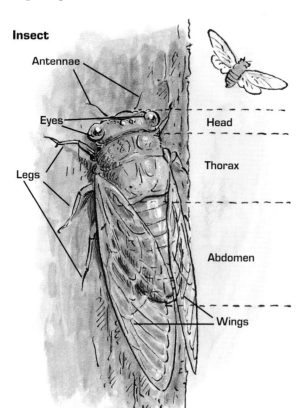

Insect
Antennae
Eyes
Head
Legs
Thorax
Abdomen
Wings

insecticide (in-**sek**-tuh-*side*)
A substance that kills insects. Many farmers spray their crops with insecticides. Also called **pesticide.**

insectivore (in-**sek**-tuh-*vor*)
Any animal that feeds mainly on insects. Bats, birds, and spiders are insectivores.

insoluble (in-**sahl**-yuh-buhl)
A substance that cannot be **dissolved.** Diamonds are insoluble. *Also,* a problem that cannot be solved.

insomnia (in-**sahm**-nee-uh)
The inability to sleep. Insomnia may be a sign of illness or stress.

inspiration (*in*-spuh-**ray**-shuhn)
Taking air into the lungs. Inspiration and **expiration** are the two parts of breathing. From the Latin *in,* meaning "in," and *spirare,* meaning "to breathe."

instinct (**in**-stingkt)
A way of behaving that is natural and inborn, rather than learned. Birds fly by instinct. See also **innate.**

insulation (*in*-suh-**lay**-shuhn)
A material that blocks the flow of **energy,** such as heat, sound, or electricity. Electric wire is covered with insulation so you do not get a shock when you touch it.

insulin (**in**-suh-luhn)
A **hormone** produced by the **pancreas gland** that helps the body control the sugar level in the blood. Most people with **diabetes** mellitus cannot use the insulin they produce and their sugar level is too high. They must take insulin as a drug.

integrated circuit
(**in**-tuh-*gray*-tid **suhr**-kit)
See **chip.**

intelligence (in-**tel**-uh-juhns)
The ability to reason, learn, remember, and solve problems. Intelligence is sometimes measured as *IQ,* which stands for **intelligence quotient.**

Internal combustion engine

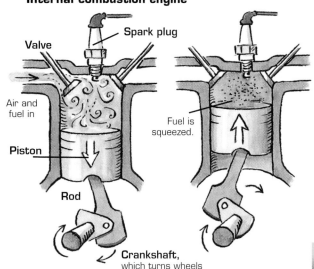

Valve — Spark plug

Air and fuel in

Fuel is squeezed.

Piston

Rod

Crankshaft, which turns wheels

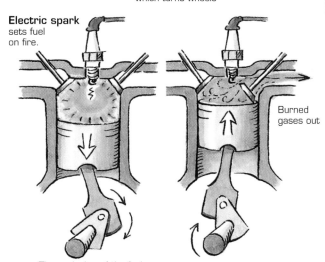

Electric spark sets fuel on fire.

Burned gases out

The explosion of the fuel forces the piston down.

intelligence quotient
(in-**tel**-uh-juhns *kwoh*-shuhnt)
A number, often called *IQ,* that indicates a person's mental ability. The IQ score is based on certain tests. But some educators question whether the IQ is a fair measure of ability.

intensity (in-**ten**-suh-tee)
The amount of force or **energy** given off or received. The intensity of sound at a rock concert is very high.

interactive (*in*-tuhr-**ak**-tiv)
Describes a machine or system that feeds information back to the operator and responds to his or her instructions.

intercom (**in**-tuhr-*kahm*)
A telephone or **loudspeaker system** that lets people communicate by voice, usually within the same building, airplane, or ship. Short for *intercommunication system.*

interface (**in**-tuhr-*fays*)
The surface between two different materials. *Also,* the connection between two parts of a computer.

interference (*in*-tuhr-**fir**-uhns)
An effect that occurs when waves bump into each other. Interference can disturb the movement of light, sound, radio, or water waves.

interferon (*in*-tuhr-**fir**-ahn)
A **protein** produced by body **cells** when they are invaded by a **virus.** Interferon interferes with the multiplication of the virus.

intergalactic (*in*-tuhr-guh-**lak**-tik)
Between **galaxies.** Most scientists believe that there is very little **matter** in intergalactic space, making it almost a complete **vacuum.**

intern (**in**-tuhrn)
A doctor working in a hospital after graduation from medical school to improve his or her skills with the help of experienced doctors. Sometimes spelled *interne.*

internal combustion engine
(in-*tuhrn*-l kuhm-**buhs**-chuhn *en*-juhn)
An engine that produces power by burning fuel. Most internal combustion engines burn gasoline.

internal medicine
(in-**tuhrn**-l **med**-uh-suhn)
The branch of medicine that deals with the **diagnosis** and treatment of diseases in adults. A doctor of internal medicine is called an *internist.*

international date line
(*in*-tuhr-**nash**-uhn-l **dayt**-*line*)
An imaginary line on the earth's surface where each calendar day first begins.

91

International date line

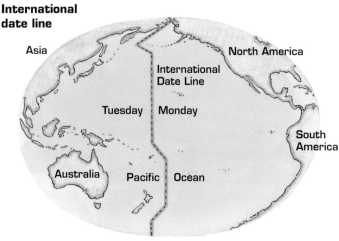

The international date line runs north and south through the Pacific Ocean, mostly along the 180th **meridian.**

Internet (**in**-tuhr-*net*)
A worldwide computer network made up of many smaller networks. The Internet includes databases, Web pages, bulletin boards, and an **e-mail** network.

interplanetary
(*in*-tuhr-**plan**-uh-*ter*-ee)
Between the planets. Interplanetary distances are measured in millions of miles or kilometers.

interstellar (*in*-tuhr-**stel**-uhr)
Between the stars. Interstellar distances are often measured in **light-years.**

intertidal zone (*in*-tuhr-**tide**-l **zohn**)
The narrow strip of land along a coast between the low- and high-**tide** lines.

intestine (in-**tes**-tin)
The digestive tube in the body that extends from the stomach to the **anus.** The intestine includes the **small intestine,** about 22 feet (7 meters) long, and the **large intestine,** about 5 feet (1.5 meters) long. Most digestion takes place in the small intestine; the large intestine mostly gets rid of undigested wastes.

intravenous injection
(*in*-truh-**vee**-nuhs in-**jek**-shuhn)
A way of putting substances directly into the bloodstream. It is usually given by **hypodermic** needle into a **vein.** See also **transfusion.**

intrusive rock (in-**troo**-siv **rahk**)
A kind of **igneous** rock formed from **magma** that became solid beneath the earth's surface. It is usually found in mines. Sometimes **erosion** exposes intrusive rock on the surface.

invention (in-**ven**-chuhn)
A new device, product, or process that solves a problem or improves a way of doing something. The person who thinks up inventions is called an *inventor.*

invertebrate (in-**vuhr**-tuh-bruht)
An animal without a **backbone.** Invertebrates include insects, worms, snails, lobsters, and starfish. About 9 out of 10 animals are invertebrates.

in vitro fertilization
(in **vee**-troh *fuhrt*-l-uh-**zay**-shuhn)
The joining of a **sperm** and egg outside the body. The **fertilized** egg is then placed into the female reproductive system to grow. From the Latin *in,* meaning "in," *vitrum,* meaning "glass," and *fertilis,* meaning "productive."

iodine (**ie**-uh-*dine*)
A **chemical element** of shiny blue-black **crystals** with an irritating odor. Humans need a tiny amount of iodine for their physical and mental growth. In a weak **solution,** iodine can be used to kill germs on wounds. Too much pure iodine taken internally is poisonous. (Symbol—I)

ion (**ie**-uhn or **ie**-ahn)
An **atom** or group of atoms with an **electric charge.** The electric charge comes from the gain or loss of **electrons.**

ionic bond (ie-**ahn**-ik **bahnd**)
The force that holds **atoms** together. In an ionic bond, **electrons** transfer from one atom to another. As an example, **sodium** (Na) and **chlorine** (Cl) combine to make **salt** (NaCl). The sodium loses an electron and becomes a sodium **ion;**

the **chlorine** gains an electron and becomes a chlorine ion. The opposite charges of the ions form the ionic bond that holds the salt **molecules** together. An ionic bond is also called a *polar bond.*

ionosphere (ie-**ahn**-uh-*sfir*)
The part of the earth's **atmosphere** with many **ions.** The ionosphere is formed as **cosmic rays** and **radiation** from the sun hit **atoms** in the atmosphere. It reflects radio waves back to earth, making long-distance communication possible. The ionosphere starts just over 30 miles (50 kilometers) above Earth and extends to a height of about 300 miles (480 kilometers).

IQ (**ie**-**kyoo**)
See **intelligence quotient.**

iris (**ie**-ris)
The colored part of the eye. The iris is a muscle that controls the amount of light that passes through the **pupil.** From the Latin *iris,* meaning "rainbow."

iron (**ie**-uhrn)
A silvery-white metal **element** used to make everything from automobiles to bridges. **Steel,** which is harder than iron, is made by adding **carbon** and other elements to iron. When iron joins with **oxygen,** it forms iron oxide, or **rust.** Small amounts of iron are found in **red blood cells.** (Symbol—Fe)

irradiate (i-**ray**-dee-*ayt*)
To expose to **radiation,** such as **ultraviolet rays, X rays,** or **gamma rays.** Doctors irradiate parts of the bodies of cancer patients to kill cancer **cells.**

irrigation (*ir*-uh-**gay**-shuhn)
Bringing water to land that is too dry for plants to grow. Irrigation spreads water taken from rivers, lakes, or wells on crops.

island (**ie**-luhnd)
Any land mass smaller than a **continent** that is surrounded by water. Hawaii is a group of islands in the Pacific Ocean.

isobar (**ie**-suh-*bahr*)
A line on a weather map that connects places with the same atmospheric **pressure.** *Also,* an **atom** with the same **mass** but a different number of **protons** in the **nucleus.** From the Greek *isos,* meaning "equal," and *baros,* meaning "weight."

isomer (**ie**-suh-muhr)
A **compound** that has the same kinds and numbers of **atoms** as another compound, but with a different arrangement of the atoms. From the Greek *isos,* meaning "equal," and *meros,* meaning "part."

isometrics
(*ie*-suh-**me**-triks)
A form of exercise in which you push or pull against another part of your body or against something that does not move.

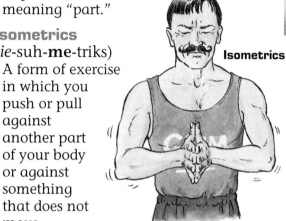

Isometrics

isotherm (**ie**-suh-*thuhrm*)
A line drawn on **weather** maps to connect places with the same **temperature.** From the Greek *isos,* meaning "equal," and *therme,* meaning "heat."

isotope (**ie**-suh-*tohp*)
An **atom** that has a different **atomic** weight from other atoms of the same **element.** Isotopes of an element have the same number of **protons** and **electrons** but different numbers of **neutrons. Hydrogen,** for example, has three isotopes: ordinary hydrogen, or *protium,* with one proton and one electron; the **deuterium** isotope with one proton, one neutron, and one electron; and the **tritium** isotope with one proton, two neutrons, and one electron. From the Greek *isos,* meaning "equal," and *topos,* meaning "place."

jaundice (**jawn**-dis)

A condition in which the skin and the whites of the eyes turn yellowish. Jaundice is caused by an extra amount of *bilirubin* in the blood. Bilirubin comes from the breakdown of **red blood cells**. From the middle French *jaune,* meaning "yellow."

Java (**jah**-vuh)

A computer language. Java **programs** can run on many different kinds of computers.

Jenner (**jen**-uhr), **Edward** (1749–1823)

An English physician who discovered a **vaccination** for the disease smallpox. Jenner found that infecting someone with cowpox, a mild disease, kept that person from getting smallpox, a more serious disease.

jet propulsion (**jet** pruh-**puhl**-shuhn)

The forward motion of an object caused by fast-moving gas or liquid rushing out the back end. A jet propulsion engine burns fuels that produce hot gases. The gases are expelled through the back of the engine, pushing the airplane or rocket forward at a high speed.

jet stream (**jet** *streem*)

A high-speed **current** of air that blows from west to east at high **altitudes.** The jet stream helps airplane pilots flying east to gain extra speed.

Jet propulsion

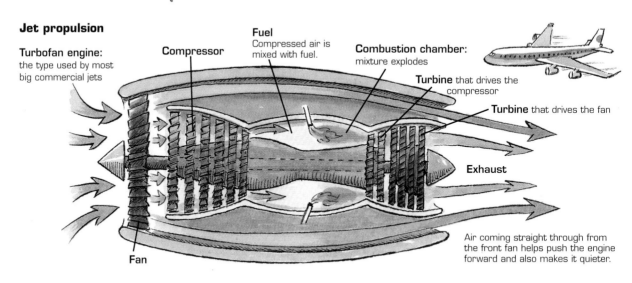

Turbofan engine: the type used by most big commercial jets

Compressor

Fuel
Compressed air is mixed with fuel.

Combustion chamber: mixture explodes

Turbine that drives the compressor

Turbine that drives the fan

Exhaust

Air coming straight through from the front fan helps push the engine forward and also makes it quieter.

Fan

Another kind of jet propulsion: human-compressed air shoots out the back of fleeing balloon

Octopus and squid squirt seawater out of a tube to shoot forward . . .

. . . or backward.

jetty (**jet**-ee)
A structure built out from the shore of an ocean or river. A jetty changes the flow of the water and protects the shoreline from **erosion**. From the Middle French *jeter,* meaning "to throw."

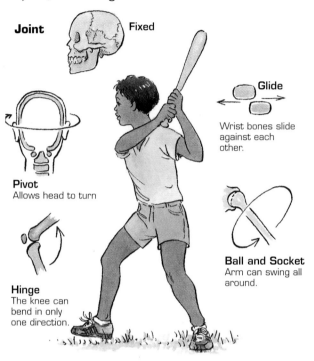

Joint

Fixed

Pivot
Allows head to turn

Hinge
The knee can bend in only one direction.

Glide
Wrist bones slide against each other.

Ball and Socket
Arm can swing all around.

joint (**joint**)
A place where two or more bones meet in the body of a human or animal. Your joints include *hinge joints* in your knees that let you move your legs back and forth; *ball-and-socket joints* in your shoulders that let you swing and turn your arms; and *pivot joints* in your neck that let you turn your head. You also have *fixed joints* in your **skull** that don't move at all, and *gliding joints* in your wrist.

Joliot-Curie (zhawl-**yoh**-kyu-**ree**), **Irène** (1897–1956) and **Frédéric** (1900–1958)
A French husband-and-wife team of physicists famous for their work with **radioactivity.** Irène Joliot-Curie was the daughter of **Marie** and **Pierre Curie.**

joule (**jool**)
A unit of **work** or **energy** in the **metric system,** named after **James Joule.** One joule equals the force of one **newton** acting over a distance of one meter. (Symbol—J)

Joule (**jool** or **joul**), **James** (1818–1889)
A British physicist, famous for helping to prove the law of **conservation of energy,** which says that **energy** can be neither created nor destroyed. Joule also showed how energy is changed from one form into another.

Jovian (**joh**-vee-uhn)
Having to do with the planet **Jupiter.**

jugular vein (**juhg**-yuh-luhr *vayn*)
One of four large **veins** in the neck. The jugular veins return blood from the head and neck to the heart.

jungle (**juhng**-guhl)
A tropical forest area overgrown with trees, vines, and other plants.

Jupiter (**joo**-puh-tuhr)
The fifth planet of the **solar system.**

Average distance from the sun— 483,000,000 miles (778,000,000 kilometers)
*Length of year—*11.99 Earth years
*Length of day—*9 hours, 55 minutes
*Diameter at equator—*88,520 miles (142,800 kilometers)

Jupiter is the largest of all the sun's planets. More than 1,400 planets the size of Earth could fit inside. Not made of rock and metal like Earth, Jupiter is mostly made up of **hydrogen** and **helium gas. Astronomers** have found 16 **satellites,** or **moons,** in **orbit** around Jupiter.

Jurassic period (ju-**ras**-ik **pir**-ee-uhd)
The period in **geological history** from about 205 to 138 million years ago. During the Jurassic period, dinosaurs reached their largest size and the first birds appeared.

K

Kelvin (kel-vin), **Lord** (1824–1907)
A British physicist who introduced the **Kelvin scale** of temperatures. Kelvin also produced 70 inventions and wrote more than 600 scientific papers. Born William Thomson, he was made Lord Kelvin for laying the first transatlantic **telegraph cable.**

Kelvin scale (kel-vin *skayl*)
A temperature scale that begins at **absolute zero** (–459.69° **Fahrenheit,** –273.15° **Celsius**), the coldest possible temperature. In the Kelvin scale, water freezes at 273° and boils at 373°. One degree in the Kelvin scale equals one degree in the **Celsius scale.** (Symbol—K)

Kepler (kep-luhr), **Johannes** (1571–1630)
A German astronomer and mathematician who published three laws describing how the planets move. Kepler noted that every planet's path around the sun is an oval, or **ellipse,** and not a circle.

keratin (ker-uht-n)
A tough **protein** found in the outer layer of skin in humans and many other animals. Keratin is also found in **horn,** nails, hair, and feathers.

kerosene (ker-uh-*seen*)
A liquid made from **petroleum** that is used mainly as a fuel in jet engines. Kerosene is also used in homes for heating, cooking, and lighting.

kettle hole (ket-l *hohl*)
A hole in the ground left behind by a buried block of ice that came from a melting **glacier.** Kettle holes often fill with water, but are not fed by streams or **springs.**

keyboard (kee-*bord*)
A set of keys used to enter **data** or other information into a computer. The keyboard keys are marked with letters, numbers, and **symbols.** Some keys, called *function keys,* direct the computer to perform special tasks.

Kingdom

MONERA (prokaryote): First life on Earth. Cells have no nucleus enclosing the DNA.

PROTISTA: Complex cells with nucleus (The members of this group are not necessarily related to one another.)

FUNGI: Eat nutrients created by the other kingdoms

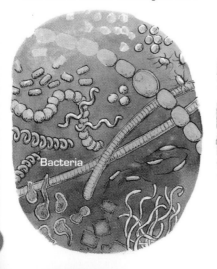

Bacteria

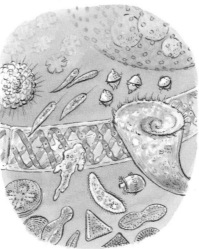

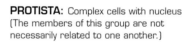

kidney (kid-nee)
The **organ** in most **vertebrate** animals that cleans the blood and maintains the proper balance of water in the body. Humans have two kidneys. They produce **urine**, which is the body's liquid waste.

kilo (kee-loh)
A prefix in the **metric system** that means one thousand. From the Greek *chilioi,* meaning "a thousand." (Abbreviation—k)

kilogram (kil-uh-*gram*)
A unit of **mass** or weight equal to 1,000 **grams** (2.2 pounds). (Abbreviation—kg)

kilometer
(kuh-**lahm**-uh-tuhr or kil-uh-*mee*-tuhr)
A distance equal to 1,000 **meters** (3,280.8 feet). To change kilometers to miles, multiply the number of kilometers by 0.6. (Abbreviation—km)

kilowatt (kil-uh-*waht*)
A unit of electric power equal to 1,000 **watts.** (Abbreviation—kW)

kinetic energy
(kuh-**net**-ik en-uhr-jee)
The **energy** in a moving body, such as the wind, a speeding train, or a flying baseball. From the Greek *kinetos,* meaning "moving."

kingdom (king-duhm)
The largest group in the **biological classification** system. All living things belong to one of five kingdoms: plants, animals, **fungi** (such as **molds** and mushrooms), **monera** (such as **bacteria** and **algae**), and **protista** (microscopic **organisms**).

Koch (kawk), Robert (1843–1910)
A German doctor who was the first to show that particular **bacteria** cause particular diseases. Koch discovered the cause of the disease **tuberculosis** in 1882.

krypton (krip-tahn)
A **chemical element** that is usually a colorless, odorless gas. Krypton is extremely rare in the earth's **atmosphere.** It is used in **lasers** and certain kinds of electric lamps. From the Greek *kryptos,* meaning "hidden or secret." (Symbol—Kr)

K

PLANTS:
Most create their own food through photosynthesis.

ANIMALS:
Do not make their own food. Mostly mobile. Complex behavior.

L

laboratory (**lab**-ruh-*tor*-ee)
A place where scientists do **research** and conduct **experiments.**

lactation (lak-**tay**-shuhn)
The secretion of milk from the body of a female **mammal.** The mammal's young offspring drink the milk she secretes.

lactic acid (**lak**-tik **as**-id)
A colorless liquid found in milk and other dairy products that have turned "sour" or fermented. Your muscles produce lactic acid after heavy exercise. From the Latin *lac,* meaning "milk."

lactose (lak-tohs)
A sugar found in milk. **Bacteria** can change lactose into **lactic acid.** *Lactose intolerance* is a condition in which the body has difficulty **digesting** milk.

lagoon (luh-**goon**)
A shallow body of salt water separated from the sea by a narrow strip of land.

lake (layk)
A large body of water surrounded by land.

Lamarck (luh-**mahrk**), **Jean Baptiste** (1744–1829)
A French biologist who developed a system for classifying animals. Lamarck incorrectly believed that **traits** acquired by parents tend to be **inherited** by their offspring. For example, he held that parents who learn to dance well will give birth to children who are good dancers.

laminate (**lam**-uh-*nayt*)
To split into very thin layers. *Also,* to glue together thin layers of material.

landfill (**land**-*fil*)
A place where garbage or solid waste is dumped and covered with soil.

landslide (**land**-*slide*)
A mass of earth, mud, or rocks suddenly sliding down a steep slope.

lanolin (**lan**-l-in)
The fat or grease obtained from **wool.** Lanolin is used in creams and cosmetics.

laptop (**lap**-*tahp*)
A small, portable computer that is either plugged into an electric outlet or run on batteries. Also called a *notebook.*

large intestine (**lahrj** in-**tes**-tuhn)
An **organ** of the **digestive system.** The large intestine absorbs **water** from undigested food and gets rid of wastes. It is about 5 feet (1.5 meters) long and reaches from the end of the **small intestine** to the **anus.**

Lagoon

Ocean

Sandbank

Lagoon

larva (**lahr**-vuh)
The early stage in the life of an insect or other animal. The larva is different in structure from the adult. For example, a butterfly larva is a caterpillar; a frog larva is a tadpole. Plural is *larvae*.

larynx (**lar**-ingks)
A structure at the upper end of the **windpipe** containing the **vocal cords.** The larynx sometimes extends forward in the throat, forming a lump called an *Adam's apple.* Also called *voice box.*

laser (**lay**-zuhr)
Short for *l*ight *a*mplification by *s*timulated *e*mission of *r*adiation. A laser produces a thin, intense, high-**energy** beam of light. *Theodore Maiman* (born 1927) built the first laser in 1960.

laser disk (**lay**-zuhr *disk*)
A device for recording sound (**compact disc** or **DVD**), sound and pictures (**DVD**), or **data** (**CD-ROM**). A laser disk has a pattern of millions of tiny holes on one side of a flat, round plastic disk covered with metal. It is played back by shining a laser at the disk as it spins around.

latent heat (**layt**-nt **heet**)
Heat taken in or given out when a substance changes state. The latent heat increases when ice melts and becomes liquid water. The latent heat decreases when water freezes and becomes ice.

lateral (**lat**-uhr-uhl)
On or to the side. A lateral **X ray** is one taken from the side.

latitude (**lat**-uh-*tood*)
The distance north or south of the **equator** in **degrees.** See also **longitude.**

lattice (**lat**-is)
The regular arrangement of the **atoms, molecules,** or **ions** in a **crystal.** The lattice of a **salt** crystal is cube-shaped.

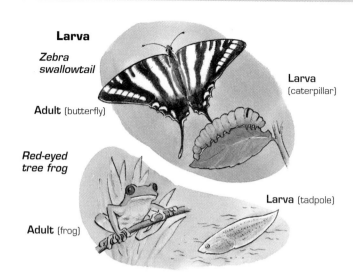

Larva

Zebra swallowtail

Adult (butterfly)

Larva (caterpillar)

Red-eyed tree frog

Adult (frog)

Larva (tadpole)

laughing gas (**laf**-ing *gas*)
See **nitrous oxide.**

lava (**lah**-vuh)
The hot, melted rock that comes out of an erupting volcano or a split in the earth's surface. Lava is also the solid rock that forms when liquid lava cools and hardens. From the Latin *labes,* meaning "sliding down or falling."

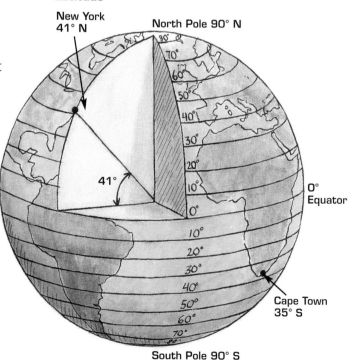

Latitude

New York 41° N

North Pole 90° N

80°
70°
60°
50°
40°
30°
20°
10°

0°
Equator

41°

0°
Equator

10°
0°
10°
20°
30°
40°
50°
60°
70°

Cape Town 35° S

South Pole 90° S

Lavoisier (lahv-*wah*-zee-**ay**), **Antoine Laurent** (1743–1794)
A French chemist who showed that **combustion** is the rapid joining of a material with a gas he discovered called **oxygen.** Lavoisier also showed that water is made up of **hydrogen** and oxygen (H_2O).

LCD (el-*see*-dee)
Short for *Liquid Crystal Display.* A display method used in many **electronic devices** to show words or numbers. See also **liquid crystal.**

leaching (**lee**-ching)
Running water or another **solvent** through a substance or material to remove something that is dissolved in it. Leaching removes sugar from plants and pure metal from ore. Rainwater can remove **nutrients** from soil by leaching.

lead (**led**)
A heavy, bluish-gray **element** that was one of the first metals to be discovered. Lead is used to make storage batteries, containers for some **chemicals,** and as a shield against **radiation.** (Symbol—Pb)

lead poisoning (**led** *poi*-zuh-ning)
A serious illness caused by too much **lead** in the body. Lead poisoning is the result of swallowing or breathing in tiny **particles** of **lead.** The illness occurs in children who eat chips of old lead paint.

leaf (**leef**)
The green, food-making part of almost every **plant.** Each leaf takes **carbon dioxide** from the **air, water** from the **soil,** and **energy** from **sunlight** to make the food the plant needs in order to grow. See also **photosynthesis.** Plural is *leaves.*

Leakey (**lee**-kee), **Louis** (1903–1972)
A British-born anthropologist who made many **fossil** discoveries in East Africa. He found that humans have been on Earth longer than once believed.

Leakey (**lee**-kee), **Mary** (1913–1996)
A British-born anthropologist who found the **skull** of an ancestor of apes and humans that is about 25 million years old and footprints of humanlike creatures that lived nearly 2 million years ago.

Leakey (**lee**-kee), **Maeve** (born 1942)
A British-born anthropologist who helped to show that humanlike creatures were walking on 2 feet about 4 million years ago.

Leakey (**lee**-kee), **Richard** (born 1944)
A Kenyan anthropologist who found several early human **fossils** in East Africa that were more than one million years old. Richard Leakey is the son of **Mary** and **Louis Leakey.**

Leavitt (**lee**-vit), **Henrietta** (1868–1921)
An American astronomer who helped find a way to measure the size of the **universe.**

LED (el-*ee*-dee)
Short for *Light Emitting Diode.* An LED is a **diode** that gives off light when a **current** flows. LEDs use little current and do not burn out. They are often found as the display in **electronic** devices.

Leeuwenhoek (**lay**-vuhn-*huk*), **Anton van** (1632–1723)
A Dutch scientist who made his own **microscopes.** Leeuwenhoek was the first to see **bacteria** and **protozoa.** He was also first to describe **red blood cells.**

legume (**leg**-yoom)
Any plant in the pea family, such as peas, beans, soybeans, or peanuts. **Bacteria** on legume roots take **nitrogen** from the air and change it into a form the plants can use.

lens (**lenz**)
A piece of clear glass or plastic with at least one curved surface. A lens bends **rays** of light that pass through it. This makes an **image** seen through the lens look larger, smaller, or different in some

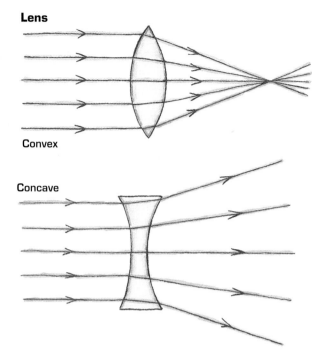

Lens

Convex

Concave

other way. *Also,* the clear part of the eye that **focuses** light rays on the **retina.**

Leonardo da Vinci
(*lay*-uh-**nahr**-doh duh **vin**-chee), (1452–1519)
An Italian scientist and artist. Leonardo drew plans for hundreds of inventions, such as a flying machine, **parachute,** movable bridge, and construction crane. His most famous painting is *Mona Lisa.*

leonids (**lee**-uh-nidz)
A shower of **meteors** that comes from the direction of the **constellation** Leo. Leonids can be seen every year around November 16 to 19.

leprosy (**lep**-ruh-see)
A **bacteria**-caused disease that produces dark lumps on the skin. Leprosy also damages the **nerves,** so patients do not feel pain when they cut or burn themselves. Also called *Hansen's disease.*

lesion (**lee**-zhuhn)
Any wound caused by injury or disease.

leukemia (loo-**kee**-mee-uh)
A type of **cancer** in which **white blood cells** grow and multiply without stop. Leukemia **symptoms** include **anemia,** frequent **infections,** and severe bleeding from cuts. The disease can be treated and sometimes cured.

leukocyte (**loo**-kuh-*site*)
A **white blood cell** that fights harmful germs and substances that enter the body. Leukocytes surround and devour the invaders or produce **antibodies** to destroy them.

lever (**lev**-uhr or **lee**-vuhr)
A bar for lifting loads. The lever rests on a **fulcrum;** to raise a heavy weight at one end, you press down at the other end. From the Latin *levare,* meaning "to raise."

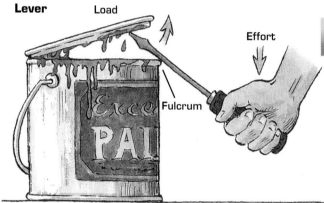

Lever   Load   Effort   Fulcrum

lichen (**lie**-kuhn)
An **organism** that contains **algae** and **fungi** growing together as a single unit. Lichen looks something like **moss,** has no roots, and mostly grows in patches on rocks or tree bark.

life (**life**)
A quality present in people, animals, plants, and other **organisms,** but not in rocks, metals, or plastic. Living beings can **reproduce** and grow, change food and **energy** into useful forms, get rid of waste, move (plants move by bending toward light or water), and **adapt** to changes in their **environment.**

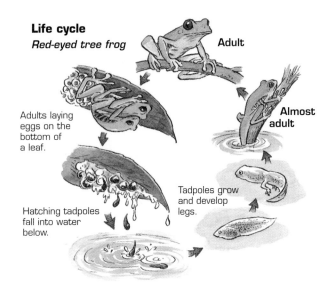

Life cycle
Red-eyed tree frog   Adult

Adults laying eggs on the bottom of a leaf.

Almost adult

Hatching tadpoles fall into water below.

Tadpoles grow and develop legs.

life cycle (**life** *sie*-kuhl)
The series of changes in living things. The life cycle of a frog includes egg, tadpole, and adult frog. When the adult frog lays eggs, the life cycle begins again.

lift (**lift**)
The upward force acting on an **aircraft**. Airplane wings and **helicopter rotors** supply lift because the air above the wings or rotors flows past faster than the air below. Balloons and **dirigibles** get lift from the lighter-than-air gases they contain.

liftoff (**lift**-*awf*)
The instant, at the end of the countdown, when a rocket leaves the ground.

ligament (**lig**-uh-muhnt)
A tough band of **tissue** that connects bones and holds the **organs** of the body in place. From the Latin *ligamentum,* meaning "band."

light (**lite**)
The form of **electromagnetic energy** that can be seen by the eye. Ordinary white light is made up of a full **spectrum** of colors. In empty space, light travels at the speed of 186,282 miles (299,792 kilometers) a second.

lightning (**lite**-ning)
A giant spark of electricity that jumps between a cloud and the earth, between two clouds, or within a cloud. Lightning can produce more than 100 million **volts** of electricity. The powerful electricity heats the air in its path to more than 50,000° **Fahrenheit** (33,000° **Celsius**). The superheated air explodes outward, which causes the roar of thunder.

lightning rod (**lite**-ning *rahd*)
A metal rod, usually on top of a building, that protects the building from being struck by **lightning**. The lightning rod conducts the electricity safely to the ground through a wire. **Benjamin Franklin** invented the lightning rod.

light-year (**lite**-*yir*)
The distance that light travels in one year. A light-year equals about 5.9 trillion miles (9.5 trillion kilometers). It is a unit for measuring the huge distances to the stars and across **galaxies.**

lignite (**lig**-nite)
A low-quality coal that is often called brown coal.

lime (**lime**)
A white **chemical** containing **calcium** and **oxygen**. Lime is made by heating **limestone**, bones, or shells. It is used in many industrial processes, to make plaster, and to improve the quality of **soil**. Also called *quicklime*. (Formula—CaO)

limestone (**lime**-*stohn*)
A type of rock made up mostly of calcite or calcium carbonate. Limestone is widely used as a building stone and to make lime. (Formula—$CaCO_3$)

limnology (lim-**nahl**-uh-jee)
The science that studies lakes, rivers, and other bodies of freshwater. Limnology also studies freshwater plants and animals. From the Greek *limne,* meaning "pool or lake."

linear accelerator
(**lin**-ee-uhr ak-**sel**-uh-*ray*-tuhr)
A **particle accelerator** that shoots particles in a straight line.

linkage (ling-kij)
Two or more **genes** joined on the same **chromosome.** Through linkage, a number of **traits** can be **inherited** together. For example, some flies show a linkage between gray bodies and long wings. *Also,* the product of the number of turns in a **coil** and the number of magnetic lines of force passing through the coil.

Linnaean system
(luh-**nay**-uhn **sis**-tuhm)
A way of naming animals and plants devised by *Carolus Linnaeus* (1707–1778). His system uses two words, the first for the **genus,** or general group, and the second for the **species,** or specific kind. For example, horses belong to the genus *Equus* and the species *caballus,* which is often shortened to *E. caballus.*

lipid (lip-id)
One of a group of oils, fats, and waxes found in living things. Lipids are an important source of food **energy.**

liquid (lik-wid)
A substance that flows freely. A liquid is not a solid, since it has no fixed shape, and not a gas, since it has a definite **volume.**

liquid crystal (lik-wid **kris**-tuhl)
A substance that flows like a liquid but has the structure of a **crystal.** A liquid crystal changes color in the presence of an **electric current.** See also **LCD.**

Lister (lis-tuhr), **Joseph** (1827–1912)
An English doctor who founded **antiseptic surgery,** insisting that doctors and nurses use **antiseptics** on their hands and **sterile** instruments in the operating room.

liter (lee-tuhr)
A measure of **volume** in the **metric system.** One liter equals 1.057 quarts.

lithosphere (lith-uh-*sfir*)
The solid **crust** of Earth. The lithosphere is between 5 and 25 miles (8 and 40 kilometers) thick. From the

Greek *lithos,* meaning "stone," and *sphaira,* meaning "ball."

litmus (lit-muhs)
A common indicator used in **chemistry** to determine whether a **solution** is **acid** or **alkali.** Blue litmus paper turns red when in acid. Red litmus paper turns blue when in alkali.

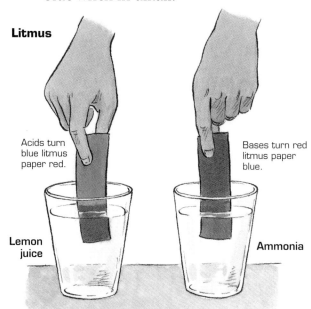

Litmus

Acids turn blue litmus paper red.

Bases turn red litmus paper blue.

Lemon juice

Ammonia

littoral (lit-uhr-uhl)
Having to do with the area along the seashore. Littoral **organisms** are those found on the shore.

liver (liv-uhr)
The largest **gland** in the human body. The liver produces **bile,** which helps the body digest food, stores vitamins, remove poisons and wastes from the blood, and makes blood-clotting **chemicals.**

load (lohd)
To enter a **program** into a computer memory. *Also,* a measure of the force or weight applied to a machine or surface.

loam (lohm)
A rich soil that contains sand, clay, and **silt.** Loam is excellent for growing plants.

lockjaw (lahk-*jaw*)
See **tetanus.**

locomotion
(*loh*-kuh-**moh**-shuhn)
The act of moving from place to place. Locomotion includes every way of moving, from walking to flying.

lodestar (**lohd**-*stahr*)
Any star that shows the way. The North Star, for example, is a lodestar.

lodestone (**lohd**-*stohn*)
A hard, black, magnetic rock that attracts iron. Lodestone is also spelled *loadstone*. It is sometimes called *magnetite*.

loess (**les** or **loh**-ihs)
A yellowish-brown kind of **silt** that is usually deposited by the wind. Loess is finer than sand, but coarser than dust or clay.

longitude (**lahn**-juh-*tood*)
The distance in degrees east or west of Greenwich, England. See also **latitude**.

loran (**lor**-an)
Short for *long range navigation*. Loran is a system of radio **navigation** that helps ships and airplanes find their positions.

loudspeaker (**loud**-*spee*-kuhr)
A device that changes electrical signals into sound waves. In a loudspeaker, the electrical signals can come from a **microphone**, a radio or television set, or a tape or **compact disc** player.

Lovell (**luhv**-uhl), Bernard
(born 1913)
An English **astronomer** who was a pioneer in the field of **radio astronomy**.

low-pressure area
(**loh-presh**-uhr *er*-ee-uh)
An air mass of lower than usual air **pressure**. Low pressure often brings storms and strong winds to an area.

low tide (**loh** tide)
The movement of ocean water away from a beach or coastline. Low tide comes to an area when the moon, with its gravitational pull, is closest to the opposite side of Earth. In most places it occurs about twice a day. See also **tide**.

LSD (**el**-*es*-**dee**)
Short for *Lysergic Acid Diethylamide*. LSD is a powerful illegal drug that causes people to see, hear, feel, and smell things that do not really exist.

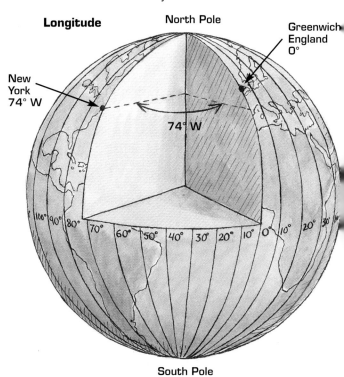

Longitude — North Pole — Greenwich England 0° — New York 74° W — 74° W — 100° 90° 80° 70° 60° 50° 40° 30° 20° 10° 0° 10° 20° 30° — South Pole

lubrication (*loo*-bri-**kay**-shuhn)
The use of oil or grease to allow surfaces to slide over each other. Lubrication makes machines and engines work better and last longer.

lumen (**loo**-muhn)
A measure of the brightness of light shining on a surface. *Also,* the space inside a tube, such as the **intestines** or blood vessels.

luminescence (*loo*-muh-**nes**-uhns)
The giving off of light with very little heat. Luminescence includes **bioluminescence**, fluorescence, and **phosphorescence**.

luminous (**loo**-muh-nuhs)
Shining with its own light. The sun is a luminous body.

lunar (**loo**-nuhr)
Having to do with the moon.

lunar eclipse (**loo**-nuhr i-**klips**)
The time when Earth comes between the sun and the moon, casting a shadow on the moon. See **eclipse**.

lung (**luhng**)
One of a pair of breathing **organs** found in humans and many other animals. The lungs take in **oxygen** from the air, exchange it for **carbon dioxide**, and breathe out carbon dioxide and water **vapor.**

Lyell (**lie**-uhl), **Sir Charles** (1797–1875)
A British geologist who found that the earth changes slowly and gradually through the ages. Before Lyell, people believed that most changes on Earth were the result of sudden upheavals. See also **erosion** and **glaciers**.

Lyme disease (**lime** di-*zeez*)
A **bacterial infection** caused by the bite of a deer tick. The **symptoms** often include a bull's-eye rash, fever, headache, and aching **joints.**

lymph (**limf**)
A liquid that seeps out of tiny blood vessels. The lymph contains many **white blood cells** that help to fight infections in body tissue. Most of the lymph later returns to the bloodstream. From the Latin *lympha,* meaning "clear water." See also **lymphatic system.**

lymphatic system (**lim**-**fat**-ik *sis*-tuhm)
A **network** of small vessels that carries **lymph** throughout the body. The lymphatic system returns lymph from body **tissues** to the bloodstream. It also carries digested fat from the **intestine** to the blood and helps remove poisons from the body.

lymphocyte (**lim**-fuh-*site*)
A kind of **white blood cell** found in the **lymphatic system.** Lymphocytes produce **antibodies** to fight **infection.**

lysergic acid diethylamide (**lie**-**suhr**-jik **as**-id die-*eth*-uhl-**am**-ide)
See **LSD.**

Lyme disease
You can get Lyme disease from the bite of the tiny deer tick.

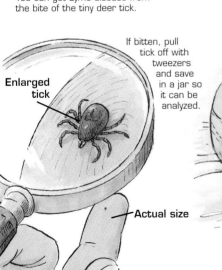

Enlarged tick

If bitten, pull tick off with tweezers and save in a jar so it can be analyzed.

Actual size

Typical rash

The first symptoms are flu-like, usually accompanied by a ring-shaped pink rash. If you think you have Lyme disease, go to a doctor right away. In its early stages, the disease can be successfully treated with antibiotics.

Prevention: In areas where there might be ticks, wear long sleeves and pants tucked into your socks. Some insect repellents may help.

Shower when you get home to wash off any unattached ticks. Check yourself carefully. Ticks especially like warm places such as the creases of elbows and knees—but look all over, including your scalp.

machine (muh-**sheen**)
A device that uses **energy** and does work. A machine can be as simple as a **lever** or **screw** or as complex as an airplane or computer.

Mach number (**mahk** *nuhm*-buhr)
The speed of a fast-moving object compared to the speed of sound. An aircraft flying 760 miles (1,216 kilometers) an hour at sea level is flying at Mach 1. Speeds below Mach 1 are *subsonic*; speeds above are **supersonic.** Named after *Ernst Mach* (1838–1916).

macro- (**mak**-roh)
In computers, a single operation that includes a number of separate steps. *Also,* macro- at the beginning of a word means "large." A *macromolecule* is a very large molecule.

macroclimate (**mak**-roh-*klie*-mit)
The climate over a large region. The macroclimate for the southwestern United States is generally warm and dry.

macrophage (**mak**-roh-*fayj*)
A large **cell** in the blood that fights **infection.** Macrophages surround any invaders and digest them. From the Greek *makros,* meaning "long or large," and *-phagos,* meaning "eating."

Magellanic Clouds
(*maj*-uh-**lan**-ik **kloudz**)
The two **galaxies** that are closest to our **Milky Way.** The Large Magellanic Cloud is 160,000 **light-years** away; the Small Magellanic Cloud is about 200,000 light-years away. The Magellanic Clouds are only visible from the Southern Hemisphere.

maggot (**mag**-uht)
The **larva** of a fly that looks like a small white worm. Maggots are often found in rotting **tissue.**

magma (**mag**-muh)
Molten rock beneath the surface of the earth that is melted by the great heat there. Magma hardens into solid rock either underground or on the surface.

magnesium (mag-**nee**-zee-uhm)
A strong, very light, silver-white metal **element.** Magnesium is often added to **aluminum, zinc,** or **manganese** to make airplane parts. (Symbol—Mg)

magnet (**mag**-nit)
An object that attracts iron, steel, cobalt, and certain **ceramics.** From the Greek *Magnes lithos,* meaning "the stone from Magnesia," where magnetic rocks were first found.

magnetic field (mag-**net**-ik **feeld**)
The space around a magnet or a wire carrying an **electric current,** where its

Magnetic field

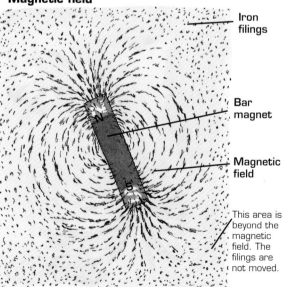

Iron filings

Bar magnet

Magnetic field

This area is beyond the magnetic field. The filings are not moved.

A magnetic field is invisible. But if we scatter iron filings around a magnet, we can see the magnetic field by the way it attracts the iron bits.

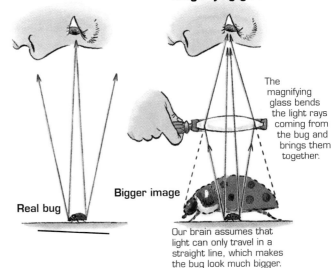

magnetic force can be felt. The earth is surrounded by a magnetic **field**.

magnetic pole (mag-**net**-ik **pohl**)
Either the north or south pole of a magnet, where **magnetism** is strongest. Opposite poles **attract** each other; like poles repel or push each other away. Since the earth is a giant magnet, **compass** needles point to the earth's poles. The magnetic poles are near, but not exactly at, the geographic North and South Poles.

magnetic storm (mag-**net**-ik **storm**)
A disturbance in the earth's upper **atmosphere** caused by high-**energy particles** and **radiation** from the sun. Magnetic storms affect the earth's **magnetic field** and **shortwave** radio signals.

magnetic tape (mag-**net**-ik **tayp**)
A long, thin strip of plastic coated with tiny **particles** of **iron oxide** that is used in audio- and videotape recorders. Tape recorders arrange the particles into patterns and then change them back into sounds or **images**. See also **tape recorder**.

magnetism (**mag**-nuh-*tiz*-uhm)
A natural force of attraction between magnets and between magnets and certain metals and **ceramics**.

magnetite (**mag**-nuh-*tite*)
See **lodestone**.

magneto (mag-**nee**-toh)
An **electric generator** found in lawn mowers, motorcycles, and some airplanes. The magneto provides a **spark** that **ignites** the fuel in the engine.

magnetometer (*mag*-nuh-**tahm**-uh-tuhr)
A device that measures the strength and sometimes the direction of a **magnetic field**. Scientists use magnetometers in mining operations and to study changes in the magnetic field of Earth.

magnification (*mah*-nuh-fuh-**kay**-shuhn)
How large an object looks compared to its real size. A magnification of 1,500 times is typical for a good **microscope**. It is usually written "1,500X."

Magnifying glass

The magnifying glass bends the light rays coming from the bug and brings them together.

Real bug

Bigger image

Our brain assumes that light can only travel in a straight line, which makes the bug look much bigger.

magnifying glass (**mag**-nuh-*fie*-ing *glas*)
A glass or plastic **lens** that makes small objects look larger than they really are. A magnifying glass usually has a double **convex** lens. It bulges out on both sides.

magnitude (**mag**-nuh-*tood*)
A measure of the brightness of objects in space. The lower the magnitude number, the brighter the object. Human eyes can see stars down to a magnitude of 5 or 6. **Astronomers** can photograph stars with a magnitude as low as 20.

mainframe (**mayn**-*fraym*)
A large, fast computer with a huge memory. Mainframes are used by the government, banks, insurance companies, laboratories, and large corporations. They can be used by many people at the same time.

malaria (muh-**ler**-ee-uh)
A serious disease in tropical areas. Malaria is caused by the **protozoa** *Plasmodia*, which are carried from person to person

by the bite of a female *Anopheles* mosquito. From the Italian *mala aria,* meaning "bad air," which was once believed to cause the disease.

male (**mayl**)
The sex of an **organism** that produces **sperm** and can **fertilize** an egg, or **ovum.**

malignant (muh-**lig**-nuhnt)
Describes any serious disease that may cause death. A malignant **tumor** is a **cancer** that can invade surrounding **tissue** and spread in the body. From the Latin *malignans,* meaning "acting from malice."

malleable (**mal**-ee-uh-buhl)
Able to be pressed or hammered into very thin sheets. Malleable metals include **copper,** gold, and silver. From the Latin *malleare,* meaning "to hammer."

malnutrition (*mal*-noo-**trish**-uhn)
Poor health caused by not having enough food to eat or not eating the right kinds of foods.

Malpighi (mahl-**pee**-gee), Marcello (1628–1694)
An Italian **scientist** who was among the first to see the **alveoli** in the lungs, the **capillaries** that connect **arteries** and **veins,** and **red blood cells.**

mammal (**mam**-uhl)
An animal that:

- has a backbone (**vertebrate**)
- nurses its offspring with mother's milk
- is **warm-blooded,** so its temperature stays about the same no matter the weather
- has hair during all or part of its life
- cares for its young longer than other animals
- and has a larger brain than other animals.

There are about 4,000 different mammals, including cats and dogs, cows and horses, whales and seals—and humans too. From the Latin *mamma,* meaning "breast."

mammary glands (**mam**-uh-ree **glandz**)
Special **glands** found in all **mammals.** Mammary glands in females produce milk to feed their young.

mammoth (**mam**-uhth)
A huge prehistoric animal closely related to the elephant. Mammoths lived from about 4 million to 10,000 years ago.

mandible (**man**-duh-buhl)
The lower jawbone. The human mandible is shaped like a horseshoe. Several insects, including ants and beetles, have two grinding jaws called mandibles. From the Latin *mandere,* meaning "to chew."

manganese (**mang**-guh-*neez*)
A silver-gray metal **element.** Manganese is used to make very hard **steel** and **stainless steel** and is also found in paints, **fertilizers,** and batteries. (Symbol—Mn)

manometer (muh-**nahm**-uh-tuhr)
An instrument used to measure the **pressure** of a gas. The manometer is a U-shaped tube containing a liquid. The gas comes in one side, which pushes the liquid up on the other side. The height of the liquid is a measure of the gas pressure.

Manometer

Liquid

Gas

mantle (**mant**-l)
A thick zone of rock within Earth that is beneath the **crust.** The mantle goes down about 1,780 miles (2,870 kilometers) and makes up almost 5/6 of the total **volume** of Earth. The upper mantle contains semisolid rock on which the **plates** of the **crust** move. *Also,* a layer of **tissue** inside the shell of many **invertebrate animals.** See also **Earth.**

marble (**mar**-buhl)
A hard, **metamorphic** rock widely used in buildings and sculpture. Marble is formed from **limestone** and is mostly made up of the **minerals** calcite and dolomite. From the Greek *marmaros,* meaning "shining stone."

Marconi (mahr-**koh**-nee), **Guglielmo** (1874–1937)
An Italian inventor who perfected the wireless **telegraph** or radio. Marconi sent the first wireless message across the Atlantic Ocean in 1901.

maria (**mahr**-ee-uh)
Dark, flat plains on the surface of the moon. (Singular *mare.*) From the Italian *mare,* meaning "seas," since early astronomers thought they were seas filled with water.

Maria the Jewess (muh-**ree**-uh thuh **joo**-is) (1st century A.D.)
An Egyptian **alchemist** who designed instruments that were later used in **chemistry.**

marijuana (*mar*-uh-**wahn**-uh)
An illegal drug made from the dried leaves and flowering tops of the hemp plant. Its scientific name is *Cannabis sativa.* Marijuana is also called *grass, pot, weed,* or *cannabis.*

marine biology (muh-**reen** bie-**ahl**-uh-jee)
The study of all life in the sea, sea birds, and land animals that depend on the sea.

marrow (**mar**-oh)
Soft **tissue** found inside most bones. Marrow produces the body's **red blood cells,** blood **platelets,** and some **white blood cells.**

Mars (**mahrz**)
The fourth planet from the sun in the **solar system.** Mars has a red surface because of all the iron in its soil, much of which has turned to rust. Because of its blood-red color, the planet was named Mars after the ancient Roman god of war.

Average distance from sun—141,600,000 miles (227,900,000 kilometers).
Length of year—About 687 Earth days
Length of day—24 hours and 37 minutes
Diameter at equator—4,212 miles (6,787 kilometers)

marsh (**mahrsh**)
Land that is sometimes under water. A marsh is home to many different kinds of plants, such as reeds and salt grass, and animals, such as frogs and turtles. Many ocean fish start life in marshes.

Marsupial
Dime-size newborn opossums attached to nipples in pouch
Two-month-olds beginning to explore the outdoors

marsupial (mahr-**soo**-pee-uhl)
A **mammal,** such as a kangaroo, koala, or opossum, whose young stay in a pouch on the mother's body for many months after birth. The young marsupial drinks the mother's milk in the pouch. From the Latin *marsupium,* meaning "pouch."

maser (**may**-zuhr)
Short for *m*icrowave *a*mplification by *s*timulated *e*mission of *r*adiation. A maser is similar to a **laser,** but it produces **microwaves** rather than light. The first maser was built by *Charles Townes* (born 1915) in 1953.

Meiosis

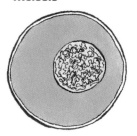

Uncoiled threads of chromosomes in cell nucleus.

Individual chromosomes can be seen.

Matching chromosomes pair up.

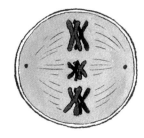

Pairs of chromosomes line up.

mass (**mas**)
The amount of **matter** in an object. Mass is also defined as the **resistance** of an object to a change in its motion. An object's mass always stays the same, while weight, which is the pull of **gravity**, can change.

mass number (**mas** *nuhm*-buhr)
The total number of **protons** and **neutrons** in the **nucleus** of an **atom**. For example, **carbon** has a mass number of 12, with 6 protons and 6 neutrons.

mass spectroscopy (**mas** spek-**trahs**-kuh-pee)
A way to identify the **elements** in a substance. Mass spectroscopy bombards a substance with **electrons** and separates them by their **mass.**

mastodon (**mas**-tuh-*dahn*)
An **extinct** form of early elephant. Mastodons first appeared about 10 million years ago and died out about 10,000 years ago.

matter (**mat**-uhr)
Anything that occupies space and has **mass.** Matter mainly exists in three common states: solid, liquid, or gas.

Maxwell (**maks**-well), **James Clerk** (1831–1879)
A British physicist who introduced the idea of the **electromagnetic field.**

McClintock (muh-**klin**-tuhk), **Barbara** (1902–1992)
An American biologist who discovered that certain **genes** can change their position on **chromosomes.**

Mead (**meed**), **Margaret** (1901–1978)
An American anthropologist who studied how different cultures influence personality. Mead's special interest was the behavior of young people.

measles (**mee**-zuhlz)
A **virus**-caused disease that produces a pink skin rash and fever. Measles has almost been wiped out by a **vaccine** developed by *John F. Enders* (1897–1985) in 1963, but there are occasional outbreaks of the disease. The scientific name is *rubeola.*

mechanical energy (muh-**kan**-i-kuhl **en**-uhr-jee)
The **energy** stored in an object that is either moving or can move. See **kinetic energy** and **potential energy.**

mechanical engineering (muh-**kan**-i-kuhl *en*-juh-**nir**-ing)
The branch of **engineering** that deals with producing and using **mechanical power.** Mechanical engineers develop, test, and operate all kinds of machines and engines.

mechanics (muh-**kan**-iks)
The study of the effect of forces on objects. The two main branches of mechanics are *statics,* which studies objects at rest, and *dynamics,* which studies objects in motion. *Celestial mechanics* is the study of the motion of bodies in space. **Quantum mechanics** is the study of the motion of **subatomic particles.** From the Greek *mechane,* meaning "machine."

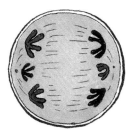

Matching pairs separate.

Separated pairs line up in two groups and each pair divides again.

Each divided pair separates again.

Four new cells form; each one has half the chromosomes of the original cell.

medicine (**med**-uh-suhn)
The science and art of healing, relieving pain, and preventing illness by means of drugs, **surgery**, **nutrition**, and so on. *Also*, a **drug** used for treating illness. From the Latin *medicina*, meaning "the art of healing."

medium (**mee**-dee-uhm)
See **culture medium**.

mega- (**meg**-uh)
A prefix in the **metric system** that means one million. *Mega*hertz (MHz) means one million **hertz**, or 1,000,000 **vibrations** per second. From the Greek *megas*, meaning "large."

meiosis (mie-**oh**-sis)
Cell division that cuts the number of **chromosomes** in a cell in half to produce a sex or **germ cell**. When two germs cells—a male and a female—unite, the result is a single cell with the proper number of chromosomes. From the Greek *meiosis*, meaning "a decrease."

Meitner (**mite**-nuhr), **Lise** (1878–1968)
An Austrian-born scientist who helped discover **nuclear fission**. Meitner made possible the development of the atomic bomb and **nuclear energy**.

melanin (**mel**-uh-nin)
The dark coloring material found in the skin and hair of humans and some animals. From the Greek *melas*, meaning "black."

melt (**melt**)
To change from a solid to a liquid by heating. For example, when solid ice is heated it melts and becomes liquid water.

meltdown (**melt**-*doun*)
A serious accident in a **nuclear reactor**. A meltdown occurs when the cooling system in the reactor fails. The heat melts the nuclear **core**, releasing dangerous **radiation**.

melting point (**mel**-ting *point*)
The temperature at which a solid melts and becomes a liquid. The melting point of ice is 32° **Fahrenheit** (0° **Celsius**).

membrane (**mem**-brayn)
A thin layer of **tissue** that covers a surface in an **organism**. *Also*, the outside surface of an animal **cell**.

memory (**mem**-uh-ree)
The ability to remember something that has been learned or to recall past events. *Also*, the computer **chips** and **disks** that store **data** and **programs**.

Mendel (**men**-duhl), **Gregor Johann** (1822–1884)
An Austrian botanist and monk who studied how **traits** are passed down from **generation** to generation. Mendel's **experiments** with the **breeding** of garden peas laid the foundation for the science of **genetics**.

Mendeleyev (*mend*-l-**ay**-uhf), **Dmitry Ivanovich** (1834–1907)
A Russian chemist who found that the properties of **elements** vary according to their **atomic weight** and arranged the elements in the **periodic table**.

M

menopause (**men**-uh-*pawz*)
The time in a woman's life, generally between the ages of 45 and 50, when **menstruation** ends and she is no longer able to bear children.

menstruation (*men*-stroo-**ay**-shuhn)
The monthly loss of blood and **cells** from the **uterus** in women of childbearing age. Menstruation begins between the ages of 10 and 16 and ends by age 50. Also called *menarche* or *menstrual cycle.*

menu (**men**-yoo)
In computers, a list of possible operations and functions. From the French *menu,* meaning "small or detailed."

Mercury (**muhr**-kyuh-ree)
The closest planet to the sun in the **solar system.** The unmanned **spacecraft** *Mariner 10* flew within 460 miles (740 kilometers) of Mercury in 1974. Mercury has no **atmosphere** and has enormous temperature differences between sunlight and shade. The planet is named after Mercury, the Roman messenger of the gods.

Average distance from sun—35,980,000 miles (57,900,000 kilometers)
Length of year—88 Earth days
Length of day—59 Earth days
Diameter at equator—3,031 miles (4,878 kilometers)

mercury (**muhr**-kyuh-ree)
A heavy, silver-colored, metal **element** that is liquid at a wide range of temperatures. Mercury is often used in **thermometers** and **barometers** because it expands and contracts evenly when heated or cooled. It is also used in some batteries and streetlights. (Symbol—Hg)

mercury barometer
(**muhr**-kyuh-ree buh-**rahm**-uh-tuhr)
See **barometer.**

meridian (muh-**rid**-ee-uhn)
An imaginary north-south circle around the earth. All meridians pass through the North and South Poles. See also **longitude.**

mesa (**may**-suh)
A hill or mountain with a flat top and steep sides. Mesas are generally found in the southwestern part of the United States. From the Spanish *mesa,* meaning "table."

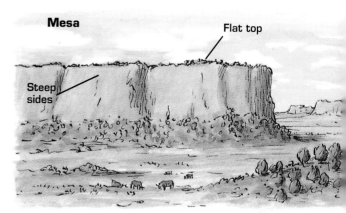

Mesa · Flat top · Steep sides

mescaline (**mes**-kuh-lin)
A powerful illegal drug that changes what users see, hear, and feel. Mescaline comes from the peyote cactus.

mesosphere (**mez**-uh-*sfir*)
The layer of the earth's atmosphere from about 30 miles (48 kilometers) above the surface to about 50 miles (80 kilometers). It is between the **stratosphere** and **thermosphere.**

Mesozoic era
(*mez*-uh-**zoh**-ik ir-uh or er-uh)
The era of **geological history** from about 225 million to 65 million years ago. Dinosaurs and **reptiles** dominated the earth during the Mesozoic era. **Mammals** and early forms of birds were also present.

Messier (mays-**yay**), **Charles** (1730–1817)
A French astronomer who prepared the first catalog of **galaxies, star clusters,** and **nebulae.**

metabolism (muh-**tab**-uh-*liz*-uhm)
All the **chemical** processes going on in the **cells** of an **organism.** Metabolism includes breaking down food **molecules** to obtain **energy** and building new molecules for body growth and repair. From the Greek *metabole,* meaning "change."

Meteor

Meteor

Meteorite

Meteoroid

metal (**met**-l)
A **chemical element**, such as gold, iron, or lead, that is usually shiny in appearance, is a good conductor of electricity and heat, and is **malleable** and **ductile**. Most **elements** are metals. A metal can also be a mixture of metals, such as **steel**, **brass**, or **bronze**.

metal detector (**met**-l di-*tek*-tuhr)
A device used to find buried or hidden metal. The metal detector sends out radio waves, which are reflected back by metal objects, and changed into sound signals. Police, prospectors, and treasure hunters use metal detectors.

metal fatigue (**met**-l fuh-*teeg*)
The weakening of metal caused by repeated bending or pulling. Metal fatigue is believed responsible for many machine breakdowns and airplane crashes.

metallurgy (**met**-l-*uhr*-jee)
The study of metals and how to remove metals from the **ores** in which they are found. Metallurgy is also concerned with finding ways to produce better metals and developing new uses for metals. From the Greek *metallon,* meaning "metal," and *ergon,* meaning "work."

metamorphic (*met*-uh-**mor**-fik)
Describes a type of rock formed when another rock is changed by the heat and/or **pressure** in the earth's **crust**. **Marble** is a metamorphic rock made from the **sedimentary** rock **limestone**. From the Greek *meta-,* meaning "change," and *morphe,* meaning "form."

metamorphosis (*met*-uh-**mor**-fuh-sis)
Changes in the life **cycles** of certain animals. The metamorphosis of a moth includes the stages of egg, **larva** (caterpillar), **pupa**, and adult.

meteor (**mee**-tee-uhr)
A streak of light in the sky caused by a hunk of rock or metal entering the earth's **atmosphere** from outer space. **Friction** with the air makes the metal or rock so hot that it vaporizes, leaving a trail of glowing gases. Sometimes called *shooting star* or *falling star.* See also **meteorite** and **meteoroid.** From the Greek *meteoron,* meaning "event in the sky."

meteorite (**mee**-tee-uh-*rite*)
A hunk of rock or metal from space that fell to Earth or another planet or moon. Meteorites are usually the size of grains of sand, but some can be huge and weigh many tons. See also **meteor** and **meteoroid.**

meteoroid (**mee**-tee-uh-*roid*)
A hunk of rock or metal in space. If it enters Earth's **atmosphere** or strikes another **planet**, **moon**, or **asteroid**, the meteoroid creates a streak of light, or **meteor.** If the meteoroid does not burn up in the air, it falls to Earth as a **meteorite.**

meteorology (**mee**-tee-uh-**rahl**-uh-jee)
The study of weather. Meteorology is concerned with temperature, wind, **air pressure**, **precipitation**, and other conditions of the **atmosphere**. From the Greek *meteoron,* meaning "an event in the sky," and *-logia,* meaning "science of."

meteor shower
(**mee**-tee-uhr *shou*-uhr)
A large number of **meteors** seen at the same time. Meteor showers occur when Earth passes through the debris left by a **comet**. The finest meteor showers occur every year around January 3 (*Quadrantids*), August 12 (*Perseids*), November 17 (*Leonids*), and December 12 (*Geminids*).

meter (**mee**-tuhr)
The basic unit of length in the **metric system**. One meter equals 39.370 inches. (Symbol—m)

methadone (**meth**-uh-*dohn*)
A drug used to help people overcome **addiction** to dangerous drugs such as **heroin** and **opium**.

methane (**meth**-ayn)
A colorless, odorless gas formed when plants decay. Methane makes up a large part of natural gas. Also called *marsh gas*. (Formula—CH_4)

metric system (**me**-trik *sis*-tuhm)
The international system of measurement widely used by scientists. In the metric system the basic units are **meter** for length and **gram** for weight.
  Each metric unit is made larger by a prefix: *deca* = 10, *hecto* = 100, *kilo* = 1,000, *mega* = 1,000,000, *giga* = 1,000,000,000, and *tera* = 1,000,000,000,000. They can also be made smaller by a prefix: *deci* = 1/10, *centi* = 1/100, *milli* = 1/1,000, *micro* = 1/1,000,000, *nano* = 1/1,000,000,000, *pico* = 1/1,000,000,000,000.
  Also called *SI* (short for *Système International*).
  The second is the basic time unit in both the metric system and in the inch-pound system.

microbe (**mie**-krohb)
An **organism** so small that it can only be seen through a **microscope**. Microbes include

M

bacteria, viruses, molds, algae, protozoa, and **yeasts**. Also called *microorganism*. From the Greek *mikros*, meaning "small," and *bios*, meaning "life."

microbiology (*mie*-kroh-*bie*-**ahl**-uh-jee)
The study of microscopic **organisms**.

microburst (**mie**-kroh-*buhrst*)
A short, sudden, downward flow of cool air from a rain cloud. Microbursts can produce **wind shear**, which is very dangerous to **airplanes**.

microclimate (**mie**-kroh-*klie*-mit)
The weather conditions over a long period of time in a small area, such as a beach or a deep valley.

micrometer (mie-**krahm**-uh-tuhr)
A device used to measure very small distances or angles. *Also,* when pronounced **mie**-kroh-*mee*-tuhr, micrometer is another name for a **micron**.

micron (**mie**-krahn)
One millionth of a meter or 1/25,400 inch; sometimes called a **micrometer**.

microorganism
(*mie*-kroh-**or**-guh-*niz*-uhm)
See **microbe**.

microphone (**mie**-kruh-*fohn*)
A device that changes sounds into patterns of **electric current**. The

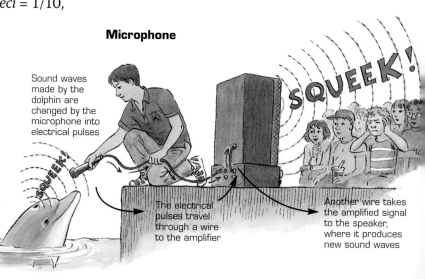

Microphone

Sound waves made by the dolphin are changed by the microphone into electrical pulses

The electrical pulses travel through a wire to the amplifier

Another wire takes the amplified signal to the speaker, where it produces new sound waves

microphone can send the electric current through wires or the air to an **amplifier** and **loudspeakers** that change the current back into sound.

microprocessor
(*mie*-kroh-**prahs**-*es*-uhr)
An important **electronic** part of computers. The microprocessor is the computer's control center, calculator, and memory bank. It is built around a **chip**. Also called **CPU**.

Microscope

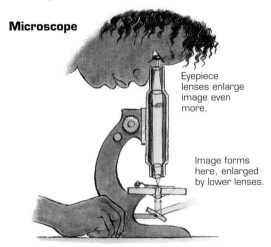

Eyepiece lenses enlarge image even more.

Image forms here, enlarged by lower lenses.

microscope (**mie**-kruh-*skohp*)
An instrument that makes small objects or details of big objects appear larger. The usual optical microscope has a tube with two or more **lenses** to magnify the object being viewed. See also **electron microscope**. From the Greek *micros*, meaning "small," and -*skopion*, meaning "means of seing."

microtome (**mie**-kruh-*tohm*)
A **laboratory** device used to cut slices of material so thin that light can pass through. Microtome slices are then examined through a **microscope**.

microwave (**mie**-kruh-*wayv*)
A very short **electromagnetic wave** used in **radar**, television, and **satellite** communications. A microwave oven uses microwave **radiation** to heat food.

middle ear (**mid**-l ir)
The air-filled gap just beyond the eardrum. The middle ear **amplifies** the sounds received by the **outer ear** and passes them to the **inner ear**. The middle ear contains the three smallest bones in the body—*malleus* (hammer), *incus* (anvil), and *stapes* (stirrup). See also **ear**.

midnight sun (**mid**-nite **suhn**)
The **sun** when it can be seen 24 hours a day. At the North Pole, the sun never fully sets from about March 20 to about September 23. At the South Pole, it does not set from about September 23 to about March 20.

midocean ridge (**mid**-*oh*-shuhn **rij**)
A series of underwater mountains. The midocean ridge is almost 40,000 miles (60,000 kilometers) long. It rises between 3,300 and 9,800 feet (1,000 and 3,000 meters) above the ocean floor.

migration (mie-**gray**-shuhn)
The regular, long-distance movement of animals to places with better living conditions. Migrations usually occur at a change of season when animals seek more comfortable weather, a greater food supply, or a place to breed or give birth.

mildew (**mil**-doo)
A kind of **fungus** that grows in damp places. Mildew leaves a white or colored coating on various materials.

mile (**mile**)
A unit of length equal to 1.6 kilometers or 5,280 feet. From the Latin *milia*

Mid-ocean ridge

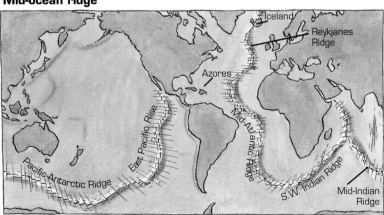

Iceland

Reykjanes Ridge

Azores

Mid-Atlantic Ridge

East Pacific Rise

Pacific-Antarctic Ridge

S.W. Indian Ridge

Mid-Indian Ridge

M

passuum, meaning "a thousand paces," since it was originally measured by the steps of marching soldiers.

Milky Way (**mil**-kee **way**)
The **galaxy** that includes Earth, the sun, the **solar system**, and many billions of stars. *Also,* the milky-colored band of stars stretching across the sky that you can see on dark, clear nights. It is made up of stars within the Milky Way galaxy.

milli- (**mil**-i)
A prefix in the **metric system** that means one thousandth. A *milli*meter is one thousandth of a meter, or about 0.04 inches.

mimicry (**mim**-i-kree)
The appearance of an **organism** that makes it look like another organism or an object. Mimicry helps living things escape danger by resembling a more dangerous **species** or confusing a **predator**.

mineral (**min**-uh-ruhl)
A nonliving substance found in nature. Each kind of mineral is made up of **crystals** and has the same general **chemical** makeup throughout. Minerals include **copper**, **gold**, **sulfur**, and **quartz**.

minute (**min**-it)
A unit of time equal to 60 seconds or 1/60th of an hour. From the Latin *minutus,* meaning "small."

Miocene epoch (**mie**-uh-*seen* **ep**-uhk)
The period of **geological history** from 24 to 8 million years ago. The first apes appeared during the Miocene epoch.

mirage (muh-**rahzh**)
A kind of **optical illusion** caused by light rays bending as they pass through air of different temperatures. A common mirage is the sight on a warm day of a wet area on a distant street.

mirror (**mir**-uhr)
A smooth, shiny surface that reflects light. A mirror is usually glass, with a thin silver backing.

missile (**mis**-uhl)
A rocket-powered weapon that is shot into the air and explodes when it strikes a target.

mission control (**mish**-uhn kuhn-*trohl*)
The headquarters on Earth from which scientists direct space exploration and keep in touch with astronauts in space.

Mississippian period (*mis*-uh-**sip**-ee-uhn **pir**-ee-uhd)
The **period** of **geological history** from 360 to 330 million years ago. During the Mississippian period **coral reefs** were forming and there were many fish and **amphibians**.

mist (**mist**)
A cloud of tiny drops of water in the air.

mistral (**mis**-truhl or mis-**trahl**)
A cold, dry, northerly wind common in southern and central France. The mistral comes most often in winter. From the Provençal *mistral,* meaning "masterful."

mitochondria (*mite*-uh-**kahn**-dree-uh)
Very small structures within **cells** that are involved in the **metabolism** of the cell.

mitosis (mie-**toh**-sis)
The division of a **cell** into two identical daughter cells. During mitosis the numbers of **chromosomes** in the cell doubles and each daughter cell gets the same set of chromosomes. From the Greek *mito,* meaning "thread," since each chromosome looks like a thread.

Mitosis

Uncoiled threads of chromosomes in cell nucleus

The chromosomes copy themselves; each strand is called a chromatid.

mixture (**miks**-chuhr)
A combination of two or more substances that are not **chemically** bound together. Air, for example, is a mixture of **nitrogen**, **oxygen**, and other gases.

Möbius strip (**moh**-bee-uhs **strip**)
A strip of paper with a half twist in the middle and with the ends attached. The Möbius strip has one side—even though the original paper had two. Named after the German mathematician *August Möbius* (1790–1868).

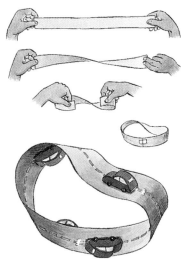

Möbius strip The Möbius strip has only one continuous surface!

modem (**moh**-duhm)
Short for *modulator-dem*odulator. The modem is a device that connects computers by telephone.

modulation (*mahj*-uh-**lay**-shuhn)
The changing of radio waves so they can carry sounds, pictures, or **data**. Radio broadcasting uses either **AM** (amplitude modulation) or **FM** (frequency modulation).

module (**mahj**-ool)
A single, complete unit. New modules are added to a space station to replace old ones or to make the space station larger.

Moho (**moh**-hoh)
Short for *Moho*rovicic discontinuity. Moho is the boundary between the **earth's crust** and **mantle**. See **Earth**.

Mohs' scale (**mohz skayl**)
A way to measure the hardness of a **mineral**. The Mohs' scale goes from 1, the hardness of **talc**, to 10, the hardness of diamond. Invented by the German scientist *Friedrich Mohs* (1773–1839) in 1812. (See pg. 118)

mold (**mohld**)
A **fungus** that grows on food that is left too long in a warm, moist place. Mold also grows on animals and plants.

mole (**mohl**)
In the **metric system**, a measure of the amount of a substance. One mole equals just over 600 billion trillion **atoms** or **molecules** of the substance. (Symbol—mol) *Also*, a colored growth on the skin. *Also*, a small **mammal** that lives under the ground.

molecular weight (muh-**lek**-yuh-luhr **wayt**)
The sum of the **atomic weights** of all the **atoms** in a **molecule**. For example, a molecule of **water** (H_2O) contains two atoms of **hydrogen** (**atomic weight**—1) and one atom of **oxygen** (atomic weight—16). Its molecular weight is $(2 \times 1) + 16 = 18$.

molecule (**mahl**-uh-*kyool*)
The smallest bit into which a **compound** can be divided without **chemical** change. A molecule consists of two or more **atoms**

Chromatids line up.

Chromosomes move to opposite sides of the cell.

The cell starts to split.

Two cells forms; each is the same as the original cell.

Mohs' scale

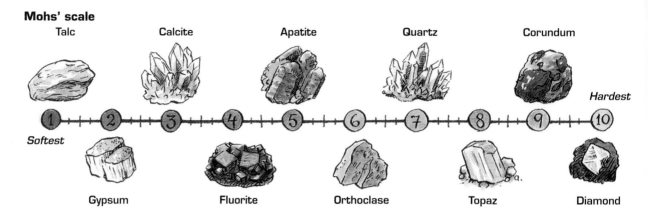

Talc — Calcite — Apatite — Quartz — Corundum

Hardest

Softest

Gypsum — Fluorite — Orthoclase — Topaz — Diamond

of different **elements** or the same element. For example, a molecule of **water** (H$_2$O) contains two atoms of **hydrogen** (H) and one atom of **oxygen** (O).

mollusk (**mahl**-uhsk)
An animal with no bones, a soft body, and often a hard shell. Mollusks include snails, clams, oysters, slugs, and octopuses. From the Latin *molluscus,* meaning "soft."

molt (**mohlt**)
To shed hair, skin, scales, feathers, fur, or other coverings and grow new ones. Many animals molt when their fur or feathers become old or worn. Insects, **reptiles,** and **crustaceans** molt as they grow larger.

molten (**mohlt**-n)
Made into a liquid by being heated. The heat inside the earth changes solid rock into molten, liquid **magma.**

momentum (moh-**men**-tuhm)
The force with which a body moves. Momentum equals the **mass** of the body times its speed. The heavier the body and the faster it is moving, the greater the momentum.

monera (muh-**nir**-uh)
One of the five **kingdoms** in the **classification system.** The *Monera* kingdom includes one-**celled organisms,** such as **bacteria** and blue-green **algae** that do not have a separate **nucleus.** From the Greek *moneres,* meaning "single."

monitor (**mahn**-uh-tuhr)
The display screen that shows the **output** of a computer. *Also,* to watch or observe something.

monocotyledon
(*mahn*-uh-*kaht*-l-**eed**-n)
A flowering plant with only one leafy structure within its seed. Monocotyledons include palms, corn, and orchids.

monomer (**mahn**-uh-muhr)
A **molecule** that can combine with the same or different molecules to form a long chain called a **polymer.**

monsoon (mahn-**soon**)
A wind that blows in one direction during the summer and in a different direction during the winter. Monsoons are caused by unequal heating of land and sea as the seasons change. From the Arabic *mawsim,* meaning "season."

month (**muhnth**)
One of the 12 divisions of the year based on the movement of the moon. The months of our calendar last anywhere from 28 to 31 days. The *lunar month*— from new moon to new moon—is 29 days and nearly 13 hours.

moon (**moon**)
Earth's only natural **satellite** and our nearest neighbor in space. In 1969, humans visited the moon for the first time. The moon has no life, **atmosphere,** wind,

or water. The moon is much smaller than Earth and has much less **gravity**.

*Average distance from Earth—238,857 miles (384,403 kilometers)
Diameter—2,160 miles (3,476 kilometers)
Length of day—about 15 Earth days
Period of rotation—27 days, 7 hours, 43 minutes
Gravity—1/6 that of Earth*

Also, the satellite of any other planet.

moraine (muh-**rayn**)
The soil and rocks that were carried by a **glacier** and then dropped as the glacier melted. The moraine can be at the sides or end of the glacier. Also called *glacial till.*

Morgan (**mor**-guhn), Garrett (1877–1963)
An American inventor who made the first gas mask and the first traffic light. Morgan's mother had been a slave, and he received no education beyond elementary school.

Morgan (**mor**-guhn), Thomas Hunt (1866–1945)
An American **biologist** who used the fruit fly to show that **genes** pass **traits** from **generation** to generation.

morning star (**mor**-ning **stahr**)
Not a star, but either **Venus** or **Mercury** as seen in the eastern sky before sunrise.

Morse (**mors**), Samuel F. B. (1791–1872)
An American inventor who made the first successful **electric telegraph.** Morse also devised the Morse code to send messages by telegraph.

moss (**maws**)
A small, green plant that grows like a soft carpet on trees, rocks, or soil. Moss has neither flowers nor roots, **reproduces** by **spores**, and is found mostly in damp, shady places.

motherboard (**muhth**-uhr-*bord*)
The main **circuit** board in a computer. The motherboard contains the **CPU.**

Moraine

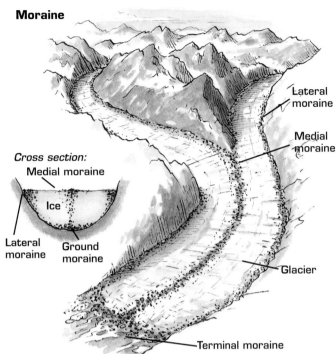

Cross section:
Medial moraine
Ice
Lateral moraine
Ground moraine
Lateral moraine
Medial moraine
Glacier
Terminal moraine

motile (**moht**-l or **moh**-tile)
Able to move by itself. A motile **microorganism** is one that has its own way of getting from place to place.

motion (**moh**-shuhn)
The act of changing position or place. The motion of a body depends on its **velocity,** which is its speed and direction.

motor (**moh**-tuhr)
A device that changes one form of **energy,** usually electricity, into **mechanical energy** or motion. See also **engine.** From the Latin *motor,* meaning "mover."

mountain (**mount**-n)
A part of the land that is much higher than its surroundings. A mountain usually has a steep slope and a sharp or slightly rounded peak or **ridge.** See also **fold mountain.**

mouse (**mous**)
In computers, a handheld device that moves the **cursor** on the **monitor.**

mouth (**mouth**)
The part of the body in animals, including humans, for taking in food and air. In

humans, the mouth has lips, a tongue, and teeth, which help us eat and speak.

MRI (em-*ahr*-ie)

Short for *Magnetic Resonance Imaging*. MRI uses a huge magnet and radio waves to allow doctors to see bones and soft **tissues** within the body.

mucus (**myoo**-kuhs)

A thick, slimy fluid found in the nose, mouth, and other parts of the body. Mucus helps to keep body passages moist and clean.

mulch (**muhlch**)

Material spread on soil to hold in moisture, keep the soil warm, and reduce **erosion**, while still allowing air to pass through. Mulch may be made of straw, leaves, wood chips, manure, or other materials.

multicellular (*muhl*-tee-**sel**-yuh-luhr)

Made up of many **cells**.

mumps (**muhmps**)

A disease caused by a **virus**. One **symptom** of mumps is a painful swelling on both sides of the face. A mumps **vaccine** protects most people from the disease.

muscle (**muhs**-uhl)

A tough, elastic **tissue** that can pull on bones to move parts of the body in humans and animals. *Striated muscles* move the body. *Smooth muscles* control digestion, blood circulation, and similar functions. *Cardiac muscles* keep the heart beating. From the Latin *musculus,* meaning "little mouse," since it was thought that a muscle looked like a small mouse.

mutant (**myoot**-nt)

An offspring that shows the result of a **mutation**.

mutation (myoo-**tay**-shuhn)

A change in the **genes** or **chromosomes** that leads to new **traits** in the offspring. A mutation may be caused by **radiation**, **chemicals**, other factors in the **environment**, or an accident during **cell** division. While most mutations are harmful, good mutations can be used to help grow better crops or improve livestock.

mutualism (**myoo**-choo-uh-*liz*-uhm)

See **symbiosis**.

mycelium (mie-**see**-lee-uhm)

The white, cottonlike mass of threads that makes up the body of a **fungus**. The mycelium part of mushrooms grows under the ground; the part we see is called the *fruiting body.*

myopia (mie-**oh**-pee-uh)

See **nearsighted.**

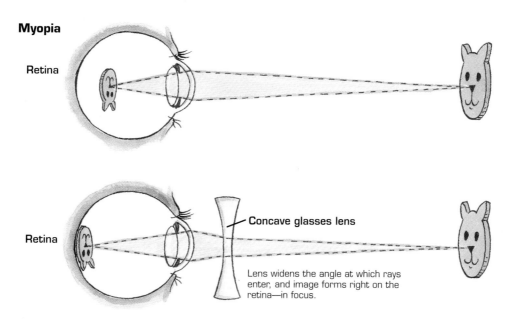

Myopia

Retina

Retina

Concave glasses lens

Lens widens the angle at which rays enter, and image forms right on the retina—in focus.

nano- (nan-oh)
In the **metric system**, a prefix meaning one billionth. A *nano*second is one billionth of a second.

narcotic (nahr-**kaht**-ik)
A drug that causes sleepiness, a lessening of pain, or a loss of consciousness. Well-known narcotics are **opium, morphine,** and codeine. Narcotics are useful in medicine but otherwise are very dangerous and **addictive.** From the Greek *narcoun,* meaning "to make numb."

NASA (nas-uh)
Short for **National Aeronautics and Space Administration.**

National Aeronautics and Space Administration (nash-uhn-l *er-*uh-**nawt-**iks uhnd **spays** uhd-*min-*uh-*stray*-shuhn)
A U.S. government agency established in 1958 to do **research** in space and launch rockets, **spacecraft,** and **satellites.** Called **NASA** for short.

natural (nach-uh-ruhl)
Something that comes from nature and is not made by humans. Wood is natural; plastic is manufactured or **synthetic.**

natural gas (nach-uh-ruhl **gas)**
A gas formed in the ground millions of years ago from the bodies of sea creatures. Natural gas is a **hydrocarbon** that mostly consists of **methane.** It is used as fuel for cooking and heating.

natural resources
(**nach-**uh-ruhl **ree-***sor*-siz)
Things in nature that support life on Earth. Natural resources include land, water, other **organisms, minerals,** sunshine, and air.

natural selection
(**nach-**uh-ruhl suh-**lek-**shuhn)
A slow, ongoing process in which living things best suited to their **environment** tend to survive, while those less suited tend to die off. When there is little food, taller giraffes find more leaves to eat than shorter giraffes. Therefore, more taller giraffes survive. And the tall giraffes are more likely to give birth to tall giraffes. The **theory** of natural selection was developed by **Charles Darwin** in the 1850s. Natural selection is also called *survival of the fittest.*

nautical mile (nawt-i-kuhl **mile)**
A length measurement used at sea. A nautical mile equals about 1.15 standard miles (1.85 kilometers).

navigation (nav-uh-**gay-**shuhn)
A way of finding the position and charting the course of a vehicle, such as a ship, airplane, **spacecraft,** or automobile. Navigation uses maps, **compasses,** stars, **satellites,** and/or radio signals. From the Latin *navis,* meaning "ship," and *agere,* meaning "to drive."

Neanderthals (nee-**an-**duhr-*tawlz*)
An **extinct** people who lived from about 100,000 to 35,000 years ago. The name comes from Neander Gorge, Germany, where **fossils** of these **prehistoric** human beings were found in 1856.

neap tide (neep *tide*)
The **tide** with the smallest range between **high** and **low tides.** Neap tides occur twice a month when the sun and moon are at right angles to each other.

nearsighted (nir-*sie*-tid)
Having a defect of **vision** in which nearby objects are seen clearly, but distant objects appear blurred. Nearsightedness can be corrected by **concave lenses** in glasses or contacts. Also called *myopia*.

nebula (**neb**-yuh-luh)
A cloud of gas and dust in space. A nebula may be the place where a new star is forming. From the Latin *nebula*, meaning "mist or cloud."

nebular hypothesis
(**neb**-yuh-luhr hie-**pahth**-uh-sis)
The belief that the **solar system** developed from a huge, hot, spinning **nebula**. It is the most widely accepted idea on the formation of the solar system.

nectar (**nek**-tuhr)
A sugary liquid made by many flowering plants. The nectar of flowers is food for many birds, bats, and insects. Bees make honey from nectar.

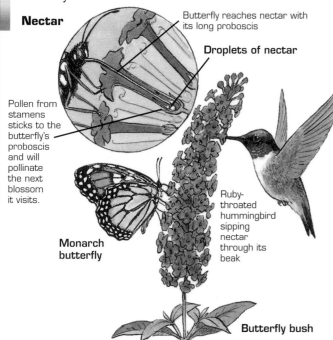

Nectar

Butterfly reaches nectar with its long proboscis

Droplets of nectar

Pollen from stamens sticks to the butterfly's proboscis and will pollinate the next blossom it visits.

Monarch butterfly

Ruby-throated hummingbird sipping nectar through its beak

Butterfly bush

needleleaf tree (**need**-l-*leef tree*)
A tree with needlelike leaves rather than broad leaves. The needleleaf trees include pine, spruce, and fir.

negative (**neg**-uh-tiv)
A number or quantity of less than zero. *Also,* a pole in a battery or electrical device that **electrons** flow away from. *Also,* developed photographic film in which dark and light are reversed. *Also,* the **electrical charge** on a substance that has more **electrons** than normal. From the Latin *negare*, meaning "to say no."

neolithic (*nee*-uh-**lith**-ik)
See **Stone Age.**

neon (**nee**-ahn)
A **chemical element** found in small quantities as a gas in the earth's **atmosphere.** Neon has no **color,** smell, or taste. Passing an **electric current** through a glass tube of neon makes the gas glow with a red-orange light. It is widely used in signs. From the Greek *neon*, meaning "new." (Symbol—Ne)

Neptune (**nep**-toon)
The eighth planet from the sun, except every 248 years when **Pluto** swings in closer and Neptune becomes the ninth planet. The flight of the **spacecraft** *Voyager II* in 1989 showed that winds on Neptune blow up to 1,240 miles (2,000 kilometers) an hour on the surface, and that the planet is surrounded by a number of faint rings and 7 **satellites.**

Average distance from sun—2,796,000,000 miles (4,500,000,000 kilometers)
Length of year—165 Earth years
Length of day—16 hours, 7 minutes
Diameter at equator—30,800 miles (49,500 kilometers)

nerve (**nuhrv**)
One of the cordlike bundles of nerve **cells,** or **neurons,** that connects the brain and **spinal cord** with every part of the body. Nerves carry messages to and from the brain at high speeds.

nerve cell (**nuhrv** *sel*)
See **neuron.**

nervous system
(nuhr-vuhs *sis*-tuhm)
The **network** of **nerves**, brain, and **spinal cord** found in almost all animals. The nervous system reacts to changes in the **environment** and controls the heart, breathing, and digestion. The two parts of the human nervous system are the **central nervous system**, which includes the brain and spinal cord, and the **peripheral nervous system** which runs to the rest of the body.

network (**net**-*wuhrk*)
A **system** that connects two or more **computers**, **telephones**, **radio** or **television** stations, or **electronic** components. *Also,* any connected arrangement of roads, canals, people, **nerves,** and so on.

neuron (**nur**-ahn)
One of the star-shaped **cells** that make up the **nerves** of the **nervous system.** Attached to the cell body is a long tubelike extension called an **axon.** The axon carries messages to other cells. Each cell also has about six shorter branches called *dendrites.* The dendrites receive messages from other cells. Also called *nerve cell.*

neurosis (nu-**roh**-sis)
A mild mental illness. The **symptoms** of neurosis may include anxiety, **depression,** or unreal fears.

neutral (**noo**-truhl)
An **electrical charge** that is neither **positive** nor **negative.** *Also,* a **chemical** that is neither **acid** nor **alkali.**

neutralize (**noo**-truh-*lize*)
The act of adding a **base** (or **alkali**) to an **acid,** or adding an acid to a base, to make the solution **neutral.**

neutrino (noo-**tree**-noh)
A **subatomic particle** with no **electrical charge.** Because it has no electrical charge, a neutrino rarely interacts with ordinary **atoms** and can pass through planet Earth with little chance of colliding with another particle. In 1998 scientists found that neutrinos have **mass,** which they have not yet been able to measure.

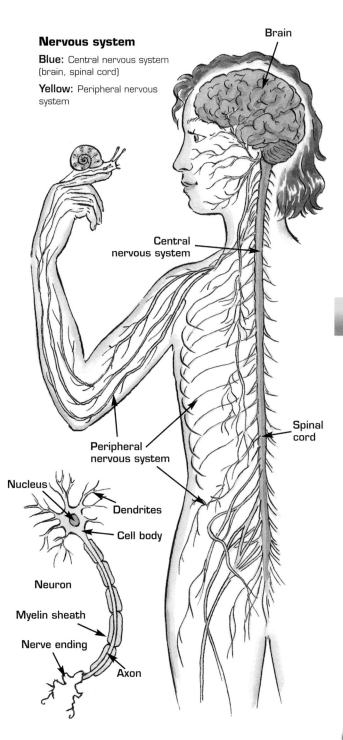

Nervous system

Blue: Central nervous system (brain, spinal cord)

Yellow: Peripheral nervous system

Brain

Central nervous system

Spinal cord

Peripheral nervous system

Nucleus

Dendrites

Cell body

Neuron

Myelin sheath

Nerve ending

Axon

neutron (noo-trahn)
A **subatomic particle** found within the **nucleus** of all **atoms** except **hydrogen**. A neutron carries no **electrical charge**, has slightly more **mass** than a **proton**, and 1,840 times more mass than an **electron**. See also **isotope**.

neutron star (noo-trahn *stahr*)
A very small and dense kind of star. A neutron star may be only about 12 miles (20 kilometers) across, but it may have more **mass** than the sun!

newton (noot-n)
A measure of force. One newton equals the force needed to increase or decrease the **velocity** of a 2.2 pound (1 kilogram) object by 3.3 feet (1 meter) per second per second.

Newton (noot-n), Isaac (1642–1727)
An English scientist who developed the law of universal **gravitation**. Newton also worked out the three basic laws of motion, found that common white light is a mixture of all other colors, explained rainbows, and built the first **reflecting telescope**—among many other important findings.

niche (nich)
The position of an **organism** in its community or **ecosystem**. The niche depends on where the organism lives, what it eats, its way of life, its enemies, and so on.

nickel (nik-uhl)
A white, metal **element** that looks like silver and is often added to **iron** or **steel** to make it stronger. The 5-cent nickel coin is made of nickel and **copper**. (Symbol—Ni)

nicotine (nik-uh-*teen*)
A highly addictive poison found in tobacco leaves. Nicotine narrows the blood vessels and strains the heart of people who smoke cigarettes. Nicotine is named after *J. Nicot* (1530–1600), who introduced tobacco into France around 1560. (Formula—$C_{10}H_{14}N_2$)

nictitating membrane (nik-tuh-*tay*-ting *mem*-brayn)
A third eyelid found in many vertebrates. The nictitating membrane covers the eye and keeps it clean. From the Latin *nictare,* meaning "to wink."

Nictitating membrane

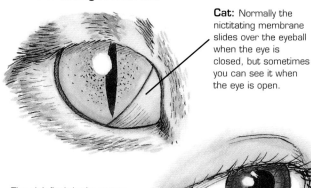

Cat: Normally the nictitating membrane slides over the eyeball when the eye is closed, but sometimes you can see it when the eye is open.

The pink flesh in the corner of our eye is the remains of a nictitating membrane present in early humans.

nimbostratus (*nim*-buh-**stray**-tuhs)
A low-hanging, dark cloud that looks like a flat layer. A nimbostratus cloud usually brings rain or snow.

nitrate (nie-trayt)
A **chemical compound** that contains **oxygen**, **nitrogen**, and at least one other **element**. Potassium nitrate (formula— KNO_3), for example, is an important **fertilizer**.

nitric acid (nie-trik as-id)
A strong **acid** widely used to make **fertilizers** and **explosives**. (Formula—HNO_3)

nitrification (*nie*-truh-fuh-**kay**-shuhn)
See **nitrogen cycle**.

nitrogen (nie-truh-juhn)
A colorless, odorless, tasteless gas **element**. Nitrogen makes up 78 percent of the earth's **atmosphere**. It is vital to all forms of life and is widely used to make **fertilizers**. (Symbol—N)

nitrogen cycle (**nie**-truh-juhn *sie*-kuhl)
The movement of **nitrogen** between the **atmosphere**, soil, and living things. Some **bacteria** change nitrogen from the air into a form that can be taken up by plants. This process is called *nitrogen fixation*. In time, the plants die, and so do the animals that ate the plants. Other bacteria then change the decaying plant and animal matter into **nitrates** and release nitrogen gas into the air, which is called *nitrification*.

nitrogen fixation (**nie**-truh-juhn fik-*say*-shuhn)
See **nitrogen cycle**.

nitroglycerin (*nie*-truh-**glis**-uh-ruhn)
A clear, oily liquid that explodes very easily. Nitroglycerin is used in **dynamite** and also to treat the pain of certain heart diseases. (Formula— $C_3H_5(ONO_2)_3$)

nitrous oxide (**nie**-truhs **ahk**-side)
A gas used by dentists and doctors as a painkiller. Nitrous oxide is also called "laughing gas" because it sometimes makes people silly. (Formula— N_2O)

Nobel (noh-**bel**), **Alfred B.** (1833–1896)
A Swedish chemist who invented **dynamite**. See also **Nobel Prize**.

Nobel Prize (noh-**bel** prize)
One of 6 annual prizes awarded to someone who has made a major contribution in **physics**, **chemistry**, **physiology** or medicine, literature, economics, or the promotion of peace; established by **Alfred B. Nobel**.

noble gases (**noh**-buhl **gas**-iz)
Six **chemical elements** that rarely react or combine with other elements. The noble gases are argon, **helium**, **krypton**, **neon**, **radon**, and xenon.

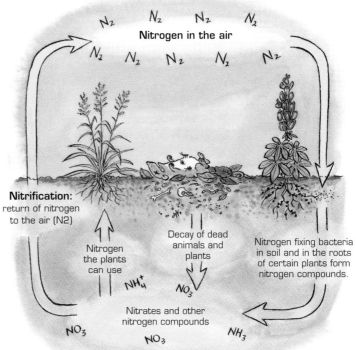

Nitrogen cycle

Nitrogen in the air

N_2 N_2 N_2 N_2
N_2 N_2 N_2 N_2 N_2

Nitrification: return of nitrogen to the air (N2)

Nitrogen the plants can use

Decay of dead animals and plants

Nitrogen fixing bacteria in soil and in the roots of certain plants form nitrogen compounds.

NH_4^+ NO_3

Nitrates and other nitrogen compounds

NO_3 NO_3 NH_3

nocturnal (nahk-**tuhrn**-l)
Having to do with the night. Owls, who are active at night, are nocturnal animals.

node (**nohd**)
The point in a vibrating body where there is no **vibration**. *Also,* a bump or swelling on a stem from which leaves or flowers grow. From the Latin *nodus*, meaning "knot."

nodule (**nahj**-ool)
A little lump on the root or stem of a plant. Some nodules contain **nitrogen-fixing bacteria**. See also **nitrogen cycle**. *Also,* a small lump of **cells** in an animal body. *Also,* a small mass of rock or mineral.

noise (**noiz**)
Unwanted, disagreeable, or loud sounds. *Also,* unwanted electrical signals or changes in **current** in an electrical **circuit**.

northern lights (**nor**-THuhrn lites)
See **aurora borealis**.

North Pole (north pohl)
The most northern point on Earth. There are actually several North poles:

North geographic pole—where all the lines of **longitude** come together.
North magnetic pole—where one end of a **compass** needle points.
Instantaneous north pole—the northern end of an imaginary **axis** around which the earth **rotates**.

north pole (north pohl)
The part of a magnet that points to the *north magnetic pole* of Earth.

North Star (north stahr)
A bright star almost directly over the earth's *north geographic pole*. Since the North Star seems to stay in one place, it has long been used for **navigation**. Also called *Polaris* or *polestar*.

nose (nohz)
The **organ** used for breathing and smelling.

nostril (nahs-truhl)
One of two openings in the nose through which air enters and leaves the body. Nostrils are also called *nares*. From the Old English *nosu*, meaning "nose," and *thyrel*, meaning "hole."

notebook (noht-*buk*)
See **laptop**.

nova (noh-vuh)
An exploding star that suddenly becomes thousands of times brighter and then gradually fades.

nuclear energy
(noo-klee-uhr en-uhr-jee)
The most powerful kind of **energy**. Nuclear energy is produced within the nuclei (plural of **nucleus**) of **atoms** and is released by **fission** or **fusion**. Also called *atomic energy*. See also **nuclear reactor**.

nuclear fission
(noo-klee-uhr fish-uhn)
See **fission**.

nuclear fusion
(noo-klee-uhr fyoo-zhuhn)
See **fusion**.

nuclear power
(noo-klee-ur pou-uhr)
Electricity produced by using the heat from a **nuclear reactor** to turn water into steam, which drives electric **generators**. Nuclear power supplies electricity to many places around the world.

North Pole

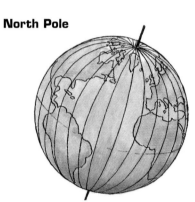

Geographic north pole
(Found near the center of the Arctic Sea)

Magnetic north pole
(Currently somewhere on a Canadian island)

Instantaneous north pole
(Moves in a small circle around the geographic north pole.)

Nuclear power

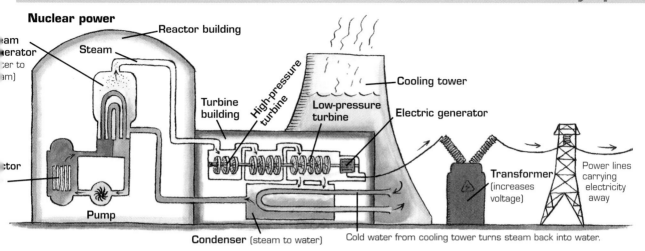

Reactor building
Steam
am erator cer to am]
ctor
Pump
Turbine building
High-pressure turbine
Low-pressure turbine
Cooling tower
Electric generator
Transformer (increases voltage)
Power lines carrying electricity away
Condenser (steam to water)
Cold water from cooling tower turns steam back into water.

nuclear reactor
(**noo**-klee-uhr ree-**ak**-tuhr)
A device that produces heat **energy** by means of a controlled **chain reaction** (nuclear **fission**). Most often, the heat from the chain reaction produces steam that drives **generators** in electric **power** plants. Also called *atomic pile.*

nucleic acid (noo-**klee**-ik **as**-id)
Any of the large, complex **molecules** that make up the genetic material of **cells. DNA** and **RNA** are nucleic acids. DNA is in the **genes** and carries **hereditary** information. RNA helps to make **proteins.**

nucleolus (noo-**klee**-uh-luhs)
A small, round body within the **nucleus** of a **cell.** The nucleolus contains **RNA.**

nucleus (**noo**-klee-uhs)
The central core of an **atom** made up of **protons** and **neutrons.** *Also,* a rounded body within most **cells** that contains the **chromosomes** and controls the work of the cell. From the Latin *nucleus,* meaning "kernel."

nutrient (**noo**-tree-uhnt)
A food substance, such as **protein, carbohydrate**, fat, vitamin, **mineral, fiber**, or water, needed for good health.

nutrition (noo-**trish**-uhn)
The science of food. Nutrition studies which foods should be eaten for good health and how the body uses food for **energy**, growth, and to build new **cells**

and **tissue.** *Also,* the process by which living things take in and use food.

nylon (**nie**-lahn)
A material made from **chemicals** that can be shaped into thin **fibers** or solid objects. Nylon was first made by the United States chemist *Wallace Carothers* (1896–1937) in 1935.

nymph (**nimf**)
A stage in the life of some insects between egg and adult. The nymphs of grasshoppers and cockroaches look like small adults. From the Greek *nymphe,* meaning "minor goddess" or "bride."

Nymph

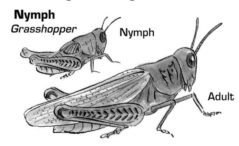

Grasshopper
Nymph
Adult

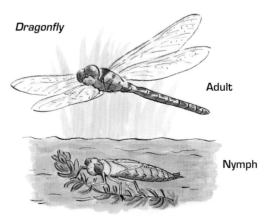

Dragonfly
Adult
Nymph

127

oasis (oh-**ay**-sis)
A **fertile** place in a **desert** where there is year-round water and where plants and trees grow.

objective lens (uhb-**jek**-tiv **lenz**)
The **microscope** or **telescope lens** that is nearest to the object being viewed.

observation (*ahb*-zuhr-**vay**-shuhn)
The act of watching something very carefully. Observation is an important part of many scientific activities. From the Latin *ob,* meaning "in front of," and *servare,* meaning "to watch."

observatory (uhb-**zuhr**-vuh-*tor*-ee)
A building or place, often on a remote mountaintop, where astronomers study the stars and other objects in space with **telescopes.** *Also,* a place where scientists study earthquakes, volcanoes, and other things happening on Earth.

occluded front
(uh-**kloo**-did **fruhnt**)
A cold **front** that has pushed under a warm front. An occluded front usually brings rain or snow.

ocean (**oh**-shuhn)
The great body of salt water that covers more than 70 percent of the earth's surface. The world's ocean is made up of 5 large, connected oceans—Atlantic, Pacific, Indian, Arctic, and Antarctic.

ocean current
(**oh**-shuhn *kuhr*-uhnt)
A river of water flowing through an ocean. The *Gulf Stream Current,* for example, flows along

the coast of the United States and across the Atlantic Ocean to Europe.

oceanography
(*oh*-shuh-**nahg**-ruh-fee)
The branch of science dealing with life in the ocean, waves and **tides, chemicals** in the water, the ocean floor, and so on.

ocellus (oh-**sel**-uhs)
One of the small, simple eyes found between the **compound eyes** of insects. *Also,* an eyelike spot, as on a peacock feather.

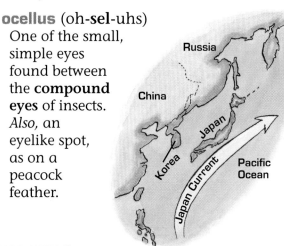

Ocean current

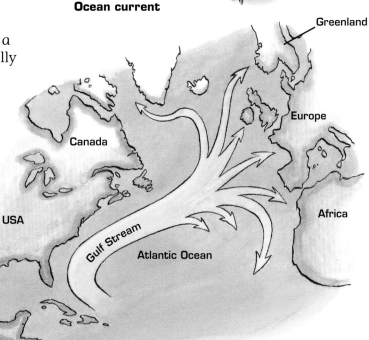

Ocellus

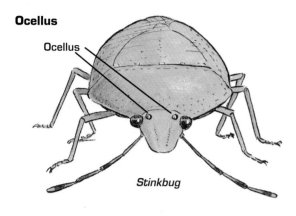

Ocellus

Stinkbug

OCR (oh-*see*-**ahr**)
Short for *Optical Character Recognition*.
The OCR is a device that allows
computers to "read" text. OCR usually
uses a **scanner** and special **software**.

octane (**ahk**-tayn)
A **chemical compound** that is an
important part of gasoline. The higher
the **octane number**, the better the
gasoline. (Formula—C_8H_{18})

ocular (**ahk**-yuh-luhr)
Having to do with the eye. *Also*, the
eyepiece of a **microscope** or **telescope**.

Oersted (**ur**-sted), **Hans Christian**
(1777–1851)
A Danish scientist who discovered
electromagnetism.

Ohm (**ohm**), **Georg** (1787–1854)
A German physicist who discovered the
relation between **voltage**, **current**, and
resistance in an **electric circuit**. The
ohm, which is the unit of resistance, is
named after him.

Ohm's law (**ohmz law**)
The law, stated by **Georg Ohm**, that
shows the relationship of **volts** (**voltage**),
ohms (**resistance**), and **amperes**
(**current**) in an **electric circuit**. The
law states: volts = amperes x ohms.

oil (**oil**)
A greasy substance that is lighter than
water and does not **dissolve** in water. Oil
comes from animals, growing plants, **fossil**

plants, or is manufactured. Most oils burn
easily and are liquid at room temperature.

oil shale (**oil** *shayl*)
Layers of **sedimentary** rock that, when
heated, release liquid oil.

ointment (**oint**-muhnt)
A substance based on oil or fat that is
spread on the skin. An ointment contains
substances to heal or protect the skin.

Olduvai Gorge (**ohl**-duh-*vie* **gorj**)
A narrow valley in Tanzania, Africa,
where **Louis** and **Mary Leakey** found the
fossil remains of early human ancestors.

olfactory (ohl-**fak**-tuh-ree)
Having to do with smelling. The **nose** is
an olfactory **organ**.

Oligocene epoch
(**ahl**-i-goh-*seen* **ep**-uhk)
The period of **geological history** from 38
to 24 million years ago. Early forms of
dogs, cats, and horses appeared during
the Oligocene epoch.

omnivore (**ahm**-nuh-*vor*)
An animal that eats all kinds of food,
both plant and animal. Omnivores
include humans, bears, monkeys, and
apes. From the Latin *omnis,* meaning
"all," and *vorare,* meaning "to eat
greedily."

opaque (oh-**payk**)
Blocking light or other **rays**. Wood is
opaque, glass is not. From the Latin
opacus, meaning "dark or shaded."

ophthalmology
(*ahf*-thuhl-**mahl**-uh-jee)
The study of the causes, treatment, and
prevention of eye disease and ways to
improve **vision**.

opium (**oh**-pee-uhm)
A powerful drug made from the juice of
the opium poppy plant. Opium is used
in several medicines that are painkillers,
such as *codeine* and *morphine*. It is also
the source of the illegal drug **heroin**.

Oppenheimer (ahp-uhn-*hie*-muhr), J. Robert (1904–1967)
An American physicist who was director of the Los Alamos National Laboratory where the first atomic bomb was built.

optical character recognition (ahp-ti-kuhl kar-ik-tuhr *rek*-ig-*nish*-uhn)
See **OCR**.

optical fiber (ahp-ti-kuhl fie-buhr)
A fine strand of pure glass surrounded by a different kind of glass that reflects light **rays** back into the center. See also **fiber optics**.

optical illusion (ahp-ti-kuhl i-loo-zhuhn)
Something that looks different from what it is. Optical illusions occur when the brain cannot properly understand what the eye sees.

optician (ahp-tish-uhn)
Someone who makes or sells eyeglasses or grinds **lenses** for optical devices.

optic nerve (ahp-tik nuhrv)
The **nerve** that carries signals from the **retina** of the eye to the brain.

optics (ahp-tiks)
The science that studies light and **vision**.

optometrist (ahp-tahm-uh-trist)
A person who examines eyes and prescribes eyeglasses or contact **lenses** to correct faulty **vision**.

orbit (or-bit)
The path of one heavenly body around another. The orbit of Earth around the **sun** is an **ellipse**. *Also*, to follow a path around a heavenly body. The planets orbit the sun. From the Latin *orbita*, meaning "track of a wheel."

orbital velocity (or-bit-l vuh-lahs-uh-tee)
The speed a rocket or **spacecraft** must maintain to stay in **orbit** around Earth. Orbital velocity in close orbit is around 18,000 miles (29,000 kilometers) per hour. The orbital velocity is lower at higher orbits.

order (or-duhr)
A group of similar plants or animals in the biological **classification** system. For example, humans belong to the order **primates**, along with apes and monkeys. From the Latin *ordo*, meaning "row."

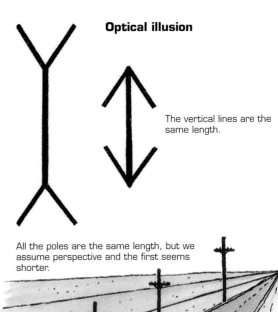

Optical illusion

The vertical lines are the same length.

All the poles are the same length, but we assume perspective and the first seems shorter.

They say vertical lines make you look thinner.

Ordovician period
(*ord*-uh-**vish**-uhn **pir**-ee-uhd)
The period of **geological history** from
about 500 to 435 million years ago.
During the Ordovician period **corals** and
trilobites were common.

ore (or)
A rock or **mineral** that contains a
valuable material such as a metal. The
ore *hematite* contains the metal iron.

organ (or-guhn)
Any part of a living thing that is
organized to do a particular job.
Mammal organs include the heart,
lungs, and brain. The **pistil** and **stamen**
are organs in flowering plants. From
the Greek *organon*, meaning "tool."

organic (or-**gan**-ik)
Describes **compounds** that contain the
element carbon. *Also,* coming from
an **organism.** *Also,* having to do with
an **organ; liver disease** is an organic
disease. *Also,* describing food from
a plant that has been grown
without any **chemical fertilizers**
or **pesticides.**

organic chemistry
(or-**gan**-ik **kem**-uh-stree)
The branch of **chemistry** that studies
compounds that contain **carbon.**

organic farming
(or-**gan**-ik **fahr**-ming)
A way of farming that uses **natural**
products rather than **synthetic chemicals**
to **fertilize** the land and rid it of insects
and other pests.

organism (or-guh-*niz*-uhm)
Any living thing.

organ transplant
(**or**-guhn *trans*-plant)
See **transplant.**

ornithology
(*or*-nuh-**thahl**-uh-jee)
The science of birds, including their body
structure, life cycle, and behavior.

orrery (or-uh-ree)
A model of the **solar system** that uses
clockwork to move the planets around
the sun. Orrery is named after the Earl
of Orrery, *Charles Boyle (1676–1731),*
who had the first orrery built in the
early 1700s.

orthodontics (or-thuh-**dahn**-tiks)
The branch of dentistry that straightens
and adjusts crooked teeth. From the
Greek *orthos,* meaning "straight," and
odous, meaning "tooth."

orthopedics (or-thuh-**pee**-diks)
The branch of medicine that deals
with the disorders of bones, joints,
and muscles. From the Greek *orthos,*
meaning "straight," and *pais,*
meaning "child."

Osborn (ahz-born), **Henry**
(1857–1935)
An American paleontologist who made
the study of **fossils** popular. Osborn
developed a theory on how animals and
plants spread out over large areas and
adapt to different **habitats.**

oscillate (ahs-uh-*layt*)
To move or swing back and forth like a
pendulum. Something that oscillates
very fast, such as a plucked guitar string,
is said to *vibrate.*

oscilloscope (uh-**sil**-uh-*skohp*)
An **electronic** device that displays
changing electric signals as patterns
of waves on a screen.

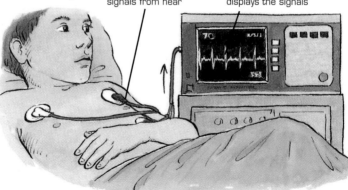

Oscilloscope   Electrode picks up   Oscilloscope on heart-
                    signals from hear   monitoring machine
                                              displays the signals

osmosis (ahz-**moh**-sis)
The movement of a liquid from a less concentrated **solution** through a **membrane** into a more concentrated solution. The result of osmosis is the same concentration in both solutions. Plants absorb water from soil by osmosis. From the Greek *osmos*, meaning "push."

ossification (*ahs*-uh-fi-**kay**-shuhn)
The process of changing into bone. Ossification in an animal **fetus** forms bones out of soft **tissue.**

osteoblast (**ahs**-tee-uh-*blast*)
A **cell** that develops into a bone. Also called *osteoplast*. From the Greek *osteon*, meaning "bone," and *blastos*, meaning "bud or germ."

osteopathic medicine
(**ahs**-tee-uh-**path**-ik **med**-uh-sin)
A medical system based on the manipulation of patients' bones and muscles. Osteopathic doctors, however, also use all the tools and methods of modern medicine.

osteoporosis (*ahs*-tee-*oh*-puh-**roh**-sis)
A weakening of bones due to the loss of bone **tissue.** Osteoporosis mostly strikes the elderly, especially women. People with osteoporosis tend to break bones more easily than others.

Otis (**oh**-tis), **Elisha Graves** (1811–1861)
An American inventor who built the first elevator with an automatic safety catch in 1853.

otoscope (**oh**-tuh-*skohp*)
An instrument doctors use to look into the ear.

Otto (**aht**-oh), **Nikolaus August** (1832–1891)
A German **engineer** who developed the **internal combustion engine** used in early versions of the modern automobile.

ounce (**ouns**)
A measure of weight equal to 1/16th of a pound (28.3495 grams). Ounce is also a measure of **volume.** One *fluid ounce* equals 1/16th of a liquid pint (29.5735 milliliters).

outcrop (**out**-*krahp*)
A piece of **bedrock** that sticks out above the soil.

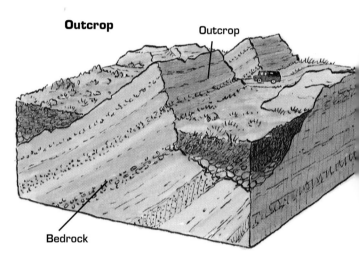

Outcrop

Outcrop

Bedrock

outer core (**out**-uhr **kor**)
The part of the **earth** and other planets beneath the **mantle.** The earth's outer core is about 1,400 miles (2,250 kilometers) thick and contains melted **iron** and **nickel.** See also **Earth.**

outer ear (**out**-uhr **ir**)
The part of the ear that can be seen on the side of the head.

outer space (**out**-uhr **spays**)
The region beyond the earth's **atmosphere.** Outer space starts where the **air** is very thin, somewhere more than 60 miles (96 kilometers) above Earth.

output (**out**-*put*)
The amount of electrical **power** produced by an electrical **circuit** or **electronic** device. *Also,* computer information displayed on a screen or printed on paper. *Also,* the **work** or **energy** produced by a machine or by a human.

ovary (**oh**-vuh-ree)
The female **organ** that produces egg **cells**. A human ovary is about the size of a small walnut. From the Latin *ovum,* meaning "egg."

overtones (**oh**-vuhr-*tohnz*)
See **harmonics**.

oviduct (**oh**-vuh-*duhkt*)
The tube through which eggs pass from the **ovary** in female animals. The oviduct in humans is called a *Fallopian tube.*

oviparous (oh-**vip**-uh-ruhs)
Describes animals that produce eggs that develop outside the mother's body. Oviparous animals include birds and most **reptiles, amphibians,** and fish. From the Latin *ovum,* meaning "egg," and *parere,* meaning "to bring forth."

ovipositer (*oh*-vuh-**pahz**-uh-tuhr)
An **organ** at the end of the **abdomen** of certain insects used to deposit their eggs. From the Latin *ovum,* meaning "egg," and *positor,* meaning "placer."

ovulation (*ahv*-yuh-**lay**-shuhn)
The release of a fully developed egg **cell** from the **ovary**. Ovulation in humans occurs at about the midpoint of the **menstrual cycle.**

ovule (**ahv**-yool or **oh**-vyool)
The part of a plant that grows into a seed following **fertilization.**

ovum (**oh**-vuhm)
An egg **cell.**

oxidation (*ok*-suh-**day**-shuhn)
A **chemical** reaction in which **oxygen** combines with a substance. Slow oxidation occurs when iron combines with oxygen to produce rust. Rapid oxidation occurs when gasoline joins with oxygen and burns.

oxide (**ahk**-side)
A **compound** of **oxygen** and some other **element**. **Carbon dioxide** is a compound of carbon and oxygen.

oxidize (**ahk**-suh-*dize*)
To combine with **oxygen**. Oxidizing means burning or rusting. See also **oxidation.**

oxygen (**ahk**-suh-juhn)
A **chemical element** important for most forms of life. Oxygen is a gas that makes up about one fifth of the **atmosphere** and nearly half of the rocks in the earth's **crust**. Oxygen combines with **hydrogen** to form water. From the Greek *oxys,* meaning "sharp," and *-genes,* meaning "born." (Symbol—O)

ozone (**oh**-zohn)
A form of **oxygen** with a sharp odor. Ozone in small amounts is found in the air, especially after a thunderstorm. Ozone **molecules** contain three oxygen **atoms;** oxygen molecules contain only two. From the Greek *ozein,* meaning "to smell." (Symbol—O_3)

ozone layer (**oh**-zohn *lay*-uhr)
A layer of **ozone**, between 12 and 30 miles (19 and 48 kilometers) thick, above the earth. The ozone layer blocks many of the sun's **ultraviolet rays** from reaching the earth. Scientists have found holes in the ozone layer over the **polar** regions. They believe the holes are caused by the use of **chemicals** such as the **CFCs.**

P

pagination (*paj*-uh-**nay**-shuhn)
The automatic numbering of pages by a **computer**.

pahoehoe (puh-**hoh**-ee-*hoh*-ee)
Lava that hardens with a smooth, ropelike finish.

palate (**pal**-uht)
The roof of the mouth. The bony front part of the palate is called the *hard palate*. The soft back part is the *soft palate*.

Paleocene epoch
(**pay**-lee-uh-*seen* **ep**-uhk)
The period of **geological history** from 65 to 57 million years ago. During the Paleocene epoch small **mammals**, including the first **primates**, were common.

paleontology
(*pay*-lee-uhn-**tahl**-uh-jee)
The study of the remains, or **fossils**, of living things from the ancient past. From the Greek *palaios*, meaning "ancient," *onta*, meaning "existing things," and *-logia*, meaning "science of."

Paleozoic era
(*pay*-lee-uh-**zoh**-ik **ir**-uh)
The **era** of **geological history** from 543 to 245 million years ago. During the Paleozoic era the first fish, insects, and **amphibians** appeared. From the Greek *palaios*, meaning "ancient," and *zoion*, meaning "animal."

pancreas (**pan**-kree-uhs)
A **gland** near the stomach in humans and animals with **spines**. The pancreas produces juices for digestion and a **hormone** called **insulin** that controls the body's use of sugar. See also **diabetes**. From the Greek *pan*, meaning "all," and *kreas*, meaning "flesh."

Pangaea
(pan-**jee**-uh)
The huge landmass that was the only **continent** on **Earth** millions of **years** ago. Pangaea began breaking into two giant masses, *Gondwanaland* and *Laurasia*, about 200 million years ago. Slowly they split into the continents we know today. From the Greek *pan*, meaning "all," and *gaia*, meaning "earth."

Pangaea

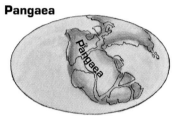

200 million years ago

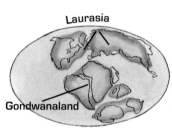

Laurasia

Gondwanaland

120 million years ago

Today's continents

parachute (**par**-uh-*shoot*)
A large piece of fabric with attached ropes. A parachute is used to slow a fall through the air from a great height. From the French *para-*, meaning "protect," and *chute*, meaning "fall."

paraffin (**par**-uh-fin)
A white, waxy solid made from **petroleum**. Paraffin is used for waterproof coatings, as in milk containers, and for making candles.

parallax (**par**-uh-*laks*)
The change in the view of an object as seen from two different points. You have parallax **vision** because your eyes are slightly apart. This helps you judge the distance to objects. Astronomers measure the distance to nearby stars by viewing them from different points in Earth's **orbit**.

parallel circuit (**par**-uh-*lel* **suhr**-kit)
An **electrical circuit** split into separate branches. In a parallel circuit each branch has the same **voltage**, but only part of the **current**.

paralysis (puh-**ral**-uh-sis)
The loss of the ability to move. Paralysis can be temporary or permanent, partial or complete. It can be caused by disease or by damage to the **spinal cord**.

paramedic (*par*-uh-**med**-ik)
A person trained to treat someone sick or hurt in an accident. A paramedic usually helps until a doctor is available. Originally a paramedic was someone who *para*chuted to a remote area to offer *medic*al help.

parapsychology
(*par*-uh-*sie*-**kahl**-uh-jee)
The branch of **psychology** that studies supernatural happenings, such as *telepathy* (mind reading), *psychokinesis* (moving things by mental power alone), *clairvoyance* (knowing about something without using the **senses**), and *precognition* (foretelling the future). See also **extrasensory perception.**

parasite (**par**-uh-*site*)
A living being that exists on another, usually larger, **organism**, called the **host**. Parasites do not usually kill their hosts. Some parasites on humans cause diseases, such as **malaria**. From the Greek *para,* "beside," and *sitos,* meaning "food."

parotid gland (puh-**raht**-id *gland*)
One of a pair of **glands**, found in front of the ears. The parotid glands supply **saliva** to the mouth and start digestion.

parsec (**pahr**-sek)
A unit of distance between stars. One parsec equals 3.26 **light-years**, or 19.2 trillion miles (30.9 trillion kilometers). The word comes from *para*llax *sec*ond.

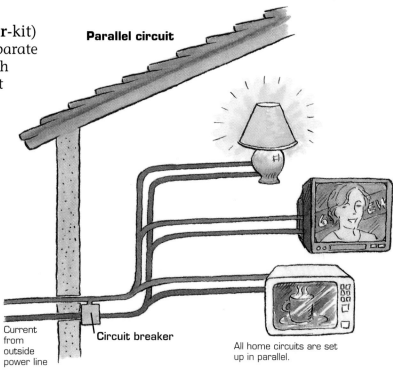

Parallel circuit

Current from outside power line

Circuit breaker

All home circuits are set up in parallel.

particle (**pahr**-ti-kuhl)
A tiny bit of matter, such as a grain of sand, a **molecule** or **atom**, or a **subatomic particle.**

particle accelerator
(**pahr**-ti-kuhl ak-*sel*-uh-*ray*-tuhr)
A device that moves **electrically charged atomic particles** at very high speeds. The particle accelerator hurls the particles at different targets. Scientists study the results of these collisions to learn more about **subatomic particles.** Also called an *atom smasher.*

Particle accelerator

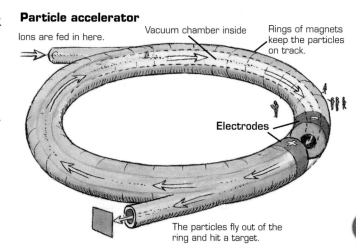

Ions are fed in here.

Vacuum chamber inside

Rings of magnets keep the particles on track.

Electrodes

The particles fly out of the ring and hit a target.

Pascal (pas-**kal**), **Blaise** (1623–1662)
A French scientist famous for his discoveries about fluids, including **Pascal's law**. The *pascal*, a unit of **pressure** in the **metric system**, was named for him.

Pascal's law (pas-**kalz law**)
The statement that **pressure** on a fluid in a closed container spreads with equal force throughout the container. Pascal's law was named for **Blaise Pascal.**

Pasteur (pas-**tur**), **Louis** (1822–1895)
A French **chemist** who found that living things only come from other living things and that **bacteria** cause many diseases. Pasteur also developed **pasteurization** to kill harmful **bacteria** in foods and **vaccination** to prevent various diseases. See also **pasteurization** and **vaccination.**

pasteurization
(*pas*-chuh-ruh-**zay**-shuhn)
A method of killing harmful **bacteria** in milk and other foods by heating them to a high temperature for a period of time. Pasteurization is named after its discoverer, **Louis Pasteur.**

pathogen (**path**-uh-juhn)
Any living thing that causes disease. From the Greek *pathos,* meaning "suffering," and *-genes,* meaning "born."

pathology (pa-**thahl**-uh-jee)
The study of the causes and results of disease. From the Greek *pathos,* meaning "suffering," and *-logia,* meaning "science of."

Pauli (**paw**-lee), **Wolfgang** (1900–1958)
An Austrian physicist who proposed a rule in 1925 that explained the behavior of **electrons** in all **atoms**. The rule is called the *Pauli exclusion principle.*

Pauling (**paw**-ling), **Linus** (1901–1994)
An American chemist who discovered the nature of the **bonds** that link **atoms** in **molecules**. Pauling also figured out the size and shape of very large molecules. In later years he worked to ban nuclear weapons.

Pavlov (**pav**-lawf), **Ivan** (1849–1936)
A Russian scientist famous for his studies of digestion and **reflexes.** Pavlov found that a dog that was always fed after hearing a bell would salivate at the sound of the bell, even without food. This reaction is called a *conditioned reflex.*

Payne-Gaposchkin
(**payn**-guh-**pahsh**-kuhn), **Helena** (1900–1979)
An English-born American astronomer who did important work on the structure of the **Milky Way galaxy.**

PC (**pee-see**)
Short for **personal computer**. A PC is a small desktop computer.

peat (**peet**)
Partly decayed **plant matter** that has been in a damp **swamp** or **marsh** for a long time. Peat is sometimes dried and burned as fuel.

pediatrics (*pee*-dee-**a**-triks)
The branch of medicine that deals with the health and growth of children. From the Greek *pais,* meaning "child," and *iatrikos,* meaning "medical."

pelvis (**pel**-vis)
The basin-shaped frame of bones that supports the lower part of the **abdomen.** The pelvis is formed by the hipbones and the bottom of the backbone. From the Latin *pelvis,* meaning "basin."

pendulum (**pen**-juh-luhm)
A freely swinging weight hung from a string or rod. In a pendulum, the path of the swinging weight is called the *arc.* The time of one arc is called the **period.** The period of a moving pendulum stays the same even if the arc gets shorter. From the Latin *pendere,* meaning "to hang."

penicillin (*pen*-uh-**sil**-uhn)
A powerful **antibiotic** drug for destroying disease-causing **bacteria.**

P

Penicillin is made from a **mold** that was discovered by accident in 1928 by **Sir Alexander Fleming.**

peninsula (puh-**nin**-suh-luh)
Land that is attached to a larger landmass and that is almost completely surrounded by water. Florida is a peninsula. From the Latin *paene,* meaning "almost," and *insula,* meaning "island."

penis (**pee**-nis)
The external sexual **organ** in men and most male **mammals. Urine** and **semen** leave the body through the penis.

Pennsylvanian period
(*pen*-suhl-**vay**-nee-uhn **pir**-ee-uhd)
The **period** of **geological history** from 323 to 290 million years ago. During the Pennsylvanian period fish and **amphibians** were common and the early **reptiles** appeared.

penumbra (puh-**nuhm**-bruh)
The lighter shadow around the dark shadow (**umbra**) during an **eclipse** or whenever a shadow is cast. *Also,* the grayish outer part of a **sunspot.** From the Latin *paene,* meaning "almost," and *umbra,* meaning "shade."

pepsin (**pep**-sin)
A powerful **enzyme** that helps to digest such **proteins** as meat, eggs, and cheese.

perennial (puh-**ren**-ee-uhl)
A plant that lives more than 2 years. From the Latin *per,* meaning "through," and *annus,* meaning "year."

perigee (**per**-uh-jee)
The point in the **orbit** of the **moon** or an artificial Earth **satellite** when it is closest to Earth. From the Greek *peri,* meaning "near," and *ge,* meaning "earth."

perihelion (*per*-uh-**hee**-lee-uhn)
The point in the **orbit** of any body in the solar system when it is closest to the sun.

From the Greek *peri,* meaning "near," and *helios,* meaning "sun."

period (**pir**-ee-uhd)
A division of time in Earth's **geological history** that is smaller than an **era.** For example, the **Cenozoic era** is divided into the **Tertiary period** and **Quaternary period.** *Also,* any interval of time, such as the time it takes for a **pendulum** to swing back and forth. *Also,* a group of **chemical elements** with similar properties and consecutive **atomic numbers.** *Also,* another name for **menstruation.**

periodic (*pir*-ee-**ahd**-ik)
Describes something that happens again and again at regular intervals. A full moon is periodic; it appears every 29½ days. *Also,* a term used to explain the **chemical** properties of a related family of **elements.**

Penumbra

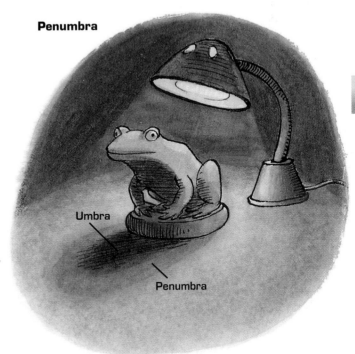

Umbra

Penumbra

periodic table
(*pir*-ee-**ahd**-ik **tay**-buhl)
A chart showing the 103 **chemical elements** arranged according to their **atomic numbers.** In the periodic table, the

Periodic Table

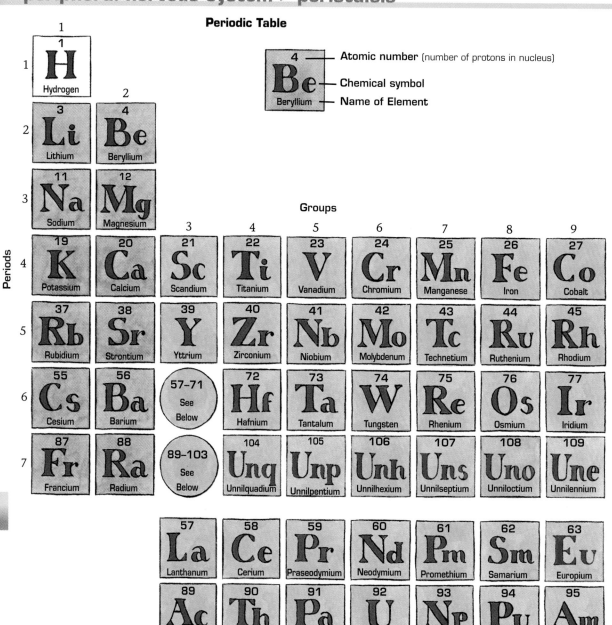

Atomic number (number of protons in nucleus)

Chemical symbol

Name of Element

elements going across, called *periods,* and the elements going up and down, called *groups,* are related. **Dimitry Mendeleyev** produced the first periodic table in 1869.

peripheral nervous system
(puh-**rif**-uh-ruhl **nuhr**-vuhs *sis*-tuhm)
The **network** of **nerves** going out from the **central nervous system** to all parts of the body.

periscope (**per**-uh-*skohp*)
An instrument that allows people to see things that are out of their field of **vision.** A simple periscope is a long tube with angled mirrors at both ends. From the Greek *peri,* meaning "around," and -*skopion,* meaning "means of seeing."

peristalsis (*per*-uh-**stawl**-sis)
Wavelike movement in the walls of the stomach and **intestine** that force the food forward. From the Greek *peri,* meaning "around," and *stellein,* meaning "to place or wrap."

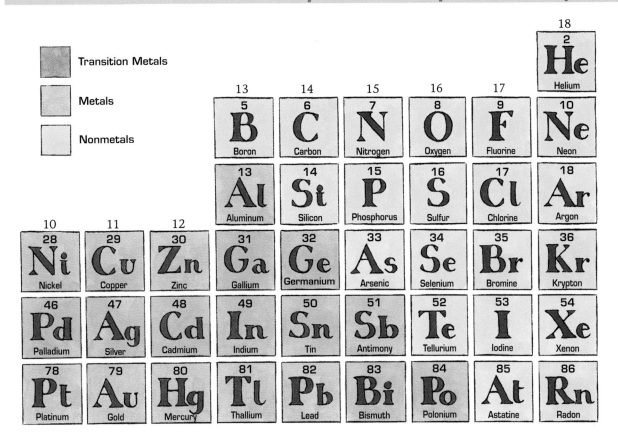

Transition Metals

Metals

Nonmetals

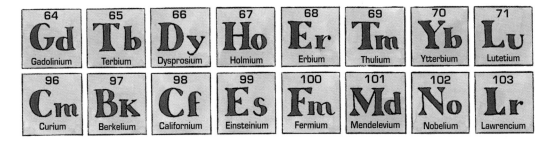

permafrost (**puhr**-muh-*frawst*)
Ground that is always frozen. Permafrost is usually found between 50° and 90° north and south **latitude.**

permeable membrane
(**puhr**-mee-uh-buhl **mem**-brayn)
A thin layer of **tissue** that allows certain substances to pass through.

Permian period
(**puhr**-mee-uhn **pir**-ee-uhd)
The period of **geological history** from

290 to 245 million years ago. During the Permian period the first plants to grow from seeds appeared.

perpetual motion machine
(pur-**pech**-oo-uhl **moh**-shuhn muh-*sheen*)
Any device that continues to move without any added **energy.**

personal computer
(**puhr**-suhn-l kuhm-**pyoo**-tuhr)
A small computer used by one person at a time. It fits on a desk or can be held on a

lap. Personal computer is often shortened to **PC**. Also called *microcomputer*.

perspiration (*puhr*-spuh-**ray**-shuhn)
Water and **salts** given off by **glands** in the skin. Perspiration helps to cool the body. Also called *sweat*. From the Latin *per*, meaning "through," and *spirare*, meaning "to breathe."

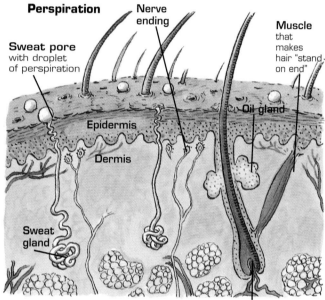

Perspiration

Sweat pore
with droplet
of perspiration

Nerve
ending

Muscle
that
makes
hair "stand
on end"

Oil gland

Epidermis

Dermis

Sweat
gland

Hair follicle

pertussis (pur-**tuhs**-is)
The medical name for **whooping cough**.

pesticide (**pes**-tuh-*side*)
A **chemical** used to kill or control pests. Pesticide is used to get rid of everything from insects and rats to weeds.

petal (**pet**-l)
The colored part of most flowers. The petal attracts the insects and birds that help to spread the flower's **pollen**.

petri dish (**pee**-tree *dish*)
A round, flat, shallow, covered glass or plastic dish used to grow and study **bacteria** and other **microorganisms**.

petrify (**pe**-truh-*fie*)
To turn into stone. Over many years, fallen trees and dead animals may petrify. Parts of their bodies are replaced by **minerals** that in time form stone

copies of the plant or animal part. From the Greek *petra,* meaning "stone," and the Latin *facere,* meaning "to make."

petrochemical (*pe*-troh-**kem**-i-kuhl)
A **chemical** made from **petroleum** or natural gas. Petrochemicals are used to produce **plastics, drugs, fibers, fertilizers**, and much more.

petroleum (puh-**troh**-lee-uhm)
A substance found under the ground that is formed from living things buried millions of years ago. **Decay, heat,** and **pressure** slowly changed these living things into petroleum. From the Greek *petra,* meaning "stone," and the Latin *oleum,* meaning "oil."

pH (**pee-aych**)
A measure of the strength of an **acid**, which is the concentration of **hydrogen ions** in a **solution**. On the pH scale of 1 to 14, water, which is **neutral**, has a pH of 7. **Acids** have a pH below 7; **bases** have a pH over 7. The *p* in pH is from the German *Potenz,* meaning "power," and *H* is the symbol of hydrogen.

phagocyte (**fag**-uh-*site*)
A type of **white blood cell** that surrounds and digests **bacteria** and other harmful substances in the body. From the Greek *phagein,* meaning "to eat," and the Latin *-kyta,* meaning "cell."

pharmacology
(*fahr*-muh-**kahl**-uh-jee)
The science of **drugs**, including their preparation, uses, and effects on living things. A *pharmacologist* is skilled in **researching**, improving, and finding drugs. A *pharmacist* or *druggist* prepares and distributes medicines.

pharynx (**far**-ingks)
A tube at the back of the nose and mouth. The pharynx lets air pass into the **trachea** and food pass into the **esophagus**.

phase (**fayz**)
A stage in the development of a living

Phase

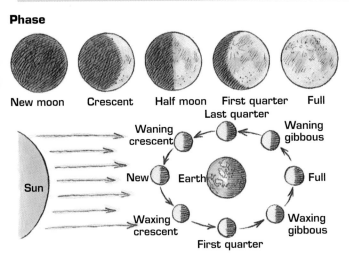

New moon Crescent Half moon First quarter Full

thing. A tadpole is one phase in the life of a frog. *Also,* a change in the apparent shape of the **moon.** A half-moon is a phase of the moon. *Also,* the size of a **wave.** When the crests of two waves move together they are said to be "in phase." *Also,* a state of **matter,** such as a "solid phase."

pheromone (**fer**-uh-*mohn*)
An odor-causing **chemical** released by certain animals to communicate with other animals of the same **species,** to ward off animals of other species, and to establish territories.

phloem (**floh**-em)
The **tissue** in plants through which food materials pass downward from the leaves to the stems and roots.

phobia (**foh**-bee-uh)
An abnormal or unreasonable fear. Phobias include fear of heights (*acrophobia*), fear of small places (*claustrophobia*), and fear of open spaces (*agoraphobia*).

phosphate (**fahs**-fayt)
A **compound** that contains **phosphorus** and **oxygen.** Phosphates are necessary for the growth of animals and plants and are widely used in **fertilizers.**

phosphor (**fahs**-for)
Any material that gives off light when exposed to light, **X rays, ultraviolet rays,** or certain other forms of **energy.** Phosphors cover the insides of computer

screens, television picture tubes, and **fluorescent** light tubes.

phosphorescence (*fahs*-fuh-**res**-uhns)
The giving off of light by a substance even after the **energy** that caused it to glow is removed. A watch dial that glows in the dark is an example of phosphorescence.

phosphorus (**fahs**-fuh-ruhs)
A solid, nonmetallic **element** found in the **cells** of nearly every living thing. Plants get phosphorus from the soil. People and animals get it from eating plants and some other foods. (Symbol—P)

photoelectric cell
(*foh*-toh-i-**lek**-trik **sel**)
A device that produces an **electric current** when exposed to light or some other forms of **radiation.** Photoelectric cells can open doors as you approach, automatically adjust camera **lenses,** and provide power for **satellites** in space. Also called **electric eye,** *photocell,* or **photovoltaic cell.**

photography (fuh-**tahg**-ruh-fee)
The process of recording an **image** on film using **light** and a **camera.** From the Greek *phos,* meaning "light," and *graphein,* meaning "to write."

photon (**foh**-tahn)
A **particle** of **electromagnetic radiation.** A photon has **energy** and behaves like a **wave.** But a photon has neither **mass** nor **electric charge.** Streams of photons make up **light rays, X rays,** and **radio waves.**

photosphere (**foh**-tuh-*sfir*)
The visible surface of the sun or another star. From the Greek *phos,* meaning "light," and *sphaira,* meaning "ball."

photosynthesis (*foh*-tuh-**sin**-thuh-sis)
The process by which **plant cells** use **energy** from the sun to combine **carbon dioxide,** water, and **minerals** to make food for plant growth. Photosynthesis releases

P

141

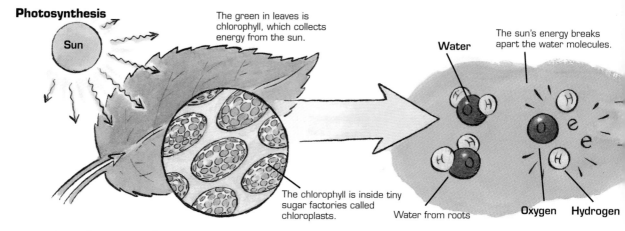

Photosynthesis

Sun

The green in leaves is chlorophyll, which collects energy from the sun.

Water

The sun's energy breaks apart the water molecules.

The chlorophyll is inside tiny sugar factories called chloroplasts.

Water from roots

Oxygen   Hydrogen

oxygen into the **atmosphere.** From the Greek *phos,* meaning "light," and *synthesis,* meaning "combination of parts into a whole."

phototropism
(foh-**tah**-truh-*piz*-uhm)
The tendency of plants to turn toward or away from **light.** From the Greek *phos,* meaning "light," and *tropos,* meaning "turn."

photovoltaic cell
(*foh*-toh-vahl-**tay**-ik **sel**)
A device usually made of **silicon** that gives off electricity when light hits the surface. Photovoltaic cells power everything from **satellites** to calculators. Also called a *solar battery* or **solar cell.**

phylum (**fie**-luhm)
A very large group of plants or animals in the **classification** plan. The phylum *Mollusca* of the animal kingdom includes clams, oysters, snails, and octopuses.

physical change (**fiz**-i-kuhl **chaynj**)
A change of **matter** from one form to another without becoming a new substance. When liquid water freezes it goes through a physical change and becomes solid ice, but it keeps the same **chemical formula** (H_2O). Physical changes can usually be reversed.

physical therapy
(**fiz**-i-kuhl **ther**-uh-pee)
The diagnosis and treatment of physical disabilities caused by various diseases and injuries. Physical therapists use exercise, **heat,** and cold to treat people.

physics (**fiz**-iks)
The science concerned with the interaction of **matter** and **energy.** The subjects of physics include **sound, heat, light, nuclear energy, force, power, motion,** the structure of the **atom, electricity, magnetism,** and so on.

physiology (*fiz*-ee-**ahl**-uh-jee)
The study of the life processes in living things. Physiology examines the purpose, function, and structure of all parts of different **organisms.** From the Greek *physis,* meaning "growth," and *-logia,* meaning "science of."

phytoplankton (*fie*-tuh-**plangk**-tuhn)
Tiny, one-**celled,** plantlike living things that often drift near the surface of oceans and are eaten by larger sea creatures.

piezoelectricity
(pee-*ay*-zoh-i-*lek*-**tris**-uh-tee)
Electric energy that is produced when certain **crystals,** such as **quartz,** are stretched, squeezed, or made to vibrate. Piezoelectricity also works in the opposite way: When electric energy is applied to these crystals, they are set into **vibration.**

pigment (**pig**-muhnt)
Natural or **synthetic** coloring matter. You have natural pigments in your skin and eyes. Most paint and printing inks use synthetic pigments. From the Latin *pigmentum,* meaning "paint."

P

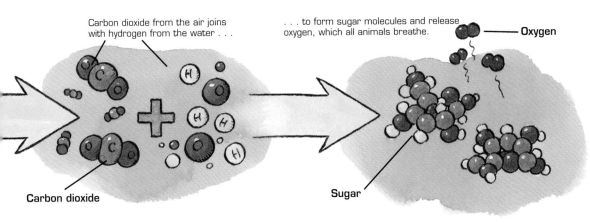

Carbon dioxide from the air joins with hydrogen from the water . . .

. . . to form sugar molecules and release oxygen, which all animals breathe.

Oxygen

Carbon dioxide

Sugar

pilot plant (**pie**-luht *plant*)
A small factory set up by scientists or engineers to solve any problems before starting full-scale production.

pimple (**pim**-puhl)
A small, inflamed swelling on the skin. Pimples are often caused by **bacteria** getting into a **pore** or a hair opening.

pint (**pinte**)
A US pint is a unit of liquid **volume** equal to 16 fluid ounces, half a **quart**, or 0.473 liters. A British pint is bigger. It equals 0.568 liters.

pipette (pie-**pet**)
A thin glass or plastic tube used in laboratories to measure or move small amounts of liquids.

pistil (**pis**-tuhl)
The part of a **flower** that produces seeds. The pistil usually contains an **ovary**, **style**, and **stigma.**

piston (**pis**-tuhn)
A round disk or closed cylinder that is moved back and forth inside a slightly larger cylinder by some force, such as **steam pressure.** The up-and-down movement of the pistons in a car **engine** turns the crankshaft, which makes the car's wheels turn.

pitch (**pich**)
The highness or lowness of a sound. Pitch depends on the **frequency** of

vibration of the **sound waves.** *Also,* the rise or fall of the nose of an airplane or the bow of a ship. *Also,* a black, sticky substance made from **coal** that is used on roads and roofs.

pitchblende (**pich**-*blend*)
A highly **radioactive** black **mineral ore.** Pitchblende contains **uranium**, which is used to produce **nuclear energy.** The scientific name for pitchblende is *uraninite.*

pith (**pith**)
The thin-walled food-storage **cells** found in the stems of some plants.

pituitary gland
(puh-**too**-uh-*ter*-ee *gland*)
A small **organ** found below the brain. The pituitary **gland** secretes **hormones** that control growth and other glands in the body. It is an important part of the **endocrine system.**

pixel (**pik**-suhl)
Short for *picture* element. A pixel is one of the tiny dots that make up the **image** on a television or computer screen.

placebo (pluh-**see**-boh)
A substance that looks like **medicine** but contains no active ingredients. Doctors doing medical experiments compare the effects of the placebo with the effects of the **drug** they are testing to see how well the drug really works.

placenta (pluh-**sen**-tuh)
An **organ** in most **pregnant** female **mammals** that brings food and **oxygen**

P

to the developing offspring and carries away its waste products. When the offspring is born, the placenta is expelled and is known as the *afterbirth. Also,* the part of the **ovary** in flowering **plants** that has the **ovules** attached.

placer (**plas**-uhr)
A deposit of **sand** or gravel that contains **gold** or other valuable **minerals.** Placers form when **rocks** containing gold, for example, crumble and wash into a riverbed or onto an **ocean** beach. The gold rush of 1849 followed the discovery of rich placer deposits in California.

plague (**playg**)
A very serious **disease** that spreads easily and can kill millions. Plague is mostly caused by the bite of a flea. The *bubonic* plague struck Europe in the 14th century and left 25 million dead.

plain (**playn**)
A large, flat area of land. *Also,* an area of the ocean bottom that is mostly flat.

Planck (**plahngk**), Max (1858–1947)
A German physicist who stated the **quantum theory.** Planck's theory holds that **energy** exists in tiny bits called quanta (plural of quantum). See also **quantum, quantum mechanics,** and **quantum theory.**

planet (**plan**-it)
A large body that travels in **orbit** around a star. A planet is usually smaller than a **star** and does not give off heat and light. From the Greek *planes,* meaning "wanderer," since when viewed from Earth, planets move among the stars.

planetarium (*plan*-uh-**ter**-ee-uhm)
A dome-covered building that shows the movements of the stars, planets, and other heavenly bodies by projecting lights onto the inside of the dome. *Also,* the device that projects the lights.

planetoid (**plan**-uh-*toid*)
A heavenly body that is smaller than a planet. Also called an **asteroid.**

plankton (**plangk**-tuhn)
Tiny living things that float or drift in ocean water. Plankton is food for many sea animals, including the giant blue whale. See also **phytoplankton** and **zooplankton.**

Plankton

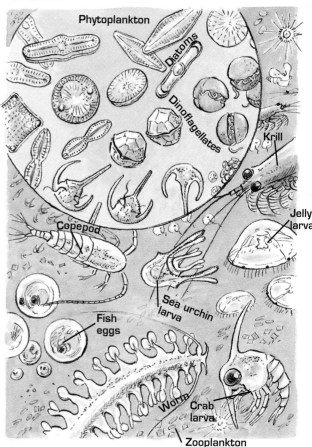

plant (**plant**)
A member of the plant **kingdom,** one of the five kingdoms of living things. A plant has many **cells** and thick cell walls, gets **energy** from the sun, needs water, and gets **minerals** from the soil. Plants supply us with food, products such as lumber, and many drugs.

plaque (**plak**)
A thin, sticky film of **bacteria** that forms on teeth. Plaque can cause tooth decay

P

or can build up into a hard substance called *calculus* or *tartar. Also,* a deposit of fatty material inside an **artery.**

plasma (**plaz**-muh)

The clear, liquid part of blood. Plasma contains various **proteins, salts,** digested foods, wastes, and other substances. *Also,* a form of **matter** made up of electrically charged atomic **particles.** Plasma is usually a **gas** and can be found in the sun, stars, lightning, and glowing **neon** signs.

plastic (**plas**-tik)

A **synthetic** material, mostly made from **petroleum,** that can be formed into any shape from a long thread to a solid object. Plastics, which are **polymers,** include **nylon, polyester,** and **acrylic.** *Also,* the nature of a material, such as clay, that can be shaped or molded.

plastic explosive
(**plas**-tik ik-**sploh**-siv)

A powerful **explosive** that looks and feels like clay. Plastic explosives can be formed into any shape.

plate (**playt**)

One of about 30 giant blocks that make up the surface of Earth. Each plate is between 30 and 150 miles (48 and 240 kilometers) thick. It floats on the molten rock of the earth's **mantle.** See also **plate tectonics.** *Also,* to cover one metal, such as **brass,** with a thin layer of another metal, such as silver. *Also,* a flat, stiff sheet used to take photographs.

plateau (pla-**toh**)

A large, flat land area at a high level. *Also,* a high, flat surface under an ocean.

platelet (**playt**-lit)

A tiny, flat body in the blood of **mammals** that helps to stop bleeding if a blood vessel is cut. A platelet is also called a *thrombocyte.*

plate tectonics (**playt** tek-**tahn**-iks)

The widely accepted **theory** that Earth's **crust** is made up of about 30 huge **plates** that are always very slowly moving. Plate tectonics explains most earthquakes, volcanoes, and mountain formation. According to plate tectonics, all the **continents** were once part of a supercontinent called **Pangaea.** About 200 million years ago, Pangaea began to split apart into smaller continents. Since then, these continents have moved to their present positions. From the Old

Plate tectonics

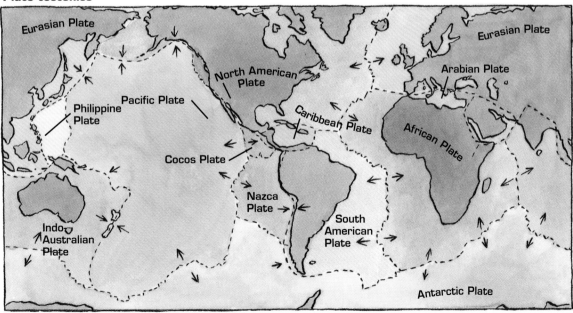

Eurasian Plate
Eurasian Plate
North American Plate
Arabian Plate
Pacific Plate
Philippine Plate
Caribbean Plate
African Plate
Cocos Plate
Nazca Plate
South American Plate
Indo Australian Plate
Antarctic Plate

French *plat,* meaning "flat," and *tekton,* meaning "builder."

platinum (**plat**-n-uhm)
A very heavy, silver-white metal **element** that is more valuable than gold. Platinum does not tarnish or melt easily. (Symbol—Pt)

Pleistocene epoch
(**plise**-tuh-*seen* **ep**-uhk)
The period in **geological history** from 1.6 million to 10,000 years ago. The Pleistocene epoch included the most recent **ice age** and the early development of humans. From the Greek *pleistos,* meaning "most," *kainos,* meaning "recent," and *epoche,* meaning "fixed point."

Pliocene epoch (**plie**-uh-*seen* **ep**-uhk)
The period in **geological history** from 5 to 1.6 million years ago. The first humans and the modern forms of many animals appeared during the Pliocene epoch.

plumage (**ploo**-mij)
A bird's feathers. The plumage of the peacock is especially beautiful.

plumule (**ploo**-myool)
A small, soft feather that grows close to a bird's skin. Plumules are also called *down. Also,* the part of a plant **embryo** from which the stem grows. From the Latin *plumula,* meaning "small feather."

Pluto (**ploo**-toh)
The ninth planet from the sun in the **solar system**—except when it crosses Neptune's **orbit** and becomes eighth. Pluto was found in 1930 by the American astronomer **Clyde Tombaugh** (1906–1997). Its one moon, Charon, was discovered in 1978. While the other outer planets are made of gas, Pluto is probably made of rock and ice. Because of its **orbit,** some scientists think Pluto was captured by the sun's **gravity** after the solar system was formed.

Distance from sun—3,666,200,000 miles (5,900,100,000 kilometers)
Length of year—248 Earth years
Length of day—6 Earth days
Diameter at equator—1,420 miles (2,284 kilometers).

plutonium (ploo-**toh**-nee-uhm)
A highly **radioactive** metal **element** widely used in **nuclear reactors** and nuclear bombs. (Symbol—Pu)

pneumatic (noo-**mat**-ik)
Having to do with air or other gases. A pneumatic drill or car lift, for example, is powered by squeezed, or **compressed,** air.

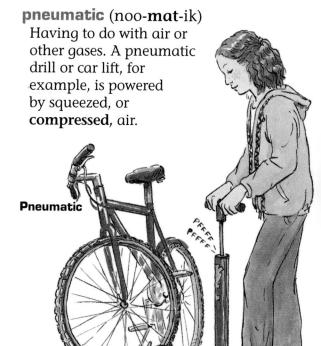

Pneumatic

pod (**pahd**)
A shell or case that holds the seeds of such plants as peas and beans. *Also,* a group of whales or seals. *Also,* a removable section of a **spacecraft.**

poison (**poi**-zuhn)
Any substance that can harm or kill a living being by being swallowed, touched, or breathed. From the Latin *potio,* meaning "drink."

polar (**poh**-luhr)
Having to do with the North or South poles of Earth. *Also,* having to do with the poles of a magnet or battery.

polar bond (**poh**-luhr **bahnd**)
See **ionic bond.**

Polaris (puh-**lar**-is)
See **North Star.**

polarized light (**poh**-luh-*rized* **lite**)
Light waves that **vibrate** in only one direction. Polarized light waves are unlike ordinary light waves, which vibrate in all directions. Some *sunglasses* and camera **lenses** polarize light to cut down glare.

pole (**pohl**)
Either the North Pole or the South Pole. The poles are the ends of the **axis** around which Earth and other heavenly bodies **rotate** or spin. *Also,* either end of a **magnet,** or either terminal of a **battery.**

pollen (**pahl**-uhn)
Tiny grains produced in the **stamen,** or male, part of flowering and cone-bearing plants. When pollen is transferred to a plant **stigma,** which is the female part, new seeds start to grow.

pollination (*pahl*-uh-**nay**-shuhn)
The transfer of **pollen** from the **stamen** or male organ of flowering and cone-bearing **plants** to the **stigma** or female organ of a flower or cone. *Cross*-pollination occurs when birds, insects, or wind carries the pollen from one plant to a different plant. *Artificial cross-pollination* occurs when people transfer pollen from one plant to another. *Self-pollination* occurs when the transfer of pollen takes place within the same plant.

pollute (puh-**loot**)
To spoil or dirty the **environment** with wastes and other materials, such as smoke, gases, **chemicals, fertilizers,** and **pesticides.**

pollution (puh-**loo**-shuhn)
The result of **polluting** the land, air, or water. Pollution makes conditions around us dirty, ugly, noisy, or unhealthy. It leads to a rise in disease and death and to the destruction of forests, farm crops, and buildings, among other harmful effects.

polyester (*pahl*-ee-**es**-tuhr)
A **synthetic** substance made from **chemicals** found mainly in **petroleum.** Polyester is used to make **fibers,** films, tapes, and plastics of all kinds.

polymer (**pahl**-uh-muhr)
A large **molecule** made by linking smaller molecules, called **monomers,** into a long chain. **Natural** polymers include wood, **starch,** and rubber. **Nylon, polyester,** and other plastics are **synthetic,** or factory-made, polymers.

polymorphism (*pahl*-ee-**mor**-*fiz*-uhm)
The appearance of three or more different types of adults within a single **species.** Honeybees, for example, have distinctive queens, workers, and drones. From the Greek *poly-,* meaning "many," and *morphe,* meaning "form."

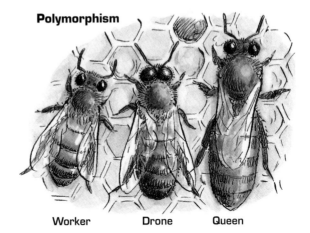
Polymorphism
Worker   Drone   Queen

polyp (**pahl**-ip)
One stage in the life of a small, soft-bodied water animal with a body shaped like a tube. A polyp, such as **coral,** attaches one end to the sea bottom and uses its other end to gather food. *Also,* a small growth on the inside of the nose, mouth, or other part of the body. From the Greek *poly-,* meaning "many," and *pous,* meaning "foot."

polyunsaturated fat
(*pahl*-ee-uhn-**sach**-uh-*ray*-tid **fat**)
Fat that is liquid at room temperature,

with many of the **carbon atoms** linked to only one **hydrogen** atom. Polyunsaturated fat is healthier for your heart than **saturated** fat.

population (*pahp*-yuh-**lay**-shuhn)
The total number of people or **organisms** in one place or group. From the Latin *populus,* meaning "the people."

pore (**por**)
A tiny opening in the skin through which sweat or oil can come out. *Also,* a space between grains in rock or soil. From the Greek *poros,* meaning "opening."

porous (**por**-uhs)
Full of **pores** or tiny holes that liquids and gases can pass through. Most cloth is porous.

positive (**pahz**-uh-tiv)
A number or quantity greater than zero. *Also,* a **pole** in a battery or **electrical** device toward which **electrons** flow. *Also,* the electric **charge** on a substance that has fewer electrons than normal. From the Latin *positivus,* meaning "formally set or established."

positron (**pahz**-uh-*trahn*)
A **subatomic particle** with the same **mass** as an **electron,** but with a **positive,** instead of **negative,** electric **charge.** Certain **radioactive** substances give off positrons. Positron is short for *positive* elec*tron.*

potassium (puh-**tas**-ee-uhm)
A soft, light, silvery, metallic **element** that combines easily with other elements. All living things need potassium. It is widely used in **fertilizers.** (Symbol—K)

potential (puh-**ten**-chuhl)
The amount of **work** necessary to move an electric **charge** from one point to another in an **electric current.** Potential is usually measured in **volts.**

potential energy
(puh-**ten**-chuhl **en**-uhr-jee)
The **energy** that is available when an

object is raised, stretched, or squeezed. Potential energy can be found in a rock on top of a mountain, a stretched rubber band, or a squeezed spring, for example. *Also,* any form of stored energy. For example, wood has **chemical** potential energy before it is burned.

Potential energy
Maximum potential energy in the squeezed spring

No potential energy— spring has returned to original shape

pound (**pound**)
A unit of **mass** equal to 16 ounces (0.454 kilograms). Pound is abbreviated *lb,* from the Latin word *libra,* which means "pound."

power (**pou**-uhr)
The rate of doing **work.** It equals work needed to do a task divided by the time it takes. It is measured in **watts** or **foot-pounds** *per second.*

prairie (**prer**-ee)
A large area of flat or hilly land, usually covered with tall grasses and many flowering plants. Prairies are hot in the summer and cold in the winter. Much of the American Midwest was prairie but is now farmland.

precipitation (pri-*sip*-uh-**tay**-shuhn)
The **rain, snow, sleet,** and **hail** that fall on Earth. *Also,* the separation of a solid from a **solution.** The precipitation reaction of soap in hard water produces a white scum or foam in the water. From the Latin *praecipitare,* meaning "to throw down or fall down."

predator (**pred**-uh-tuhr)
An animal that hunts and eats other animals. Lions, sharks, and eagles are examples of predators. From the Latin *praedator,* meaning "robber."

pregnant (**preg**-nuhnt)
Carrying a developing **embryo** or **fetus** inside the body. A woman is pregnant for about 9 months before she gives birth. From the Latin *prae,* meaning "before," and *gnasci,* meaning "be born."

prehistoric (*pree*-his-**tor**-ik)
Anything that dates back to a time before recorded history. Prehistoric usually means more than 5,000 years ago.

prenatal (pree-**nayt**-l)
Before birth. Good prenatal care of the **pregnant** woman is important for the future health of the baby.

pressure (**presh**-uhr)
The force acting over a given area of a surface. Pressure is equal to the strength of the force divided by the area. It is measured in **pounds** per square inch or *pascals.*

prevailing wind (pri-**vay**-ling **wind**)
A wind that usually blows in the same direction. The prevailing wind in North America blows from west to east.

prey (**pray**)
An animal that is hunted or eaten by other animals. Mice are the prey of cats.

Priestley (**preest**-lee), **Joseph** (1733–1804)
An English **chemist** and clergyman who was one of the discoverers of **oxygen.** Priestley later identified **nitrous oxide** (laughing gas) and **sulfur** dioxide.

primary color (**prie**-mer-ee **kuhl**-uhr)
A color that cannot be made by mixing colors. The primary colors of paint, ink, and dye are red, yellow, and blue. The primary colors of light beams are red, green, and blue.

primate (**prie**-mayt)
Any of the order of **mammals** that includes humans, apes, and monkeys. Primates usually live in groups, have large brains, can grasp with hands and feet, and have eyes that look forward. From the Latin *primus,* meaning "first."

prime meridian (**prime** muh-**rid**-ee-uhn)
The imaginary north-south line that passes through Greenwich, England. The prime meridian is known as 0° **longitude.**

printer (**prin**-tuhr)
A device attached to a computer that produces **text** or **graphics** on paper. Printer **output** is called hard copy.

prism (**priz**-uhm)
A **transparent** solid of glass, plastic, or **quartz** that can bend or reflect light. The prism separates light into the colors of the rainbow. A prism has two parallel bases and three or more sides.

probability (*prahb*-uh-**bil**-uh-tee)
The chance that something will happen. The probability that the sun will rise tomorrow morning is very high.

Primary color

Paint

BLUE YELLO RED

Light beams

probe (**prohb**)

An unmanned **spacecraft** sent to explore, photograph, or measure bodies in space. *Also,* an instrument used to gather information from inside the human body or other hard-to-reach places. *Also,* to search or examine.

processing (**prahs**-es-ing)

The calculations and handling of **data** by a computer. From the Latin *procedere,* meaning "to go ahead or proceed."

producer (pruh-**doo**-suhr)

See **food chain.**

program (**proh**-gram)

The set of instructions that a computer follows to solve a problem or accomplish a given task.

projectile (pruh-**jek**-tuhl)

An object, such as a baseball or bullet, that can be thrown or shot into the air. From the Latin *pro,* meaning "forward," and *jacere,* meaning "to throw."

prominence (**prahm**-uh-nuhns)

A bright arch of *gas* that rises above the sun's surface. A typical prominence is 20,000 miles (32,000 kilometers) high and 120,000 miles (190,00 kilometers) long. Some prominences stay the same for months; others change after a few hours.

prompt (**prahmpt**)

A computer message that tells the user what to do next in order to complete a task.

propagate (**prahp**-uh-*gayt*)

To **reproduce** and have offspring. Animals propagate by eggs; many plants propagate by seeds. *Also,* to send some form of **energy** through a gas, liquid, or solid.

propane (**proh**-payn)

A colorless *gas* found in natural gas and **petroleum** that becomes liquid under **pressure** and burns easily. (Formula— C_3H_8)

propellant (pruh-**pel**-uhnt)

Something that drives an object forward. The propellant that speeds a bullet out of a gun is **gunpowder.**

propeller (pruh-**pel**-uhr)

Two or more blades on a shaft that spin around at high speed. Propellers move ships through water and airplanes through the air. From the Latin *pro,* meaning "forward," and *pellere,* meaning "to drive."

Propeller
A propeller moves because:

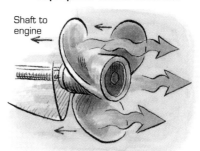

Shaft to engine

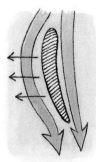

1 The blades shove water back behind the propeller, which pushes the propeller forward.

2 In cross section, each blade is an airfoil. Lower pressure in front sucks the blade forward.

The principle is the same in water and in air.

prophylaxis (*proh*-fuh-**lak**-sis)

Any medicine, treatment, or device that protects against disease. Brushing your teeth daily is a prophylaxis to prevent tooth decay. From the Greek *pro,* meaning "before," and *phylassein,* meaning "to guard."

prosthetics (prahs-**thet**-iks)

The branch of medicine that is concerned with artificial limbs and other body parts that are designed to replace those missing through accident, disease, or birth defect. The artificial part is called a *prosthesis.*

protease inhibitor
(**proh**-tee-*ays* in-*hib*-uh-tuhr)
A drug used to treat **AIDS**. The protease inhibitor slows down the **reproduction** of **HIV**, the **virus** that causes the disease.

protein (**proh**-teen)
A substance necessary for life that is found in all living **cells**. Every protein **molecule** contains **carbon**, **hydrogen**, **nitrogen**, and **oxygen**. Foods high in protein are cheese, eggs, meat, milk, and beans. From the Greek *protos,* meaning "first."

protist (**proh**-tist)
Any member of the *Protista* **kingdom** in the **classification system**. A protist is a tiny, one-celled **organism** with a **nucleus**. Protists include **diatoms**, **protozoa**, and blue-green **algae**. See also **classification**.

proton (**proh**-tahn)
A tiny **subatomic particle** with a **positive** electric **charge**. An **atom** usually has the same number of protons in its **nucleus** as it has **electrons** outside its nucleus. See also **atomic number**.

protoplasm (**proh**-tuh-*plaz*-uhm)
The jellylike living matter of most plant and animal **cells**. Protoplasm includes both the **cytoplasm** and the **nucleus** of the cells. It is a mixture of **proteins** and other substances.

protozoan (*proh*-tuh-**zoh**-uhn)
A tiny **organism** with only a single **cell**. Protozoa are classified as **protists**. The **amoeba** is a well-known protozoan.

psychoanalysis
(*sie*-koh-uh-**nal**-uh-sis)
A method of treating some mental illnesses devised around 1900 by **Sigmund Freud**. Psychoanalysis helps patients become aware of **unconscious** fears, desires, and childhood experiences that might have caused their illness. A person trained to use psychoanalysis

in treating some forms of mental illness is called a *psychoanalyst.*

psychology (sie-**kahl**-uh-jee)
The science of the human mind. Psychology tries to explain why people act, think, and feel as they do.

pterosaur (ter-uh-*sor*)
A member of an **extinct** group of flying **reptiles** that had large, batlike wings. Pterosaurs lived from about 210 to 65 million years ago. From the Greek *pteron,* meaning "wing," and *sauros,* meaning "lizard."

Ptolemy (**tahl**-uh-mee) (323–32 B.C.)
A Greek astronomer and geographer who believed that the stars and planets move around Earth. His ideas were accepted until well after 1543, when **Copernicus** proposed that the sun, not the earth, was the center of the **solar system**.

puberty (**pyoo**-buhr-tee)
The time of rapid physical growth, when boys and girls become sexually mature and develop into men and women. Puberty comes at about age 10–12 years in girls and about 12–14 years in boys. From the Latin *pubes,* meaning "adult."

pulley (**pul**-ee)
A wheel with a rope, chain, or belt passed

Pulley

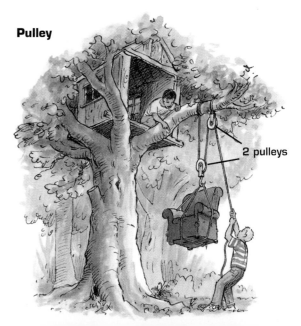

2 pulleys

over it. A load is attached to one end of the rope and the other end is pulled. A single pulley lets you change the direction of the pull. A set of pulleys makes it possible to lift heavy loads with less effort.

pulmonary (**pul**-muh-*ner*-ee)
Having to do with the **lungs**. Pulmonary disease in humans often results from smoking cigarettes.

pulsar (**puhl**-sahr)
Short for *pulsating radio star*. A pulsar is a rapidly spinning object in space that sends out regular bursts of **radio waves**. The narrow beam of **radiation** sweeps very quickly over Earth, like the beam from a lighthouse. English astronomers discovered pulsars in 1967.

pulse (**puhls**)
The regular beating of the **arteries** caused by surges of blood from the heart. *Also,* a short burst of **energy**, such as a pulse of electricity. From the Latin *pulsus,* meaning "beating."

pump (**puhmp**)
A machine to move or compress liquids or gases. Pumps are used for everything from bringing water up from a well to forcing air into a bicycle tire.

pupa (**pyoo**-puh)
A stage between **larva** and adult in the life cycle of most insects. A pupa usually forms a **cocoon** around itself and does not eat or move until it has changed into an adult. Plural is pupae. From the Latin *pupa,* meaning "doll."

pupil (**pyoo**-puhl)
The black, round opening in the center of the **eye**. The pupil is the place where light enters the eye. See also **eye**.

purify (**pyur**-uh-*fie*)
To make pure by getting rid of all unwanted substances. You can purify water by passing it through a **filter**.

pus (**puhs**)
A yellow-white substance produced by the body when it fights **infection**. Pus contains **white blood cells**, dead and live **bacteria**, and **blood plasma**.

pustule (**puhs**-chool)
A pimple containing **pus**.

putrefy (**pyoo**-truh-*fie*)
To rot or decay. An old apple will putrefy as it is attacked by **bacteria** and **molds**.

P-wave (**pee** *wayv*)
Short for *Primary wave*. A wave of **energy** produced by an earthquake. The P-wave pushes and pulls on the rock in the ground. A P-wave is fast-moving. See also **S wave**.

Pupa   **Stag Beetle** and pupa

Swallowtail butterfly and pupa

Adult honeybee

Honeybee pupae in their cells

quadruped (**kwahd**-ruh-*ped*)
An animal that has four feet, such as a cow or dog. From the Latin *quadri-,* meaning "four," and *pes,* meaning "foot."

quantum (**kwahn**-tuhm)
A very small, fixed amount of **energy.** The quantum of **electromagnetic** energy is the **photon.** The plural of quantum is *quanta.* From the Latin *quantum,* meaning "how much."

quantum mechanics
(**kwahn**-tuhm muh-**kan**-iks)
The branch of **physics** that shows that **electrons** only move in **orbits** at fixed levels around the **nucleus.** When an electron gains a quantum of **energy,** it jumps a level. When it falls back a level, it gives off a quantum of light energy.

quantum theory
(**kwahn**-tuhm
thee-uh-ree)
The idea that **atoms** or **molecules** gain or lose **energy** in steps. The amount of energy gained or lost at each step is a **quantum.** Quantum theory explains the **uncertainty principle** and the fact that **electromagnetic radiation** acts as both **waves** and **particles.**

Quantum Theory

Energy

Light

When energy is added to an atom, an electron may jump from its shell to a higher shell. When it falls back to its home shell, it releases energy in the form of a flash of light.

quark (**kwork** or **kwahrk**)
A very tiny **particle** believed to be the building block of **protons, neutrons,** and some other **subatomic particles.** There are 6 known quarks; they are called *up* and *down, strange* and *charm, truth* and *beauty.*

quarry (**kwor**-ee or **kwahr**-ee)
A large pit for digging blocks of stone out of the earth. Quarries contain large **deposits** of **marble, slate, granite,** or **limestone.** *Also,* an animal hunted by other animals.

quart (**kwort**)
A unit of liquid **volume** equal to 2 **pints,** 1/4 **gallon,** or 57.8 cubic inches (0.95 liters). *Also,* a unit of dry capacity equal to 1/32 bushel or 67.2 cubic inches (1.1 liters).

quartz (**kworts**)
A hard **mineral** found in many kinds of rock. Quartz is widely used in **radar,** radio, television, and many watches and clocks because of its **piezoelectric** qualities. Pure quartz is colorless and **transparent.** But other kinds of quartz are colored gemstones such as *amethyst* or *citrine.* (Formula—SiO_2)

quasar (**kway**-zahr)
Short for *quasi-*stel*lar* object. A quasar is an extremely bright, starlike object at a very great distance from Earth. Quasars give off immense amounts of **electromagnetic radiation.**

Quaternary period
(kwah-**tuhr**-nuhr-ee **pir**-ee-uhd)
The period of **geological history** from 1.6 million years ago to the present. During the Quaternary period human beings spread over the entire earth and made huge advances in **technology** and culture.

queen (**kween**)
The egg-laying female in a colony of insects such as ants or bees. Most colonies have only one queen.

quicklime (**kwik**-lime)
See **lime.**

quicksand (**kwik**-sand)
Very deep, fine, water-soaked sand.

R

rabies (**ray**-beez)
A deadly disease caused by the bite of an animal infected with the *rhabdovirus*. From the Latin *rabies*, meaning "madness," because animals with rabies act in crazy ways.

radar (**ray**-dahr)
Short for *radio detection and ranging*. An **electronic** device used to locate and track airplanes, ships, speeding automobiles, or rain or snow clouds. Radar sends out short pulses of **microwaves** and receives the waves that bounce back.

Radar Radar sends out a beam of high-frequency radio waves. The beam bounces off a passing car and back to a detector, which uses the Doppler effect to calculate the speed of the car.

Radar display

radiant (**ray**-dee-uhnt)
Giving off **rays** or **waves** of **energy**. Radiant sources include the sun, fire, and light bulbs. *Also,* the direction from which a **meteor shower** comes into sight.

radiation (*ray*-dee-**ay**-shuhn)
A form of **energy**, such as **heat, light, X rays, microwaves,** or **radio waves.** Radiation also includes dangerous, high-energy **nuclear radiation** and **cosmic rays.** Electromagnetic radiation travels in **waves.** It can pass through empty space and through some materials.

radiator (**ray**-dee-*ay*-tuhr)
Anything that produces **radiant energy.** *Also,* a device used to give off heat. A home radiator warms a room; a car radiator releases the heat of the engine into the air.

radical (**rad**-i-kuhl)
A group of **atoms** that acts as a single unit during a **chemical reaction.** Two common radicals are **nitrate** (NO_3) and sulfate (SO_4).

radio (**ray**-dee-*oh*)
A way of sending and receiving sounds using **electromagnetic waves** instead of wires. The radio **transmitter** changes sounds into radio waves, which it sends out through the air by means of a tall **antenna.** A small antenna in or on the radio receiver picks up the waves and changes the waves back into the original sounds. See also **television.**

radioactive decay
(*ray*-dee-oh-**ak**-tiv di-**kay**)
The emission of **atomic particles** and **rays** from a **radioactive** substance. Radioactive decay causes one **element** to change and become a different element.

radioactivity
(*ray*-dee-oh-ak-**tiv**-uht-ee)
The process by which the *nuclei* (plural of **nucleus**) of certain **atoms** give off high energy **particles** and **rays.** Radioactivity occurs naturally in the **elements radium** and **uranium.** Human beings are harmed when exposed to radioactivity.

radio astronomy
(**ray**-dee-*oh* uh-**strahn**-uh-mee)
The branch of **astronomy** that studies the natural radio waves given off by objects in space. The main tool of radio astronomy is the **radio telescope,** which

picks up radio signals from such objects as **quasars** and **pulsars**.

radiocarbon dating
(*ray*-dee-oh-**kahr**-buhn *day*-ting)
A way of finding the age of **fossils** of living things. All living things take in some **atoms** of radiocarbon, which is a radioactive form of **carbon**. These atoms undergo **radioactive decay** to form **nitrogen**. By measuring the ratio of radiocarbon to nitrogen, scientists learn how long ago the **organism** lived.

radioisotope (*ray*-dee-oh-**ie**-suh-*tohp*)
Short for *radioactive isotope.* A radioisotope is the radioactive form of an **element**. It occurs naturally or can sometimes be made by bombarding an element with **neutrons**. A doctor can give a patient a radioisotope and then trace the **radioactivity** in the body to see how an **organ** is working. In higher doses, radioisotopes can be used to kill **cancer cells.**

radio telescope
(**ray**-dee-*oh* **tel**-uh-*skohp*)
Usually one or several large metal dish **antennas** that pick up natural radio waves coming from space. The radio telescope is the main tool used in **radio astronomy.**

radio wave
(**ray**-dee-*oh wayv*)
An **electromagnetic wave** that can be used for both radio and television broadcasting and **microwave** communication. The radio waves for radio broadcasts are longer than those for television.

radium (ray-dee-uhm)
A silvery-white, highly **radioactive metal element.** Radium is very dangerous and harmful to humans because of its **radioactivity.** Radium was discovered by **Marie Curie** and her husband, **Pierre,** in 1898. (Symbol—Ra)

radon (ray-dahn)
A radioactive **element** produced by the decay of the **radium** found in some soil and rocks. Radon, an odorless gas, sometimes seeps into houses and settles in basements since it is so heavy. Radon can cause lung **cancer.** (Symbol—Rn)

rain (rayn)
Drops of water that fall from clouds. Rain also falls when **snow, hail,** or **sleet** melts as it comes down. Raindrops are bigger than 0.02 inches (0.5 millimeters). When smaller drops fall it is called *drizzle.*

R

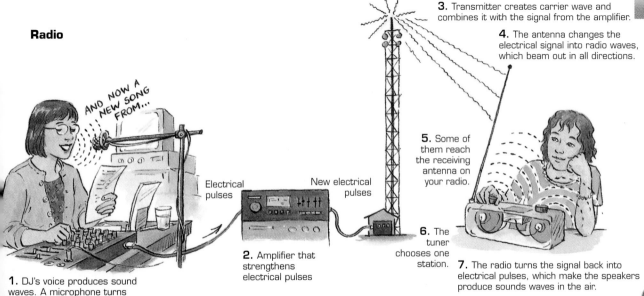

Radio

3. Transmitter creates carrier wave and combines it with the signal from the amplifier.

4. The antenna changes the electrical signal into radio waves, which beam out in all directions.

5. Some of them reach the receiving antenna on your radio.

Electrical pulses

New electrical pulses

6. The tuner chooses one station.

2. Amplifier that strengthens electrical pulses

7. The radio turns the signal back into electrical pulses, which make the speakers produce sounds waves in the air.

1. DJ's voice produces sound waves. A microphone turns them into electrical pulses.

Rainbow

Light entering raindrop is broken into colors.

Sunlight

The back of the raindrop reflects the color back toward the observer.

Many raindrops together give us a complete rainbow.

rainbow (rayn-*boh*)
An arc of colors that appears in the sky, usually when the sun shines after a rain shower. The raindrops still in the air break the sunlight into its separate colors—red, orange, yellow, green, blue, indigo, and violet.

rain forest (rayn for-*uhst*)
An area of very tall trees and much rainfall—more than 70 inches (180 centimeters) each year. A rain forest has a great variety of trees but few bushes or small plants, since the trees block the sunlight from reaching the ground. Most rain forests are found in tropical areas near the **equator.**

RAM (ram)
Short for *Random-Access Memory.* The part of a computer's memory where **data** can be added, changed, erased, or called up.

ramjet (ram-*jet*)
A type of jet engine that is mostly used in guided **missiles.** The ramjet burns fuel in air that is **compressed** as it enters the engine.

Ramsay (ram-zee), William (1852–1916)
A British chemist who discovered the gases *argon,* **neon,** *xenon,* and **krypton,** and was the first to isolate **helium.** These gases are called the **noble gases** or **inert gases.**

range (raynj)
A chain of mountains, such as the Alps or Rockies. *Also,* the area in which a living thing is found. For example, the range of the polar bear is around the Arctic Ocean. *Also,* the difference between two values. For example, the range of average temperatures in New York City is from 25° to 82° **Fahrenheit** (-4° to 28° **Celsius**). *Also,* a measure of distance. For example, the range of a 747 airliner is more than 6,000 miles (9,650 kilometers) on one tank of fuel. From the Old French *ranc,* meaning "line or row."

rarefaction (*rer*-uh-fak**-shuhn)**
The part of a sound wave or other wave where the **particles** are spread apart. From the Latin *rarus,* meaning "rare," and *facere,* meaning "to make."

ray (ray)
A narrow beam of some sort of **radiation,** such as **light, heat, X rays,** or **cosmic rays.** *Also,* a kind of **fish,** such as the *stingray* or *manta ray.*

rayon (ray-ahn)
A **synthetic fiber** made from **cellulose,** which is obtained from wood or cotton.

reaction (ree-ak-shuhn)
A **chemical** process in which substances combine and change, such as heating **iron** and **sulfur** together to produce *iron sulfide. Also,* an **organism's** response to a **stimulus,** such as a plant bending toward the sun. *Also,* a process in which the **nucleus** of an **atom** is changed by being struck by an outside **particle.** *Also,* movement in one direction caused by a force working in the opposite direction, such as an airplane flying forward as gases from its jet engines push backward.

reactor (ree-ak-tuhr)
See **nuclear reactor.**

reagent (ree-ay-juhnt)
Any substance that takes part in a **chemical reaction.** *Also,* something

used to test for the presence of other substances. For example, **iodine** is a reagent that turns foods blue-black if they contain **starch.**

real time (**ree**-uhl **time**)
Getting instant results from a computer. For example, computers that help fly an airplane operate in real time. They react at once to the information they receive.

receiver (ri-**see**-vuhr)
A radio or television set or a telephone. A receiver gets **electromagnetic waves** from the air or through a wire and changes them into sound or pictures.

receptor (ri-**sep**-tuhr)
An **organ** or individual **cell** that reacts to a **stimulus** and sends a signal to a **nerve.** For example, the ear is a receptor that reacts to **sound waves** in the air.

recessive (ri-**ses**-iv)
Describes a **gene** or **trait** that is masked or not expressed in the offspring of a plant or animal. A recessive gene is passed down from parent to offspring. It has instructions for one trait (say, blue eyes) but is overruled by instructions for a different trait (say, brown eyes). A blue-eyed man married to a brown-eyed woman would usually have a brown-eyed child, though the child still carries the recessive gene for blue eyes.

recombinant DNA
(ri-**kahm**-buh-nuhnt **dee**-*en*-**ay**)
A **molecule** of **DNA** that is formed by splitting a DNA molecule from one **organism** and combining it with DNA from a different organism. The recombinant DNA is often put into a third organism to get a desired result, such as cows that give more milk or **microbes** that produce certain drugs. The process is called **genetic engineering** or **gene splicing.**

rectum (**rek**-tuhm)
The lower part of the **large intestine.**

The rectum ends at the **anus,** through which solid wastes leave the body.

recycling (ree-**sike**-ling)
Saving waste materials and using them to make new materials. Recycling paper, glass, plastic, and metal lets us make new products without using up **natural resources.** Nature recycles by **decomposing** dead **organic** material and adding it to the soil.

Recycling

red blood cell (**red bluhd** *sel*)
A **cell** in the blood that brings **oxygen** to the **tissues** and carries away **carbon dioxide.** Also called **erythrocyte.**

red dwarf star (**red dworf stahr**)
A star that is cooler, smaller, and less bright than the sun. Red dwarf stars are common in our **galaxy.**

red giant star (**red jie**-uhnt **stahr**)
A star that is cooler, larger, less dense, and brighter than the sun. Red giants are very old stars.

red shift (**red** *shift*)
The change in **wavelength** of light toward the red, or longer, end of the

spectrum. The red shift occurs when a light source speeds away from the viewer. Light coming from **galaxies** is red-shifted. Scientists believe this red shift shows that the galaxies are speeding away from Earth and from each other and that the **universe** is growing larger.

red tide (red tide)
A red or brown area in an ocean, lake, or river. A red tide is often caused by huge numbers of tiny, one-celled **organisms**, called *dinoflagellates,* in the water. Poisons these organisms release into the water can kill fish.

reduction (ri-**duhk**-shuhn)
A **chemical reaction** in which **oxygen** is taken from a substance. An example of reduction is removing the oxygen from rust, or **iron oxide** (Fe_2O_3), to produce pure iron (Fe). *Also,* a reaction in which a substance gains **electrons.**

Reed (reed), Walter (1851–1902)
A doctor in the US Army who helped show how to control **yellow fever** and **typhoid fever** by getting rid of the mosquitoes whose bite caused the diseases.

reef (reef)
A **ridge** of **coral**, rock, or sand that forms at or near the surface of the sea. Most often, reefs build up slowly from layers of **coral**. Reefs are dangerous for ships but important for life in the ocean.

refining (ri-**fie**-ning)
Removing unwanted matter from **metal, petroleum, sugar,** or other substances.

reflecting telescope
(ri-**flek**-ting **tel**-uh-*skohp*)
A **telescope** that uses a **concave** mirror to collect and **focus** the light from objects in the sky. The **Hubble** Space Telescope is a reflecting telescope. Also called *reflector telescope.*

reflection (ri-**flek**-shuhn)
The change in direction of a wave of **energy** bouncing off a surface. The reflection of a light, sound, heat, or radio wave by a flat, smooth surface sends it in one direction. A bent or rough surface scatters the wave. The reflection of sound waves from any surface is called an **echo.** From the Latin *re-,* meaning "back," and *flectere,* meaning "to bend."

reflex (**ree**-fleks)
An automatic, unthinking **reaction** to a **stimulus.** The reflex action when you touch a hot stove is to pull your hand away immediately.

refracting telescope
(ri-**frak**-ting **tel**-uh-*skohp*)
A **telescope** that uses two **convex lenses** to collect and **focus** the light from objects in the sky. The world's largest refracting telescope—40 inches (102 centimeters)—is at the Yerkes **Observatory** in Wisconsin. Also called *refractor telescope.*

refraction (ri-**frak**-shuhn)
The bending of light **rays,** or other waves, as they pass through different substances at an angle. Refraction makes a tilted pencil standing in a glass of water look as though it is broken. Refraction in the **lens** of your eye or your eyeglasses lets you see the words in this book clearly.

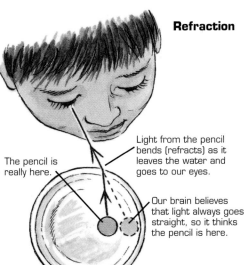

Refraction

The pencil is really here.

Light from the pencil bends (refracts) as it leaves the water and goes to our eyes.

Our brain believes that light always goes straight, so it thinks the pencil is here.

refrigeration (ri-*frij*-uh-**ray**-shuhn)
The process of cooling or keeping cold by removing heat from an enclosed space. Refrigeration is mostly used to keep food from spoiling. It is also used in air conditioning to keep indoor temperatures at a comfortable level.

regeneration (ri-*jen*-uh-**ray**-shuhn)
Growing new body parts to replace those that are lost or damaged. Regeneration is common in worms, sponges, sea stars, tadpoles, and some lizards.

relative humidity
(**rel**-uh-tiv hyoo-**mid**-uh-tee)
A comparison between the amount of water **vapor** actually in the air and the total amount of water vapor the air can hold at that temperature. A relative humidity of 50 percent means the air is holding only half the amount it can hold.

relativity (*rel*-uh-**tiv**-uh-tee)
A two-part theory stated by **Albert Einstein.** The *special theory of relativity* (1905) holds that when an object moves at a very high **speed** its **mass** increases, its length decreases, and time slows down—changes that can only be noted when the object is moving at close to the **speed of light.** The famous **equation, $E=mc^2$,** shows the connection between **energy** and mass. According to the equation, energy equals mass times the speed of light squared. The *general theory of relativity* (1915) states that the **gravity** of huge objects, such as stars, bends or curves time and space. Both theories have been proven in **experiments.**

relay (**ree**-lay)
An electric switch that uses a weak **current** to turn on or off a much stronger current. An elevator button is a relay that uses its small current to turn on the strong current needed to raise or lower the elevator.

REM (**rem**)
Short for *Rapid Eye Movement.* REM is the movement of the eyes when dreaming. REM sleep periods can occur as often as 5 times a night and last up to 30 minutes each. *Also,* short for *Roentgen Equivalent Man,* a measure of the body damage caused by exposure to **radioactivity.**

remission (ri-**mish**-uhn)
The disappearance or reduction of the symptoms of a disease. A patient is in remission when there are no **symptoms** for a period of time. From the Latin *re-,* meaning "back," and *mittere,* meaning "to send."

remote control
(ri-**moht** kuhn-**trohl**)
A way of directing a machine or system from a distance. The remote control for a television uses **infrared rays.**

renal (**reen**-l)
Related to the **kidneys.** The **artery** going to the kidneys is called the renal **artery.**

rendezvous (**rahn**-day-*voo*)
A meeting in space in which one **spacecraft** joins with another. From the French *rendez vous,* meaning "present yourselves."

renewable energy
(ri-**noo**-uh-buhl **en**-uhr-jee)
Energy from an unlimited source. Renewable **resources** include the wind, flowing water, and sunlight. *Nonrenewable* energy sources include coal, oil, natural gas, and **minerals;** they can be used up.

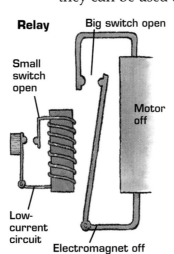
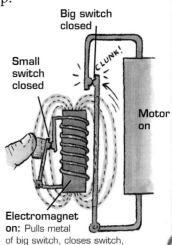

Relay

Big switch open

Small switch open

Motor off

Low-current circuit

Electromagnet off

Big switch closed

CLUNK!

Small switch closed

Motor on

Electromagnet on: Pulls metal of big switch, closes switch, and turns the motor on.

repel (ri-**pel**)
To push away. The **south poles** of two magnets repel each other.

reproduce (*ree*-pruh-**doos**)
To have offspring. Living things reproduce to keep their **species** alive.

reproduction (*ree*-pruh-**duhk**-shuhn)
The process by which living things create more of their own kind. In *sexual reproduction* a **sex cell** from the male **organism** joins with a sex cell from the female organism, leading to the new organism. Humans and most animals **reproduce** sexually. In *asexual reproduction* the new organism develops from one parent and is identical to that parent. **Bacteria** and some other simple organisms reproduce asexually.

reptile (**rep**-tile)
One of about 6,000 different kinds of **cold-blooded** animals with a **spine** and a skin of **scales** or plates. All reptiles breathe with lungs. Most **reproduce** by laying **eggs**. They shed their skin several times a year. Snakes, lizards, alligators, crocodiles, and turtles are all reptiles. From the Latin *repere,* meaning "to crawl."

repulsion (ri-**puhl**-shuhn)
A force that pushes objects apart. You see repulsion when the same **poles** on two **magnets** move away from each other. From the Latin *repulsus,* meaning "driven back."

research (ri-**suhrch**)
Experiments, observations, and study to learn new facts, develop new products or methods, or discover natural laws. From the French *re-,* meaning "again," and *cerchier,* meaning "to search."

reservoir (**rez**-uhr-*vwahr*)
A place to store a large amount of water, such as the water supply for a big city. *Also,* a place in a body or machine where **fluids** are stored. From the Middle French *reserver,* meaning "to reserve."

resin (**rez**-uhn)
A natural yellow or brown liquid that comes from the wood or bark of certain trees and hardens when exposed to air. Resins are used in varnishes, medicines, soaps, paints, and other products.

resistance (ri-**zis**-tuhns)
A measure of how strongly a substance opposes the flow of electricity. The unit of resistance in an **electric circuit** is the **ohm.** *Also,* a force, such as **friction,** that slows down or stops a moving object. From the Latin *re-,* meaning "back," and *sistere,* meaning "to take a stand."

resistor (ri-**zis**-tuhr)
A device in an **electric circuit** that controls the flow of **current.** The resistor adds **resistance** to the circuits in computers and other electronic devices.

resonance (**rez**-uh-nuhns)
An increase in the size of **vibrations** caused by applying a **force** that vibrates at the natural **frequency** of the object. For example, singers can shatter glass by singing a note that vibrates at the natural frequency of the glass. You use resonance when you push a swing in time with the swing's back-and-forth motion. From the Latin *re-,* meaning "back," and *sonare,* meaning "to sound."

resources (**ree**-*sor*-siz or ri-**sor**-siz)
The materials and **energy** that make life on Earth possible. The vital resources include air, land, water, **minerals,** fuels, the energy we get from the sun, and the living things that directly or indirectly provide the foods and products we need.

respiration (*res*-puh-**ray**-shuhn)
The process by which most living things take in **oxygen** and get rid of **carbon dioxide.** Respiration occurs in individual **cells** and entire **organisms.** Land animals use their **lungs** to get oxygen from the air. Fish use their **gills** to get it from water. From the Latin *re-,* meaning "again," and *spirare,* meaning "to breathe."

respirator
(**res**-puh-*ray*-tuhr)
A machine that helps
a person breathe. A
respirator is used to
help someone who is
having difficulty
breathing because of sickness
or injury. Also called a *ventilator*
or *resuscitator*. Also, a mask worn
to prevent breathing harmful
substances.

respiratory system
(**res**-puh-ruh-*tor*-ee *sis*-tuhm)
The parts of the body needed for breathing.
It includes the **nose**, **mouth**, **throat**,
trachea, **larynx**, **bronchial tubes**, **lungs**,
and **diaphragm**.

Revolve/Rotate

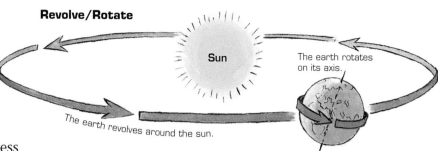

Sun

The earth rotates
on its axis.

The earth revolves around the sun.

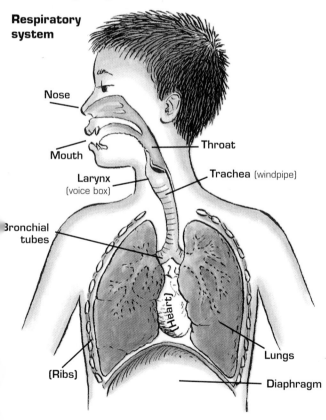

**Respiratory
system**

Nose

Mouth

Throat

Larynx
(voice box)

Trachea (windpipe)

Bronchial
tubes

(Heart)

(Ribs)

Lungs

Diaphragm

response (ri-**spahns**)
The way a living thing acts or behaves
when it receives a **stimulus**. Fright is the
usual human response to the stimulus
of a sudden, loud noise.

resuscitator (ri-**suhs**-uh-*tay*-tuhr)
See **respirator**.

retina (**ret**-n-uh)
A layer of **cells** at the back of the **eye**.
The retina **reacts** to light by sending
electrical signals to the brain. The retina
includes two kinds of cells that are
stimulated by light: **cones**, that see
colors and produce sharp, clear **images**;
and **rods**, for seeing in dim light.

revolution (*rev*-uh-**loo**-shuhn)
Movement in a circle or curve around a
central point or **axis**. One revolution of
Earth around the sun takes a year. See
also **rotation**.

revolve (ri-**vahlv**)
To move around a central point or **axis**.
In **astronomy**, the word usually refers
to a body in **orbit** around another body.
The earth revolves around the sun. From
the Latin *re-*, meaning "back," and *volvere*,
meaning "to roll." See also **rotate**.

Rh factor (**ahr-aych** *fak*-tuhr)
A **protein** substance found in blood.
If you have the Rh factor in your blood
you are *Rh* **positive**. Your blood will not
mix well with the blood of someone
without the Rh factor, who is *Rh*
negative. The term comes from the
*rh*esus monkey, in whose blood the
factor was first found.

rheostat (**ree**-uh-*stat*)
A device to change the **resistance** in an
electrical circuit. A rheostat is a **resistor**
whose value can be changed. The
volume control in a radio or television
set is a rheostat. From the Greek *rhein*,

meaning "to flow," and -*states,* meaning "to make stand."

rhizome (**rie**-*zohm*)
A horizontal, underground plant **stem** that produces leaves and **flowers** above the soil and **roots** below. Ferns, water lilies, gingers, irises, and some grasses are plants with rhizomes.

rib (**rib**)
One of the pairs of bones in the chest that protect the heart and lungs. The ribs move up and down, which expands or contracts the chest and helps with breathing. Most **vertebrates** have ribs, but the number varies from **species** to species.

Richter scale (**rik**-tuhr *skayl*)
A measure of the **energy** released by an **earthquake.** The Richter scale was developed in 1935 by the American scientists *Charles F. Richter* (1900–1985) and *Beno Gutenberg* (1889–1960). The most powerful earthquake to be measured reached 9.5 on the Richter scale.

ridge (**rij**)
A long, narrow strip of hills or mountains on land or in the ocean. *Also,* an area of high **barometric pressure** in the **atmosphere.**

rift valley (**rift** *val*-ee)
A broad stretch of low land between two parallel mountain slopes. A rift valley forms when two pieces of the earth's **crust** pull apart and the land in between drops down. A rift valley is also called a *graben.*

Ring Nebula (**ring** *neb*-yuh-luh)
A well-known cloud of dust and gas seen in the **constellation** Lyra. The Ring Nebula was formed from the explosion of a star. It is shaped like a bagel.

ringworm (**ring**-*wuhrm*)
The name of several skin diseases caused by *fungi* (plural of **fungus**). Ringworm usually starts as a small, round, itchy, red spot that grows bigger and takes on a ring shape.

rip current (**rip** *kuhr*-uhnt)
A strong, dangerous ocean **current** moving away from the shore. Also called *riptide.*

river (**riv**-uhr)
A large stream of water that usually starts high in the mountains and flows over land to another river, lake, or ocean.

RNA (**ahr**-*en*-**ay**)
Short for *RiboNucleic Acid.* RNA is a **molecule** found in all **cells.** It carries instructions for making **proteins.** See also **DNA.**

robot (**roh**-baht)
A machine that does work usually done by humans. A robot is especially useful in handling jobs that are boring, difficult, or dangerous. From the Czech *robota,* meaning "work."

rock (**rahk**)
The hard material that makes up the **crust** of the earth. The rock is sometimes hidden under soil, ice, or water. The three main kinds of rock are **igneous, sedimentary,** and **metamorphic.** Most rock is made up of two or more **minerals.**

Rock

1. Igneous rock forms from magma.

2. Ice, water, and plants start to weather and erode the rock.

3. The bits of rock, along with the remains of plants and animals, are deposited in rivers, lakes, and oceans.

4. Over time, these deposits form sedimentary rocks . . .

rocket (rahk-it)

A very powerful **engine.** The rocket burns a mixture of fuel and oxygen that produces expanding gases. The gases rush out the back, sending the rocket forward at great speed. Since the engine does not need **oxygen** from the **air,** rockets can fly in outer space. *Also,* the craft driven by a rocket engine.

Rocket

Rocket fuel, such as liquid hydrogen

Liquid oxygen

Combustion chamber where they mix burn

The resulting hot gases shoot out the back, pushing the rocket forward.

rod (rahd)

The type of **cell** found in the **retina** of the eye that allows us to see in dim light. *Also,* a unit of length. A rod equals 16.5 feet (5 meters). *Also,* the metal bars placed in **nuclear reactors** to control the speed of the **reaction.**

5. . . . which may be raised to the surface and erode again . . .

6. . . . or may be buried deep in the ground and turned into metamorphic rock.

7. The metamorphic rock may also rise and erode . . .

8. . . . or be pushed under and melt into magma—starting the cycle all over again.

rodent (rohd-nt)

A **mammal** with a large pair of sharp front teeth used for gnawing. A rodent's teeth wear away but continue to grow until old age. Mice, rats, beavers, and squirrels are rodents.

Roentgen (rent-guhn), Wilhelm Conrad (1845–1923)

A German physicist who discovered **X rays** in 1895. Roentgen's discovery gave doctors a valuable tool for seeing into the body.

ROM (rahm)

Short for *Read Only Memory.* ROM is the part of a computer's memory that contains **data** and instructions that cannot be changed. See also **RAM.**

root (root or rut)

The part of a plant that grows under the ground or sometimes in water or air. The root anchors the plant, absorbs the water and **minerals** the plant needs, and in some cases stores food for the plant. *Also,* in the body, the hidden bottom part of a tooth or hair.

root hair (root *her* or rut *her*)

A tiny hairlike growth on a plant **root** that absorbs water and **minerals** from the soil.

rot (raht)

To **decay** or spoil because of **bacteria** or other **microorganisms.** *Also,* a disease of plants that causes them to decay.

rotate (roh-*tayt*)

To move around a central point or **axis.** In astronomy, the word usually refers to a body spinning around itself. The earth rotates around an imaginary axis that runs from the North to the South Pole. *Also,* to make repeated changes in a regular pattern or **cycle.** Farmers rotate their crops by changing what they plant in the same field. See also **revolve.**

R

rotation (roh-**tay**-shuhn)
The act of spinning or turning around a central point or **axis**. One rotation of the earth takes 24 hours, or one day. The rotations of a **helicopter's** blades keep it in the air. See also **revolution**.

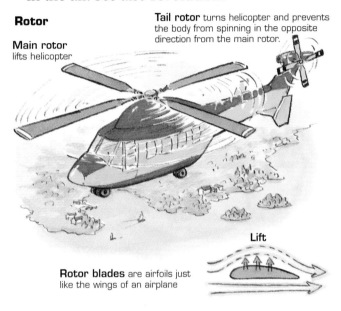

Rotor

Main rotor
lifts helicopter

Tail rotor turns helicopter and prevents the body from spinning in the opposite direction from the main rotor.

Lift

Rotor blades are airfoils just like the wings of an airplane

rotor (**roh**-tuhr)
The blades that spin around on a **helicopter**. The rotor provides the lift to raise the helicopter in the air. *Also,* the **rotating coil** in an **electric motor**, which is also sometimes called an **armature**.

roughage (**ruhf**-ij)
The rough, coarse parts of cereals and vegetables. Roughage, which is sometimes called **fiber**, helps food move through the digestive system.

rubber (**ruhb**-uhr)
A tough, elastic substance made either from the juice of a rubber tree or from **petroleum**. Rubber is airtight and watertight and springs back into shape after being stretched.

rudder (**ruhd**-uhr)
A movable, hinged plate on the back of a boat or airplane. The rudder is used for steering the craft. From the Old English *rothor,* meaning "oar."

ruminant (**roo**-muh-nuhnt)
A grazing animal that chews its food, swallows it, brings it up, and chews it again. Most ruminants have a stomach with three or four separate parts. Cows, sheep, deer, and giraffes are ruminants.

run (**ruhn**)
To operate a computer **program**. *Also,* to turn on the **power** of an electrical or mechanical device.

runoff (**ruhn**-*awf*)
Water from rain or melted snow that flows into a river, lake, or ocean. The runoff often contains **sediment** that may hold **fertilizers**, **pesticides**, and other poisons or harmful substances.

Russell (**ruhs**-uhl), **Henry Norris** (1877–1957)
An American astronomer who showed that the brightness of a star is related to its surface temperature. See also **Hertzsprung-Russell** diagram.

rust (**ruhst**)
The reddish-brown substance that forms on **iron** or **steel** that is exposed to dampness. Rust is the result of the **oxygen** in the air joining with iron. (Formula—$2Fe_2O_3$) *Also,* a brownish **fungus** disease in certain plants.

Rutherford (**ruh**TH-uhr-fuhrd), **Ernest** (1871–1937)
A British physicist who is considered the father of **nuclear** science. In 1911, Rutherford proposed a model of the **atom** with a heavy central **nucleus** and **electrons** moving around the outside. He also discovered that **radioactive elements** give off radioactive **rays** and change into other elements.

Sabin (say-buhn), Albert (1906–1993)
An American doctor who developed an oral **vaccine** against polio in 1960. Polio is a disease caused by a **virus**. The Sabin vaccine uses weakened **viruses** to protect against the disease.

saccharin (sak-uh-rin)
An artificial sweetener made from **petroleum**. Saccharin is sweeter than sugar and has no **calories**.

Sagan (say-guhn), Carl (1934–1996)
An American astronomer who used unmanned space probes to make discoveries about **Mars** and **Venus**.

sailplane (sayl-playn)
See **glider**.

saline (say-leen)
Having to do with **salt**. A saline **solution** is usually salt **dissolved** in water.

salinity (suh-lin-uh-tee)
The amount of **salt dissolved** in a **solution**. The salinity of oceans is much greater than that of lakes and rivers.

saliva (suh-lie-vuh)
A liquid made in certain **glands** that lead into the mouth. Saliva keeps the mouth moist, softens food, and contains the **enzyme** amylase, which starts digestion.

Salk (sawk), Jonas (1914–1995)
An American doctor who developed the first polio **vaccine** in 1952. The Salk vaccine injects dead polio **viruses** into the body to protect against the disease.

salt (sawlt)
A **mineral** used to flavor and preserve food. Salt comes either from **evaporating** seawater or digging up deposits in the ground. The **chemical** name of salt is sodium chloride. (Formula—NaCl) *Also,* a **compound** that forms when an **acid** and **base** are combined or when a metal is **dissolved** in an acid.

saltpeter (sawlt-pee-tuhr)
The **mineral** *potassium nitrate* or *niter* (Formula—KNO_3), which is used to make matches, **explosives**, and **fertilizers**. From the Latin *sal petrae,* meaning "salt of the rock."

San Andreas Fault (san an-dray-uhs fawlt)
A crack in the earth's **crust** in California. The San Andreas Fault marks the border between 2 of the earth's **plates**. Sudden shifts along the fault have resulted in severe earthquakes.

San Andreas fault

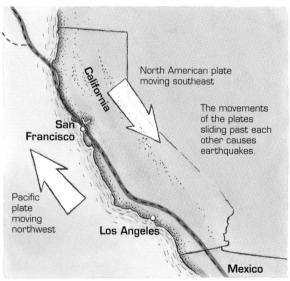

California

North American plate moving southeast

The movements of the plates sliding past each other causes earthquakes.

San Francisco

Pacific plate moving northwest

Los Angeles

Mexico

sand (sand)
Very tiny pieces of rock that have crumbled or been worn down.

sandstone (sand-stohn)
A **sedimentary** rock formed mostly of grains of sand that have been cemented together by **pressure** or **minerals**.

sandstorm (**sand**-*storm*)
A windstorm that carries a cloud of sand through the air. Most sandstorms occur in deserts or along beaches.

sap (**sap**)
The liquid in a plant that carries water and **dissolved minerals** from the roots up to the leaves. Sap also carries sugar dissolved in water from the leaves to other parts of the plant.

sapling (**sap**-ling)
A young tree.

saprophyte (**sap**-ruh-*fite*)
A **fungus** or *bacterium* (singular of **bacteria**) that lives on dead and decaying **organisms**. From the Greek *sapros,* meaning "rotten," and *phyton,* meaning "plant."

sapwood (**sap**-*wud*)
The new, soft wood between the bark and the hard inner wood of most trees. The thick-walled **cells** of the sapwood carry water and **minerals** from the roots to the leaves.

satellite (**sat**-l-*ite*)
A smaller body that **revolves** around a larger body such as a planet. The moon is a natural satellite of Earth. An *artificial satellite* is an object launched into **orbit** around Earth. From the Latin *satelles,* meaning "attendant."

satellite dish (**sat**-l-*ite dish*)
A bowl-shaped **antenna** that picks up radio signals from an artificial **satellite** in the sky. Home satellite dishes can receive television programs from an artificial satellite.

saturate (**sach**-uh-*rayt*)
To soak thoroughly or to **dissolve** the greatest possible amount of a substance in a **solution.**

saturated fat (**sach**-uh-*ray*-tuhd **fat**)
Fat that is hard at room temperature, such as meat fat, butter, and cheese.

In saturated fat, the **carbon atoms** are linked to as many **hydrogen** atoms as possible. Saturated fat is bad for your heart.

Saturn (**sat**-uhrn)
The 6th planet from the sun in the **solar system.** Saturn is a giant ball of gas surrounded by *rings* made of ice and rock and about 20 moons.

Average distance from sun—888,200,000 miles (1,429,400,000 kilometers)
Length of year—nearly 30 Earth years
Length of day—10 hours, 39 minutes
Diameter at equator—74,810 miles (120,660 kilometers)

savanna (suh-**van**-uh)
A tropical grassland with few trees or shrubs. Savannas cover nearly half of Africa. Lions, leopards, and zebras live on the African savannas. Sometimes spelled *savannah.*

save (**sayv**)
To place a document or **data** into a computer's **memory.**

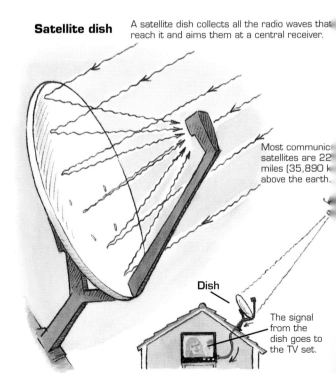

Satellite dish A satellite dish collects all the radio waves that reach it and aims them at a central receiver.

Most communic: satellites are 22 miles (35,890 k above the earth.

Dish

The signal from the dish goes to the TV set.

scale (skayl)
One of many flat plates that make up the outside covering of most fishes and some snakes and lizards. *Also,* a weighing device. *Also,* the size of a map or model compared to the size of the original. A map may have a scale of one inch for 100 miles.

scanner (skan-uhr)
An **input** device that reads text and **images**, and changes them into **digital** signals that go to a computer.

scar (skahr)
A mark left on the skin after an injury heals.

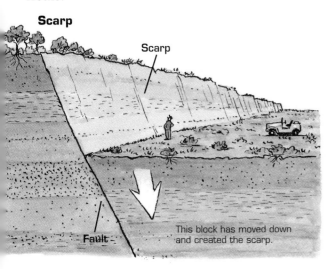

Scarp

Scarp

This block has moved down and created the scarp.

Fault

scarp (skahrp)
A steep slope along a line of cliffs. A scarp is usually formed by movements in the earth's **crust** or by **erosion**. Short for *escarpment.*

scattering (skat-uhr-ing)
The change in direction of **particles** or **waves** of **energy**. The scattering that occurs when sunlight strikes tiny particles of dust and water in the air makes the sky look blue. See also **dispersion**.

scavenger (skav-uhn-juhr)
An animal that feeds on a dead or decaying animal that it did not kill. Hyenas and vultures are scavengers.

schist (shist)
A **metamorphic** rock that splits easily into layers. The layers of schist often have shiny surfaces because the *mica* in the rock reflects light.

science (sie-uhns)
A vast system of facts and natural laws that puts our understanding of the world into an orderly form. Science is largely based on **observation**, **research**, and **experiments**. Its main branches include **astronomy, biology, chemistry, geology,** and **physics**. From the Latin *scientia,* meaning "knowledge."

scientific method (sie-uhn-tif-ik meth-uhd)
A way scientists seek to understand the world and living things. The scientific method usually includes finding a problem, making observations, forming a **hypothesis,** doing **experiments** to test the hypothesis, and drawing conclusions.

scientist (sie-uhn-tist)
Someone who is trained in one of the branches of science and works in that field.

screw (skroo)
A kind of simple machine. A screw is actually an **inclined plane** that twists around a central **axis**. *Also,* the **propeller** on a ship.

scroll (skrohl)
To move an **image** up, down, or sideways on a computer screen.

sea level (see lev-uhl)
The level of ocean water, halfway between **low tide** and **high tide**. Sea level is used to measure heights on Earth.

Seaborg (see-borg), Glenn Theodore (1912–1999)
An American **chemist** who led the team that discovered **plutonium** and 7 other **elements**.

Seashore

Muddy

Sandy

Rocky

seamount (**see**-*mount*)
An underwater mountain formed by a volcano whose peak is at least 3,300 feet (1,000 meters) above the sea floor.

search engine (**suhrch** *en*-juhn)
A site on the **Internet** that searches the **World Wide Web** for the word or phrase that you type in.

seashore (**see**-*shor*)
The land along the edge of the sea. The three main kinds of seashores are: *rocky*, where most sea creatures live; *muddy*, where most plants grow; and *sandy*, where you find few plants or animals. Also known as the **littoral** *zone*.

season (**see**-zuhn)
One of the 4 periods of the year—spring, summer, autumn, and winter. Each season has different average temperatures, weather conditions, and lengths of daylight. Some tropical areas have only 2 seasons—rainy and dry. The seasons are opposite in the Northern and Southern Hemispheres.

sebaceous gland
(si-**bay**-shuhs **gland**)
A **gland** that supplies oil to the skin and hair. The sebaceous glands are found below the hair **follicles** in the skin. From the Latin *sebum,* meaning "grease."

second (**sek**-uhnd)
A small unit of time. There are 60 seconds in a minute, 3,600 in an hour, and 86,400 in a day.

secretion (si-**kree**-shuhn)
A useful substance given off by certain **cells** in the body. Secretions include sweat, tears, **saliva, mucus,** and many different **hormones.** From the Latin *secretio,* meaning "separation."

section (**sek**-shuhn)
A slice of matter cut so thin that light can pass through. A section is often studied under a **microscope.** From the Latin *sectio,* meaning "cut."

sedative (**sed**-uh-tiv)
A drug that slows down the action of the **nervous system.** Doctors prescribe sedatives to help people relax or to help them fall asleep. From the Latin *sedare,* meaning "to calm."

sediment (**sed**-uh-muhnt)
Material that settles to the bottom of a **liquid.** The sediment of a **river** includes **sand, silt,** clay, and **rocks.** From the Latin *sedere,* meaning "to sink down."

sedimentary rock
(*sed*-uh-**men**-tuh-ree **rahk**)
A kind of rock that forms in one of 3 ways: Fine grains of **sediment** become cemented

together, as in **sandstone;** water **evaporates,** leaving behind a **precipitated mineral,** as in **limestone;** or the buried remains of animals or plants are heated and **compressed** under the ground, as in chalk. Sedimentary rock makes up about ¾ of the earth's land surface.

seed (**seed**)
The part of a plant from which a new plant will grow. A seed includes an **embryo,** food **tissue,** and the seed coat.

seed leaf (**seed** *leef*)
See **cotyledon.**

seedling (**seed**-ling)
A young plant grown from a seed.

segment (**seg**-muhnt)
A separate part of something. Each segment of a worm's body looks like a ring. From the Latin *segmentum,* meaning "piece or fragment."

seismic (**size**-mik)
Having to do with earthquakes. Seismic waves are the shock waves of an

earthquake. From the Greek *seismos,* meaning "shock or earthquake."

seismograph (**size**-muh-*graf*)
An instrument that records the time, strength, and duration of earthquakes and of **explosions** used to study the earth's interior or to search for oil.

seismology (size-**mahl**-uh-jee)
The study of **earthquakes** and other movements of the earth's **crust.**

semen (**see**-muhn)
A fluid containing male **sex cells.** From the Latin *semen,* meaning "seed."

semiconductor
(**sem**-ee-kuhn-*duhk*-tuhr)
A material that controls the flow of electricity in many **electronic** devices. Most semiconductors are made of **silicon.** The

You can imitate the squiggly line of a seismograph by holding a pencil motionless over a pad while a friend shakes the pad and slides it away from you.

Seismograph

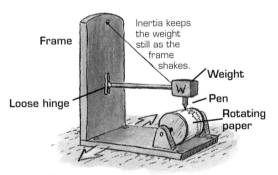

Frame
Inertia keeps the weight still as the frame shakes.
Loose hinge
Weight
Pen
Rotating paper

This seismograph records side-to-side movement.

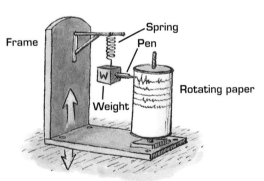

Frame
Spring
Pen
Weight
Rotating paper

This seismograph records up-and-down movement.

At many modern earthquake stations, the seismographs are in the ground. They send signals (via phone or radio) to a computer.

resistance of a semiconductor falls between that of a **conductor** and an **insulator**.

semipermeable

(*sem*-i-**puhr**-mee-uh-buhl)
Describes a material that allows some substances to pass through but not others. The semipermeable **membranes** that surround living **cells** allow only small **molecules** in and out.

Semmelweis (**zem**-uhl-*vise*), Ignaz (1818–1865)

A Hungarian doctor who developed **antiseptic** methods of childbirth.

senses (**sen**-siz)

The means by which an animal learns what is happening outside, or inside, its body. Most humans, for example, have 5 senses—hearing, sight, smell, taste, and touch—for knowing what happens in the outside world. We have many more senses—hunger, thirst, pain, and so on—for knowing what happens inside ourselves. From the Latin *sentire,* meaning "to feel."

sensor (**sen**-suhr)

A device that can detect heat, sound, light, **pressure**, **magnetism**, or other signals. A **thermostat** and an automatic door opener are examples of sensors.

sensory (**sen**-suhr-ee)

Having to do with the **senses**. The main sensory **organs** in humans are the eyes, ears, nose, and skin.

sepal (**see**-puhl)

A green, leaflike structure that protects a flower when it is still a bud. Sepals also help to support the flower when the bud opens.

septic system (**sep**-tik *sis*-tuhm)

A system in which **sewage** from sinks and toilets flows into an underground tank and then through pipes into the soil. **Bacteria** in the septic system tank and soil digest the sewage and turn it into harmless materials.

series circuit (**sir**-eez *suhr*-kit)

An **electric circuit** in which the parts are connected one after the other. In a series circuit, the electricity follows a single path. All the parts share the same **current.**

serum (**sir**-uhm)

Blood plasma without the *fibrinogen* that causes clotting. Serum is the watery, pale-yellow liquid that separates from blood when a **clot** forms. *Also,* a liquid containing **antibodies** that can protect a person against certain diseases.

servomechanism

(**suhr**-voh-*mek*-uh-*niz*-uhm)
A control system that corrects errors made by a machine, sensing the problem and acting to solve it. The *automatic pilot* in an airplane is an example of a servomechanism.

SETI (**set**-ee)

Short for *Search for ExtraTerrestrial Intelligence.* SETI scientists believe that there may be intelligent beings out in space. These scientists use **radio telescopes** to listen for radio signals from other civilizations. Thus far no signals have been received.

sewage (**soo**-ij)

Water containing waste matter that humans produce. In cities, most sewage

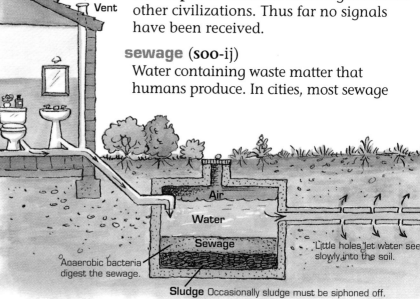

Septic System

Vent

Air

Water

Sewage

Little holes let water seep slowly into the soil.

Anaerobic bacteria digest the sewage.

Sludge Occasionally sludge must be siphoned off.

Series Circuit

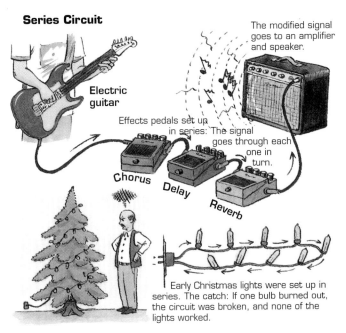

The modified signal goes to an amplifier and speaker.

Electric guitar

Effects pedals set up in series: The signal goes through each one in turn.

Chorus

Delay

Reverb

Early Christmas lights were set up in series. The catch: If one bulb burned out, the circuit was broken, and none of the lights worked.

is treated and then released into a lake, ocean, or river. In rural areas, the sewage goes into an underground tank where **bacteria** digest the harmful matter. See also **septic system.**

sex cell (**seks** *sel*)
See **gamete.**

sex linkage (**seks** *ling*-kij)
See **linkage.**

sex-linked characteristic
(**seks**-*lingkt kar*-ik-tuh-**ris**-tik)
A **trait** whose **genes** are on the **chromosome** that determines sex or gender. Color blindness and **hemophilia** are sex-linked characteristics. Males are much more likely to have these particular disorders than females.

sextant (**seks**-tuhnt)
An instrument used to measure the angle between two objects, such as the **horizon** and a star. Sailors use sextants to help them find their position.

sexual reproduction (**sek**-shuh-wuhl *ree*-pruh-**duhk**-shuhn)
The union of a female **egg** and a male **sperm** to produce an offspring.

shadow (**shad**-oh)
The dark **image** or shade cast by an object where it blocks the light. See also **penumbra** and **umbra.**

shale (**shayl**)
A smooth **sedimentary** rock made up of very small **particles** originally found in **silt** and clay. Shale was formed into layers by extreme **pressure.** It can be split into thin, flat pieces.

Shapley (**shap**-lee), **Harlow** (1885–1972)
An American astronomer who figured out that the sun is 30,000 **light-years** away from the center of our **galaxy.** Shapley also did important work on our **galaxy** and on **globular clusters** of stars.

shell (**shel**)
The hard outer covering of some animals, eggs, nuts, and seeds.

shellfish (**shel**-*fish*)
An animal, such as a clam, oyster, or lobster, that lives in the water and has a hard outer shell.

shoal (**shohl**)
A place where the water is shallow because of a sandbank or sandbar. *Also,* a large number of fish swimming together.

shock (**shahk**)
The jolt produced by an **electric current** passing through a person's body. *Also,* a sudden attack of illness caused by heart failure or blood loss.

shock wave (**shahk** *wayv*)
A powerful disturbance in air, water, or another substance caused by a sudden change in **pressure.** A shock wave in the air can cause a loud bang called a **sonic boom.** See also **seismic** wave.

shooting star (**shoo**-ting **stahr**)
Not a **star,** but a **meteor.** Also called a **falling star.**

short circuit (**short suhr**-kit)
A very strong **current flowing** through a **circuit** because of an accidental drop

in **resistance**. A short circuit can melt wires or start a fire. **Circuit breakers** and **fuses** protect against a short circuit.

shortwave (short wayv)
A **radio wave** with a wavelength between 33 and 264 feet (10 and 80 meters). Shortwaves are shorter than the radio waves used for ordinary broadcasts.

shrub (shruhb)
A woody plant that is smaller than a tree. A shrub usually has many stems starting from or near the ground. Also called a *bush*.

shutter (shuht-uhr)
The device that lets light into a camera. The shutter, which is in front of the **lens**, opens for a fraction of a second when you take a photo.

SI unit (ess-ie *yoo*-nit)
Short for *Système International,* French for "international system." It is used by scientists around the world. The 7 basic SI units are: Length—meter (m); **Mass—**kilogram (kg); Time—second (s); **Electric current—ampere** (A); Temperature—**Kelvin** (K); Light intensity—**candela** (cd); Amount of a substance—**mole** (mol).

siderial time (sie-dir-ee-uhl time)
A way of measuring time in relation to the stars. It is about 4 minutes shorter than a **solar** day, which is measured in relation to the sun.

signal (sig-nuhl)
A radio, sound, or light wave that sends information from one point to another. A red traffic light is a signal to stop.

silica (sil-i-kuh)
A **compound** of **silicon** and **oxygen**. Silica is the main ingredient of **sand**, **flint**, and **quartz**. (Formula—SiO_2)

silicate (sil-i-kit)
One of a group of **minerals** that makes up 95 percent of the earth's **crust**, soil, and rocks. Silicates are **compounds** of **silicon, oxygen,** and one or more metals.

silicon (sil-uh-*kahn*)
The second most abundant **element** on earth; only **oxygen** is more abundant. Silicon is found only combined with other **elements**, as in **silica**. It is widely used in computer **chips, transistors, solar cells,** and other types of **semiconductors**. (Symbol—Si)

silicon chip (sil-uh-*kahn* chip)
See **chip**.

silicone (sil-uh-*kohn*)
A manmade plastic with very large **molecules** that contain **silicon** and **oxygen**. It has great value because it is waterproof, nonsticky, a good **insulator**, and does not melt or get stiff at very high or low temperatures.

silk (silk)
A fine thread taken from the **cocoons** of *silkworms*. Silkworms are the caterpillars of large white moths known as *Bombyx mori*. The silk **fiber** is woven into fine fabric.

silt (silt)
Very tiny bits of soil and rock that settle to the bottom of rivers and other bodies of water. Silt is part of **sediment**.

Silurian period (si-lur-ee-uhn pir-ee-uhd)
The period of **geological history** from 435 to 408 million years ago. During the Silurian period land plants appeared and **coral reefs** formed.

silver (sil-vuhr)
A soft, white, shiny, metal **element**. Silver is used to make coins, jewelry, and many products for industry. It is a precious metal that does not easily corrode. (Symbol—Ag)

silviculture (sil-vi-*kuhl*-chuhr)
Planting and raising forest trees. From the Latin *silva*, meaning "forest," and *cultura*, meaning "the tilling of land."

simulation (*sim*-yuh-lay-shuhn)
A computer-operated model used to mimic a real-life situation. Simulation is used to train airplane pilots. They

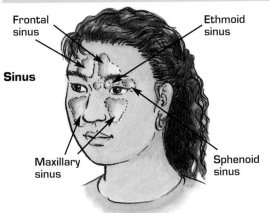

Sinus

Frontal sinus

Ethmoid sinus

Maxillary sinus

Sphenoid sinus

Africa across the Mediterranean Sea and southern Europe. The sirocco may be damp and warm or dry and filled with sand.

skeleton (skel-uht-n)
The bones of any animal with a **backbone**. The skeleton gives the body its shape, protects the inner **organs**, and

practice flying in a machine on the ground that looks and feels like the cockpit of a real plane.

sinkhole (singk-hohl)
A large hole in the ground where water collects. A sinkhole often forms when rainwater drips through the soil and **dissolves** rock under the ground.

sinus (sie-nuhs)
A cavity in a bone that is filled with either air or blood. Humans have 4 pairs of air-filled sinuses. A sinus **infection** is called *sinusitis*.

siphon (sie-fuhn)
A tube used for moving liquid from a higher container to a lower one. One end of a siphon is placed in the higher container and liquid is sucked into the tube. Liquid then continues to flow through the tube to the lower container. *Also*, a tube-shaped **organ** of some **shellfish** that they use to draw in and expel water. From the Greek *siphon*, meaning "pipe."

Sirius (sir-ee-uhs)
The brightest **star** in the **sky**; also called Dog Star.

sirocco (suh-rahk-oh)
A hot wind that blows northward from North

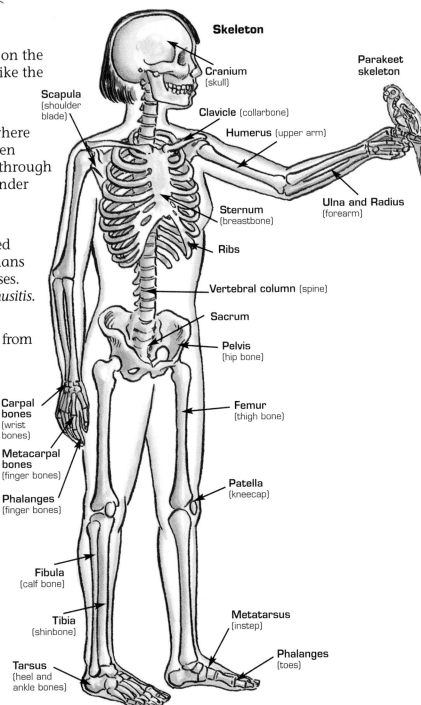

Skeleton

Cranium (skull)

Scapula (shoulder blade)

Clavicle (collarbone)

Humerus (upper arm)

Parakeet skeleton

Ulna and Radius (forearm)

Sternum (breastbone)

Ribs

Vertebral column (spine)

Sacrum

Pelvis (hip bone)

Carpal bones (wrist bones)

Metacarpal bones (finger bones)

Phalanges (finger bones)

Femur (thigh bone)

Patella (kneecap)

Fibula (calf bone)

Tibia (shinbone)

Tarsus (heel and ankle bones)

Metatarsus (instep)

Phalanges (toes)

173

allows the body to move. The human skeleton has more than 200 bones. See also **exoskeleton.** From the Greek *skeletos,* meaning "dried up."

skin (**skin**)

The **organ** that covers the body of a person or animal. The skin is the largest organ in the human body. It is waterproof, keeps body fluids in, and keeps most harmful germs and **chemicals** out. The outer layer, called the **epidermis,** is as thick as a sheet of paper. Under the epidermis is the thicker *dermis,* which contains blood vessels and **nerve** endings.

skull (**skuhl**)

The bones of the head of human beings and other animals with **backbones.** The skull of humans is made up of 22 bones.

sky (**skie**)

The region above the earth that extends hundreds of miles (kilometers) into space. The sky's blue color comes from the **scattering** of sunlight by dust **particles** in the **atmosphere.** From the Old Norse *sky,* meaning "cloud."

slag (**slag**)

The rough, hard waste that is left over after metal is taken from its **ore.** Slag is sometimes used to make **cement.**

slate (**slayt**)

A gray or black rock that can easily be split into thin slabs. Slate is a **metamorphic** rock formed underground from **shale,** a **sedimentary** rock. It is used for roof tiles and as paving stones.

sleet (**sleet**)

Small bits of ice formed by raindrops that freeze or by partly melted snowflakes freezing again.

slurry (**sluhr**-ee)

A mixture, or **suspension,** of very fine material in water. One kind of slurry is made by adding **cement** powder to water.

small intestine (**smawl** in-**tes**-tuhn)

An important part of the **digestive system.** The small intestine is a tube about an inch (2.5 centimeters) wide and 20 feet (6 meters) long. It runs from the stomach to the **large intestine.** The 3 parts of the small intestine are the **duodenum,** *jejunum,* and *ileum.*

smell (**smel**)

An important sense that lets animals and human beings detect odors. The chief organ of smell is the nose. It picks up **molecules** of gases that come from different objects. *Also,* an odor.

smelting (**smel**-ting)

A way of getting pure metal out of its **ore** by melting. During smelting, workers sometimes add **chemicals** to the ore to remove unwanted substances.

smog (**smahg** or **smawg**)

Short for *smoke* and *fog.* The **pollution** caused by gases in the air. Smog includes harmful **chemicals** that enter the air from automobiles, factories, and **power plants.**

smoke (**smohk**)

A mixture of gases and **particles** of **carbon** and other solids. Smoke forms when something burns.

sneeze (**sneez**)

A sudden and uncontrolled rush of air out of the nose and mouth. A sneeze is often caused by something that irritates the inside of the nose.

snow (**snoh**)

Tiny ice **crystals** that fall in soft, white flakes from cold clouds. Snow is an important source of water. Most snowflakes have 6 sides. It is said that no 2 are exactly the same.

soap (**sohp**)

A substance used for washing. Soap cleans in 3 steps: It helps water work its way into the material; it removes

particles of dirt; and it holds the particles of dirt in the water until they are rinsed away. Soap is made from fat and **chemicals** known as **alkalis**.

Soddy (**sahd**-ee), **Frederick** (1877–1956)
A British chemist who won fame for his **research** on **isotopes**.

sodium (**soh**-dee-uhm)
An **element** found only together with other elements. Sodium **compounds** have many uses. *Sodium chloride* (NaCl) is common table **salt**. *Sodium carbonate* (Na_2CO_3) is used in making glass, soap, paper, and water softeners. (See **soft water**.) *Sodium hydroxide* (NaOH) plays a part in making many other **chemicals**. (Symbol—Na)

software (**sawft**-*wer*)
The instructions that direct a computer to perform many tasks. Different software allows the same computer to be used to play games, get information, write and send letters, and so on.

soft water
(**sawft wawt**-uhr)
Water that contains few **minerals**. Soft water does not leave deposits in pipes and easily lathers and forms suds.

softwood
(**sawft**-wud)
The wood from trees with needle leaves, such as pine and fir.

soil (**soil**)
The covering of most of the earth's land surface. Soil is made by the breakdown of rocks into small **particles**, plus material from dead and decaying plants and animals.

solar (**soh**-luhr)
Having to do with the sun.

solar cell (**soh**-luhr **sel**)
A device that creates electricity from sunlight. Solar cells power most **artificial satellites**, some small calculators, and some highway signs.

solar energy (**soh**-luhr **en**-uhr-jee)
Radiation given off by the sun, which can be turned into light, heat, and electricity. Solar energy is the result of the **nuclear fusion** going on inside the sun.

solar flare (**soh**-luhr **fler**)
A sudden burst of **radiation** from the sun. Most of the **energy** from a flare is **ultraviolet light** and **X rays**. A solar flare may last several hours.

solar heating (**soh**-luhr **hee**-ting)
Using the sun's **energy** directly to heat water, heat or cool buildings, or cook food.

solar plexus (**soh**-luhr **plek**-suhs)
The **network** of **nerves** behind the stomach. A solar plexus punch is a blow

Solar cell

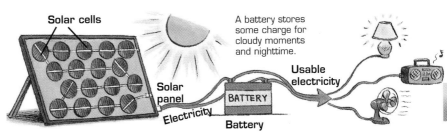

Solar cells

A battery stores some charge for cloudy moments and nighttime.

Usable electricity

Solar panel

Electricity

BATTERY

Battery

How it works: Each cell is a very thin sandwich of two materials.

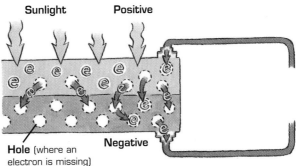

Sunlight   Positive

Negative layer: silicon and a bit of arsenic, which provides extra electrons

Positive layer: silicon and a bit of boron, which supplies lots of "holes"

Hole (where an electron is missing)

Negative

The photons in sunlight knock electrons loose from their atoms.

Loose electrons in the top layer go to the bottom layer to fill "holes" where electrons are missing. This makes the top layer positive so it attracts electrons, which flow out from the cell.

Solar System

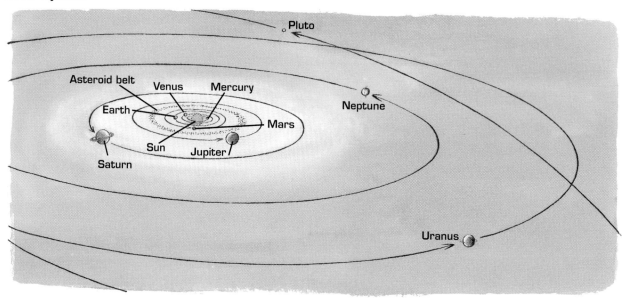

to the stomach just above the navel. A hard solar plexus punch can knock out a fighter.

solar system (**soh**-luhr *sis*-tuhm)
The sun and the planets, moons, **asteroids**, **comets**, and dust **particles** that are in **orbit** around the sun.

solar wind (**soh**-luhr **wind**)
A stream of **electrically charged particles**, or **ions**, flowing out of the sun. Solar wind travels at a speed of about 300 miles (500 kilometers) a second.

solder (**sahd**-uhr)
A metal or **alloy** that is heated and used to join or mend metal surfaces. Solder must melt more easily than the metal on which it is used. An alloy of **lead** and **tin** is a common solder.

solenoid (**soh**-luh-*noid*)
A coil of wire around a movable iron rod. In a solenoid, electricity flows through the coil, which becomes a magnet and pulls on the rod. Solenoids are used as **circuit breakers** and in other **electrical** devices. From the Greek *solen*, meaning "pipe."

solid (**sahl**-uhd)
A substance with a definite shape. Solids include wood and metal.

solidify (suh-**lid**-uh-*fie*)
To make or become hard, or solid. To solidify liquid water into solid ice, you need to remove heat from the water.

solid-state physics
(**sahl**-uhd **stayt fiz**-iks)
A branch of physics that deals with the physical properties of solids, including their **magnetism** and how well they conduct heat and electricity. Solid-state physics also studies solid **electronic** devices, such as **semiconductors**, **transistors**, and computer **chips**.

solstice (**sahl**-stis or **sohl**-stis)
The time of the year when the sun is farthest north or farthest south of the **equator**. In the Northern Hemisphere, the summer solstice comes around June 21 when the sun is most northerly. That is the longest day of the year. The winter solstice comes around December 21 when the sun is farthest south. That is the shortest day of the year. In the Southern Hemisphere the dates are reversed. From the Latin *sol*, meaning "sun," and *sistere*, meaning "to stand still."

soluble (**sahl**-yuh-buhl)
Able to be **dissolved**. **Salt** is soluble in water. From the Latin *solvere*, meaning "to dissolve."

solute (**sahl**-yoot)
A substance that **dissolves** in another substance to make a **solution**. **Salt** is a solute in **seawater**.

solution (suh-**loo**-shuhn)
A solid, liquid, or gas **dissolved** in another solid, liquid, or gas. The solution contains **solute** (the substance that is **dissolved**) and **solvent** (the substance in which the solute is dissolved). *Also,* the solving of a scientific problem. Scientists try to find solutions to their problems.

solvent (**sahl**-vuhnt)
A substance that can **dissolve** other substances. Water is a solvent of **salt**.

soma (**soh**-muh)
Cells that form the **tissue** and **organs** of living things, except for the sex cells. From the Greek *soma,* meaning "body."

sonar (**soh**-nahr)
Short for *sound navigation and ranging*. Sonar helps find underwater objects. The device sends out short bursts of sounds that are **reflected** back when they hit an object. The time it takes for the sound to bounce back shows where the object is. See also **echolocation**.

sonic boom (**sahn**-ik **boom**)
A loud bang heard when an airplane flies at or faster than the speed of sound. See also **shock wave**.

sound (**sound**)
Something that can be heard. Sound is produced by **vibrations**, or a rapid shaking back and forth, that create **sound waves**. Sound waves can travel through the air or through some solids or liquids, but not through a **vacuum**. *Also,* to measure the depth of water by lowering a weight fastened to the end of a line. *Also,* a narrow passage of water between 2 seas.

sound wave (**sound wayv**)
The **vibrations** that carry sound through the air and some solids and liquids. A sound wave's **frequency** and size

determine the **pitch** and tone quality of the sound.

Southern Cross (**suh**TH-uhrn **kraws**)
A **constellation** of 4 bright stars seen in the Southern Hemisphere. The Southern Cross was so named because the 4 stars outline a cross. Also called *Crux*.

southern lights (**suh**TH-uhrn **lites**)
See **aurora australis**.

South Pole (**south pohl**)
The most southern point on Earth. There are actually 3 South poles. The place where all the lines of **longitude** come together is the *south geographic pole*. The place where one end of a **compass** needle points is the *south magnetic pole*. The earth **rotates** around an imaginary **axis** whose southern end is the *instantaneous south pole*. The south magnetic pole and instantaneous south pole move every year.

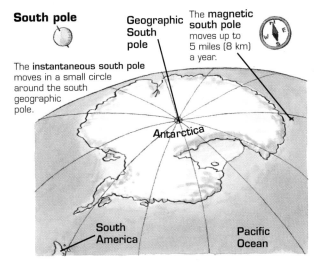

South pole

Geographic South pole

The magnetic south pole moves up to 5 miles (8 km) a year.

The **instantaneous south pole** moves in a small circle around the south geographic pole.

Antarctica

South America

Pacific Ocean

south pole (**south pohl**)
The part of a magnet that points to the earth's south magnetic pole.

space (**spays**)
The giant, near-empty region in which the planets, stars, and **galaxies** are found. Space begins beyond the earth's **atmosphere**. Above about 60 miles (95 kilometers) the atmosphere is so thin that it can be called the beginning of outer space.

S

spacecraft (**spays**-*kraft*)
Any vehicle designed for travel into space, such as a **space shuttle.**

space shuttle (**spays** *shuht*-l)
A **spacecraft** with wings. The space shuttle takes off like a rocket and lands like an airplane. It can make trips into space over and over again.

space station
(**spays** *stay*-shuhn)
A large artificial **satellite** in which **astronauts** can live and work for long periods of time. Space stations are now used for scientific **research.**

Spallanzani (*spah*-luhn-**zah**-nee), **Lazzaro** (1729–1799)
An Italian biologist who discovered that air contains tiny **microbes.**

spark (**spahrk**)
A brief flash that occurs when **electrons** jump across an open space. The spark from a *spark plug* **ignites** the fuel inside an automobile engine.

spawn (**spawn**)
The eggs of fish, **amphibians, crustaceans,** and **mollusks.** *Also,* the young of various sea animals. *Also,* to produce eggs. From the Old French *espandre,* meaning "to expand."

speaker (**spee**-kuhr)
A device used to reproduce sounds. The speaker receives electric signals from an **amplifier** and uses an **electromagnet** to change the signals into **vibrations,** which we hear as speech or music. Speakers are found in tape recorders, **CD** players, radios, televisions, and in theater sound systems. **Headphones** are small speakers.

species (**spee**-sheez or **spee**-seez)
A group of living things that are the same in many ways. Members of a species are able to mate and produce offspring that are also able to mate and produce offspring. Human beings belong to the species *Homo sapiens*.

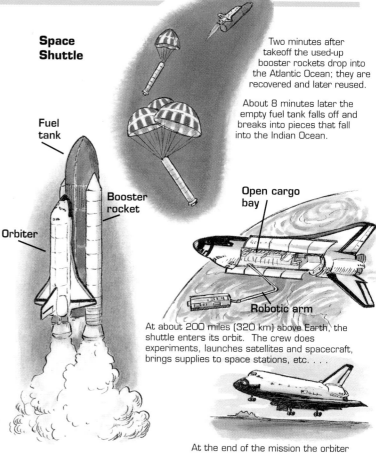

Space Shuttle

Two minutes after takeoff the used-up booster rockets drop into the Atlantic Ocean; they are recovered and later reused.

About 8 minutes later the empty fuel tank falls off and breaks into pieces that fall into the Indian Ocean.

Fuel tank

Booster rocket

Orbiter

Open cargo bay

Robotic arm

At about 200 miles (320 km) above Earth, the shuttle enters its orbit. The crew does experiments, launches satellites and spacecraft, brings supplies to space stations, etc. . . .

At the end of the mission the orbiter uses some power to get out of orbit and then glides down to land.

From the Latin *species,* meaning "appearance."

specific gravity
(spuh-**sif**-ik **grav**-uh-tee)
The **density** of a substance compared to the density of water at 39° **Fahrenheit** (4° **Celsius**). The specific gravity of gold, for instance, is 19.3. That means that gold's density is 19.3 times greater than the density of water. Any substance with a specific gravity under 1 will float in water; anything over 1 will sink.

specimen (**spes**-uh-muhn)
One member of a group that is an example of other members of the group. For instance, a doctor may check a few blood cells to test for disease. From the Latin *specere,* meaning "to look at."

spectrometer (spek-**trahm**-uh-tuhr)
An instrument that separates the different **wavelengths** of light given off by a

substance when it is heated. The spectrometer also measures the different wavelengths to identify the **elements** in the substance. See also **spectroscope.**

spectroscope (**spek**-truh-*skohp*)
An instrument that breaks light apart into separate color bands according to their different **wavelengths.** See also **spectrometer.** From the Latin *spectrum,* meaning "appearance," and the Greek *-skopion,* meaning "means of seeing."

spectrum (**spek**-truhm)
The band of different colors produced when white light is broken up by a **prism** or similar device. The spectrum has the same colors as a rainbow—red, orange, yellow, green, blue, indigo, violet. *Also,* the range of all **electromagnetic waves,** from **gamma rays** to **radio waves.**

speed (**speed**)
The rate of movement of an object.

speed of light (**speed** uhv **lite**)
The rate at which light travels in empty space. The speed of light is 186,282 miles (299,792 kilometers) per second.

sperm (**spuhrm**)
A male sex **cell** that may **fertilize** an egg of the female. Also called a **gamete** or **germ cell.**

sphere (**sfir**)
A figure shaped like a globe or baseball.

spinal cord (**spine**-l *kord*)
The thick bundle of **nerve cells** in the **spine** that connects the brain to nerve cells in the arms, legs, and trunk of the body.

spine (**spine**)
A column of small bones down the middle of the back from the head to the tailbone. The spine supports the body and holds the **spinal cord.** Sometimes called the *backbone. Also,* any short, sharp growth on an animal or plant, such as a porcupine's hair or the needles on a cactus. From the Latin *spina,* meaning "thorn."

spinneret (**spin**-uh-*ret*)
The fingerlike **organ** with which spiders spin their webs. Most spiders have 6 spinnerets at the rear of their **abdomens.**

spiracle (**spir**-i-kuhl or **spie**-ri-kuhl)
A breathing hole. Insects have spiracles along the sides of their body. The blowhole is the spiracle for whales and porpoises. From the Latin *spirare,* meaning "to breathe."

spiral galaxy (**spie**-ruhl **gal**-uhk-see)
A vast system of stars, dust, and gas that looks like a giant pinwheel in space. The stars of a spiral galaxy form a thick, round center with long, coiled arms.

spleen (**spleen**)
A spongy **organ** near the stomach that helps the body to fight **infection** and **filter** waste from the blood.

spore (**spor**)
A tiny body that can grow into a new **organism.** Spores are produced by most plants, some kinds of **bacteria,** fungi

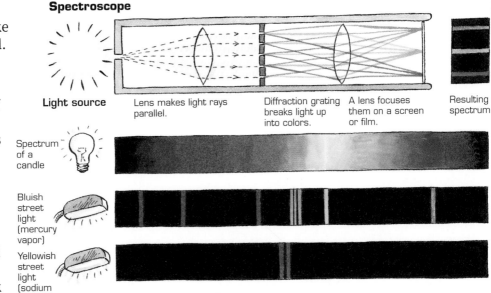

Spectroscope

Light source — Lens makes light rays parallel. — Diffraction grating breaks light up into colors. — A lens focuses them on a screen or film. — Resulting spectrum

Spectrum of a candle

Bluish street light (mercury vapor)

Yellowish street light (sodium vapor)

(plural of **fungus**), **algae**, and **protozoa**. From the Greek *spora*, meaning "seed."

spring (spring)
The season between winter and summer. In the Northern Hemisphere it starts on or about March 21 (**vernal equinox**) and ends on or about June 21 (summer **solstice**). In the Southern Hemisphere it starts on or about September 22 and ends on or about December 21. *Also*, an elastic device that returns to its original shape after being pulled or held out of shape. *Also*, a small stream of water coming from the earth.

spring tide (spring tide)
The very **high tide** that comes at a new moon or full moon. At spring tide, the sun and the moon are in a line and pull on the water creating a tidal bulge. See also **tide**.

Sputnik I (sput-nik wuhn)
The first of a series of unmanned **satellites** launched by the Soviet Union. Sputnik I, sent up on October 4, 1957, was the first artificial satellite.

squall (skwawl)
A sudden gust of wind, often with rain, snow, or **sleet**.

stabilize (stay-buh-lize)
To keep steady or make firm. Ships are stabilized with a keel or underwater fins. Airplanes are stabilized with the flat part of the tail, which is called a *stabilator,* a combination of *stabil*izer and elev*ator*.

stainless steel (stayn-luhs steel)
Steel that does not rust or tarnish. Stainless steel is made from **iron** with added **carbon** and **chromium**.

stalactite (stuh-lak-tite)
A **mineral** deposit that hangs down from the roof of some caves. A stalactite forms from water containing **calcium** carbonate seeping through a cave

ceiling. It may take thousands of years for a stalactite to develop. From the Greek *stalaktos*, meaning "dripping."

stalagmite (stuh-lag-mite)
A **mineral** deposit that builds up on the floor of some caves. A stalagmite forms from water containing **calcium** carbonate seeping through a cave ceiling and dripping onto the cave floor. It may take thousands of years for a stalagmite to develop. From the Greek *stalagma*, meaning "drop."

Stalactite

Stalagmite

stamen (stay-muhn)
The male part of a **flower**. The stamen consists of an **anther** and **filament**. It produces **pollen**.

star (stahr)
A huge ball of glowing gas that appears as a bright point in the night sky. The star that is closest to Earth is the sun. Astronomers now think there are more than 200 billion stars in the **universe**.

starch (stahrch)
A natural substance found in potatoes, wheat, corn, rice, and oats. Starch is a complex **carbohydrate**. It contains **carbon, hydrogen,** and **oxygen**.

star cluster (stahr kluhs-tuhr)
A group of stars held together by **gravity**. A star cluster in the shape of a ball is called a **globular cluster**. It may have up to a million stars. An irregular star cluster is called an *open cluster*. An open cluster usually has no more than a few hundred stars.

static (**stat**-ik)

A hissing or crackling sound coming from a radio or television set. Static is caused by electricity in the **atmosphere**. *Also*, describes an object that is not moving. The study of such objects is called *statics*. From the Greek *statikos*, meaning "to make stand."

static electricity

(**stat**-ik i-*lek*-**tris**-uh-tee)

Electricity that stays in one place instead of flowing in a **current**. You can feel the discharge of static electricity when you slide your foot on a carpet and then touch a metal doorknob. You can hear it when you pull off a wool sweater.

statistics (stuh-**tis**-tiks)

The science of collecting, classifying, and analyzing **data**. Statistics tell us that in Los Angeles it rains an **average** of one day a month in August and September.

steam (**steem**)

Very hot water in the form of a gas. Steam is produced when liquid water is heated to its boiling point of 212° **Fahrenheit** (100° **Celsius**) at standard atmospheric **pressure**. Steam has no color. The white cloud you see over a teakettle spout is steam that has **condensed** into tiny drops of water.

steel (**steel**)

A very hard, strong metal made of **iron** mixed with **carbon** and other **chemicals**. See also **stainless steel**.

stem (**stem**)

The part of a plant that holds the flowers, fruit, and leaves of the plant. The stem carries water and **minerals** from the roots to the leaves. It also carries sugar from the leaves to other parts of the plant. Most small plants have soft or *herbaceous* stems; tree stems are hard or *woody*.

steppe (**step**)

A vast, treeless area mostly covered by short grasses. A steppe usually has a dry **climate** with hot summers and cold winters.

stereo (**ster**-ee-oh)

Short for a *stereo*phonic sound system that uses 2 separate sound channels. A stereo recording is made with 2 **microphones** or groups of microphones at a distance from each other. The recording is played back with 2 **speakers** or **headphones** to give a feeling of direction to the sound.

sterile (**ster**-uhl)

Free of germs. A sterile bandage protects an open cut. *Also*, unable to **reproduce**. A sterile cat is not able to have kittens.

sterilization (*ster*-uh-luh-**zay**-shuhn)

Killing germs to prevent **infection** and the spread of disease. *Also*, treating people or animals so they are unable to bear offspring.

sternum (**stuhr**-nuhm)

A bone in the center of the chest. The sternum connects the collarbone to the ribs. It is also called the *breastbone*.

steroid (**ster**-oid or **stir**-oid)

A **chemical compound** made in the body that is important to good health.

Stem
Flowers
Leaves
Fruit
Stem
Roots

Cross section of stem: Bundles of tubes, called xylem, carry water and minerals up from roots.

Other tubes, called phloem, carry food made by the leaves to the rest of the plant.

Different cells help support the plant.

Some of the many kinds of stems:

Woody   Grassy   Climbing   Fleshy

Steroids, which include **cholesterol, bile,** and sex **hormones,** can also be made in **laboratories** and given to patients who need them.

stethoscope (**steth**-uh-*skohp*)
An instrument doctors use to hear sounds made by the heart, lungs, and other **organs** of the body.

Stethoscope

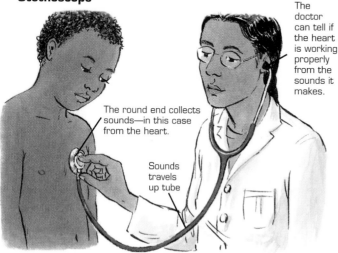

The round end collects sounds—in this case from the heart.

Sounds travels up tube

The doctor can tell if the heart is working properly from the sounds it makes.

stigma (**stig**-muh)
The female part of a **plant** at the top of the **pistil.** The stigma receives **pollen** from a **stamen.** *Also,* a spot, mark, or **pore** on an animal or **organ.** From the Greek *stigma,* meaning "tattoo or brand."

still (**stil**)
A device for refining, or distilling, liquids. The **distillation** of crude oil is done in huge, industrial stills.

stimulant (**stim**-yuh-luhnt)
Any substance that increases the activity of some part of the body, such as the **nervous system.** A stimulant found in coffee and cola drinks is **caffeine.**

stimulus (**stim**-yuh-luhs)
Anything that causes a **reaction** in a living thing. Dust is a stimulus that makes people **sneeze.** See also **response.**

sting (**sting**)
The pointed part of an **organism** that it uses to prick or wound its enemy or **prey.** The sting often carries some sort of poison. It is sometimes called a *stinger. Also,* the act of pricking or wounding an enemy or prey with a sting.

stolon (**stoh**-lahn)
A thin plant stem that grows on or beneath the ground. New plants grow from the stolon. Also called a *runner. Also,* a bud on some **organisms,** such as **coral,** from which new individuals grow.

stoma (**stoh**-muh)
A small opening or **pore** in a leaf. Gases pass through the stomata (plural of stoma). *Also,* any small opening in an **organism.** From the Greek *stoma,* meaning "mouth."

stomach (**stuhm**-ik)
The **organ** of the human body between the **esophagus** and the **small intestine.** The stomach is where chewed food is held and partially digested. The stomach mixes the food with **chemicals** from the lining of the stomach. The food, which is now a liquid, then moves to the **small intestine.**

stone (**stohn**)
A hard mass of **minerals** that is not metal. *Also,* a piece of **rock.** *Also,* a hard mineral mass that sometimes develops in a body **organ,** such as a *kidney stone.*

Stone Age (**stohn** *ayj*)
The period, beginning about 1.6 million years ago, when human beings first began to use crude tools made of stone. The Stone Age is usually divided into *Paleolithic, Mesolithic,* and *Neolithic.* It ended about 5,000 years ago, when people began to make tools of metal.

storage battery (**stor**-ij *bat*-uhr-ee)
See **battery.**

S

storm (storm)
A heavy downfall of **rain, snow,** or **hail.** A storm may also have strong winds and thunder and lightning. The air **pressure** is usually low during a storm.

strait (strayt)
A narrow body of water connecting 2 larger bodies of water. The Bering Strait is between the Pacific Ocean (Bering Sea) and the Arctic Ocean. From the Latin *strictus,* meaning "narrow or drawn tight."

stratified rock (strat-uh-*fide* rahk)
A rock, such as **shale, sandstone,** or **limestone,** that is formed in layers. Each layer of stratified rock is called a *stratum;* the plural is *strata.*

stratosphere (strat-uh-*sfir*)
The region in the **atmosphere** from about 4 to 11 miles (6 to 17 kilometers) to 30 miles (48 kilometers) above the earth's surface. The stratosphere is where many airplanes fly because there are few clouds or storms at this level. From the Latin *stratus,* meaning "spreading out" and *sphaera,* meaning "globe."

stratus (strat-uhs or stray-tuhs)
A low, gray cloud that spreads over a large area. A stratus cloud usually brings light rain. From the Latin *stratus,* meaning "spreading out."

stream (streem)
A continuous flow of water. A stream can be as small as a brook or as large as an ocean **current.** *Also,* the flow of wind in the **jet stream, electrons** in electricity, blood through the body, and light from its source.

streamlined (streem-*lined*)
Describes a shape that offers the least **resistance** as it moves through air or water. The streamlined shape is usually pointy in front with smooth, rounded sides. A streamlined airplane moves easily through air. The streamlined shape of sharks allows them to swim easily through water.

striated (strie-*ay*-tid)
Describes something that is striped or streaked. The striated muscles have dark and light bands and are used for most bodily movements.

sty (stie)
A small, red swelling on an eyelid. A sty is an infection usually by *staphylococcus* **bacteria** at the root of an eyelash or in a **gland** in the eyelid.

style (stile)
The thin, stemlike part of the **pistil** of a flower. The style contains the **ovary** at the bottom of the structure and the **stigma** at the top. *Also,* a general term for a thin or pointed part of an animal. From the Latin *stilus,* meaning "tool for writing."

subatomic particle
(suhb-uh-tahm-ik pahr-ti-kuhl)
Any tiny **particle** found within an **atom.** The best-known subatomic particles are **protons, neutrons,** and **electrons.** Lesser-known particles include **quarks,** *leptons, gluons, hadrons,* and *muons.* Scientists have described more than 200 subatomic particles.

Streamlined

Fish are beautifully streamlined in order to slice easily through water.

Sports cars are streamlined letting the air flow smoothly.

Many trucks are not streamlined. Their square shape makes the air flowing over them break up into eddies which slows them down.

subconscious (suhb-**kahn**-shuhs)
Describes thoughts and feelings below the level of awareness. A subconscious fear of flying in airplanes is common.

subcutaneous
(*suhb*-kyu-**tay**-nee-uhs)
Under the skin. Subcutaneous **injection** is a way to deliver drugs to body **tissues.**

subduction (suhb-**duhk**-shuhn)
The process of one **plate** of the earth's **crust** pushing under another plate, sometimes causing **earthquakes.**

sublimation (*suhb*-luh-**may**-shuhn)
The change from a solid to a gas or from a gas to a solid without passing through the liquid state. *Dry ice,* which is solid **carbon dioxide,** undergoes sublimation when heated. It changes directly into a gas.

subsoil (**suhb**-*soil*)
The soil just beneath the **topsoil.** Subsoil is usually lighter in color and contains more clay than topsoil.

succession (suhk-**sesh**-uhn)
A natural series of changes over time in a **species.** *Also,* the **chemical changes** that occur as a result of heating or mixing different substances together.

succulent (**suhk**-yuh-luhnt)
A plant, such as a cactus, that has thick, fleshy stems or leaves in which it stores water. Many succulents grow in deserts.

sucrose (**soo**-krohs)
The **chemical** name for table sugar. Sucrose is a **carbohydrate.** (Formula—$C_{12}H_{22}O_{11}$)

sugar (**shug**-uhr)
A food substance usually made from sugarcane or beets. Sugar is added to foods to make them taste sweeter. It is a **carbohydrate** that is manufactured by plants during **photosynthesis.**

sulfa drug (**suhl**-fuh *druhg*)
A **chemical compound** that helps the body fight invading **bacteria.** The sulfa drug does not kill the bacteria, it just stops them from multiplying. Today, doctors use **antibiotics** more than sulfa drugs.

sulfur (**suhl**-fuhr)
A yellow **chemical element** that reacts easily with other substances. Sulfur is often made into *sulfuric acid* (H_2SO_4), which has many industrial uses. Sulfur joins with **oxygen** in the air to form *sulfur dioxide* (SO_2), a major cause of air **pollution,** which mixes with rain to form **acid rain.** (Symbol—S)

summer (**suhm**-uhr)
The warmest season of the year. Summer comes between spring and autumn. In the Northern Hemisphere it starts on or about June 21 (*summer* solstice) and ends on or about September 22 (*autumnal* **equinox**). In the Southern Hemisphere it starts on or about December 21 and ends on or about March 21.

sun (**suhn**)
A huge ball of gases around which the earth and other planets of the **solar system revolve.** The sun is a **star** that provides Earth with most of its heat and light **energy.** The sun has a **diameter** of about 865,000 miles (1,392,000 kilometers) and is about 93 million miles (150 million kilometers) from earth. Its temperature is about 10,000° **Fahrenheit** (5,500° **Celsius**) on the surface and 27,000,000° **Fahrenheit** (15,000,000° **Celsius**) at the center.

sundial (**suhn**-*die*-uhl)
An instrument for telling time by the sun's light. The sundial has an upright piece of metal (the *gnomon*) that casts a shadow on a dial. As the sun crosses the sky, the shadow moves and shows the time.

sunspot (**suhn**-*spaht*)
A dark area that appears on the surface of the sun. Sunspots usually come in pairs. They are caused by magnetic storms on the sun. Sunspots look darker than the rest of the sun because they are cooler.

S

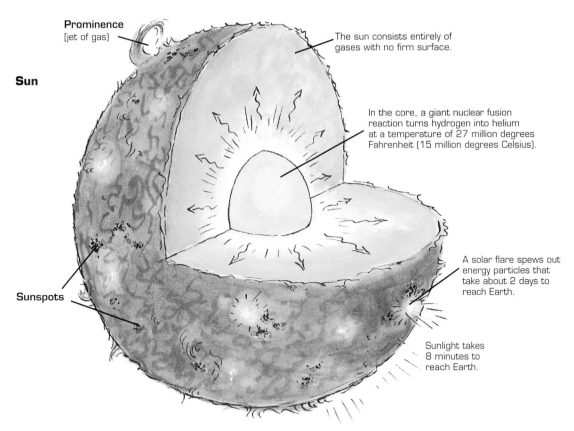

Sun

Prominence
[jet of gas]

The sun consists entirely of
gases with no firm surface.

In the core, a giant nuclear fusion
reaction turns hydrogen into helium
at a temperature of 27 million degrees
Fahrenheit (15 million degrees Celsius).

A solar flare spews out
energy particles that
take about 2 days to
reach Earth.

Sunspots

Sunlight takes
8 minutes to
reach Earth.

supercollider (**soo**-puhr-kuh-*lide*-uhr)
A circular track many miles (kilometers)
long that flings **subatomic particles**
against each other. The supercollider uses
powerful magnets to send the particles
racing around the track. The results help
physicists learn the basic laws of **matter**
and **subatomic particles.**

superconductivity
(*soo*-puhr-*kahn*-duhk-**tiv**-uh-tee)
The ability to conduct electricity without
resistance. Certain metals and **ceramics**
show superconductivity at very low
temperatures, around -418° **Fahrenheit**
(-250° **Celsius**). Scientists now want to
achieve superconductivity at higher
temperatures. This will let them build
electronic devices that use less **energy.**

supernova (*soo*-puhr-**noh**-vuh)
A **star** that explodes and then dies. A
supernova suddenly becomes several
thousand times brighter than normal.
It throws out huge amounts of gas and
dust at the moment of the **explosion.**

supersonic flight
(**soo**-puhr-**sahn**-ik **flite**)
Flying faster than the speed of sound. At
a height of 36,000 feet (11,000 meters)
the speed of sound is about 660 miles
(1,070 kilometers) per hour, depending
on temperature and **humidity.** Any faster
speed is supersonic. Supersonic speeds are
usually measured in **Mach numbers.** See
also **shock wave** and **sonic boom.**

superstring theory
(**soo**-puhr-*string* **thee**-uh-ree)
The idea that **subatomic particles** are
made of tiny lengths of stringlike
structures. A superstring may be a line or
a loop but not a point. It is many times
smaller than the smallest **particles.**

surface tension
(**suhr**-fuhs *ten*-chuhn)
The pull on the surface of liquids caused
by the attraction of the **molecules** to one
another. Surface tension makes it seem
that there is a thin, elastic cover on the
liquid. It allows insects to walk on water.

surfing (suhr-fing)
In computers, searching through the
Internet or **World Wide Web.**

surgery (suhr-juh-ree)
A medical treatment in which a doctor
repairs or removes a part of the body
that is diseased or injured. Also called an
operation.

survival of the fittest
(suhr-**vie-**vuhl uhv thuh **fit-**uhst)
See **natural selection.**

suspension (suh-**spen-**chuhn)
A mixture of very small **solid particles**
in a liquid or gas. Muddy water and
smoke are suspensions.

swamp (swahmp)
Low or coastal land that is covered
with water at least part of the year.
A swamp has very poorly drained
soils. More trees and shrubs grow in
a swamp than in a **marsh.**

S wave (es *wayv*)
Short for *Secondary wave.* A wave of
energy produced by an earthquake. The
S wave shakes the rocks in the ground up
and down. An S wave moves more
slowly than a **P-wave.**

symbiosis (*sim*-bie-**oh-**sis)
Two **organisms** living together.
Symbiosis includes *mutualism,* in
which the 2 organisms help each
other; **commensalism,** in which one
gains without harming the other; and
parasitism, in which one gains and the
other is harmed. From the Greek *syn,*
meaning "together," and *bios,*
meaning "life."

symbol (sim-buhl)
One or 2 letters that stand for the name
of an **element** in **chemistry.** The symbol
for **calcium,** for instance, is Ca.

symptom (sim-tuhm)
A change in the way your body works or

looks that shows that you are sick. A
runny nose is a symptom.

synapse (sin-aps)
One of many places in the **nervous
system** where impulses pass from one
nerve cell to another. A synapse is
where the *dendrite* of one nerve cell
meets the **axon** of another. From the
Greek *syn,* meaning "together," and
haptein, meaning "to fasten."

synchrotron (sing-kruh-*trahn*)
A device for sending **electrons** and
protons at very high speeds crashing
into a target of some sort. Scientists study
the results of the collisions to learn more
about the structure of the **atom.**

synthesizer (sin-thuh-*sie*-zuhr)
An **electronic** musical instrument
that can imitate the sounds of other
instruments. Most synthesizers have
keyboards like pianos. Players press the
keys to produce tones of different **pitch.**
Other switches and connections control
loudness and tone quality.

synthetic (sin-**thet-**ik)
An artificial substance made by combining
2 or more **elements** to create a new
compound. An example of a synthetic
fiber is **nylon,** which is made from
carbon, hydrogen, and other **chemicals.**
From the Greek *syn,* meaning "together,"
and *theinai,* meaning "to put."

system (sis-tuhm)
A number of separate parts that work
together to do a certain job. Your body's
digestive system contains the **mouth,
esophagus, stomach, small** and **large
intestines,** and other **organs.** It changes
the food you eat into the **nutrients** your
body needs.

syzygy (siz-uh-jee)
Two or more heavenly bodies in a line.
Syzygy occurs when the sun, moon, and
Earth are lined up.

tachometer (ta-**kahm**-uh-tuhr)
A device to measure the speed of a turning wheel or shaft. A tachometer usually gives the speed as **revolutions** per minute, or RPM.

tactile (**tak**-tuhl or **tak**-tile)
See **touch.**

taiga (**tie**-guh)
A forest in a region of very cold winters and short growing seasons. In a taiga, most of the trees are evergreens, such as spruce and fir. See also **biome.**

tail (**tayl**)
The part of an animal that extends behind its body. The tail may help the animal move, balance, or grasp. *Also,* the back part of an airplane. It includes the up-and-down fin and **rudder** and the side-to-side *stabilator.* The airplane's tail keeps it steady in the air and helps it make turns.

talc (**talk**)
A soft **mineral** that is used in talcum powder, crayons, face powder, and plastics.

talon (**tal**-uhn)
The claw of a bird of prey, such as an eagle or hawk. The birds use their talons to grasp the animals that they eat.

talus (**tay**-luhs or **tal**-uhs)
A pile of broken rock at the bottom of a cliff or mountain. The talus comes from the **weathering** of the solid rock above.

tannin (**tan**-in)
An **acid** found in the bark and leaves of oak, chestnut, hemlock, and other trees. Tannin is used to tan animal hides. Also called *tannic acid.*

tape (**tayp**)
See **magnetic tape.** *Also,* a device for measuring distance.

tape recorder (**tayp** ri-*kord*-uhr)
A device to record sound, sound and pictures, or computer **data** on **magnetic tape.** A tape recorder changes electric signals from a **microphone,** video camera, or computer into patterns of magnetized **particles** on the tape. When the tape is played, the magnetic pattern is changed back into electric signals that reproduce the original sound, pictures, or computer data.

tar (**tahr**)
A thick, black liquid used in dyes, perfumes, and to cover roofs. Tar is made from coal, **petroleum,** or wood. *Also,* a substance found in cigarettes that can cause lung disease.

taste (**tayst**)
An important sense that helps us identify foods. Humans recognize 4 basic tastes—salty, sour, sweet, and bitter.

taste bud (**tayst** *buhd*)
One of the small bumps on the **tongue** and in the mouth that pick up the different flavors of food. See also **taste.**

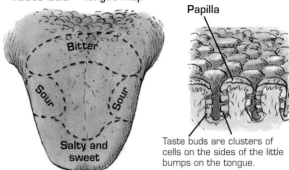

Taste bud Tongue map
Papilla
Bitter
Sour   Sour
Salty and sweet

Taste buds are clusters of cells on the sides of the little bumps on the tongue.

taxonomy (tak-**sahn**-uh-mee)
A branch of science that deals with the **classification** of all living things. See also **classification.**

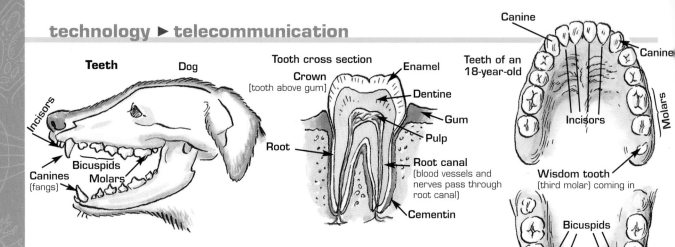

Teeth

Dog

Incisors

Bicuspids

Canines (fangs)

Molars

Tooth cross section

Crown [tooth above gum]

Root

Enamel

Dentine

Gum

Pulp

Root canal (blood vessels and nerves pass through root canal)

Cementin

Teeth of an 18-year-old

Canine

Canine

Molars

Molars

Incisors

Wisdom tooth (third molar) coming in

Bicuspids

technology (tek-**nahl**-uh-jee)
The practical use of science to make life better and easier for people. Technology has produced a huge number of things, from airplanes to zippers.

tectonics (tek-**tahn**-iks)
See **plate tectonics**.

teeth (**teeth**)
Hard, bonelike structures in the jaws of humans and many kinds of **vertebrate** animals. Teeth are the hardest material in the body. Humans use teeth for chewing and speaking. Some animals use teeth only for catching and eating **prey**. *Also,* the regular ridges around the edge of a **gear**.

Teflon (**tef**-lahn)
A **plastic** material used to put nonstick coatings on pots and pans. **Chemical** name—polytetrafluoroethylene resin.

tektite (**tek**-tite)
A glassy stone that is usually round in shape and black or green in color. Scientists believe tektites were formed when **meteorites** from space crashed into **sedimentary** rocks on Earth. From the Greek *tektos*, meaning "melted."

telecommunication (**tel**-uh-kuh-*myoo*-nuh-**kay**-shuhn)

Television

SCIENCE QUIZ

CONTESTANT A

Studio

Local TV studio

Sending and receiving sounds or **images** over long distances by telephone, radio, or television. Telecommunication sends electric signals, radio waves, or light waves through the air or wires. They go from **transmitter** to **receiver** or from computer to computer. From the Greek *tele,* meaning "far off," and the Latin *communicare,* meaning "to share."

telegraph (**tel**-uh-*graf*)
A way to send written messages electrically through wires. The **electromagnetic** telegraph was developed by **Samuel F. B. Morse** in 1837. Today messages are mostly sent by telephone or radio. From the Greek *tele,* meaning "far off," and *graphein,* meaning "to write."

telemetry (tuh-**lem**-uh-tree)
Measuring something from a distance, such as a distant planet. A telemetry system has **sensors** to make the measurements, a **radio transmitter** to send out the measurements, and a receiver to collect the information. From the Greek *tele,* meaning "far," and *metron,* meaning "measure."

telepathy (tuh-**lep**-uh-thee)
See **extrasensory perception.**

telephone (**tel**-uh-*fohn*)
A device for sending and receiving voice messages. The telephone changes **sound waves** into electrical signals and sends them through wires or on **radio waves** to another telephone. Here the signals are changed back into sound waves. The telephone lines can also carry **facsimile images, video** signals, and **data** for computers. From the Greek *tele,* meaning "far off," and *phone,* meaning "sound."

telephoto (*tel*-uh-**foh**-toh)
Describes a camera **lens** that makes distant objects appear larger and closer.

telescope (**tel**-uh-*skohp*)
An instrument that makes distant objects appear larger. Telescopes are mostly used to view various bodies in space. See also **reflecting telescope, refracting telescope, radio telescope.** From the Greek *tele,* meaning "far off," and *skopion,* meaning "means of seeing."

television (**tel**-uh-*vizh*-uhn)
A way of sending pictures and sound by radio waves or cable over great distances. In television, cameras and **microphones** change pictures and sound into electrical signals. The signals

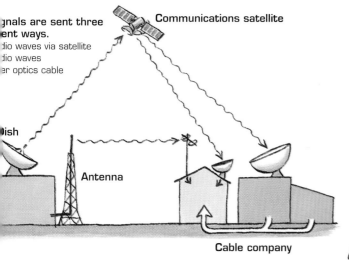

gnals are sent three ent ways.
dio waves via satellite
dio waves
er optics cable

Communications satellite

Dish

Antenna

Cable company

Home

travel on radio waves or through cable to television receivers. Here the signals are changed back to pictures and sound.

temperate (**tem**-puh-ruht)
Not very hot or very cold. A temperate **climate** is found in most of the United States.

Temperate Zone (**tem**-puh-ruht *zohn*)
The parts of Earth that are not too hot or cold. The Temperate Zone in the Northern Hemisphere is between the *tropic of Cancer* and the *Arctic Circle*. In the Southern Hemisphere, it is between the *tropic of Capricorn* and the *Antarctic Circle*.

temperature (**tem**-puh-ruh-chuhr)
A measure of how hot or cold something is. Temperature is measured on either the **Fahrenheit** (F), **Celsius** or centigrade (C), or **Kelvin** (K) scale.

temperature-humidity index (**tem**-puh-ruh-chuhr hyoo-**mid**-uh-tee *in*-deks)
A measure of how comfortable people feel in hot weather. The temperature-humidity index, or *THI,* is based on the air temperature and the **relative humidity.** Most people feel comfortable with a THI below 75.

tempering (**tem**-puhr-ing)
A process that hardens metal or glass. Tempering is usually done by heating and quickly cooling the material.

tendon (**ten**-duhn)
A strong band of **tissue** that attaches a muscle to a bone. The tendons make it possible for the muscles to move the bones.

tendril (**ten**-druhl)
The part of a climbing plant that attaches itself to something to support the plant. Tendrils often look like short, extra lengths of stem.

tensile (**ten**-suhl)
A measure of how much force is needed to pull a material apart. The tensile strength

Temperature

Oven temperature to roast turkey: 375°

There is no known upper limit to temperature.

	C	F	K
Water boils	100°	212°	373
		200°	350
	75°	150°	
	57.7°	136°	330.7
	50°		325
Human body	37°	98.6°	310
	25°		300
		50°	
Water freezes	0°	32°	272
		0°	250
	−25°		
	−50°	−50°	225
	−75°	−100°	200
	−89.2°	−128.6°	184
	−100°	−150°	175
	−125°	−200°	150
Nitrogen becomes liquid	−150°	−250°	125
	−175°		100
	−190°	−300° −310°	83
	−200°		75
	−220°	−350° −360°	53
	−225°		50
		−400°	
	−250°		25
Absolute zero	−273°	−475°	0
	Celsius	Fahrenheit	Kelvin

of **steel** wire, for example, is much greater than the tensile strength of cotton thread.

tentacle (**ten**-ti-kuhl)
A long, thin growth on the head of an **invertebrate** animal. The animal uses the tentacle for feeling, holding, or moving. From the Latin *tentare,* meaning "to touch."

terminal (**tuhr**-muhn-l)
The point at which an electric wire brings **current** into or out of an electrical device. *Also,* a computer that is part of a computer **network**. *Also,* the rocks and soil at the end of a **glacier**; sometimes called terminal **moraine**.

terrarium (tuh-**rer**-ee-uhm)
A glass or plastic container in which small plants or land animals are kept. From the Latin *terra,* meaning "land."

terrestrial (tuh-**res**-tree-uhl)
Having to do with the land part of the earth, not the water or air. Humans are terrestrial creatures; fish are not.

Tertiary period
(**tuhr**-shee-*er*-ee *pir*-ee-uhd)
The period of **geological history** from 65 to 1.6 million years ago. During the Tertiary period the early ancestors of humans appeared and the Alps, Andes, and Rocky mountains were formed.

Tesla (**tes**-luh), **Nikola** (1856–1943)
An American **engineer** who made many important discoveries dealing with motors and electricity.

testes (**tes**-teez)
See **testicle**.

testicle (**tes**-ti-kuhl)
One of the 2 male **glands** found in most **vertebrates**. The testicles produce the **sperm cells** necessary to **fertilize** an egg. The testicles are found in a sac behind the **penis** called the *scrotum*. A single testicle is also called a *testis;* the plural is *testes*.

testosterone (tes-**tahs**-tuh-*rohn*)
A **hormone** from the **testicles** that controls sexual development, the development of body hair, and a deep voice in human males. The testicles produce more testosterone as a teen-aged boy enters **puberty**.

text (**tekst**)
In computers, the words, sentences, and paragraphs produced by a **word processor**.

thallophyte (**thal**-uh-*fite*)
A plantlike **organism** that has no root, stem, or leaves. The thallophytes include **bacteria, fungi, algae,** and **lichens**. From the Greek *thallos,* meaning "green shoot," and *phyton,* meaning "plant."

thaw (**thaw**)
To melt anything that is frozen. *Also,* weather that melts ice and snow coming after a period of freezing temperatures.

theodolite (thee-**ahd**-l-*ite*)
An instrument surveyors use for measuring angles and directions. The theodolite is usually mounted on a tripod to hold it steady.

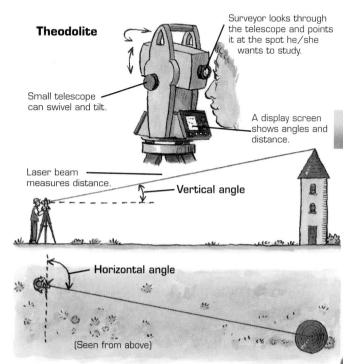

Theodolite

Surveyor looks through the telescope and points it at the spot he/she wants to study.

Small telescope can swivel and tilt.

A display screen shows angles and distance.

Laser beam measures distance.

Vertical angle

Horizontal angle

[Seen from above]

theory (**thee**-uh-ree)
A possible explanation. To test a theory, scientists do **experiments** and make **observations**.

theory of relativity (**thee**-uh-ree uhv *rel*-uh-**tiv**-uh-tee)
See **relativity**.

therapy (**ther**-uh-pee)
A way of treating or curing a disease or unwanted condition. See also **chemotherapy, drug**, psychotherapy, and **physical therapy**.

thermal (**thuhr**-muhl)
Anything to do with heat. A thermal spring bubbles hot water out of the ground. *Also,* a rising column of warm air. **Gliders** rise and fly on thermals.

thermal inversion
(**thuhr**-muhl in-**vuhr**-zhuhn)
A condition in the **atmosphere** when a layer of warm air settles over a layer of cooler air. It can trap gases and **particles** that cause **pollution** close to the ground. Also called a *temperature inversion. Also,* a condition in the ocean when a layer of warm water settles over a layer of cooler water.

thermal pollution
(**thuhr**-muhl puh-**loo**-shuhn)
The heating of water that occurs when hot waste water is released into an ocean, river, or lake. Thermal pollution can harm the **organisms** that live in the water.

thermocouple (**thuhr**-moh-*kuhp*-uhl)
A device that changes **heat** into **electricity**. A thermocouple is made of 2 different metal wires joined at their ends. If one end is warmer, an **electric current** flows in the wires. Since the amount of current depends on the difference in temperature, the thermocouple can be used as a **thermometer**. Also called a *thermal junction.*

thermodynamics
(*thuhr*-moh-die-**nam**-iks)
The branch of science that studies **heat**

and **work.** Thermodynamics has two basic laws: **Energy** cannot be created or destroyed, it can only be changed; heat always flows from a hotter object to a colder one.

thermometer
(thuhr-**mahm**-uh-tuhr)
An instrument for measuring temperature. Liquid thermometers have **mercury** or colored **alcohol** in a thin, sealed tube. The liquid expands and moves up the tube when heated and contracts and moves down when cooled. Electronic thermometers use a **thermocouple** to measure temperature. From the Greek *therme,* meaning "heat," and *metron,* meaning "measure."

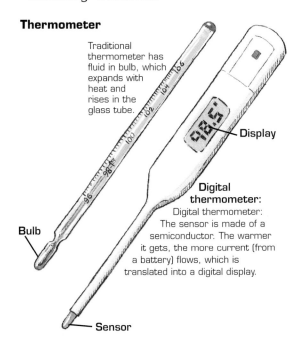

Thermometer

Traditional thermometer has fluid in bulb, which expands with heat and rises in the glass tube.

Display

Bulb

Digital thermometer:
Digital thermometer: The sensor is made of a semiconductor. The warmer it gets, the more current (from a battery) flows, which is translated into a digital display.

Sensor

thermonuclear reaction
(*thuhr*-moh-**noo**-klee-uhr ree-**ak**-shuhn)
See **fusion**.

thermosphere (**thuhr**-muh-*sfir*)
The layer of the earth's **atmosphere** below the **exosphere**. The thermosphere extends from about 50 to 400 miles (80 to 650 kilometers) above the earth's surface. The temperature ranges from about -135˚ **Fahrenheit** (-93˚ **Celsius**)

at the bottom to more than 2700°
Fahrenheit (1500° Celsius) at the top.
From the Greek *therme,* meaning "heat,"
and *sphaira,* meaning "globe."

thermostat (**thuhr**-muh-*stat*)
A device that automatically controls the
temperature of a place or object. The
thermostat detects the temperature and
then turns heating or cooling devices on
or off. Thermostats are found in buildings,
ovens, refrigerators, air conditioners,
and heaters. From the Greek *therme,*
meaning "heat," and -*states,* meaning
"one that stops."

THI (**tee**-*aych*-**ie**)
See **temperature-humidity index.**

Thomson (**tahm**-suhn), **Sir Joseph
John** (1856–1940)
A British physicist who proved that
cathode rays consist of **electrons.**

thorax (**thor**-aks)
The chest or the part of the body
between the neck and **abdomen.** The
thorax contains the heart and lungs.
Also, the middle part of an insect's body,
where the wings and legs are attached.

throat (**throht**)
The passage from the mouth and nose
to the lungs and stomach. The throat
contains the structures necessary for
breathing and eating. The **larynx** and
pharynx are found in the throat.

thrust (**thruhst**)
A force or push. The thrust of a jet engine
moves an airplane forward. *Also,* the
push of one block of rock over another
block, which is called a thrust **fault.**

thunder (**thuhn**-duhr)
The loud noise caused by the sudden
expansion of air that has been heated
by lightning. Thunder can sound like
a sharp crack or a long, deep rumble.

thymus (**thie**-muhs)
A **gland** in the upper chest that helps
the body fight disease. The thymus

produces **white blood cells** that attack
bacteria, viruses, cancer cells, and other
harmful **organisms.** The thymus is biggest
in children and shrinks with age.

thyroid (**thie**-roid)
A **gland** in the neck that produces
thyroxine and other **hormones** that
control body growth and the rate of
energy production in **cells.** A thyroid
that is too active or too slow affects a
person's growth and causes other serious
health problems.

tidal pool (**tide**-l *pool*)
An area near a coast or shore that is
always covered with seawater, though
more water enters during **high tide.** A
tidal pool is home to many sea creatures.

tidal wave (**tide**-l *wayv*)
See **tsunami.**

tide (**tide**)
The regular rise and fall of ocean water
caused by the pull of the moon and
sun's gravity. **High tide** comes about
every 12 hours and 26 minutes; **low tide**
comes in between. See also **neap tide**
and **spring tide.**

Tide

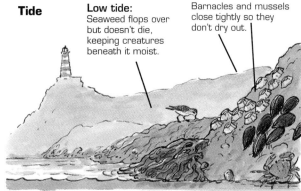

Low tide:
Seaweed flops over
but doesn't die,
keeping creatures
beneath it moist.

Barnacles and mussels
close tightly so they
don't dry out.

High tide:
Fish move
in to feed.

Seaweed
rises up.

Barnacles and mussels
open to feed.

timber line (tim-buhr *line***)**
The limit of the area where trees will not grow because of the cold. Timber lines are found near the top of tall mountains and in the **polar** regions.

time (time)
A measure of the past, present, and future. Time can be based on natural events, such as the earth's **rotation** on its **axis** (a day), the **phases** of the moon (a month), or the earth's **revolution** around the sun (a year). Time can also be based on a time keeper, such as a clock.

tin (tin)
A soft, silvery, metal **element** that is widely used to coat **steel** and make so-called tin cans for food. Tin is also used to coat pins, paper clips, and staples. (Symbol—Sn)

tissue (tish-oo**)**
A group of similar **cells** joined together to form part of the structure of a living thing. Human body tissue includes muscle tissue, **nerve** tissue, and fat tissue. From the Old French *tissu,* meaning "fine fabric."

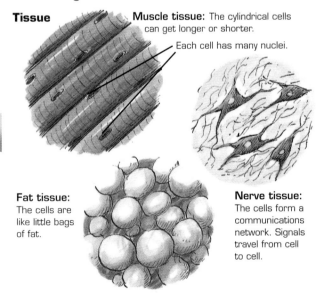

Tissue

Muscle tissue: The cylindrical cells can get longer or shorter.

Each cell has many nuclei.

Fat tissue: The cells are like little bags of fat.

Nerve tissue: The cells form a communications network. Signals travel from cell to cell.

tissue culture (tish-oo *kuhl*-chuhr**)**
Growing **tissue** in a **laboratory.** Tissue culture provides scientists with living tissue for study and **research.**

titanium (tie-tay-nee-uhm)
A hard, light, white, metal **element** that can withstand high temperatures and does not rust or corrode. Titanium is widely used in rockets and airplanes. (Symbol—Ti)

titration (tie-tray-shuhn)
A way to determine the makeup of a **compound.** In titration, a known substance is slowly added to a **solution** or compound to see how much is needed to cause a **chemical reaction.** The amount added tells the scientist the contents of the original compound.

TNT (tee-en-**tee)**
Short for *TriNitroToluene.* A very powerful **explosive** used in bombs, **missiles,** mining, and construction. (Formula—$CH_3C_6H_2(NO_2)_3$)

Tombaugh (tahm-boh**), Clyde W.** (1906–1997)
An American astronomer who discovered the **planet Pluto** in 1930.

tomography (tuh-mahg-ruh-fee)
A way of diagnosing disease by taking **X-ray** pictures of cross sections of parts of the body. From the Greek *tomos,* meaning "slice or section," and *graphein,* meaning "to write." See also **CAT** scans.

ton (tuhn)
Three different units of weight. The *short ton,* widely used in the United States, is 2,000 pounds (907 kilograms). The *metric ton* (or *tonne*), used in most other countries, is 2,204.6 pounds (1,000 kilograms). The *long ton,* used in coal mines, is 2,240 pounds (1,016 kilograms).

tongue (tuhng)
The **organ** in the mouth used for tasting, chewing, swallowing, and speaking. Frogs use their tongue to catch food. Snakes use their tongue to detect smells.

tonsil (tahn-suhl**)**
A mass of **tissue** in the throat that is thought to protect against **infection.**

T

An **inflammation** of the tonsil is called *tonsilitis*.

tooth (**tooth**)
See **teeth**.

topography (tuh-**pahg**-ruh-fee)
The surface of the land, including mountains, rivers, roads, and cities. *Also*, a way to show the surface features of an area on a map. From the Greek *topos*, meaning "place," and *graphein*, meaning "to write."

Topography

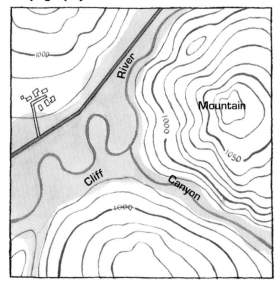

topsoil (**tahp**-*soil*)
Usually the top 4 to 10 inches (10 to 25 centimeters) of soil. Topsoil is generally dark brown and contains the **minerals** and **humus** necessary for plant growth.

tornado (tor-**nay**-doh)
A powerful, narrow, funnel-shaped wind that usually cuts a path of destruction less than a mile (1.6 kilometers) wide. Tornado winds of up to 300 miles (480 kilometers) an hour destroy everything in their way. Also called *twister*.

torque (**tork**)
A turning or twisting effort that causes **rotation**. Torque is usually measured in **pound**-feet. Examples of torque include turning a doorknob and pedaling a bicycle.

Torricelli (*tor*-i-**chel**-ee), **Evangelista** (1608–1647)
An Italian physicist who invented the **mercury barometer** in 1644. Torricelli also improved the **telescope**.

Torrid Zone (**tor**-id *zohn*)
See **Tropics**.

torsion (**tor**-shuhn)
Twisting an object by applying forces in opposite directions at its ends. A *torsion bar* helps a car absorb the shock when it goes over a bump.

touch (**tuhch**)
The sense that helps you learn the shape, hardness, and heat of objects by feeling them. Your skin is your main touch **organ**. Also called *tactile sense*.

toxic waste (**tahk**-sik **wayst**)
Chemical, medical, **nuclear**, or **petroleum** waste that can poison humans and other living things. Also called *hazardous waste*.

toxin (**tahk**-suhn)
A poison produced by a living **organism**. Toxins from **bacteria** can cause disease. Toxins from some snakes, spiders, and insects can kill. *Also*, any substance poisonous to living things. *Toxicology* is the science that deals with poisons and their effects on living things.

trace element (**trays** *el*-uh-muhnt)
A **mineral** needed in very small amounts by the body. Trace **elements** that humans need include **copper**, **manganese**, **iodine**, and **zinc**.

trachea (**tray**-kee-uh)
The air passage from the nose and the mouth to the lungs. Also called *windpipe*.

traction (**trak**-shuhn)
The ability to move over a surface without slipping. Traction lets cars drive on icy roads. *Also*, pulling on a muscle to correct a medical condition. From the Latin *trahere*, meaning "to pull or drag."

trade wind (**trayd wind**)
A strong, steady wind blowing toward the **equator** from the northeast and the southeast. The trade winds were very important in the days of sailing ships.

trait (**trayt**)
A special quality of a person or object, such as shyness or courage. *Also,* a feature, such as red hair or blue eyes, which is inherited.

trajectory (truh-**jek**-tuhr-ee)
The path of an object, such as a rocket or **missile,** flung into space. Trajectories are usually curved because of the pull of **gravity.** From the Latin *trans,* meaning "across," and *jacere,* meaning "to throw."

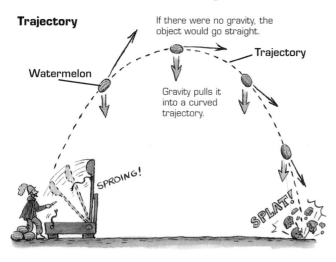

Trajectory

If there were no gravity, the object would go straight.

Trajectory

Watermelon

Gravity pulls it into a curved trajectory.

SPROING!

SPLAT!

tranquilizer (**trang**-kwuh-*lie*-zuhr)
A drug that helps people relax and feel calm. Tranquilizers work on the **nervous system.**

transducer (trans-**doo**-suhr)
A device that changes one form of **energy** into another. A transducer that changes sound waves into electrical signals is called a **microphone.**

transformer (trans-**for**-muhr)
A device that raises or lowers the **voltage** of an **electric current.**

transfusion (trans-**fyoo**-zhuhn)
Injecting blood taken from one person into a **vein** of someone else. From the Latin *trans,* meaning "across," and *fundere,* meaning "to pour."

transistor (tran-**zis**-tuhr)
A small **electronic** device that can amplify an **electric current** or switch it on or off. A transistor is a part of computers, radios, and other electronic equipment. It was invented in 1948.

transition element
(tran-**zish**-uhn *el*-uh-muhnt)
An **element** with an incomplete inner shell of **electrons.** The transition elements include the metals iron, **nickel, copper, silver,** and **gold.**

translucent (trans-**loo**-suhnt)
Letting light pass through, but not **transparent.** Frosted glass is translucent. From the Latin *trans,* meaning "across," and *lucere,* meaning "to shine."

transmission (trans-**mish**-uhn)
Sending a radio or television signal from a **transmitter** to a **receiver.** *Also,* the system in a vehicle that sends **power** from the engine to the wheels.

transmit (trans-**mit**)
To send a signal of some sort from one place to another. Communication **satellites** transmit television programs all over the world. From the Latin *trans,* meaning "across," and *mittere,* meaning "to send."

transmitter (trans-**mit**-uhr)
A device for sending out some kind of signal. Every radio and television station has a transmitter to send out radio waves that carry the programs.

transmutation
(*trans*-myoo-**tay**-shuhn)
The change of one **element** into another. Natural transmutations occur mostly through **radioactive decay.** Artificial transmutations can be caused by bombarding **atoms** with **subatomic particles.** From the Latin *trans,* meaning "across," and *mutare,* meaning "to change."

transparent (trans-**per**-uhnt)
Letting light through so things on the other side can be clearly seen. Windows are usually made of transparent glass.

transpiration
(*tran*-spuh-**ray**-shuhn)
The giving off of water **vapor** by plant leaves. Transpiration usually takes place through tiny openings, called stomata (plural of **stoma**), on the leaf's surface. From the Latin *trans,* meaning "across," and *spirare,* meaning "to breathe."

transplant (**trans**-*plant*)
In medicine, the transfer of living **tissue** from one **organism** to another. Also called a *graft. Also,* to move a plant from one place to another (pronounced trans-**plant**).

transuranium element
(*trans*-yu-**ray**-nee-uhm *el*-uh-muhnt)
An **element** with a higher **atomic number** than **uranium**, which is 92. There are 17 transuranium elements; they are all **radioactive**. See also **periodic table**.

trauma (**traw**-muh or **trou**-muh)
A severe physical or psychological wound. A broken arm is physical trauma. The loss of a pet is psychological trauma.

tree (**tree**)
The largest of all plants. A tree has a stiff, woody stem and branches with leaves. Many trees bear flowers, fruit, or **cones** once a year.

trefoil (**tree**-*foil*)
A plant having 3 leaflike parts. Trefoils include clover and some kinds of lotus. From the Latin *tri,* meaning "three," and *folium,* meaning "leaf."

Triassic period (trie-**as**-ik *pir*-ee-uhd)
The period of **geological history** from 245 to 208 million years ago. During the Triassic period early dinosaurs and the first **mammals** appeared.

triglyceride (trie-**glis**-uh-*ride*)
A fatty substance in the blood. Too much triglyceride can lead to heart disease.

trilobite (**trie**-luh-*bite*)
A small sea animal that lived from about 543 to 251 million years ago. Trilobite **fossils** are found all over the world.

Tropics (**trahp**-iks)
The area of Earth around the **equator** where it is warm or hot all year long. The Tropics reach about 1,600 miles (2,575 kilometers) north and south of

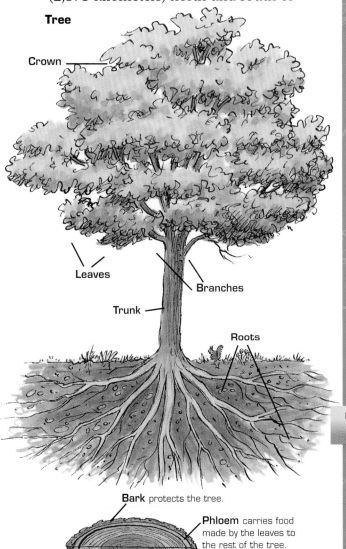

Tree

Crown

Leaves

Branches

Trunk

Roots

Bark protects the tree.

Phloem carries food made by the leaves to the rest of the tree.

Xylem carries water and minerals from the roots to the leaves.

Cambium makes new wood on the inside and phloem on the outside.

Heartwood, made of dead xylem, helps support the tree.

the equator, from the *tropic of Cancer* in the north to the *tropic of Capricorn* in the south. Also called *Torrid Zone.*

tropism (**troh**-*piz*-uhm)
The movement of living things toward or away from a **stimulus.** Many plants show tropism by bending toward light, which is **phototropism.**

tropopause (**troh**-puh-*pawz*)
The boundary in the **atmosphere** between the **troposphere** and **stratosphere.** The tropopause is about 10 miles (16 kilometers) high above the **equator** and 6 miles (10 kilometers) high above the North Pole and South Pole.

troposphere (**troh**-puh-*sfir*)
The layer of the **atmosphere** closest to Earth. The troposphere is where almost all of Earth's weather occurs. It is about 10 miles (16 kilometers) thick at the **equator** and 6 miles (10 kilometers) thick at the North Pole and South Pole.

Troy weight (**troi** *wayt*)
A system for weighing gold, silver, and most jewels. In Troy weight, one pound equals 0.822 standard pounds (0.373 kilograms). There are 12 ounces in a Troy pound; 20 pennyweights in a Troy ounce; and 24 grains in a pennyweight. From the French *Troyes,* the French town where these weights were first used.

trunk (**truhngk**)
The main, woody stem of a tree, not including the branches and roots. *Also,* an elephant's snout, which is a combination nose and upper lip. *Also,* the central part of a human or animal body, without arms, legs, or head. *Also,* the **circuit** that connects telephone exchanges.

tsunami (su-**nah**-mee)
A giant wave that travels across the **ocean** at high speed. A tsunami may be 100 feet (30 meters) high when it hits the shore. It is caused by an earthquake or volcano under the water. Also called *tidal wave.* From the Japanese *tsu,* meaning "harbor," and *nami,* meaning "wave."

tuber (**too**-buhr)
A thick part of a stem that grows underground. White potatoes and yams are tubers. From the Latin *tuber,* meaning "lump."

tumor (**too**-muhr)
An abnormal growth of **tissue.** A tumor that is *benign* does not spread and can be removed without growing back. A tumor that is *malignant* is a **cancer** that can spread and damage other tissue.

tundra (**tuhn**-druh)
A vast, flat, treeless region with long, snowy winters and short, cool summers.

T

Tsunami

The biggest tsunamis occur when part of the seafloor lifts suddenly along a fault, shoving water up.

Long, very low waves that travel very fast—up to 500 miles (800 kilometers) an hour—but are so low that ships barely notice them.

Grasses, **mosses**, **lichen**, and low shrubs grow in the tundra. *Arctic tundras* surround the Arctic Circle; *alpine tundras* are found on high, snowy mountaintops. See also **biome.**

tuner (**too**-nuhr)
The part of a radio or television set that lets the user select a particular station or channel. The tuner is built around a **capacitor** that lets you choose the **frequency** to get the station or channel you want.

tungsten (**tuhng**-stuhn)
A white, metal **element** used in making **steel** and light bulbs. Tungsten does not melt at high temperatures and does not corrode easily. Also called *wolfram.* (Symbol—W)

tuning fork (**too**-ning *fork*)
A narrow, U-shaped metal device that produces a clear musical tone when hit. A tuning fork is often used to give the **pitch** for tuning musical instruments.

turbine (**tuhr**-buhn)
A device in which a flowing liquid or gas turns a set of blades. Turbines range from simple windmills and waterwheels to giant **electric generators.**

turbojet (**tuhr**-boh-*jet*)
A jet engine that uses a **turbine** to **compress** the air entering the engine.

Turing (**tur**-ing), **Alan** (1912–1954)
A British mathematician who helped to develop the first computer.

tusk (**tuhsk**)
A long, pointed tooth that extends out from the jaw of some animals. Tusks in pairs are common to elephants, walruses, and warthogs, among others. The narwhal has only one tusk.

twin (**twin**)
One of two children born at the same time to the same mother. *Identical twins* come from the same egg and are very similar in appearance and other characteristics. *Fraternal twins* come from separate eggs and are as different as any brothers or sisters born of different pregnancies are from each other. *Also,* a cluster of **mineral crystals** growing together.

tympanum (**tim**-puh-nuhm)
See **eardrum.**

typhoon (tie-**foon**)
A violent tropical storm in the western Pacific Ocean. A typhoon is the same as a **hurricane.** From the Chinese *tai fung,* meaning "big wind."

By the time the waves hit land, they may be higher than a 6-story building.

As the water gets shallower, the waves lose speed, but grow taller.

UFO (yoo-*ef*-oh)
Short for *Unidentified Flying Object*. A UFO is an unknown object that people see in the sky. UFOs are sometimes thought to be spaceships from other planets, though there is no evidence that this is true.

UHF (yoo-*aych*-ef)
Short for *UltraHigh Frequency*. UHFs are very short **radio waves**. They are used in television broadcasting for channel 14 and higher. UHFs are also used to communicate with emergency vehicles and with **satellites** in space.

ulcer (**uhl**-suhr)
An open sore in the skin or on a **membrane** of the body. A *peptic ulcer* is found in the **intestines** or stomach.

ulna (**uhl**-nuh)
The long bone that goes from the elbow to the wrist.

ultrahigh frequency
(**uhl**-truh-*hie* **free**-kwuhn-see)
See UHF.

ultrasonic (*uhl*-truh-**sahn**-ik)
Having to do with **ultrasound**.

ultrasound (**uhl**-truh-*sound*)
Sound with a **vibration** speed above 20,000 times a second, which is too high to be heard by humans. Ultrasound is widely used in medicine and industry. Doctors use ultrasound to see inside the body. From the Latin *ultra,* meaning "beyond," and *sonus,* meaning "sound."

ultraviolet rays
(**uhl**-truh-**vie**-uh-lit **rayz**)
An invisible form of light with a higher **frequency** (shorter **wavelength**) than visible light. Ultraviolet rays can kill bacteria and **viruses**. They cause sunburn in humans and are also linked to skin **cancer**. Sometimes shortened to *UV*.

umbilical cord (uhm-**bil**-i-kuhl **kord**)
The thin, ropelike tube that connects the unborn baby to the mother. The umbilical cord is used by the developing **fetus** to get **nutrients** and **oxygen**. The doctor cuts the umbilical cord after the baby is born. The place where the umbilical cord was connected is called the *umbilicus, navel,* or *belly button.*

Umbilical cord

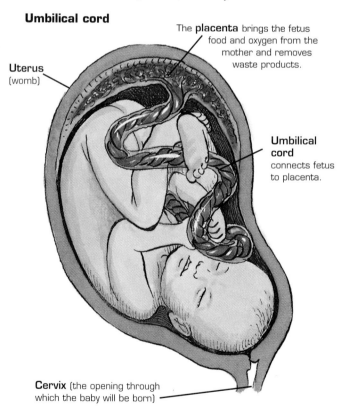

The **placenta** brings the fetus food and oxygen from the mother and removes waste products.

Uterus (womb)

Umbilical cord connects fetus to placenta.

Cervix (the opening through which the baby will be born)

umbra (**uhm**-bruh)
The dark central part of a shadow. Umbra describes the shadow cast by the earth or moon during an **eclipse** or the center of a **sunspot**. See also **penumbra**.

uncertainty principle
(uhn-**suhrt**-n-tee *prin*-suh-puhl)
The idea that we cannot measure both the position *and* **momentum** of a **subatomic particle** at the same time. The uncertainty principle was stated by **Werner Heisenberg** in 1927.

unconscious (uhn-**kahn**-shuhs)
In **psychology**, the thoughts, ideas, and feelings that a person has without being aware of them. The unconscious is believed to control many of the things we do. See also **Sigmund Freud**. *Also,* describes the mental state of not being aware of one's surroundings.

ungulate (**uhng**-gyuh-lit)
Any **mammal** with **hoofs**. Ungulates include horses, cows, and pigs, for example.

unidentified flying object
(*uhn*-ie-**dent**-uh-*fide* flie-ing **ahb**-jikt)
See **UFO**.

unified field theory
(**yoo**-nuh-*fide* feeld *thee*-uh-ree)
The idea that **gravity** and electromagnetism could be linked together into one **theory**. The theory was first proposed by **Albert Einstein** in the late 1920s. Since then, scientists have also tried to include *nuclear forces* in the theory. The unified field theory has not yet been proved, but work on it continues.

uniformitarianism
(*yoo*-nuh-*for*-muh-**ter**-ee-uh-*niz*-uhm)
The **theory** that the earth is slowly changing and will continue to change in the same ways. Uniformitarianism holds that what is happening now is a key to what happened in the past. The theory was first stated by a Scottish doctor, *James Hutton* (1726–1797).

Universal Product Code
(*yoo*-nuh-**vuhr**-suhl **prahd**-uhkt *kohd*)
See **bar code**.

universe (**yoo**-nuh-vuhrs)
Everything that exists anywhere in space. The universe includes all the **galaxies** and the stars, planets, and other bodies that they contain. Scientists believe the universe extends out at least 13 billion **light-years**. They also think the universe is growing larger.

UPC (**yoo**-*pee*-**see**)
Short for *Universal Product Code*. See **bar code**.

uranium (yu-**ray**-nee-uhm)
A heavy, white, metal **element** that is **radioactive**. Uranium is made into the fuel for **fission** in **nuclear reactors**. (Symbol—U)

Uranium 235 (**yoo**-too-*thuhr*-tee-**five**)
The form, or **isotope**, of **uranium** widely used as the fuel in **nuclear reactors** and nuclear weapons. Commonly known as U-235. See **fission**.

Uranus (**yur**-uh-nuhs or yu-**ray**-nuhs)
The 7th planet from the sun in the **solar system**. Uranus has at least 15 moons and 11 rings around it. It is named after the Greek god of the sky.

Average distance from sun—1,786,400,000 miles (2,871,000,000 kilometers)
Length of year—30,685 Earth days
Length of day—17 hours, 8 minutes
Diameter at equator—32,240 miles (51,800 kilometers)

urea (yu-**ree**-uh or **yur**-ee-uh)
An **organic compound** made in the bodies of humans and other animals. Urea is a white **crystal** that is rich in **nitrogen**. In 1828, urea became the first organic compound to be manufactured artificially from **inorganic** substances.

ureter (**yur**-uh-tuhr)
One of 2 tubes that lead from the **kidneys** to the bladder in **vertebrates**.

urethra (yu-**ree**-thruh)
The tube through which **urine** passes from the bladder and out of the body.

Urey (**yur**-ee), **Harold** (1893–1981)
An American chemist who discovered *deuterium* and **researched isotopes** as a young man. Urey later studied the **chemicals** in the sun, moon, and planets. He also worked on the **experiment** that showed that life on Earth could have started from **inorganic** chemicals.

urine (**yur**-uhn)
Liquid waste produced by humans and other **vertebrates**. Urine is mostly water with dissolved **urea**, **salts**, and other **chemicals**.

urticaria
(*uhr*-tuh-**ker**-ee-uh)
See **hives**.

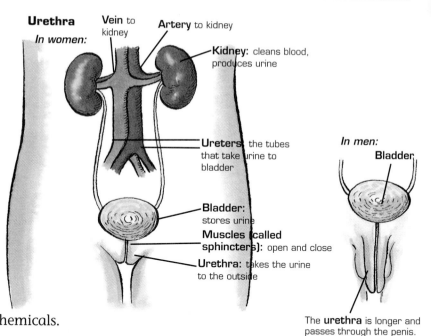

Urethra
In women:
Vein to kidney
Artery to kidney
Kidney: cleans blood, produces urine
Ureters: the tubes that take urine to bladder
Bladder: stores urine
Muscles (called sphincters): open and close
Urethra: takes the urine to the outside

In men:
Bladder

The **urethra** is longer and passes through the penis.

uterus (**yoo**-tuhr-uhs)
A hollow, muscular, pear-shaped **organ** in women and most female **mammals**. The uterus holds and nourishes the **fetus** until birth. Also called *womb*.

UV (**yoo**-vee)
Short for *UltraViolet*. See **ultraviolet rays**.

U

vaccination (*vak*-suh-**nay**-shuhn)
A way to protect against disease. Vaccination introduces dead or weakened germs into the body, which cause the body to produce **antibodies.** The antibodies attack the germs and remain in the blood to fight off any similar germs that come later. Vaccinations today protect people against **measles, mumps, influenza**, polio, and **whooping cough.** Also called **immunization.**

vaccine (vak-**seen** or **vak**-seen)
The substance used in **vaccination.**

vacuole (**vak**-yoo-*ohl*)
A tiny space in a living **cell** that is filled with fluid. A vacuole is generally used for digestion, storage, or getting rid of wastes.

vacuum (**vak**-yoom or **vak**-yu-uhm)
A space that contains no air or other matter. A perfect vacuum cannot exist, since it is impossible to remove every bit of air. From the Latin *vacuum,* meaning "empty."

vagina (vuh-**jie**-nuh)
The tube in women and female **mammals** that extends from the lower end of the **uterus** to the outside of the body. The vagina is the birth canal for a newborn baby.

valence (**vay**-luhns)
The number that shows how well a **chemical element** combines with other elements. Valence is based on the number of **electrons** an element can give, take, or share when joining with another element. For example, **hydrogen** has a valence of 1 and **oxygen** has a valence of 2.

valley (**val**-ee)
A stretch of low land between hills or mountains. A valley is often formed by a river or **glacier** flowing across the land.

valve (**valv**)
A device that starts, stops, and controls the flow of a liquid or gas. A sink faucet is one kind of valve. Natural valves in the heart regulate the flow of blood. *Also,* one of the two shells of a **mollusk.** *Also,* one part of a ripe seedpod. From the Latin *valva,* meaning "folding door."

Van Allen belts
(*van*-**al**-uhn **belts**)
Two zones of **charged electrical particles** that surround the earth. The inner Van Allen belt stretches from about 600 to 3,000 miles (1,000 to 5,000 kilometers) above Earth. The outer belt reaches from 9,300 to 15,500 miles (15,000 to 25,000 kilometers). Named after their discoverer, the American physicist *James Van Allen* (born 1914).

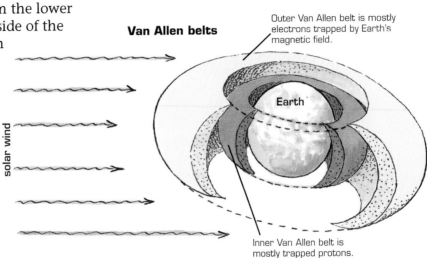

Van Allen belts

Outer Van Allen belt is mostly electrons trapped by Earth's magnetic field.

solar wind

Earth

Inner Van Allen belt is mostly trapped protons.

Van de Graaff generator
(**van**-duh-*graf*
jen-uh-*ray*-tuhr)
A device that generates a
powerful **electrical charge**
by passing a belt over a row
of metal points. The Van de
Graaff generator was
invented in 1931 by *Robert
J. Van de Graaff (1901–1967)*,
an American physicist.

vapor (**vay**-puhr)
The result of heating a solid
or liquid until it becomes a
gas. But vapor and gas are
different. Vapor becomes
a solid or liquid when
compressed at an ordinary
temperature. Gas does not.

variable
(**ver**-ee-uh-buhl)
Likely to change. Variable
winds keep shifting their
direction. *Also,* a condition in
an experiment that can be
changed to affect the result.

variable star
(**ver**-ee-uh-buhl **stahr**)
A star whose brightness seems to
change. The variable star may grow
brighter and dimmer by itself or because
dust or another star blocks its light.

variation (*ver*-ee-**ay**-shuhn)
Differences that occur among the offspring
of any **species.** Variation explains why
humans differ in height, weight, hair color,
and in many other ways.

varicella (*var*-uh-**sel**-uh)
The medical name for **chicken pox.**

variety (vuh-**rie**-uh-tee)
A division within a **species** based on too
small a difference to make a new species.
The variety of cats within the *Felis
domesticus* species includes Siamese cats,
Persian cats, Manx cats, and many others.

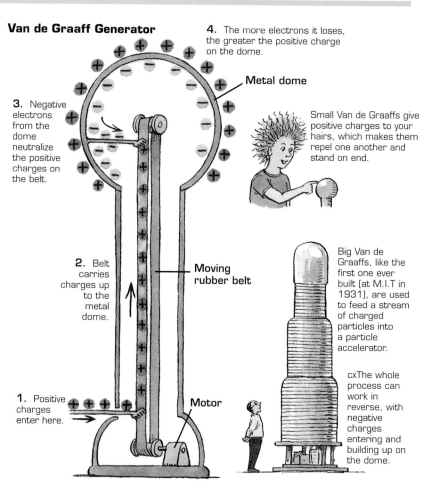

Van de Graaff Generator

4. The more electrons it loses,
the greater the positive charge
on the dome.

Metal dome

3. Negative
electrons
from the
dome
neutralize
the positive
charges on
the belt.

Small Van de Graaffs give
positive charges to your
hairs, which makes them
repel one another and
stand on end.

2. Belt
carries
charges up
to the
metal
dome.

Moving
rubber belt

Big Van de
Graaffs, like the
first one ever
built (at M.I.T in
1931), are used
to feed a stream
of charged
particles into
a particle
accelerator.

cxThe whole
process can
work in
reverse, with
negative
charges
entering and
building up on
the dome.

1. Positive
charges
enter here.

Motor

vascular (**vas**-kyuh-luhr)
Having to do with the vessels that carry
blood, sap, or other **liquids** in living
things. From the Latin *vasculus,* meaning
"small vessel."

VCR (vee-*see*-**ahr**)
Short for *VideoCassette Recorder.* A VCR
is the device attached to or built into a
television set that plays back videotapes.
It is also the **video** camera that records
television pictures and sound on a
magnetic videotape cassette. The video
camera is sometimes called a **camcorder.**

vector (**vek**-tuhr)
A living thing, such as an insect, that
carries a disease-causing **organism.**
Also, the size and direction of a force.
Also, a line showing length and
direction. From the Latin *vehere,*
meaning "to carry."

V

vegetable (**vej**-tuh-buhl)
A food that comes from the seeds (corn), leaves (spinach), root (carrot), stem (asparagus), flower buds (capers), bulb (onion), fruit (tomato), or **tuber** (white potato) of a plant. From the Latin *vegetare,* meaning "to grow."

Vegetable

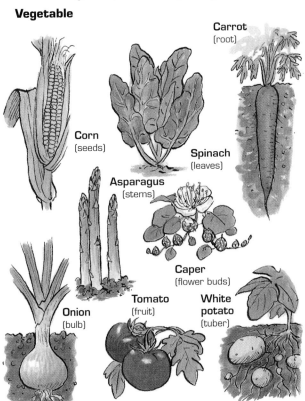

Carrot
(root)

Corn
(seeds)

Spinach
(leaves)

Asparagus
(stems)

Caper
(flower buds)

Onion
(bulb)

Tomato
(fruit)

White
potato
(tuber)

vegetation (*vej*-uh-**tay**-shuhn)
Plant life. Vegetation often refers to plants growing in one particular area.

vegetative reproduction
(**vej**-uh-*tayt*-iv *ree*-pruh-**duhk**-shuhn)
A way of creating a new plant from the stem, root, or leaf of a growing plant. Vegetative reproduction can grow a new plant from a part of a potato, onion, tulip, or geranium plant, for example.

vein (**vayn**)
A tube in **vertebrates** that carries blood toward the heart. *Also,* a thin tube that carries **nutrients** and gives structure to plant leaves. *Also,* one of the supports

in an insect wing. *Also,* a crack or layer in a rock filled with material that differs from the rest of the rock.

velocity (vuh-**lahs**-uh-tee)
The speed *and* direction of a moving object. The velocity of a car could be 50 miles (80 kilometers) an hour heading west.

venom (**ven**-uhm)
A poison produced by certain animals to kill or paralyze their **prey.** Some animals use their venom for defense only. The venom of some animals can cause death in humans.

vent (**vent**)
The opening on the top of a volcano through which **lava** and gases come out. *Also,* a device to release **pressure** in machines. *Also,* the act of releasing a gas. From the Latin *ventus,* meaning "wind."

ventilator (**vent**-l-*ay*-tuhr)
See **respirator. ventral** (**ven**-truhl)

ventral (**ven**-truhl)
Having to do with the front side of a body. Your chest is on the ventral side of your body. Your back is **dorsal.** From the Latin *venter,* meaning "belly."

Venus (**vee**-nuhs)
The second planet from the sun in the solar system. Venus is covered with thick clouds of yellow poisonous gas that make it the brightest body in the sky, except for the sun and moon. It is also the only planet with longer days than years and that spins backward.

Average distance from sun—67,230,000 miles (108,200,000 kilometers)
Length of year—225 Earth days
Length of day—243 Earth days
Diameter at equator—7,521 miles (12,104 kilometers)

verify (**ver**-uh-*fie*)
Prove something by testing. To verify results, scientists may repeat the

experiments done by others. From the Latin *verus,* meaning "true."

vernal equinox
(**vuhrn**-l ee-kwuh-*nahks* or ek-wuh-*nahks*)
The time in the spring when day and night are the same length all over Earth. The vernal equinox is around March 21 in the Northern Hemisphere and around September 22 in the Southern Hemisphere. See **equinox.**

vertebra (**vuhr**-tuh-bruh)
One of the bones of the **spine,** or **backbone.** Its plural is *vertebrae.*

vertebrate
(**vuhr**-tuh-bruht or **vuhr**-tuh-*brayt*)
Any animal with a **spine,** or backbone. There are about 40,000 different kinds of vertebrates, including fish, birds, **reptiles, amphibians,** and **mammals.**

very high frequency
(**ver**-ee **hie free**-kwuhn-see)
See **VHF.**

Vesalius (vuh-**say**-lee-uhs), **Andreas** (1514–1564)
A Flemish doctor who is called the founder of human **anatomy.** Vesalius wrote the first book of human anatomy in 1543, based on direct observations.

veterinarian (*vet*-uh-ruh-**ner**-ee-uhn)
A doctor who treats diseases and injuries of animals.

VHF (**vee**-*aych*-**ef**)
Short for *Very High Frequency.* VHF **radio waves** are used for broadcasting television channels between 2 and 13 and for some **FM** radio broadcasts.

vibration (vie-**bray**-shuhn)
The rapid back-and-forth motion of an object or wave. The vibrations of a plucked guitar string produce the sounds you hear.

video (vid-ee-*oh*)
Having to do with television or just the picture part of television. *Also,* a recording

of sound and pictures on **videotape** or videodisc that can be played back on a **VCR** or a **videodisc** player.

videocassette recorder
(**vid**-ee-*oh* kuh-**set** ri-**kord**-uhr)
See **VCR.**

videodisc (**vid**-ee-*oh disk*)
A recording of a movie, television show, or concert on a **disc.** It is played on a player like a **CD** player attached to a television set. See also **laser disc.**

videotape (**vid**-ee-oh-*tayp*)
Magnetic tape on which sound and pictures can be recorded. See also **VCR.**

villi (**vil**-ie or **vil**-ee)
Tiny, fingerlike projections growing from the lining of the **small intestine** or any **membrane.** The villi in the intestine **absorb** some **nutrients** and pass them into the bloodstream. Its singular is *villus.*

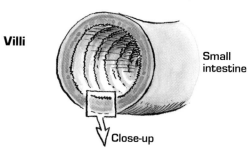

Villi
Small intestine
Close-up

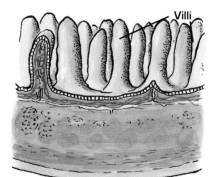

Villi
Intestinal wall

vine (**vine**)
A plant with a long, thin, flexible stem.

virtual reality
(**vuhr**-choo-uhl ree-**al**-uh-tee)
A 3-dimensional **environment** that is created by a computer but that seems

real to the user. In virtual reality, you wear a *head-mounted display* with a screen for each eye, sound in both ears, and **data** gloves and trackers to follow hand and head movements.

virus (**vie**-ruhs)
A very tiny structure that can only grow inside a living **cell**; outside a cell, a virus is a lifeless **particle**. In a **cell**, the virus multiplies hundreds of times and destroys the cell. The new viruses then look for other cells in which to **reproduce**, causing such diseases as the cold, **influenza**, and **measles**. *Also,* a **program** that can destroy information stored in a computer. From the Latin *virus,* meaning "poison," since it was originally thought to be poison that was carried in the night air.

viscosity (vis-**kahs**-uh-tee)
A measure of how strongly a liquid or gas resists flowing. A substance with high viscosity, such as honey, flows very slowly. Water has a very low viscosity and flows easily.

visible light (**viz**-uh-buhl **lite**)
Electromagnetic waves that can be seen by the human eye. Visible light has **wavelengths** between 350 and 750 *nanometers.* (A nanometer is one billionth of a meter.) Electromagnetic waves with longer wavelengths (**infrared rays** and **radio waves**) and those with shorter wavelengths (**X rays** and **ultraviolet rays**) are invisible.

vision (**vizh**-uhn)
The sense of sight. The *eye* is the **organ** of vision.

vitamin (**vite**-uh-min)
A substance that people need in small amounts for good health. The 13 best-known vitamins are: A (retinol), B_1 (thiamine), B_2 (riboflavin), niacin, B_6, pantothenic acid, B_{12}, biotin, folate, C (ascorbic acid), D (cholecalciferol), E (tocopherol), and K.

viviparous (vie-**vip**-uhr-uhs)
An animal that bears live young. Humans and most **mammals** are viviparous. From the Latin *vivus,* meaning "alive," and *parere,* meaning "to bring forth."

Vocal cords

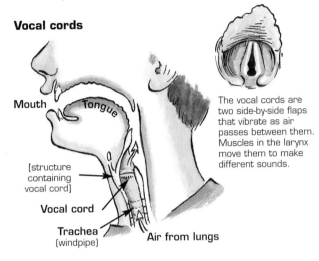

Mouth
Tongue

[structure containing vocal cord]

Vocal cord

Trachea (windpipe)

Air from lungs

The vocal cords are two side-by-side flaps that vibrate as air passes between them. Muscles in the larynx move them to make different sounds.

Vocal cords tight and together produce high sounds.

Vocal cords loose and apart produce low sounds.

vocal cord (**voh**-kuhl *kord*)
A structure within the **larynx** or voice box. The vocal cords vibrate to produce sounds in humans and other animals. Also called *vocal fold.*

voiceprint (**vois**-*print*)
A visual record of the length, loudness, **pitch,** and tone quality of human speech. Voiceprints sometimes help police officers solve crimes. Also called *voice spectrograph.*

volatile (**vahl**-uht-l)
Describes a liquid that **evaporates** quickly, such as **gasoline** or perfume. *Also,* describes a substance that is explosive or reacts easily with other substances. From the Latin *volare,* meaning "to fly."

volcano (vahl-**kay**-noh)
An opening in the earth's surface through which **lava**, gases, ash, and

Volcano

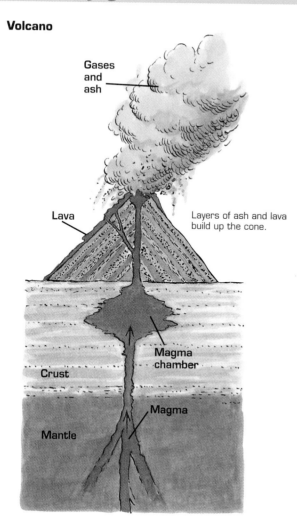

Gases and ash

Lava

Layers of ash and lava build up the cone.

Magma chamber

Crust

Magma

Mantle

rocks pour out. A volcano forms when melted rock (**magma**) from under the ground breaks through the earth's surface. From the Latin *Vulcanus,* the name of the Roman god of fire.

volt (**vohlt**)
A unit of **electrical pressure** or **potential**. One volt causes a **current** of one **ampere** to flow through a **resistance** of one **ohm**. The volt is named for **Count Alessandro Volta**.

Volta (**vohl**-tuh), **Count Alessandro** (1745–1827)
An Italian physicist who invented the first electric **battery**. The **volt** is named after Count Volta.

voltage (**vohl**-tij)
The **electromagnetic force,** or **potential,** of a **current** measured in **volts**. The voltage of most home appliances is 110 volts.

voltmeter (**vohlt**-*mee*-tuhr)
An instrument that measures the **voltage** between 2 points on an **electric circuit.**

volume (**vahl**-yuhm)
The amount of space an object occupies. The basic unit for measuring volume is either a *cubic* foot or a *cubic* meter. *Also,* the loudness of a sound. Extremely high volume on the radio hurts the ears.

vomit (**vahm**-it)
To expel the contents of the stomach through the mouth. Vomiting usually follows *nausea,* the feeling that one is about to throw up.

vortex (**vor**-teks)
A whirling, spinning mass of liquid or gas. A vortex of water is sometimes called a *whirlpool.* A vortex of air is sometimes called a *whirlwind* or **tornado.**

Voyager (**voi**-i-juhr)
One of 2 **spacecraft** that were launched in 1977 to fly by the distant planets of the **solar system.** *Voyagers 1* and *2* sent back to Earth photographs of **Jupiter, Saturn, Uranus,** and **Neptune,** their **moons,** and their rings.

Waksman (waks-muhn), Selman Abraham (1888–1973)

An American bacteriologist who discovered the **antibiotic** *streptomycin*.

Wallace (wahl-uhs), Alfred Russel (1823–1913)

A British naturalist who arrived at the theory of **natural selection** at about the same time as **Charles Darwin**.

wane (wayn)

To become smaller. The moon wanes after it has become full. See also **wax**.

warm-blooded (wawrm bluhd-id)

Describes animals whose temperature stays about the same no matter the surrounding temperature. Warm-blooded animals include **mammals** and birds. Also called *endothermic*.

wart (wawrt)

A hard growth on the skin. A wart is caused by a **virus**, not by touching a toad as some wrongly believe.

water (wawt-uhr)

The most common substance on Earth. Water covers more than 70 percent of the earth's surface and makes up most of every plant and animal.

Water can exist in 3 states: It is usually liquid water. When it is cooled below 32° **Fahrenheit** (0° **Celsius**) water becomes ice, a solid. When it is heated above 212° Fahrenheit (100° **Celsius**) it becomes **water vapor**, a gas.

Water is a **compound**. Each **molecule** of pure water contains 2 **atoms** of **hydrogen** and one atom of **oxygen** (H_2O). Pure water is colorless, tasteless, and has no smell. Salt water or ocean water has various salts **dissolved** in the water.

water cycle (wawt-uhr sie-kuhl)

The continuing movement of water from the earth's surface to the air and back to Earth. The water on Earth **evaporates**. It changes into **water vapor**. The water vapor rises in the air, cools, and **condenses** into tiny drops of liquid water. The drops form clouds. In time, the drops fall as rain or snow. This water then evaporates — and the cycle starts all over again.

Water Cycle

As the water vapor cools, it condenses into clouds.

Water in the clouds falls to Earth as precipitation on lakes, land, and oceans.

Water from lakes, land, plants, and oceans evaporates and becomes water vapor.

water pollution
(**wawt**-uhr puh-*loo*-shuhn)
Making water unfit for drinking, swimming, or other purposes. Water **pollution** comes from adding industrial wastes, sewage, farm wastes, animal wastes, or heat to water.

watershed (**wawt**-uhr-*shed*)
An area where rainwater soaks into the soil and drains into a river or stream. In some watersheds the rainwater flows over the surface and into a river or stream. Most forests are watersheds. Also called a *drainage basin. Also,* in popular use, a stretch of high land between 2 rivers.

waterspout (**wawt**-uhr-*spout*)
A tall column of water drawn up into the air by a **tornado** passing over an ocean or large lake. A waterspout can be as wide as to 200 feet (60 meters) across.

water table (**wawt**-uhr *tay*-buhl)
The top level at which the ground is **saturated** with water. The water table rises when heavy rain soaks into the ground. It falls during dry spells. To get water, a well must be dug deep enough to reach beneath the water table.

water vapor (**wawt**-uhr *vay*-puhr)
Water in the form of a gas that is usually present in the air. Water vapor consists of **molecules** of water that enter the air when liquid water **evaporates.**

Watson (**waht**-suhn), **James Dewey** (born 1928)
An American biologist. Watson discovered the structure of **DNA**, working with **Francis H.C. Crick** and others.

watt (**waht**)
A unit of **electric power** named after **James Watt.** One watt equals the **current** multiplied by the **voltage.** For example, a 60-watt bulb has a current of 0.5 amperes and a voltage of 120 volts (120 X 0.5 = 60). The power from an electrical **generator** is usually measured in *kilowatts* (kw)(1,000 watts) or *megawatts* (Mw) (one million

watts). *Also,* one **joule** of **work** per second. (Symbol—W)

Watt (**waht**), **James** (1736–1819)
A Scottish engineer and inventor who perfected the **steam** engine in 1768 and made steam **power** practicable. The unit of power, called the **watt**, is named for him.

wattmeter (**waht**-*mee*-tuhr)
A device used to measure **electric power.**

wave (**wayv**)
A continuing up-and-down or back-and-forth motion that carries **energy,** but not **matter,** from one place to another. In an ocean wave, the water does not move forward, but just goes up and down in place. Sound, light, and heat also move in waves.

Wave

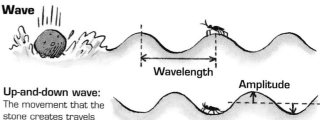

Wavelength

Amplitude

Up-and-down wave: The movement that the stone creates travels through the water. But the water itself—and the water strider on it—stays in one place.

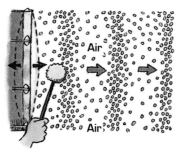

Back-and-forth waves: The vibrating surface of a drum flexes in and out, alternately squeezing air molecules closer together and stretching them apart. This energy travels through the air as sound waves.

wave theory (**wayv** *thee*-uh-ree)
The idea that **subatomic particles,** such as **photons** and **electrons,** behave like waves of **energy,** as well as like **particles** of **matter.**

wavelength (**wayv**-*length*)
The distance between the crests, or peaks, of a wave. The wavelength of a **microwave** is a fraction of an inch (few centimeters).

wax (waks)
A fatty solid material that comes from **petroleum**, animal sources (beeswax), plants (bayberry), or is made in a factory. Wax is used to make candles, crayons, polishes, and a coating on paper. *Also,* to grow bigger. The moon waxes until it becomes full. See also **wane.**

weather (weTH-uhr)
The changing conditions of temperature, rainfall, **pressure**, **humidity**, wind, and clouds in one area at one time. Weather differs from **climate**, which is weather over a long period of time.

weather forecasting
(weTH-uhr *for-kas*-ting)
Predicting what the weather will be. Using collected **data** and a knowledge of weather patterns, weather forecasting tells what to expect over the next hours, days, and weeks. See also **meteorology.**

weathering (weTH-uhr-ing)
The breaking up of rocks on the earth's surface by rain, ice, changes in temperature, **chemicals dissolved** in the rain, and growing plants.

weather map (weTH-uhr *map*)
A chart that shows weather conditions at a particular time. The weather map is based on **observations** and reports from weather **satellites** and **radiosondes.**

weather satellite
(weTH-uhr *sat-l-ite*)
An orbiting object in space that monitors weather conditions on Earth. Most weather satellites have television cameras that take pictures of clouds, storms, and snow on the ground. They also have **sensors** to measure temperature and **humidity** conditions. The satellite beams the pictures and **data** to Earth.

web (web)
The net of very fine silken threads spun by a spider to trap the insects that it eats. *Also,* the **tissue** between the toes of ducks, frogs, and some other animals to help them move through water. *Also* short for **World Wide Web.**

wedge (wej)
A simple machine with 2 or more sloping surfaces. An ax is a wedge used to split wood.

weed (weed)
Any plant that grows where people don't want it to grow. A daisy growing in a cornfield is a weed.

weed killer (weed *kil*-uhr)
See **herbicide.**

Wegener (vay-guh-nuhr), Alfred (1880–1930)
A German geologist who was the first to suggest that the **continents** move, or drift, on the surface of Earth.

weight (wayt)
The pull of **gravity** on an object. Weight is different from the **mass**, or amount of **matter**, in the object. Mass stays the same. But weight changes, depending on where the object is being weighed.

Weather Map

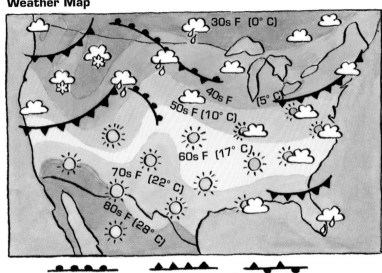

Warm front   Cold front   Stationary front

weightless (**wayt**-lis)
Not feeling the pull of **gravity**. Objects in an **orbiting spacecraft** are weightless, and float freely about. The spacecraft is also weightless because it is in "free fall," always falling down to Earth. Since the earth curves away under it, the craft stays in **orbit**, and everything inside stays weightless. You sometimes feel weightless in an elevator that suddenly starts going down.

well (**wel**)
A hole in the ground that reaches down to water, natural gas, or **petroleum** under the surface. A well usually has a **pump** to bring up the liquid or gas.

Westinghouse (**west**-ing-**hous**), **George** (1846–1914)
An American inventor and industrialist who created *air brakes* and an improved pipeline for carrying natural gas. Although he did not invent **alternating current**, Westinghouse helped make it the standard for **electric power**.

wetland (**wet**-luhnd)
Land covered with water for all or part of the year. A wetland is home to many kinds of living things and helps to control **flooding**.

wheel (**weel**)
A round frame that turns on a central shaft or rod called an **axle**. A wheel is a simple machine. Wheels are found on almost all vehicles that move on land.

whirlpool (**wuhrl**-*pool*)
Water that spins around at great speed and with great force. A whirlpool can be caused by the shape of the shoreline, wind blowing in a certain way, or 2 **currents** meeting.

whirlwind (**wuhrl**-*wind*)
Air that spins around at great speed and with great force. A whirlwind usually twirls around an area of low **pressure**. Whirlwinds are usually not

as strong as **hurricanes** or **tornados**, which also have spinning winds. Also called a *dust devil*.

white blood cell (**wite bluhd** *sel*)
See **leukocyte**.

white dwarf (**wite dwawrf**)
A very old star that has shrunk into a small ball. The **matter** of a white dwarf is so dense and heavy that a spoonful weighs many tons.

Whitney (**wit**-nee), **Eli** (1765–1825)
The American inventor of the *cotton gin,* which separates the seeds from cotton **fibers**.

whooping cough (**hoo**-ping *kawf*)
A serious disease, especially in children, caused by **bacteria**. Whooping cough takes its name from the sound victims make when they try to catch their breath after a coughing attack. Also called **pertussis**.

Wiener (**wee**-nuhr), **Norbert** (1894–1964)
An American mathematician who started the field of study known as

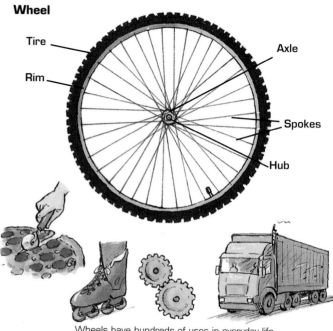

Wheel

Tire

Rim

Axle

Spokes

Hub

Wheels have hundreds of uses in everyday life.

cybernetics. Cybernetics compares control and communication in human beings and machines.

wildlife (**wild**-*life*)
Nonhuman living things, especially wild animals. Wildlife usually refers to animals in their natural surroundings. *Also,* animals that are hunted for food or sport.

Wilkins (**wil**-kinz), **Maurice H. F.** (born 1916)
A British biophysicist whose **X rays** of the **DNA molecule** helped **James D. Watson** and **Francis H. C. Crick** work out the exact structure of DNA.

Williams (**wil**-yuhms), **Daniel** (1856–1931)
An American doctor who, in 1893, was the first to operate on the heart.

wilt (**wilt**)
To droop or turn yellow. Wilt usually refers to the withering of a plant's leaves and stem because of disease or too little water.

wind (**wind**)
The movement of air from areas of high **pressure** to areas of low pressure. A wind can vary from a gentle breeze to the powerful gusts of a **hurricane** or **tornado.**

windchill (**wind** *chil*)
A measure of the effect on humans of wind speed and temperature.

windmill (**wind**-*mil*)
A machine, usually with blades or sails, that is run by wind power. A windmill may be used to pump water, grind grain, or generate electricity. Also called a *wind turbine.*

window (**win**-doh)
A box on a computer **monitor** that covers part or all of the screen. The window can contain **text** or an **image.** *Also,* an opening in a wall or side of a building or automobile to let in light and air. From the Old Norse

vindr, meaning "wind," and *auga,* meaning "eye."

windpipe (**wind**-*pipe*)
See **trachea.**

wind shear (**wind** *shir*)
A sudden change in wind speed or direction. Wind shear is sometimes caused by the downward flow of cool air during a rainstorm or ice storm. Many airplane takeoff and landing accidents are blamed on wind shear.

wind tunnel (**wind tuhn**-l)
A structure built to test the effect of wind on airplanes and other vehicles and structures. A very large fan or **propeller** creates the wind in the wind tunnel.

wing (**wing**)
The part of the body of birds, insects, and bats that allows them to fly. The same part in a nonflying animal, such as an ostrich or penguin, is also called a wing. *Also,* that part of an airplane that extends out from each side of the body. The wing

Windchill Chart
Equivalent windchill temperatures:

Wind speed in miles per hour

	0	5	10	15	20	25	30	35	40
35	35	32	22	16	12	8	6	4	3
30	30	27	16	9	4	1	-2	-4	-5
25	25	22	10	2	-3	-7	-10	-12	-13
20	20	16	3	-5	-10	-15	-18	-20	-21
15	15	11	-3	-11	-17	-22	-25	-27	-29
10	10	6	-9	-18	-24	-29	-33	-35	-37
0	0	-5	-22	-31	-39	-44	-49	-52	-53
-5	-5	-10	-27	-38	-46	-51	-56	-58	-60
-10	-10	-15	-34	-45	-53	-59	-64	-67	-69

Air temperature in degrees Fahrenheit

has a flat bottom and curved top, which helps keep the plane in the air. *Also,* the projecting part of some plants and seeds.

winter (**win**-tuhr)
The coldest season of the year. Winter comes between autumn and spring. In the Northern Hemisphere it starts on or about December 21 (winter **solstice**) and ends on or about March 21 (**vernal equinox**). In the Southern Hemisphere it starts on or about June 21 and ends on or about September 21.

wire (**wire**)
A long, thin, flexible thread of metal. Wire used to carry electricity is usually made of **copper** or **aluminum**. Wire used in suspension bridges or to pull heavy loads is often **iron** or **steel**.

wirephoto (**wire**-*foh*-toh)
A way of sending pictures by wire or by radio.

wolfram (**wul**-fruhm)
See **tungsten**.

womb (**woom**)
See **uterus**.

wood (**wud**)
The tough material of the trunk and branches of trees and shrubs. The scientific name for wood is **xylem**. See also **hardwood** and **softwood**.

woodland (**wud**-luhnd)
Land covered by trees. Much of the earth's woodland is being destroyed to build houses, roads, and farms. See also **forest**.

Woods (**wudz**), **Granville** (1856–1910)
An African-American scientist who invented a telephone and telegraph for use on railroads, an air brake, an electric battery, an egg incubator, and other devices.

wool (**wul**)
A **fiber** spun from the fleece, or curly hair, of sheep, goats, and some other animals. Wool is used to make clothing, blankets, rugs, and other items. *Also,* fiber made from **steel** (*steel wool*) or **glass** (*glass wool*).

word processor (**wuhrd** *prahs*-es-uhr)
A computer **program** for typing, editing, and printing a letter, report, book, or other document. The word processor lets you change, add, erase, and move words and paragraphs around. At the end, it prints what you have written and stores it for future use.

work (**wuhrk**)
Moving an object by applying force to the object. The amount of work is the force times the distance the object is moved. The unit of work is the **foot-pound**. The work done to lift a 2-pound (0.9-kilogram) book to a height of 3 feet (0.9 meters) is 6 foot-pounds (2 x 3 = 6). The unit of work in the **metric system** is the **joule**. One joule equals 0.7 foot-pounds.

World Wide Web (**wuhrld** *wide* web)
A huge collection of information, such as **databases**, Web sites, and library holdings, that you can see and copy with a computer **Internet** service.

Wright (**rite**), **Orville** (1871–1948) and **Wilbur** (1867–1912)
Two American brothers who flew the first motor-powered airplane in 1903. The basic principles of that plane are still in use today.

X chromosome
(**eks** *kroh*-muh-*sohm*)
A **chromosome** that determines a person's gender. Male sex **cells** have one **Y chromosome** and one X chromosome. Female sex cells have 2 X chromosomes.

xerography (zi-**rahg**-ruh-fee)
A way to copy documents using a machine called a **copier**. From the Greek *xeros,* meaning "dry," and *graphein,* meaning "to write," since xerography does not use liquid ink.

xerophyte (**zir**-uh-*fite*)
A plant that needs little water to live. Xerophytes include many desert plants, such as cacti. From the Greek *xeros,* meaning "dry," and *phyte,* meaning "plant."

X ray (eks-*ray*)
An invisible **electromagnetic ray** of very high **frequency** that can pass through many materials that block **visible** light. X rays can be produced in an X-ray tube where **electrons** strike a metal plate, which then emits the X rays. Doctors use X rays to see bones and **organs** in the body. Dentists use X rays to see inside teeth. See also **Wilhelm Roentgen.**

X-ray astronomy
(**eks**-*ray* uh-**strahn**-uh-mee)
The study of **X rays** given off by objects in space in order to learn more about the objects. X-ray astronomy **research** uses **satellites** in **orbit** to detect the X rays since X rays cannot pass through the **atmosphere** to reach Earth.

X-ray diffraction
(**eks**-*ray* di-**frak**-shuhn)
Sending **X rays** through a **crystal** to learn the **atomic** structure of the crystal. X-ray diffraction was used to discover the structure of **DNA.** Also called *X-ray crystallography.*

xylem (**zie**-luhm)
The woody **tissue** of a plant root or stem. The xylem carries water and **minerals** upward to the leaves in seed plants and ferns. From the Greek *xylon,* meaning "wood."

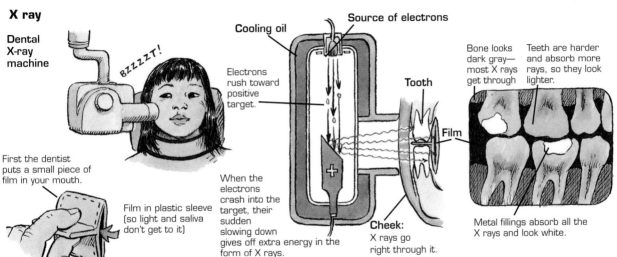

X ray

Dental X-ray machine

BZZZZT!

First the dentist puts a small piece of film in your mouth.

Film in plastic sleeve (so light and saliva don't get to it)

Cooling oil

Source of electrons

Electrons rush toward positive target.

When the electrons crash into the target, their sudden slowing down gives off extra energy in the form of X rays.

Tooth

Cheek: X rays go right through it.

Film

Bone looks dark gray— most X rays get through

Teeth are harder and absorb more rays, so they look lighter.

Metal fillings absorb all the X rays and look white.

Y

Yalow (yal-oh), **Rosalyn** (born 1921)
An American physicist who showed how
radioisotopes could be used to trace
hormones in the blood.

yaw (yaw)
A turn to the left or right by an airplane
or **spacecraft**.

Y chromosome
(wie *kroh*-muh-*sohm*)
A **chromosome** that determines a
person's gender. Male sex **cells** have
one Y chromosome and one **X
chromosome**. Female sex cells have 2
X chromosomes.

year (yir)
The time it takes Earth to make one
complete **revolution** around the sun.
A year lasts exactly 365 days, 5 hours,
48 minutes, and 46 seconds. A calendar
year is divided into 12 months and runs
from January 1 to December 31. *Also,*
the time it takes any planet to finish
a revolution, which can be longer or
shorter than a year on Earth.

yeast (yeest)
A tiny **fungus** that is used in making
bread, beer, and wine. Yeast breaks down
sugar to produce **alcohol** and **carbon
dioxide**. In bread baking, the alcohol
evaporates while tiny bubbles of carbon
dioxide gas make the dough rise.

yellow fever (yel-oh **fee**-vuhr)
A serious disease of the **Tropics**. Yellow
fever is caused by a **virus** carried by a
mosquito. The symptoms include fever,
headache, dizziness, muscle pain, and
yellowing of the skin. See also **William
Gorgas** and **Walter Reed**.

yolk (yohk)
The central, yellow part of an egg. The
yolk contains the food for the **embryo**
that develops in the egg. From the Old
English *geolu,* meaning "yellow."

Yukawa (yu-**kah**-wah), **Hideki**
(1907–1981)
A Japanese physicist who explained the
force that holds the **protons** and **neutrons**
together in the **nucleus** of an **atom**.

Y chromosome

This pair
determines
whether we are
male or female.

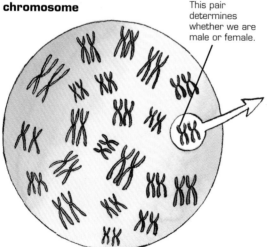

We have 23 pairs of chromosomes
in every cell in our body.

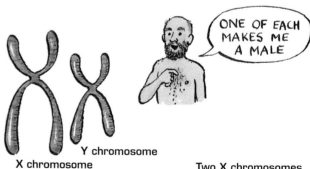

ONE OF EACH
MAKES ME
A MALE

Y chromosome

X chromosome

Two X chromosomes

BOTH THE
SAME... I'M
A FEMALE

zero (zir-oh)
The starting point or neutral point for most scales of measurement.

zinc (zingk)
A bluish-white metal **element** that is often combined with other metals. Zinc plus **copper** makes *brass*. Zinc plus copper and **tin** makes *bronze*. Zinc is also used as a coating on **iron** and **steel** (called *galvanizing*) to prevent rust. (Symbol—Zn)

zodiac (zoh-dee-ak)
The 12 **constellations** that the sun passes through in a year. The zodiac marks the **ecliptic**. The constellations are: Capricorn (Goat), Aquarius (Water Bearer), Pisces (Fishes), Aries (Ram), Taurus (Bull), Gemini (Twins), Cancer (Crab), Leo (Lion), Virgo (Virgin), Libra (Scales), Scorpio (Scorpion), and Sagittarius (Archer). From the Greek *zoidion*, meaning "circle of animals."

zone (zohn)
One of the five **climate** bands of Earth. The zones include *South Frigid Zone, South Temperate Zone*, **Torrid Zone**, *North Temperate Zone*, and *North Frigid Zone. Also*, one of the 24 time zones of Earth. The time zones start at the prime **meridian**, which runs through Greenwich, England. Each time zone to the west is one hour behind. Each time zone to the east is one hour ahead. From the Greek *zone*, meaning "girdle."

zoo (zoo)
Short for zoological garden. Zoos are places where wild animals are kept for public viewing and for education and **research**. Zookeepers also protect and breed animals in danger of **extinction**.

Zone

Climate Zones

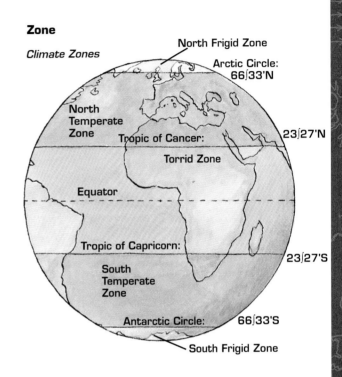

North Frigid Zone
Arctic Circle: 66|33'N
North Temperate Zone
Tropic of Cancer: 23|27'N
Torrid Zone
Equator
Tropic of Capricorn: 23|27'S
South Temperate Zone
Antarctic Circle: 66|33'S
South Frigid Zone

Time Zones

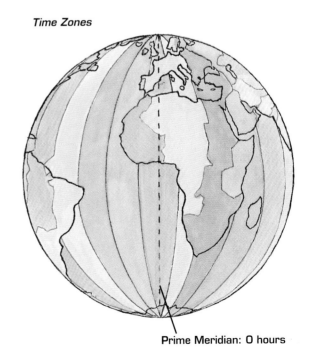

Prime Meridian: 0 hours

zoology (zoh-**ahl**-uh-jee)
The study of different **animal species**, of which there are more than a million. A *zoologist* is a scientist who works in this field. From the Greek *zoion,* meaning "animal," and *-logia,* meaning "science of."

zoom lens (**zoom** *lenz*)
A **lens** in a camera that can change from a long, wide view of an entire scene to a close-up enlargement of one small part. A zoom lens can make you feel far away from or close to the subject of the photograph.

zooplankton (*zoh*-uh-**plangk**-tuhn)
Tiny living things that drift near the surface of the ocean. Zooplankton include microscopic **protozoa** and such small creatures as copepods and water fleas. They feed on smaller plant **plankton** called **phytoplankton.**

Zworykin (**zwawr**-i-kin), **Vladimir** (1889–1982)
A Russian-born American engineer who invented the first television camera and television picture tube. Zworykin also helped to develop the **electron microscope.**

zygote (**zie**-goht)
The **fertilized egg cell** of a plant or animal. The zygote holds **genes** from both parents and has all the information necessary to make a complete, new **organism.** From the Greek *zygotos,* meaning "joined together."

Index of Picture Labels

Resources

MUSEUMS

American Museum of Natural History
Central Park West at 79 Street
New York, NY 10024-5192
212-769-5100
http://www.amnh.org

Arizona Science Center
600 E. Washington Street
Phoenix, AZ 85004-2394
602-716-2000
http://www.azscience.org

California Science Center
700 State Drive
Exposition Park
Los Angeles, CA 90037
323-SCIENCE
http://www.casciencectr.org

Detroit Science Center
5020 John R Street
Detroit, MI 48202
313-SCIENCE or 313-577-8400
http://www.sciencedetroit.org

Discovery Center of Idaho
131 Myrtle Street
Boise, ID 83702
208- 343-9895
http://www.scidaho.org

Family Museum of Arts and Science
2900 Learning Campus Drive
Bettendorf, IA 52722
319-344-4106
http://www.qconline.com/arts/family

Great Lakes Science Center
601 Erieside Avenue
Cleveland, OH 44114
216-694-2000
http://www.greatscience.com

Headwaters Science Center
PO Box 1176
413 Beltrami Ave.
Bemidji, MN 56601
218-751-1110

http://www.spacestar.net/users/oishsc

The Imaginarium
737 West 5th Avenue #G
Anchorage, AK 99501
907-276-3179
http://www.imaginarium.org

Imagination Stations Science Museum
P.O. Box 2127
224 E. Nash St.
Wilson, NC 27893
252-291-5113
http://www.imaginescience.org

Lawrence Hall of Science
University of California Berkeley
Lawrence Hall of Science #5200
Berkeley, CA 94720-5200
510-642-5132
http://lhs.berkeley.edu

Liberty Science Center
Liberty State Park
251 Phillip Street
Jersey City, NJ 07375-4699
201-200-1000
TDD: 201-200-1993
http://www.lsc.org

Louisville Science Center
727 West Main Street
Louisville, KY 40202
502-561-6100
http://www.louisvillescience.org

Maryland Science Center
601 Light Street
Baltimore, MD 21230
410-685-5225
http://www.mdsci.org

Miami Museum of Science and Space Planetarium
3280 South Miami Avenue
Miami, FL 33129
305-646-4200
http://www.miamisci.org

Montshire Museum of Science
1 Montshire Road
Norwich, VT 05055
802-649-2200
http://www.montshire.net

Museum of Science
Science Park
Boston, MA 02114
617-723-2500
http://www.mos.org

Museum of Science and Industry
57th Street and Lake Shore Drive
Chicago, IL 60637
800-GO TO MSI
773-684-1414
http://www.msichicago.org

New York Hall of Science
47-01 111th Street
Corona, NY 11368
718-699-0005
http://www.nyhallsci.org

Oregon Museum of Science and Industry
1945 SE Water Avenue
Portland, OR 97214-3354
503-797-OMSI (6674)
http://www.omsi.edu

Pacific Science Center
200 Second Avenue North
Seattle, WA 98109-4895
206-443-2880
http://www.pacsci.org

Science Museum of Minnesota
120 W Kellogg Boulevard
St. Paul, MN 55102
651-221-9444
http://www.smm.org

Science Museum of Virginia
2500 West Broad Street
Richmond, VA 23220
804-367-6552
http://www.smv.org

St. Louis Science Center
5050 Oakland Avenue
St. Louis, MO 63110
(800) 456-SLSC
http://www.slsc.org

MAGAZINES

Audubon
National Audubon Society
700 Broadway
New York, NY 10003
212-979-3000
http://www.audubon.org

Discover
114 Fifth Avenue
New York, NY 10011
212-633-4400
http://www.discover.com

Dolphin Log
The Cousteau Society
870 Greenbrier Circle
Suite #402
Chesapeake, VA 23320
800-441-4395
http://www.dolphinlog.org

National Geographic World
National Geographic
1145 17th Street N.W.
Washington, DC 20036-4688
800-NGS-LINE (800-647-5463)
http://www.nationalgeographic.
com

Odyssey
Cobblestone Publishing
Company
30 Grove Street, Suite C
Peterborough, NH 03458
603-924-7209
http://www.odysseymagazine.
com

OWL Magazine
179 John Street, Suite 500
Toronto, Ontario M5T 3G5
CANADA
416-340-2700
http://www.owl.on.ca

Ranger Rick
National Wildlife Federation
8925 Leesburg Pike
Vienna, VA 22184
800-822-9919
http://www.nwf.org

Science News
Science Service
1719 N Street NW
Washington DC 20036
202-785-1243
http://www.sciencenews.org

Scientific American
415 Madison Avenue
New York, NY 10017
212-754-0550
http://www.sciam.com

Scientific American Explorations
179 South Street
Boston, MA 02111
800-285-5264
http://www.explorations.org

SCIENCE COMPETITIONS

Intel Science Talent Search
Science Service
1719 W. Street NW
Washington, DC 20036
202-785-2255
http://www.sciserv.org/sts

Siemens Westinghouse Science and Technology Competition
1301 Avenue of the Americas
New York, NY 10019
877-822-5233
http://www.siemens-
foundation.org/index.htm

Youth Science Foundation
(an organization that
coordinates science fairs in
Canada)
1985 Merivale Road, Suite 2
Nepean, Ontario K2G 1G1
CANADA
613-727-8475
http://www.ysf.ca

WEB SITES

AltaVista's Science Directory
http://dir.altavista.com/Science.
shtml

America Online's Science Directory
http://www.aol.com/webcenters/
research/science.adp

Discovery Channel Homepage
http://www.discovery.com

National Aeronautics and Space Administration Homepage
http://www.nasa.gov

National Science Teachers Association
http://www.nsta.org

National Space Society
http://www.nss.org

Scholastic's Web Guide
http://teacher.scholastic.com/
webguide/index.htm

Scientific American (magazine) Homepage
http://www.sciam.com

Scientific American Explorations (magazine) Homepage
http://www.explorations.org

Yahoo's Science Directory
http://dir.yahoo.com/Science

About the Author

Melvin Berger has been writing science books for children, both on his own and with his wife, Gilda Berger, for over forty years. The *Scholastic Science Dictionary* draws on the knowledge that the author has gathered from study and from researching the more than 200 books he has published. Melvin Berger understands what young people find interesting and delights in conveying new information to them in a fresh and accessible way. A number of his books have been cited as excellent by the National Science Teachers Association and he has been elected to membership in the prestigious New York Academy of Sciences. The Bergers live and write in East Hampton, New York, when not traveling or enjoying their grandchildren.

About the Illustrator

Hannah Bonner is an American who grew up on the Spanish island of Mallorca, where she learned to speak Spanish, English, and Catalán like a native. She began drawing at an early age, choosing as her subjects many of the creatures she saw around her. When she was ten, her father bought her a microscope, and from then on she was fascinated by the tiny world she observed with it. She moved to the United States in 1988, where she studied studio art and science, perfecting her drawing, research, and observational skills that are all called upon in her illustrations in this book. Hannah lives with her husband, Rick, in Watertown, Massachusetts, on the banks of the Charles River.